A Social Theory of Corruption

A Social Theory of Corruption

NOTES FROM THE
INDIAN SUBCONTINENT

Sudhir Chella Rajan

HARVARD UNIVERSITY PRESS
Cambridge, Massachusetts, and London, England · 2020

Copyright © 2020 by the President and Fellows of Harvard College
All rights reserved
Printed in the United States of America

FIRST PRINTING

Library of Congress Cataloging-in-Publication Data
Names: Rajan, Sudhir Chella, 1961– author.
Title: A social theory of corruption : notes from the Indian subcontinent /
   Sudhir Chella Rajan.
Description: Cambridge, Massachusetts : Harvard University Press, 2020. |
   Includes bilbiographical references and index.
Identifiers: LCCN 2020018588 | ISBN 9780674241275 (cloth)
Subjects: LCSH: Corruption—India—History. | Dominance (Psychology)—India—
   History. | Elite (Social sciences)—India—History. | India—Social conditions.
Classification: LCC HV6771.I4 R35 2020 | DDC 364.1/3230954—dc23
LC record available at https://lccn.loc.gov/2020018588

In memory of my father, Sunder Rajan,
whose learning was graced with patience and humility

Contents

Preface ix

PART I: POSITIONS

1 Introduction 3
2 Thinking Clearly about Corruption 31
3 The Corruption of Society: Locating Kernels of Mistrust 66

PART II: TALES

4 Early Symptoms of Corruption: Harappan Routines of Bodily Practice 115
5 The Vedic Period: The Esoteric Rhythm of Sacrifice 148
6 Dharma Yuga: Contentions over Justice 186
7 Trade Winds: Building Global Connections of Corruption 237
8 Conclusions: Corporate Power and Its Dissolution, or The Future of Corruption 265

Notes 291
Acknowledgments 361
Index 363

Preface

I owe inspiration for this book to an extraordinary panel discussion I attended at an international conference in Guatemala City on anti-corruption in 2004. I do not remember all the details, except that at one point several prominent scholars and policy practitioners, on the dais and in the audience, agreed that fighting corruption is principally about identifying small but overlapping elite networks of wealth and power. Such networks drive all criminal activity—from terrorist financing to manipulation of huge tax write-offs through shell companies and offshore accounts to protect ill-gotten wealth. Over time, laws may be changed to normalize these activities and, in particular, to legalize the laundered financing of political campaigns, which entrenches white-collar criminal control of democracy.

This perspective was unconventional at the time and is not popular even now. It is a networked assessment of political corruption that does not point fingers solely at those individual bureaucrats and politicians who distort public goods for private gain. Instead, it suggests the need to move toward a macro-sociological interpretation in which an inner circle, comprising prominent and wealthy individuals, political machines, and corporations, may be involved in deceiving the public over a much longer time frame than a mere election cycle.[1]

A few years after my minor epiphany in a conference room in Guatemala City, the US Supreme Court in *Citizens United vs. Federal Election Commission* ruled to remove limits on private corporations' financial contributions to political campaigns. As many have pointed out, this opened the door to amplifying the scope of party collusion with giant businesses. These conditions allowed their joint power to manipulate information technology and altered the very shape of how news was consumed and political campaigns were run. News reporting, which had already turned into skillfully crafted sound bites, morphed into full-fledged fabrications produced by rumor factories.

My trip to Guatemala was funded by a "blue-sky" grant to review a vast literature on corruption. I did not, however, have a chance to work more on the subject until I met Sharmila Sen from Harvard University Press in 2014, thanks to Ram Guha's generous introduction. Somewhat rashly, I suggested to her that I would like to work on the "history of corruption in India." Sharmila patiently spent several weeks ironing out a short proposal, and I had my nose to the grindstone for another half-decade.

The outcome of these efforts, I fear, may seem inconsequential or unproven to many historians and traditional scholars of corruption. My inability to do justice to the sheer volume of historical material available for the most important periods pertaining to the formation of elite networks in India reflects my utter lack of training as a historian. Many rational choice scholars of corruption will also be put off by my reasoning, at least in part because I have set aside the majority of their findings over the past few decades. Still, I am eager to advance a theory of grand corruption as a provocation for others to respond to.

The argument is simple: many societies have long collective memories traversing multiple symbolic and physical spaces. What if the stories they tell themselves about their pasts were somehow connected with the ways in which they justify their current lifestyles—the given social conditions of their lives, as well as their ways of living within them? How deeply linked to these lifestyles are the actions and motives of elite groups operating over several generations in close-knit and well-functioning networks?

What I am calling "grand corruption" is the long-term, collective, and colossal human failure to acknowledge the illegitimacy of elite networks exercising power over diverse social groups and ecosystems. Paying close attention to the accompanying violence and destruction that the actions of elite networks engender over generations is almost as rare. In our time, the corruption of the people is revealed in our collective incapacity to see our complicity in maintaining the elite collusion of economic and political power, which is manifested in our own daily habits and routines. Detailing each example of grand corruption in our deep histories might display its own rivulets and tributaries that give it its particular features or syndromes.

This is not an easy proposition to defend. But the tapestry of Indian pasts available to us in scholarship promises a tantalizing journey. I have gathered together a modest collection of sweeping tales that prompts other, more rigorous scholars to ask if there is stronger evidence of elite roles in political control through various patterns of deception in long histories. A provocation such as this may be seen as a call to arms through disrespect. I mean no disrespect. Rather, I draw inspiration from scholars of recent fame, such as Thomas Piketty, James C. Scott, and Charles Tilly, who have demonstrated that inequality is not a natural phenomenon of societies but is born out of entrenched political power and has gathered deep ideological roots over several generations. Paying attention to the role of elite networks might lead to ways to strengthen our democratic imagination.

Currently, many of our formal political and legal institutions seem to be barely capable of addressing even proximate concerns, let alone planetary crises of democracy. But if republicanism has a moral force, then those who endorse it would agree that forming good laws, including having consensual social and ecological order, and restoring popular sovereignty against oligarchies must be a collective goal. But forming good laws also requires having some clarity about the guiding principles of correct action. In the long tradition of "unmaking" our various forms of domestication or of our continuing willingness to support institutions of grand corruption, it seems central that, at a time of immediate peril, we must expand our democracy ethic to nonhuman life and to non-life in a rich and plural invocation of "Gaia," our collective divinity of Earth.

The corruption literature is delightfully vast and diverse. Perhaps this exercise too will find its rightful place in the jumble.

A Social Theory of Corruption

Stories are not lived but told

—Louis O. Mink (1970)

na paśyāmo 'napahṛtaṃ dhanaṃ kiṃ cit kva cid vayam |
rājarṣayo jitasvargā dharmo hy eṣāṃ nigadyate ||

Nowhere do we see wealth that was not acquired through plunder . . . the royal sages who have attained heaven describe this as dharma

—Arjuna, to placate his anguished brother, the Crown Prince Yudhishthira (Chapter 8, Śāntiparvan, Mahābhārata)

PART I

Positions

1

Introduction

In Indonesia today, there are only two real choices: to be a "critical partner" or to be an underground subversive . . . most people choose the former.

This Sounds like Corruption

The United Nations Office on Drugs and Crime (UNODC) estimates that more than US $2 trillion of international criminal proceeds are laundered each year, with much of the money circulating in so-called corporate vehicles involving businesses, foundations, and trusts. Significant amounts are buried in elaborate multiparty transactions and shell companies that conceal the names of the few thousands of individuals who actually control the funds. An equally spectacular sum—US $1 trillion—changes hands as bribes each year; these are best described as under-the-table payments that help "smooth" transactions by circumventing the law or by simply providing discretion. UNODC also estimates that tax evasion from offshore banking amounts to US $7.6 trillion annually.

Government officials are often key players in these murky activities, either by exchanging political favors with each other and with wealthy individuals and corporations or receiving bribes to facilitate some inappropriate activity. But as political campaigns, organized crime, sports franchises, media moguls, terrorist organizations, universities, the military, mining companies, banks, the health care industry, Big Tech, and other mega-corporations progressively expand their constellations to camouflage multiple transactions and linkages involving money and other forms of mutual support, a nested but tightly restricted set of networks and their associated politics around the world are implicated in the imposing phenomenon of *grand* or political corruption.[1]

"Something is rotten in the state of Denmark," says the character Marcellus in *Hamlet,* darkly portending its tragic story of medieval palace intrigues, deception, and murder. Across cultures, over time—and hardly ever lost in translation—this is the foul sense in which corruption is generally understood. According to the *Oxford English Dictionary,* the word "corruption" originates in the obsolete English "corrump," to decompose or rot, and the Latin "corrumpere," to adulterate, violate, falsify, or bribe. The Hindi and Sanskrit word is *bhrashtaachar,* which is a combination of *bhrasht* (degenerate, rotten) with *aachar* (custom, practice, code, or institution). It is the stink of decay in the putrid sense of *fubai* in Chinese and *oozhal* in Tamil, representing the slow attrition of basic human decency. It connotes venality, selling offices, being mercenary, or otherwise forsaking principles that, when held jointly, would denote solidarity and shared community life. It is disgraceful because it implicates a substantial number of people acting in collusion who betray such ideals. But it is additionally wretched because it causes people to lose trust in staple institutions and even their own ways of living, as familiar actions and entities come under suspicion.[2]

Something is indeed rotten in today's world if racketeers of various sorts routinely skim off a good chunk of the world's annual income. When combined with extreme levels of inequality across the world, that corruption is an indicator of great social injustice. Only rarely do the media find ways to dig into the murky warrens of the powerfully criminal, depths that even well-meaning law enforcement agencies may fail to probe. But in recent times, stunning exposés by the International Council for Investigative Journalists (ICIJ) have given us a glimpse of large-scale, everyday deception in clandestine global arrangements.

In 2016, a pair of German journalists, with the help of ICIJ, published their findings from the so-called Panama Papers, nearly twelve million documents that were leaked from a single law firm, Mossack Fonseca, located in Panama. The emails, contracts, and other materials in these leaks revealed the secret holdings of dozens of world leaders and other prominent personalities. Their networks with powerful European and Latin American banks were linked to several thousand offshore shell companies having complex arrangements that helped keep hidden drug money laundering, terrorist financing, and child trafficking. Further implicated were gigantic military contractors, purveyors of global finance, and highly respectable engineering companies. The following year, another similarly sized trove of leaked financial documents from an informal clique of firms having offshore practices yielded the Paradise Papers. These documents pointed to even more intricate patterns of suspicious financing mechanisms used for corporate tax avoidance, as well as criminal activity, political campaigns, the illegal trafficking of drugs, humans, and arms, and other clandestine undertakings involving political leaders and royals.[3]

In the Panama Papers' case, Byzantine connections among dozens of reputable individuals and firms and their shadowy counterparts were discovered from documents obtained from just one organization. Even with the addition of the Paradise Papers, from which a broader assessment of offshore activity was conducted, experts have suggested that the revelations are still only the tip of the iceberg; there are possibly hundreds of other illegitimate transnational businesses and tens of thousands of allied shell companies having ties to the powerful that are yet to be discovered.[4]

These events suggest that the persistent nexus of criminals, politicians, and the wealthy is not accidental, after all. People in all sorts of ordinary jobs, the frenetic pace of deployment of natural resources, and the rising prominence of a small and interlinked group of individuals heading institutions are systematically tied to the growing wealth of a tiny segment of the population and a tide that does lift several boats, but only at the expense of the despair of the vast global majority. The extensive and yet deeply selective networks found in present-day secretive and extractive operations are themselves only the latest instance of similar large-scale maneuvers used in predatory forms of capitalism for at least 200 years and in other economic and political regimes for millennia earlier. The patterns of control and social transformation associated with grand corruption seem to get cemented through complicated arrangements that develop over extended periods. Many, in turn, coalesce into "customs" that are bred and maintained in bloodlines. Some become so familiar as to be incorporated into fairy tales about benevolent kings and queens or "social contracts" as cultural routines become traditions.[5]

This is not just a repetition of the familiar leftist refrain about class exploitation being structurally tied to social injustice and conflict. It points instead to a related chronic feature of human and ecological pasts that provides just as helpful a reading of history: the underhanded interests of bands of violent and strong-armed men have for long caused wealth and political power to remain closely held among their associates and relatives, sometimes across generations. They drew their power from the habits of larger populations forming specific patterns of daily life and social arrangements and places, otherwise known as the institutions making up a culture. These mass habits, in turn, drove the very machinery that maintained extraordinary wealth inequality. The disparity in wealth was closely connected with equally vast imbalances in people's control over their own lifestyles.

What is characteristically tragic in this situation is that a politically passive majority of the people tend to misread and support the very regimes and social routines that continually harm them. As sordid as the dramatis personae are in these stories—crooked bankers, fraudulent dictators, and greedy celebrities—there is an even more disastrous tale—of how societies seem everywhere to sustain the criminally powerful for surprising lengths of time, aiding their own degeneration and corruption.[6]

In Indonesia, President Muhammad Suharto's vast political and business operations flourished for thirty-two years during a reign made rich by a peculiar combination of repression, liberality, co-optation of different constituencies, and mineral resources. Until he resigned unexpectedly in 1998 under the pressure of the Asian financial crisis, Suharto enjoyed enormous popular support, despite the harsh and heavy hand of his military on dissidents. A small elite group of business magnates, military officers, professional bureaucrats, and former journalists around the president's office controlled access to petroleum resources and windfall rents from it while they managed an elaborate network of political patronage that dispensed favors to businesses and local leaders in carefully calibrated ways.

The Indonesian nation itself had been forged in 1949, not even two decades before Suharto came to power, after a small but determined armed struggle against Dutch colonial rule. It was a remarkable transition for a profoundly multicultural population spread out across an enormous archipelago of tens of thousands of islands. The newly formed country was characterized by a strong army, a politicized Islam, and centralized political power. Its very identity was built around the motto, "unity in diversity," which became the basis for a durable nationalist sentiment.

Suharto was an army officer under Sukarno, Indonesia's first president. He came to prominence in 1965, when he led the military in a bloody purge of communist dissidents with the active support of the US government. After he formally took over the reins of government on March 11, 1966, he replaced military chiefs with loyalists, purged dissidents in the parliament, changed the educational system, positioned the military's ruthless force to quell protests, invited foreign investors to extract the country's rich oil and mineral resources, and built a team of mostly Berkeley-educated advisers to direct the regime's economic policy. The government only gave limited voice for the opposition and was careful to distribute rewards widely to all those who participated in its formal structures, while threatening sanctions against those who opposed them.

In the course of three decades, Suharto stole as much as US $35 billion in public funds, but he also helped the economy grow sevenfold in real terms by creating enormous oil wealth that made many Indonesians rich, while carrying along a burgeoning middle class. Although there is little evidence to show that returns to the economy were spread extensively, there is enough to inform us that money, political favors, and sweet deals were carefully dispensed to sustain a complex but tight web of military officers, legislators, advisers, political officials, and a global network of company executives, bankers, and world leaders. Each of these elite groups supported each other through preferential deals and other forms of patronage, whose patterns were reproduced across scales all the way down to local gang leaders and thugs.

The flow of information was also carefully controlled. The Indonesian press, which had a glorious history of independent views dating back to the eighteenth century, was mobilized to serve as a partner of the government, with editors receiving periodic telephone calls from the authorities on how to handle the news. Those papers that resisted the official line, like the newspaper *Indonesia Raya*, the newsmagazine *Detik*, and a few others, were banned, with some of their editors facing incarceration by the state as well as vilification by more pliant members of the fourth estate, thereby breeding a culture of compliance and self-censorship.

By 1990, the Suharto family business was so big that any large project had to include one or the other of its many subgroups. It was even involved in the country's poverty reduction efforts: the central government directly provided benefits to provinces and villages through the "Inpres" or "Presidential Instruction" programs, which were executed at the discretion of the president and constituted a major portion of the country's development budget. The government's semi-authoritarian style meant that opposition was always circumscribed and co-opted by the regime, whereas any open rebellion was immediately crushed. But Suharto did not need to use violence to keep revolt in check. He relied instead on the elite's fears of religious extremism and social disorder to constrain opposition, even while he pitted various factions that were loyal to him against each other.[7]

As the chapter's epigraph suggests, Indonesian society under Suharto had somehow become distorted into bipolar political stances that required radical adjustments be made to everyday life. Either one blithely ignored the brutal police violence of the government and its suppression of human rights, or one found oneself in the extremely dangerous position of being a covert dissident, "an underground subversive": there was no middle ground. For ordinary Indonesians, Suharto brought prosperity; for elites and the military, much more. Only those concerned with human rights and democracy were appalled at what was going on, but they too mostly kept their silence.

Throughout history, publics have been critical or uncritical partners in most political regimes, often being misled into trusting their intentions and operations. This introduces another aspect of corruption that seems to be relevant: ordinary people are forced to learn everyday informal give-and-take practices that are necessary for them to stay prosperous or just make do. These routines may range from pulling strings for getting one's children better opportunities in life to cooking the books for others or looking the other way to avoid reporting felonious acts, so as not to "rock the boat." In Indonesia under Suharto, these practices ran the gamut from violence and loosely dispersed arrangements of patronage in local neighborhoods to extraordinary levels of privilege among the most powerful; elsewhere, the rule of law sometimes prevailed but simply kept invisible the actual dealmaking among the most powerful. Elsewhere these patterns may occur across larger geographical and temporal scales and result in even more dramatic social transformation.

What I term *grand* or *political corruption* (or mostly just corruption, for short) typically appears in the form of a set of powerful arrangements that perpetuate various types of injustice, while leading to long-term outcomes of rising symbolic and financial wealth and political dominance for a powerful few. It generally involves three concentric circles of actors: a closed coterie of rulers and members of propertied classes; a large group of administrators, scholars, and others who are overtly paid for services or otherwise persuaded to provide ideological or justificatory support for the regime through direct and indirect means; and an even bigger and somewhat politically enfranchised public. Elite networks are formed through interlocking connections between those in the inner circle and select members elsewhere. Those in the inner circle often use their rulemaking power to sustain themselves over generations by demanding certain actions of their networks, which successfully shape the actions of the larger society to conform to preferred patterns of ordered collective behavior.

Starting at least with the Middle Kingdom (*c.* 2000 BCE) in ancient Egypt, through the more recent Gilded Age and the 1920s in North America, astonishing inequalities in wealth and power have been rampant. It is not that access to exceptional wealth, whether self-made or inherited, is a criminal exercise in itself. It is not. Today, the ultra-rich are legally entitled to maintain their legacies and grow their wealth and routinely store it offshore and find other ways to bypass the laws that apply to ordinary people. But, more importantly, extreme wealth inequality and admiration for the super-rich in the media normalize massive wealth formation, whose production, maintenance, and inheritance invariably cause harm to other humans, lawmaking practices, and ecosystems. The extraordinarily wealthy are suspect not because each of them stole their money from someone or because they paid goons to incite violence. But one could use the term "structural violence" to describe their lobbying efforts to chip away at labor security laws and their willingness to burn through fossil fuels rapidly, overleverage finance and threaten the banking system, and avoid paying taxes through instruments that are back channels for violent crime.[8]

Wealth concentration in a small group of culturally, if not filially, interlinked families is a mark of Europe and much of Asia. But elsewhere, too, inner cores of control over political power and financial wealth are familiar features in the twenty-first century. Elite networks wield enormous influence and political authority in major governments and global institutions and rely significantly on public trust and collective resources. In fact, an elite network is the distinctive feature of large-scale or grand corruption everywhere.

The most powerful entities in the network are aided and abetted by hordes of accountants, asset managers, bankers, crisis managers, lawyers, and their organizations. These agents and the institutions they represent make up a reputable web of associations—generating jobs, businesses, mortgages, laws, and so on. Together, they shape the daily pattern of ordinary people's lives through the occupations they create, the consumerist lifestyles they spawn, the types of health care they make available, and the credit they are linked up with. The average person's success or failure in life is deeply interlinked with how the economy as a whole performs, because everyone is codependent on a well-functioning "habits-forming" machine, which standardizes almost every element of human activity—from education to work practices and home life.

In 2011, 147 companies, many of them banks, were linked to each other and controlled about 40 percent of global wealth. An astonishing 80 percent of the wealth was in the hands of only 737 companies. Individual members of these circles might be unwitting in their complicity with the corrupt system in place but may discover too late that they also have been betrayed in their daily lives, along with the poorest and most vulnerable in their society. As long as the prevalent belief is that elites acquired their positions by playing by the rules, a sense of fairness may prevail. But at some point, a chorus of voices may arise to point out that the aura of legitimacy the regime enjoys is in fact a false veneer. [9]

Throughout history, despotic autocracies, whose rulers seek a "scorched earth" strategy of plundering their countries' resources, tend to be both rare and short-lived. In contrast, corrupt regimes are usually constituted according to rule-bound processes and seek to stay in control over several centuries. Their rulers (and their associates) typically deploy a combination of secrecy and deception, as well as inherited cultures and traditions, rather than brute force, to consolidate power and wealth in a few hands. To the public at large, they seem to say, "Trust us—we will all gain from these actions, no matter how onerous!" Yet, these promises prove false once it becomes clear that the bulk of the benefits accrue to those already in power and their inner circle, rather than to those most needy.

Valuable lessons about corruption would be lost if attention were paid primarily to the biography of Suharto or even just to his lieutenants, rather than to the ways in which most Indonesians distorted their lives and collectively fed themselves lies for more than three decades. It would truly be a gross misreading of corruption to focus only on those principal actors who get caught in the net of corruption scandals and whose thefts and ensuing violence are dwarfed by the much wider and long-term distributed impacts of their elite networks on several successive generations of large societies.

It is not just the fact that Suharto appropriated shocking amounts of public money that ought to concern ordinary Indonesians. Rather, they should ask

Introduction

themselves in what equally hidden but abiding ways did their own behavior and patterns of life get contorted to accommodate his regime. Who made up the elite classes that benefited most from political and economic decisions and quietly ended up with prominent positions in post-Suharto society and government? And why did the public find comfort in maintaining the status quo? Finally, if similar patterns are common across societies, what does this tell us about corruption and its opposite, our common capacity for democracy, to free ourselves finally from oligarchs?

It is useful to recall that if Suharto had not personally amassed vast amounts of stolen money, it is unlikely that the rest of the world would have called his regime corrupt. Like many authoritarian leaders, he cultivated a strongman image of himself from the start and, at least from the mid-1970s, came to be identified as a national hero in Indonesia. Over time, he made use of the old Javanese term *Pancasila,* or Five Principles involving unity, justice, and consensus building as state philosophy; he thereby legitimated the strong arm of the state to intrude and engage deep into Indonesian life, which hitherto had been a largely ungoverned patchwork of assorted self-sufficient communities living as forager-hunters and occasionally as farmers.

Given his strong anticommunist stance, Suharto was espoused as a valuable ally in the United States and Western Europe. Meanwhile, he, his favored friends, and their networks violently extended their tentacles deep into everyday lives of Indonesian society, inflicting lasting pain and injustice on vast publics and institutions. Even today, many Indonesians avoid talking about the harm perpetrated by the Suharto regime, preferring instead either to remain silent or praise their former dictator. It is these elements of the story that tell us something about the sustaining, or "settling down," institutional qualities of corruption, a hitherto underexamined question of great relevance to the autonomy of ordinary people.[10]

What Is This Book About?

This book presents a social theory of corruption—a word easier to use than define—against the backdrop of India's long record of more than 4,000 years. Why corruption, why India?

Corruption is worthy of study because, when experienced at the scales described earlier, it signals enduring collusion among very powerful individuals and their familial and other proximate descendants to engage in massive public deception and fraud. Often, these cartels are linked to and even powered by strong institutions built on trust, such as government and other regulatory associations—indeed, the very entities that are meant to protect people from harm and disorder.

Corruption, it turns out, is most active when societies are actually doing quite well in terms of some measures of collective prosperity. Yet, from an ethical perspective, it does not matter whether the ultra-wealthy and powerful collude lawfully or unlawfully, as long as the long-term outcome of ongoing collusion is the suffering of many. "Do no harm" is a self-evident principle in any ethical framework. This means that some revered institutions are also open to investigation. In fact, the types of corruption I am most interested in are less likely to be prominent during times of substantial economic decline or collapse. A thriving economy and government may still be accompanied by the erosion of societal trust and mutual respect, indicating a deeper malaise that seems almost inexplicable.

That oddity about corruption—its hidden presence and relative long-term stability, sometimes over centuries—is one of the key features I emphasize in this book. I make the case that it is these very conditions that permit small groups at different geographical scales but intricately connected to each other—elite networks—to enjoy benefits as a multigenerational club while not causing so much general unhappiness as to cause widespread unrest. Often, they deploy strongmen and other exclusive groups to form exchange networks in overlapping hierarchies that are difficult to unravel in the abstract or even to detect during short periods in history. But over the course of generations, these networks make up a secure set of rules governing wealth collection and protection. As the political scientist Jeffrey Winters suggests, the continued dominance of oligarchies is principally dependent on their successfully defending their massive fortunes by forming elaborate but secure complexes of control and widespread complicity that seem to steer social and economic life to their advantage.[11]

In due course, corrupt practices may escalate uncertainty and deepen social conflicts around axes of power. They then cause institutions that ought to be stable to become off-centered by rewarding ill-gotten gains and creating a race all the way down to the moral abyss. The race is not for the competent, but for the luckiest and wiliest individuals, who end up catching all the breaks and becoming successful brokers, forming ever-stronger alliances with the most powerful agents and their networks. This unholy nexus manages to benumb the rest of society to the virtues of solidarity and democratic courage. What remains, instead, are people who forsake their promised ideals and hopes by reason of their willing, though often unsuspecting, participation in larger-scale forms of connivance among a much smaller collective. In its most insidious sense, corruption turns out to be *the disproportionate and duplicitous sustenance of groups who manage to retain control of vast resources and profit from the everyday ways of society at large, often with the cynical or beguiled support of the public.*[12]

Writing about corruption across historical contexts means looking for ways in which different configurations of elite networks might have worked systematically behind the scenes in different eras and political regimes to aggrandize wealth and power. In this pursuit, elite configurations must have caused not only the disempowerment of prevailing institutions but, eventually, also the loss of faith in them. They may even have sustained their grip over societies by making false claims about a "greater good." Oddly, those claims seemed adequate justification to acquire, manage, and defend wealth extracted from others' labor and social and cultural reorganization, while buttressing already highly gradated lifestyles.

My choice of the Indian subcontinent in presenting a series of historical case studies is deliberate, although I have no desire to be needlessly sensational in the sense of muckraking by presenting accounts of debauchery and corruption in a region already rife with exotic fables. Instead, I point to sociopolitical patterns one might discover in almost any place with a deep and rich history. I am driven by the idea, which I explain subsequently, that habits developed over time carry with them both long memories of how to behave with each other and a few clues about the highly unevenly networked arrangements of many societies, which are best described as cultures or syndromes. Such syndromes can frequently be linked through social practices to the close alliances of specific persons, along with their kin and other dependents. I ask whether the coincidental or socially produced effects of elite networks that build up alliances of mutual engagement and collective action have the effect of creating cultures of corrupt custom over protracted historical time.

In our times, the worst corruption scandals typically unfold as ever more secretive networks that systematically plunder public investments, often involving political and business magnates holding the highest office. These usually come as a shock to the public, who do not suspect that things are as bad as they are discovered to be. Corruption is therefore confusing and promotes deep cynicism, especially when encountered at close quarters as widespread bribery, cronyism, extortion, embezzlement, fraud, graft, nepotism, and other exclusive forms of patronage or its associated violence. Only after a time, when it is discovered in its fusty depths, does corruption sting collectively, because many ordinary people too have been disloyal to humanity. That is also why we seem so tragically affected by corruption. In its grand, systematic forms, corruption takes on a particularly wily and elusive character where there is no one left to blame but the social order itself.

Making Sense in a Flurry of Corruption

I have three broad strategies in this book. First, I provide a fresh interpretation of the term "political corruption" by treating it as a multiscale, macrosocial phenomenon. In addition to the familiar way in which corruption is treated, as the abuse of public office for personal advancement, I consider a slower mode of large-scale public deception that can also be termed corruption. This is something that can be attributed to many societies and that can only be fully discerned over intervals of considerable length, as the sustaining principles and public values of a political society crumble and the impacts of corruption's dissimulation tend to accumulate. Revolutions are typically understood as large-scale social phenomena that are more than the sum of individual actions. As an event, corruption, too, can be understood in this way, although its slow, festering, and mostly hidden manifestations are almost the inverse of explosive revolutionary activity. But like revolutions, corruption is associated with a diversity of agents, from individual provocateurs to crowds following orders or acting under their own logic, together spawning processes that transform society. This type of reading will help broaden the study of corruption beyond policy prescriptions that wrongly view it primarily in terms of behavior associated with individual deviance or poor judgment arising out of bad incentives.[13]

Second, I use this construal of corruption to reinterpret the locally specific, put-together set of relations we call "society." In doing so, I also hope to discover something useful about society's correlative feature—politics—

which describes processes of sustaining authority through some combination of coercion and consent. By inverting the lens to focus on the essential networked elements that shape the formation of societies, I introduce a sociological dimension into extant political and economic studies of corruption. I suggest, following the political scientist Michael Johnston, that these social relations constitute "syndromes." Some features of these syndromes are shared across contexts, but others give shape to a unique cultural makeup and associated customs that persist over generations.

Third, by using South Asia as the site for these investigations, I construct an alternative frame for reviewing the region's remarkable history and thereby find new sources of inspiration for its continuing democratic journey. The details of this conceptual architecture may emerge only indirectly, but I hope that these studies will open up unorthodox but practical avenues of inquiry into the troubling subject of corruption. The astute reader will note that what I refer to as "India" was neither an independent actor in the world nor a coherent entity for much of the time considered in this book (from around 2600 BCE to the present). It is also not the same as the largest country in the region with that name. Still, with apologies to the country's neighbors, I use the identification here as shorthand for South Asia, to describe a sizable terrain where most of the action described in the book took place and whose collective memories continue to animate politics and cultural life vigorously.

Similarly, I do not treat "corruption" as if it meant the same thing in times past as it does now, or in ancient Athens as in early India. But just as "patriarchy" and "slavery" have universal signatures, corruption too denotes comparable patterns of societal harm that have persisted for several generations across many cultures. In fact, patriarchy, slavery, and associated forms of totalizing bodily violence on the majority may be treated as the betrayal of freedom in the service of oligarchies. For millennia, they sustained elites who formed enduring alliances across vast landscapes to establish regimes of control over the bodies of women, slaves, and various other captive populations. These alliances were typically organized to extract vastly superior advantages for the controlling authority. As these patterns of practice evolved, they resulted in the cultivation and maintenance of belief systems, rituals, and so on, which together constituted a complex set of ordered performances of service to some shared vision while fattening the pockets of the few and heightening their prestige.

Each occurrence of these deep patterns of corruption has an extended history of formation and resembles, even as it differs from, the next one. To research corruption means looking at each situation separately, as would a detective or an investigative reporter. Much like those specialists, one gains knowledge by examining a broad range of incidents. It is tempting to group together cases quickly under several broad categories and find corresponding solutions for each of them. Instead, it is more meaningful to make sense of corruption by considering a *gestalt* of illustrations that reveal a medley of congruences and striations.[14]

Does every elite network produce corruption? The answer depends on the timescale under consideration. Over the *longue durée,* elite network societies, or social formations that are built on vastly unequal relationships, become so entrenched that their amalgam of exploitative relationships seem "normal" and even comforting in their familiarity to ordinary people. Elite networks do not, however, spring up from nowhere. Their initial formation and growth are dependent on the ability of dominant groups to deliver results on promises of security and prosperity to a substantial constituency. In their early phases, elite groups take on positions of leadership and show sincerity toward the people dependent on their largesse and authority. These periods need not be termed "corrupt." But over time, this very paternalism almost inevitably engenders a complex set of strategies that consolidate the power of an interlocking elite network in particular ways, spawning what I term "corruption syndromes" but more commonly known as "ideology." Elite members in the network are themselves often fragmented and may engage in conflict with each other, although prolonged conflict of this nature typically serves to shift the gears of history toward new corruption syndromes.

I do not presume that every society is corrupt or that there is an "iron law" of oligarchy. Quite often, in various forms, democratic arrangements—in the sense of spaces of relative social independence, if not self-rule and collective freedom—do come to pass. Sometimes, as a result of popular revolts and demands for change, laws that are deemed to be fair by a majority of parties are passed. These tend to yield relative equality of access to goods and services, mutual respect, bonds of unity, and opportunities to strengthen the collective vigilance against corruption. Over ages, however, many societies show signs of degeneration expressed as the loss of trust and a palpable sense of betrayal; they may sometimes be identified as a growing sense of collective embarrassment. Yet even as scandals break, ever larger segments of society are exposed as being coconspirators in the very deception that initially stung them.[15]

Even when one recognizes the various duplicities one may be part of, it may simply be easier to hold one's tongue and pretend as if the "normality" of it all is a virtue. Notably, for most human beings these patterns align nicely with their own desire for order, routine, and structure in their lives. Only too late, if ever, may people recognize themselves in the long historical mirror as having been lied to and deceived by the sunniest of promises made to them by those in authority. These lies may become etched into the collective memory of a culture in lofty terms such as "republic," "religion, "nation," or indeed as any other expression signifying organic solidarity or the ability to form networks of cooperation for the common good. Many of these associations lead to positive outcomes linked to democracy and may be the only buffer against the power of elite networks. But even then, in the cacophony of different practices that these enterprises demand, it is often hard to distinguish those that generate positive results from the human-institutional networks that wield the most authority and influence while accumulating wealth through various forms of dispossession.[16]

For instance, even when outraged at the mistreatment of factory workers in countries with poor labor protection, we overcome our distress when we rush to discount stores and find that the devices, clothes, and other products we desire are available at a fraction of what they would cost if similar wages were to prevail everywhere. We may have become too comfortable with the most recognizable routines of exploitation that underlie the structures and spaces of our own consumption, in spite of our occasional concern about news of exploitative garment factories in Bangladesh or the terrible conditions of electronics manufacturing in China. Our acquiescence in such systematic structures of abuse—a subterranean complicity—is what makes the corruption of everyday life all the more appalling. Indeed, exposing all these structures may make it difficult to sustain larger zones of contentment for wider groups of people.[17]

The dissident artist Ai Weiwei, commenting on the system of self-censorship in China, writes, "The self-silenced *majority*, sycophants of a powerful regime, resentful of people like me who speak out, are doubly bitter because they know that their debasement comes by their own hand." But such forms of debasement are not just found in overtly authoritarian regimes: they also persist in diverse, subtle forms as part of the lifestyles of billions of people across continents over long stretches of time.[18]

The Panama Papers case is a familiar motif in my investigations, even though I am concerned with places and times far from Panama. Mine is the archetypal tale of a society in continuous change that developed ordered forms over the course of many generations of largely migrating but also sedentary peoples, in particular geographies, and leading quotidian, everyday lives. Over time, one can identify the consolidation of oligarchies that have direct links of coercion (and the generation of consent) to certain entrenched structures within this society. Those institutions are significant, because they fostered enduring collective memories that are remembered through storylines in various romances, some of which may reappear today in attenuated forms.

Only occasionally do links to criminal elite networks get so fully exposed that the gravity of a scandal can no longer be ignored. But even that may not matter very much. In the film version of the novelist John Le Carré's remarkably prescient novel, *Our Kind of Traitor*, whose central premise of large-scale deception and treachery is more or less confirmed by the Panama Papers, there is a telling moment in the penultimate scene.

It is an unusually sunny workday morning in Canary Wharf, the "new" financial district of London. Perry Makepeace, the accidental hero of the undercover world, has finally unraveled an extraordinary case of collusion involving payoffs and deals among high-ranking politicians, bureaucrats, bankers, and the Russian mafia. The culprits have at last been discovered, and there is hope for resolution. But in a long tracking shot, Perry is seen walking, struggling his way past a swarm of traders in business suits, who are apparently either ignorant of or unperturbed by the scandal. There is no indication that those in whose hands lies the law will bring the criminals to justice. It is yet another day of falling or rising markets.

This scene is an apt allegory for the power of large-scale chicanery: a legally accepted system—namely, a well-organized network of extremely successful firms that ruthlessly manipulate financial markets and also help launder funds—is itself deeply harmonized into the common and prevailing forms of daily life that coordinate an entire world's economy. To recognize the betrayal is hard enough: to initiate action against it is almost impossible because it would also mean radically changing many existing societal practices.

The Deep Politics of Corruption

My social theory of corruption is this: over long periods and in many contexts, a set of processes make up the very original character of a society, with its typical routines and dominant ideas. The engine or order of this social formation, usually until it is transformed, supports and is sustained by an elite network of political (territorial) power that is built on the disproportionate control of wealth.

That network can be associated with the term "state" but is not always or necessarily identical to it. Rather, the network's central spine comprises specific agents interacting with one another but playing important roles in enabling social compliance with preferred modes of routines and everyday practices. The state's instruments of power—the police, financial institutions, the military—and a mid-level entrepreneurial class together make up a major axis in a larger interlocking relationship with dominant and subordinate elites who are linked to each other in complex but mutually beneficial ways. The nonstate members are typically the largest business houses and their associated firms, priesthoods, subterranean criminal networks, and other motley entities that collectively possess undue influence over ordinary people's habits and routines through rich, interconnected cultures of practice.[19]

I have no intention of shaming any particular group or groups in Indian history. But I suspect that vast regions with deep histories are likely to have had significant continuities in family relationships, wealth creation, and other legacies that produce important sociological effects. When grand corruption is unraveled, the roles played by the powerful are banal yet upsetting, because they disclose a pattern of deep exploitation and deception whose basic elements were built long ago but remain hidden even to protagonists who stand to gain most from the arrangements. Present-day elites, whether self-made or through inheritance, can thereby proclaim their innocence in the way social and political arrangements just happen to align themselves as to benefit them disproportionately while causing great harm to the majority.

In due course, even grand betrayals may fade from collective memory or acquire new meanings. Daily routines may also change, forming entirely new patterns in relatively short periods of time. Historians have described countries after the fall of apartheid, communism, fascism, slavery, or other regimes in which general support for and commitment toward particular ideologies suddenly collapsed for a variety of reasons. Afterward some societies preferred to forget their past, as did Russia; others fiercely reversed it, such as Germany; still others, like South Africa, attempted peace and reconciliation for past injustices. None of these developments were preordained in the DNA of their societies; rather, they stemmed from proximate circumstances that may have been influenced both by past habits and external events.

On multiple occasions, the masses react to grand corruption not by demanding change but by becoming politically apathetic and indifferent: this is a sign that ordinary people themselves have become corrupt and distracted. Some political scientists suggest that the US citizens during various periods have demonstrated such apathy. As I describe later, there is evidence that ancient and medieval societies too were sometimes alert to threats to their freedom and at other times indifferent to them. In still other contexts, the machinations of elite networks were often transparent, and their members even brash and boastful about their power; for example, in the eighteenth- and nineteenth-century slavery system in Europe and the Americas, in sweatshops in Asia and elsewhere today, and in recent celebratory mega-mergers in key economic sectors.[20]

Even when the actions of elites are notorious, corrupt activity on the part of the powerful attracts far less attention than generally assumed. As political scientist Gregg Barak writes,

> The crimes and victims of the powerful remain relatively *invisible* thanks to the concerted efforts of lawyers, governments, and corporations to censor or suppress these disreputable pursuits from going viral when they succeed. . . . Historically, [they] have managed to avoid or escape criminalization and stigmatization. Time and again, these powerful criminal activities have been conventionalized or neutralized by way of alliances, negotiations, and justifications that undermine the moralizations of these offenses.[21]

Barak goes on to provide examples of the brutal conditions of factory life in the nineteenth century and of the enormous harm wrought by the 2008 economic crisis. In both cases, those responsible directly for these situations were clearly identifiable, but these perpetrators were either let off with a slap on the wrist or went on to gain enormous respectability as "business tycoons" rather than as "robber barons." Remarkably some of the financial manipulations that led to the 2008 crisis are still being practiced; they are still keeping afloat certain sectors of the economy, such as the aerospace, energy, finance, land and construction, military suppliers, and information technology industries. Meanwhile, a prolonged age of "jobless growth" seems built into the very logic of the liberalized trade economy.[22]

During the twentieth century, social welfare programs uplifted the working classes and brought them into the middle class as they attained comfortable living standards. Still, their political and economic distance from elite prestige and influence has remained substantial. In contrast to a revolution, which is a relatively short-lived event, corruption breeds its own special forms of collective disorder that persist for some time. The social philosopher, Emile Durkheim, refers to collective disorder as *dérèglement*—declining levels of confidence in fellow members of society and mutual feelings of disengagement, expressed sometimes in actions and moods, such as displays of rage at workplaces and attitudes of extreme xenophobia. Such social patterns may be evident only over long periods and may be expressed by the ability of some to generate wealth for themselves and their partners within conclaves as well as at bigger scales, all at the expense of the long-term interests of common people.[23]

What conditions have led to these perversions of justice? What similar patterns of practice lie hidden from view when we focus solely on the personal motivations of individuals and their behavior? By doing so, are we not ignoring the organized patterns of activity of groups of people and their apparent willingness to oversee structures of power that support elite cartels, kleptocracies, or neo-patrimonial regimes? Why is it that the privileges accorded to the most powerful networks in these societies find no place in the news, even when sensational reports of corruption are publicized? And, just as importantly, how are all of us implicated in this growing strength of corrupt networks? Indeed, what socializing mechanisms provide implicit acceptance or legitimation for these "criminal" activities, which cause harm to ordinary people and yet seem to be normalized?

The answers provided in Barak's handbook on the crimes of the powerful are instructive. Even though citizens are most often harmed by the powerful organizations of the world, they perceive that the actions of particular individuals are to blame. Standardized approaches and languages and frameworks, such as those of mainstream psychology and economics, seek explanation solely at the level of the individual, who supposedly acts based on his or her own motivations. Vincenzo Ruggiero claims, "By denying the reality of *collective phenomena,* [the] mere interest of individuals comes to be recognized. This strategy does not amount to deceit but is inspired by a serious imperative to justify acts; it is not a pretext, but a genuine attempt to present actions as conducts which withstand the test of justification."[24]

There surely are no simple ways to find answers to the many questions raised by corruption. Presumably, studying the slowly developing formations and patterns of corruption over time will provide suitable clues to our quest. A look at two well-known societies—ancient Rome and the Vatican in the medieval period—should prove useful in this regard. They are both examples of deeply corrupt formations becoming exposed and yet persisting over time. Eventually they each generated other, more tolerable, patterns of political and religious life. In both these societies, tight networks of those having political authority or those having privileged access of one sort or another enlisted a significant coterie of administrative supporters and other allies. This eventually created a gaping abyss between the masses who were subject to the resplendent spectacle of secular power (Rome) or divine power (the Vatican) and those sources of power. The authority of the elites had extraordinarily *affective* ways of influencing the collective of ordinary bodies to coalesce as a "people." Yet, these conditions did not last forever.[25]

In Rome, around the birth of the Common Era, the political order after Augustus Caesar was being managed increasingly by an uneasy coalition among the *potentes,* the "Haves"—some of whose families had endured for several generations in conditions of obscene wealth and prosperity—and their bureaucratic and political connections. The classicist Ramsay Macmullen describes how officialdom (including office-bearers and those directly in the employ of government) and wealthy merchants and traders were locked into thick patterns of interdependence involving the mutual exchange of favors, and their top layer constituted the Haves. But it was the reckless flaunting of their wealth that turned the nobility's public image sour. This, in turn, led to the growing recognition of the regime's betrayal of the ideals of the republic.[26]

The moral scandal of the corrupt and insensitive power exercised by Roman officials and nobles eventually led to the downfall of Rome. Indeed, early Christianity's stark message, pointing out that the self-righteous republic was in fact unjust, fostering the decadence of the few at the cost of vast misery for the many, seemed to be a critical factor in leading to a prolonged and slow downfall of the regime. Long after the decay first became evident, it was the relentless sale of power through the privatization of public office that led to the collapse of the empire, as the power of the state was rendered effectively useless, most seriously in the military. It could no longer protect Rome from the periodic attacks of the Huns, Vandals, Visigoths, and other "barbarians."

Early Christianity grew rapidly as a thorn in the side of the Roman Empire and was variously persecuted by Roman administrators until the fourth century, when it was first legalized and then adopted as a state religion. The Vatican arose out of this conflict but was itself prone to degeneration. It was a strange mix of oligarchy and monarchy. Popes had absolute sovereignty, with sole divine and political power at least among humans, but they were often the compromise candidates selected by a small, powerful coterie and were therefore significantly in their debt. In addition to such palace intrigues, the Vatican elite, usually but not always led by the popes, formed dubious strategic alliances with sovereign partners within Christendom, often exceeding the bounds of ethical conduct. In the late Middle Ages, the Vatican infamously fleeced the public to fill its coffers. Altogether, a highly venerated institution ended up deceiving its vast congregation and undermining much of the faith vested in it. Reform was inevitable by the fifteenth century, but trouble had been brewing for some time.

Well before the collapse of confidence in Rome in 450 CE and in the Vatican about a millennium later, bands of robber barons controlled access to land and consolidated elite relationships, gaining enormous political power through their patronage networks. In ancient Rome, a new feudal order—in the economy, in ecclesiastical practice, and in other parts of social and cultural life—came into place, disrupting traditional arrangements for nearly a millennium. In Europe, from the fifteenth century onward, various developments—collectively termed "capitalism and modernization"—changed the world as part of the unraveling of the corruption of the old order.

Each long-drawn-out case, in the manner of a syndrome or slowly changing condition, was characterized by different forms of order and routine. These new routines gave rise to new ideologies, or ways of interpreting the world, some having more democratizing effects than others. What is important to remember is how various forms of broad social consent and of coercion emerged, were rendered normal, and were maintained as such. These routines typically hid patterns of social injustice from ordinary people. Although a slowly increasing erosion of trust or reduced expectations of reasonableness and fairness may have arisen soon enough, most people were supporters of a corrupt regime without being aware of the breach of public trust—even betrayal—inherent in such support. Indeed, in most of these instances, the gravest injustices and their associated structures of power came to light only as they were being slowly dismantled. Were the transitions painful for different groups of society even as resentments, resistance, and the gradual realization of the extent of the state's perfidy began to surface?[27]

Perhaps such occasions resemble what the philosopher Georg W. Hegel described as the spreading wings of the owl of Minerva, the goddess of wisdom, at the dusk of a historical epoch. They characterize diverse conditions of political corruption and their social impacts in times past, but with lasting legacies that we comprehend only after a time lapse. And we may also see in their midst the emergence of new social conditions of stability, predicated on fresh hopes, promises, and frameworks of solidarity.

Each of these interludes also reveals something about a society's ability to look at itself and find something morally wrong with it. With any luck, that society may change its practices at least significantly enough to register a voice of protest against the elite consolidation of power, while leaving its mark in history. What I am calling corruption here may be identified as the growing discomfort and disorder in societies from time to time against the background of the elite capture of and violence over a typical person's lifeworld, often with earlier and far more disastrous impacts on women, the elderly, the differently abled, and other outcasts. Over long stretches of time, one might discern similar social responses to such violence, even if they are initially perceived as shock rather than outrage at discoveries of corruption. Only occasionally do they give voice to resistance, possibly achieving a measure of social change. In ancient Rome and the medieval church, thick elite formations were unable to distribute goods fairly. The social movements that led to transformation helped reveal the character or syndrome of the political corruption that was flourishing at great popular expense.

Corruption and India

South Asia is a special context for a study on political corruption. Its complex history and geography make it a rich site for investigation into variously manifest forms of protracted societal betrayal. It is a vast subcontinent sitting on one edge of Asia, with over five thousand miles of coastline and an immense mountain range to the north that together give it the illusion of being somewhat cut off from other parts of the world. On that subcontinent, substantial churnings and contact took place for about four millennia, including incursions by adventurers and their armies and shifting power struggles for dominance by multiple elite configurations.

With its open borders and access to trade routes in many directions, India experienced significant migration and exchange with groups originating across a broad swath of Asia, Europe, and Africa, and as far away as the edges of the Indian Ocean. None of the exchanges remained frozen, but continuously changed the cultural practices of the different groups involved through various forms of intermarriage, social learning, and systemic transformation. India remains enormously diverse in terms of language, social customs, artistic traditions, forms of livelihood, and so on. Still, for much of its history, large parts of Indian society were (or were intended to be) governed by endogamous hierarchical groups within small-scale village societies.[28]

The religious studies scholar, Ariel Glucklich cites his teacher, David Eckel, who compared India to a pan of lasagna, having multiple layers of culture in any given location:

> Layering can be found in Europe and the Near East, too, of course: the difference is the sauce, if you will. In India, rising civilizations have tended to embrace or encompass existing ones instead of annihilating them. The result is a single multi-flavored dish. . . . Perhaps a better metaphor than the lasagna pan would be the whole kitchen. This diversity raises questions of definition in regard to Hinduism: Is it a single religion or is "Hinduism" a convenient (and imported) term that masks and does not fully unify a whole range of Indian cultures and traditions? . . . [In fact,] Hinduism is decisively not a single narrative: the metaphor of one tree with one root system simply does not work. It is a constellation

of religions only some of which look back to a primordial past for their origins.[29]

The word "Hindu" was coined by the British in the eighteenth century but was much earlier associated by Persians and others with the land of the Sindhu (or the region to the east of the Indus River). As a religious practice, today it is best described as having a strong ceremonial liturgical tradition, but one markedly different from many other such traditions, such as the Abrahamic, in the sense that there is no authentic book or single doctrine that guides its diverse forms of worship. Common to Hindu practice in nearly all its manifold forms is a generalized claim to a Vedic past through "community"-defining texts known as the Puranas. Virtually all of Hindu custom is connected through gods and goddesses that are sanctified as various incarnates of grander Vedic and allied divinities in later narratives. But they are also cosmically linked to the great order of the universe and the self. In several local traditions, other divinities and familiar spirits may also play either dominant or submissive roles. Most Indian faiths are blends of canonical forms and a plethora of local traditions, although there is a trend toward more orthodox rigor, especially within Brahmin communities.

What I am calling "India" is, of course, much larger than Hindu practices, whose scope and geographical extent are legion. One way to describe India is in terms of the mobility of contact and the fluidity of faiths; in addition to a range of Hindu practices, these include different manifestations of agnosticism, Buddhism, Christianity, Islam, Jainism, materialism, Sikhism, and Zoroastrianism. In fact, there is no reason to doubt that all of Indian interchange has been cosmopolitan in practice and ideas for eons, making up various hybrid cultures. Trade and migration with Mesopotamia took place 4,500 years ago; later, there were strong cultural links and trade with East Africans, Arabs, Chinese, Greeks, Indonesians, Italians, Malays, and others. Although many endogamous kinship groups may have existed earlier, there is evidence of multiple forms of genetic diversity until around the early first millennium, even within orthodox upper-caste communities.[30]

First-time visitors to India often come away with a transformative experience, reporting that it is world-changing in some way. Native Indians, including those with no other experiences to compare it against, also treat India with some awe not only because of its vast social and political panorama but also primarily for the way its rich forms of interaction continue to be demonstrated in its many languages, rituals, and cuisines across a vast, ecologically diverse area. Most modern Indians are aware, to some degree at least, of their striking diversity as a nation, capable of a "million mutinies" perhaps and yet bearing a complex though strongly discernible set of identities with dense layers of pride and honor. Still, Indian society is by no means utterly fragmented into varied and separate identities. Instead, both its dominant and its many subordinate forms and institutions remain fairly discernible over its ancient history as the "wonder that was India," no matter how contestable such a characterization may be. To describe political corruption in India over several millennia, as I choose to do here, means having to cross difficult terrain in every sense of the term. And that is the earnest mission of this book, as intractable as it may seem.[31]

My immediate task is to resist defining India as having a separate and unique culture with an essential set of customs or—even more narrowly—that it has an inner, immutable core, despite all the "foreign" influences implying contact and transformation. I also do not want to use this opportunity to "periodize" Indian history in familiar or new ways. Instead I propose that long-term motivations to maintain advantages for certain groups created important social forces, along with external events, surprises, and resistance to (or re-appropriation of) elite intentions by less advantaged peoples. Another pitfall I hope to avoid is the assumption that numerous vitalizing terms in circulation today, such as history, justice, freedom, and, indeed, corruption, are principally "Western" concepts and, furthermore, that they have been colored in their meaning by the rise of European and North American powers during the past two hundred years.

A flawed interpretation that follows from these three types of framing is that it is impossible to find an "authentic" way to represent India's pasts without making serious compromises in one's own situated intellectual judgment. An alternative question might instead be whether a shared, meaningful, and practical interpretation is possible. The one proposed here seems plausible at first blush and also points to patterns of action among purposive collectives of actors with each other over several generations: it singles out elite actor-networks as being behind a collective type of grand deceit. This deceit becomes epiphanic only because it frequently affects the day-to-day, mundane elements of people's expectations and lifestyle.[32]

An expectation that the rules that govern everyday life are reasonably credible has been common among functioning societies for much of history. Unless a populace is fighting a war or revolution, it expects just arbitration of disputes and other forms of fairness in at least a few aspects of its lifestyles. The alternative is a continual state of friction among the masses and between them and the organs of government. The fact that many territorial regimes have been stable over more than a few generations is telling. So too is the fact that the majority of the people in the wild evidently lived healthy and fulfilling lives without being governed. What gave kingdoms and empires the legitimacy they still enjoy in present-day collective memory, even though in actuality the masses preferred to live outside them? That is an important question having to do with the enduring ideological power of elites.

The spectacle of kingship (its pomp and splendor) is an expression of the longer-term festering corruption in much of the globe. It is expressed in royalty's rapid accumulation of wealth and territory by making unsubstantiated claims that were never properly questioned. Elite family clubs of rājās in India and of kings and emperors elsewhere were formed only because they had the ability to overwhelm opposition through physical strength, intimidation, divine invocation, and hereditary mythology. The evidence suggests that high levels of inequality—sometimes extreme inequality—have been fairly common for much of history. The presence of palaces indicates the presence of kings and their entourage who not only flagrantly hoarded rents by engaging in little or no physical labor but also successfully created a storybook universe of beneficence, edification, and war.[33]

Although certain patterns of monarchy in particular were prominent in West Asia more than five millennia ago, Indian kingship only appeared after 800 BCE. The stories of kings and queens that render their behaviors as normal courses of action in India and elsewhere are at the very heart of what I am terming corruption at a grand scale. For what they hid were the elaborate mechanisms stemming from the court outward that maintained the myth that kings could legitimately control vast territory and all its material wealth. But even though this pattern appeared late in India, its characteristic features of pomp, battle, ritual identification with sacrality, and hereditary rule emerged quickly and remained unbroken. Although kingship patterns did vary in strength over time, where a king's divine genealogy was ever more firmly encased in myth, his authority was greater.

Yet again, the beguiling twentieth and twenty-first centuries' nationalist idea of India is the modern figment of a generalized spatial imagination of a territory of grand economic and cultural significance, with an unbroken sense of history, notwithstanding several deep and unknown corners. It stands now as a nation with global ambition. These two features, one physical and tangible, and the other the product of imagination, are not unrelated. An imagined entity can come to life through the actions of human bodies within it, by creating emergent processes that are irreducible to its individual materials and exchanges. Think of Disneyland, a university, or the inside of a commercial airplane, each of which becomes an institution, the noun form of a collective of designs, a set of practices and physical objects. Similar social-individual-geographical assemblages and the processes they spawned will also be relevant in my study.

Outline of the Book

My aim, as mentioned, is to discern singular syndromes of elite network duplicity that have misled publics into pursuing lifestyles that were used to unfair advantage during nearly four millennia in India. It is a complicated journey, involving many layers and themes, as intricate as the Panchatantra and the Mahābhārata—the first an interlinked set of fairy tales involving animal characters, the second the much-told nested story of a war and its preparation involving humans, spirits, animals, gods, and demons. For want of skill, I can scarcely recount only some of the surprises that I came across in my research.

Chapters 2 and 3 elaborate the main elements of my framework on corruption in relation to existing theories. They also break down my journey into discernible themes. Chapters 4–7 identify a few significant intervals in a "big" history of India's corruption syndromes: the Harappan and Vedic civilizations until the rise of the Mauryas; the coming into significance of legal texts and new religious practices; and the long trade relationships ending in colonialism, its political opposition, and present-day inheritors of these multiple legacies. I do not promise the reader scandalous stories of the corrupt in India's past or even very clear patterns that develop as distinct syndromes. But the shapes that occasionally appear vividly propose some interesting arrangements of how elite networks were often connected with social formations over long time frames.

Chapter 8, in conclusion, attempts to reorganize these strata into a perspective for the future that could be realized by seeking a democratic and cosmopolitan escape from the corruption that also seems essential in the planetary age. Having started in an arbitrary part of the world that also happens to be my birthplace and current home, this book tells a useful tale not just of the subcontinent but also about some subtle long-term collections of processes associated with both stabilizing and changing social mores. These processes may be more common and connected to most other lands and contexts than may be evident at first.

To my reader, hence, I promise to describe how in different places in India, in different times past, the emergence of corruption—appearing as the unequal power of cartels—generated varying forms of collective action among a subaltern or largely disempowered majority. Over the course of generations, that could mean one of the following: accommodation, acquiescence, or agitation. For tomorrow, I can only hold onto the hope, along with others, of building greater democracy and planetary sustenance on the ruins of a corrupted present.

2

Thinking Clearly about Corruption

The Grand Stances of Corruption

As I stated in the introduction, attention to corruption today focuses on individuals and those in their immediate circle who cheat the public by breaking the rules of decency and fair play. But what happens if the formal rules themselves are rigged or, worse, if most people do not realize that the system itself is skewed in favor of the powerful? How do rulers (rule makers and enforcers) give themselves the legitimacy to govern, and how do others come to accept their legitimacy? What processes of governance are thereby followed? Finally, how does one differentiate between just and unjust forms of rule?

Politics, the fraught process of shaping social order, inevitably raises questions of trust and legitimacy. One of its principal features is the claim of justification for kings, presidents, and representative forms of government, as well as for priests, prophets, landlords, and tax collectors. In each long-evolving social formation, these various authority figures and links across them become well established and recognized over time as being the necessary forms of order for a society to grow and enrich itself. Historically, all such claims were predicated on authority derived from some combination of divinity (e.g., the divine rights of kings and priests), wisdom (e.g., the superiority of philosopher-kings), property (e.g., the natural right to inherit and to draw income from assets), age (e.g., the natural right of the elderly to make decisions based on their experience), and popularity (e.g., the will of the *demos* or people). Bolstering these claims were extensive and specialized administrative systems with ever more complex strata of control over populations and the flow of tribute upward to rulers through territorial expansion.[1]

In more recent times, constitutions have come to define the basic rules for wielding political power, including checks and balances and the means for any person to seek remedies for infraction of these rules. The reasonable assumption here is that the authority of a particular regime is not arbitrary but is derived from procedures established in its formal constitution, whose writing itself went through a publicly justifiable process. As constitutional democracies established themselves, they put in place two features to protect them from outright capture by elite groups. One was the use of reasoning (justification) around (defensible) principles of justice against violence, exploitation, and cheating by special groups or interests. The other feature was processes for representation and the use of well-positioned checks and balances. Both, however, could be subverted through some combination of artifice and violence, as the history of the last few centuries has shown.[2]

In *Nicomachean Ethics,* Aristotle describes how regimes tend to have three basic forms: rule of one over the many, rule of the few over the many, and rule of the many over the many. Each of these archetypes is subject to corruptions, especially when those in charge lose sight of their appropriate roles in safeguarding society: "There are three species of polity, and an equal number of deviations from them—corruptions of them, so to speak. The three are kingship, aristocracy, and a third based on ownership of property (*timema*), which it seems proper to call 'timocratic' though most people usually call it a 'polity.' The best of these is kingship, the worst timocracy."

Aristotle believed that if the goodness inherent in the figures of the king, aristocrat, or timocrat is lost, their regimes degenerate into tyranny, oligarchy, or democracy, respectively. These deviations from legitimate forms of rule arise primarily because of the vices of individuals; they also harm what Aristotle terms "friendship" (*philia*), a sense of mutual good between persons that creates the very bonds of community. For Aristotle, democracy was the somewhat disenchanted view of rule based on the whims of people who refuse to look for shared goals around collective values and whose individual, self-seeking interests prevail over those of the city as a whole. The rise of demagogues in Athenian democracy justified such fear, and Aristotle and Plato before him had reasons to be dissatisfied with the pattern of direct democracy that was prevalent in their time. It was a democratic majority, after all, that put Socrates to death because he dared to provoke the youth to ask dangerous questions.[3]

Aristotle's view of corruption is a useful springboard for my analysis. Like him, I am interested in the betrayals of those who are charged with serving the public good. Kings, generals, and other persons in authority make various promises of security in return for people's trust and support. To trust an institution, a set of sustained social practices, is also to feel a sense of mutual commitment to respect and honor one another. Frequently, however, elite formations emerge that betray that trust by hoarding resources in exploitative ways. Over time, the exploitation has a societal effect: a growing gap between the rich and the poor, which is fueled by the entrenchment of identifiable social orders of dependence and their associated cultural beliefs and practices.

In the course of these changes, the more subterranean operations of what may best be described as "hives" or "colonies" of highly placed and connected individuals exercise greater control over systems that become part of a society's habits and dispositions. This control generally comes at a great cost to the larger public, who in response might lose faith in the value of mutual respect and social justice. When misdeeds of the powerful are persistently unpunished as a result of these maneuvers, the institutions of administration and justice regulated by them turn sour, and even ordinary people may become mistrustful toward each other. But many may also become habitually complicit and subservient to rulers and their allies in the hope of gaining rewards for themselves. It is these very conditions that generate even more collective harm over the long term.

Stories of original contract and the divine right of kings make up two of the grandest deceptions of human history. Social contract theory assumes that a political society is made up of individual members who share an implicit or explicit agreement on the composition and legitimacy of those who rule over them. This idea has been used to justify historical as well as present-day states, but despite the formation of modern constitutions and their manifest rules making up law, there is scant evidence of any actual contract in the history of territorially bound political formations. Modern constitutions were written by a small body of influential and propertied men on the basis of rules of deliberation and fairness. Constitutions are contracts, to be sure, but not social contracts in the way in which the latter are usually understood. From the late eighteenth century onward, some political theorists have put forward the idea of a hypothetical contract, but such a notion of an imagined ideal order stretches the limits of justification for actually existing social orders. Even less persuasive is the idea that rulers were preordained to rule on account of divine sanction, although this model enjoyed the longest run in territorial societies around the world.[4]

Nevertheless, for millennia, and to this day in many parts of the world, mythologies of one sort or the other have bolstered public acceptance of, if not reverence for, certain ways of organizing societies hierarchically. Their weak underpinnings notwithstanding, kingdoms and empires did serve small parts of the population extremely well. Chroniclers made distinctions between good kings and tyrants, but these too were mostly cover-ups of time-honored patterns of exclusivity to rationalize rule by elite networks. Occasionally, after generations of such validation, the effect of the legendary boy shouting, "The emperor has no clothes!" resulted in the internal disruption of many tyrannies and oligarchies. Although such actions sometimes generated conditions ripe for political revolution and democratizing institutions, they more often than not led to despotic regimes, which openly used the raw force of the stick to demonize their own people whom they kept bound to the powerful. Eventually, a prince with a far gentler demeanor arose from within the nobility to help restore the facade.[5]

Across the world, corrupt elites persisted because they managed to develop deep roots and interconnected networks of favors along with markets of exchange of these favors. They developed strong commitments both with economically and political well-endowed notables, as well as with those engaging in maintaining social order through intimidation and subterfuge. In the process, powerful alliances systematically exploited these relationships to consolidate political control over populations and land. The social historian Charles Tilly writes,

> I know of no European national regime, past or present, in which *a small number of rich and well-connected men*—I mean men—did not wield disproportionate influence over the government. In every formally democratic regime of which I am aware, stigmatized minorities have lacked protection from arbitrary governmental action.... "[D]emocratic" simply means less undemocratic than most other regimes—escaping to some extent from the petty tyranny and monolithic authoritarianism that have been the two usual forms of government throughout the world over the last 5,000 years.[6]

Inequality, hierarchy, and political tyranny may be common features of Indian and European history, but elite networks hiding their power within sovereign political regimes (when detected) express a more profound betrayal of public confidence. Each time this deception causes collective harm, it means that large populations had followed customs and engaged in certain actions under false assumptions of good faith by their rulers. Occasionally within long time frames, one finds certain periods when substantial numbers of people feel especially insecure because of the direct and indirect harm generated by elite power. Then, either through revolution or slow shifts in political conditions, what had seemed normal earlier may convey a sense of horror to later observers.

For instance, over the course of several lifetimes during which the enslavement of Africans was normalized in Europe and the Americas, political changes took place in the nineteenth century, leading to the wider recognition of slavery's inherent violence and injustice. These shifts in perception and social practice did eventually lead to vast changes, but after emancipation, many leading brokers and captains of slavery and their inheritors simply altered some of the social arrangements of their productive processes and remained respectable tycoons.[7]

Power is therefore a critical parameter in this investigation, which I explore more fully in various parts of the narrative. For now, I define power as the intent and actions to dominate others. There are many ways in which domination is expressed, but they usually involve some sort of identifiable authority that can exercise physical force, as well as subtler forms of influence. The identity of this authority over large geographies is usually termed "sovereign power," represented most potently in the bodily presence of the king. More generally, sovereign power is associated with the state, an authority exercised over a given people and territory.[8]

To examine the elite actors and alliances that benefit from these arrangements of government in its broadest sense is to trace political partnerships and influences, as well as conflicts, and to recognize small- and large-scale transitions of power. These arrangements may be overt or hidden: it may be that everyone knows the rules of authority and influence, which are often codified as laws and regulations, or they could be unstated and implicit. Whether described as kingdoms, empires, or city-states, these arrangements acquire a certain legitimacy, an expectation of how those asserting charge should conduct themselves—by decree or through negotiated settlements with larger publics. As Tilly points out, at least for the past 5,000 years, these forms of justification have been asserted simply as the symbolic right of who wears the crown or, in more common terms, as "might is right," although this assertion has not gone unchallenged.

Concealed within the pomp and glory associated with the sovereign authority of emperors, federations, and even many republics that are made up of popular representatives are more elusive networks of actors, who manage to appropriate most of the capital or wealth generated from collective labor. These cartels find ways to maintain advantages by putting their delegates in positions of dominance. Different types of elite groupings—based on economic wealth, political control, and status gained from knowledge and other forms of cultural capital—may form special linkages. An exclusive few preserve their activities and gains within bloodlines or other alliances across generations, capturing both physical assets and cultural prestige. Physical assets, such as crown, scepter, and throne, also become vivid symbolic assets of the court and give it the remarkable ability to have limited but sure command over the affective or sentimental feelings of entire societies. Throughout this book, I describe these privileged and influential connections among different patterns of human actors and material landscapes and the advantages accrued to the few, who somehow manage to capture territory and political power in many forms, as "elite actor-networks" or simply "elite networks."[9]

Elite networks do not necessarily turn corrupt as a result of some preordained betrayal of public ideals. But early in their formation, windfall gains may accrue to relatively advantaged groups attempting to form complex alliances while responding to the vagaries of history. In these moments, profoundly divergent patterns of wealth and hard labor might build up, with elites gaining overwhelming control over surplus from land in the form of agricultural surplus, mostly grain, but also from trade in luxury goods. These conditions might incentivize elite networks to create strategies of "enclosure," to consolidate their gains and build legacies for future generations. These highly unequal societies develop into "territorial sovereignties," meaning polities or states, which in turn require the means to defend them in the form of armies and militias, systems of public and private law, and a whole arrangement of discourses and social practices. The emergence of elites with physical assets may complement those accumulating symbolic wealth having a "hierophanic" or sacred dimension. These orders may then become hierarchically ordered in the form of priestly classes and social castes, with substantial links to those extraordinarily wealthy with material assets, including arms and armaments. Together, these alliances generate a system of rule with routines of community behavior that make up that political society. In due course, justification for elite privilege might wear thin as the harsh effects of inequality and slavery become widely felt. Each such long pattern of history thus constitutes a "corruption syndrome," a term I expound on subsequently.[10]

What Are the Manifestations of Corruption?

In recent years, the multiple uses of the word "corruption" have led to the creation of a typology in the scholarship: petty, administrative, and grand or political corruption.[11]

Petty Corruption

Petty corruption is the most familiar form of corruption and is associated with having to pay individuals or small groups who have some type of gatekeeping role to allow access, legally or illegally, in relation to some activity. In the Middle East and South Asia, it is connected with the term *baksheesh*, traditionally signifying a gift or tip, but more recently rendered as a bribe. It could mean, for example, paying off a policeman to overlook a fine, getting a driver's license by bribing someone in the Department of Motor Vehicles, or going to the front of a line in a government medical facility by providing the doctor a personal favor.

The ubiquity of such bribery in countries like India, Nigeria, or Mexico gives petty corruption prominence, but it is common to view baksheesh more as a nuisance than as a deep social malady. Partly, this has to do with the social circumstances of public sector employees in these countries. Public sector jobs are highly coveted in developing countries, because they offer more stability and a safer haven than the norm. Nevertheless, jobs at the lowest levels of the bureaucracy and allied services usually provide modest earnings that are barely sufficient. For poorly paid workers who are increasingly uncertain about their futures, there are strong incentives to sell official favors on the private market. Worse still, an ideology of neoliberalization has recently shifted many of these jobs to contractual positions, where stability and security are fragile and real wages lower than career government positions.

Where formal rules and laws provide for the just dispensation of public resources, we are rightly chagrined when individuals misappropriate public funds or charge "fees" for legitimate goods we have already paid for. Thus, a policeman who functions in his official role in one manner, and then looks the other way when his friend, kinsman, or village superior does something illegal, is clearly violating commonsensical rules of fairness. But even here, it would be useful to ask what broad shifts in society brought about these particular patterns in law and order, and whether both existing and new hierarchies, networks of domination and influence, and meeting the needs of everyday life in conditions of poverty are predicated on the continuation of the exchange of petty favors.[12]

Baksheesh is also an example of what the anthropologist and political scientist, James C. Scott, calls everyday forms of resistance that make up "weapons of the weak." It is a resistance to or even re-appropriation of the tools generally deployed by the dominant groups in a society to maintain their status and wealth. Viewed as a gift or tip, baksheesh represents rightful demands for respite from an unfair set of relationships and alliances involving hierarchies and domination, but that are camouflaged as a gift, respect, or gratitude. But such forms of resistance also emulate some of the duplicitous methods deployed by more powerful men who routinely engage in extortion and gatekeeping, stealing, telling elaborate lies, and so on. Forms of baksheesh, in other words, are minor, hidden strategies that the poor and underprivileged use simply to maintain and reproduce themselves. Still, because they so often get caught up in the deceits of bigger and more elaborate criminal and government networks, the poor engaging in petty corruption typically become trapped in them. Their entrapment may result in various degrees of violence and harm to each other and the rest of society, as with mafias anywhere. It is equally impressive to note how vast systems have operated as smoothly as they have for several generations in spite of the ever-present possibility of the destabilizing effects of petty corruption snowballing out of control.[13]

The spiraling impacts of the everyday transactions of petty officials who engage in baksheesh are that they distort personal lives and create unusual difficulties, especially for those who are the most vulnerable in society. More troubling is the way the quantum of bribes and the severity of criminal activity increase markedly on the higher rungs of the ladder on which senior and executive levels of government and business perch, where some of the worst offenders are routinely let off the hook or even rewarded in elections or otherwise. Even as almost every member of the public has to bribe policemen on the street, security guards, and attendants acting as gatekeepers to bigger offices, high-ranking officials in the hierarchy typically demand—discreetly—larger sums in cash and other forms of value. At the highest levels, money may not even change hands, but special favors and privileges almost certainly do. Petty corruption may indeed be a subtle expression of more deeply hidden patterns of corruption that are rampant across societies, including those where baksheesh is severely frowned on.[14]

Administrative Corruption

Administrative or middle-level government and sometimes private sector companies often aggregate small payoffs, taking them to a more "officially sanctioned" level. For instance, a country's department of land revenue collection may pool bribes obtained by individual staff members and redistribute them among members of the office staff. Given their frequency and the relatively low pain to those people anxious to engage in land transactions, these practices become normalized. Similarly, electric line workers may demand baksheesh for doing what they are already paid to do, but both a cut of that payment and the materials they skim off may be siphoned off in larger aggregate quantities at higher levels. Extortion is another common form of administrative corruption; for instance, officials may threaten to condemn a building nearing construction unless a substantial bribe is paid.

Usually, administrative corruption redistributes funding and political influence through hierarchy-based unequal shares among a substantial set of office staff within confined groups. As its name implies, it typically operates within government, but one can also find cartels and complex regimes of payoffs and influence at different scales in private businesses operating international networks such as sports franchises, quasi-public entities like school boards, and community groups such as church or temple trusts and other neighborhood associations.

In its more advanced stages, administrative corruption may resemble the case of Tammany Hall in New York City in the nineteenth and early twentieth centuries, where a tight private club of the Democratic Party's political and financial leadership became a hub controlling the municipal and state administration. In the 1860s, after getting himself elected to the New York Board of the Supervisors, William Magear Tweed, better known as "Boss" Tweed, was appointed to be on the boards of several large banks, hotels, railroad companies, and utilities. That put him at the cusp of Tammany Hall's "machine politics" to oversee the open sale of government assets and services to the highest bidders among bankers, criminal mafias, industrialists, land developers, and other key figures seeking to be the first movers in capturing valuable political and economic markets in the city. Over time, the machine grew even more powerful, using the funds to distribute private largesse across a large number of key constituents.

Tammany Hall epitomized US politics as a battleground for trading interests such as jobs, services, and votes. But its machine politics may also have represented a collective approach to solving the problem of the needs of multiple ethnic subgroups vying for political gain. Elites within these groups effectively parlayed agreements around criminal territories and interests, creating a morass of lawlessness with ordinary people left to fend for themselves.[15]

Grand or Political Corruption

Grand corruption, also known as political or systemic corruption, involves larger scales and more complex forms of action than the other types. It arises when the government's center of political power is almost entirely shaped by elite interests. One might imagine how criminal cartels and other groups of actors characterizing administrative corruption of the Tammany Hall type might gather steam and join forces with bigger territorial players. In contemporary democratic political systems, it is also routine for donors and large sponsors of political parties to expect returns on campaign contributions as political favors. States often change the rules to protect special interests even though doing so harms the public good. Moreover, social practices may change substantially to accommodate these interests, generating new patterns and consequences that give us clues to how elite networks of power manage to stay entrenched.[16]

In the corruption literature, contemporary Russia is frequently cited as the paradigmatic case of grand corruption. In the early 1990s during the transition from communism to capitalism, vast state interests were privatized to benefit an ensemble of *apparatchiks*—former senior government officials, mercenaries, and KGB agents —together with a small group of powerful local warlords across the former Soviet Union. During this transition, which involved the rapid redistribution of giant industrial, land, and natural resource assets, especially energy and minerals, from the state to the private sector, an oligopoly (of wealth and political power) just as quickly and firmly established tight control over these assets. This control was facilitated by several, mutually reinforcing features that had characterized Soviet Russia, which the political scholar Alena Ledeneva terms *blat*: the use of friends, acquaintances, and occasional contacts for mutual favors; the provision of influence and protection; and gaining exclusive access to goods and services in short supply and also to jobs and special privileges. These informal, unwritten rules of conduct that ordinary people had to engage in to stay alert to the use of their personal connections to exchange favors simply to survive changed shape to become the basis on which post-Soviet society was organized.[17]

When the Soviet Union disintegrated, decentralized networks gave way to the *sistema*, power networks forming the state-led political machine, which was operated by insiders maintaining informal arrangements of loyalty and compensation for favors delivered. Ledeneva describes the sistema:

> The leader's inner circle provides support for agenda setting, vision, or program. The leader's core contacts provide structure and organization to ensure public policy implementation and mobilization of cadres. Useful friends help mobilize and control resources and support important projects. Mediated contacts serve to communicate policies, to create a buffer with the public and to ensure legitimacy and stability.[18]

The net result was a small but resilient oligarchy powered by oil resources, which continues to provide a steady and significant source of revenue with shared and carefully distributed windfalls. In a recent twist, resembling the Indonesia case under Suharto, the original oligarchy formed in the late twentieth century appears to have effectively been stripped of its political influence by the Kremlin, which maintains dominance. In the process, Russian society has been reshaped through various patterns of intrigue, violence, and strong forms of mistrust operating at multiple levels. The leader and his inner circle have a strong grip on resources and maintain primary authority, with subsidiary, globally connected elite networks holding tight reins over the routine operations of (apparently) multiple societies. Their effects are expressed in Russia's vast, globally powerful organized crime syndicates, high levels of economic inequality, and growing social isolation experienced by most of the people.[19]

The United States exemplifies a qualitatively different form of grand corruption, which has taken shape for more than a century. Its extensive and complex rules appear to be constructed to benefit elite interests in arenas where the stakes are high, such as political campaigns, speculative financial markets, and the defense business, previously known as the military-industrial complex. In geopolitical terms, the United States more than dominates the global conventional military order, which makes multipower nuclear parity almost irrelevant. This assures a formidable defense and security industry, which drives about 3 percent of the US economy. Its firms operate in cartel-like ways when they help direct government policy, occasionally collaborating with the big banks, chemicals, electronics and software, oil and gas, retail, and the transportation industries—indeed, many of the wealthiest firms in the Fortune 500. In those other industries, private arrangements among business owners, bankers, government clients, and regulators are also the key to the ability of elite power networks to capture extraordinary wealth and privilege, but they do not penetrate all parts of government as they do in Russia. This system nevertheless exhibits a post–Tammany Hall syndrome of corruption, where many of the most blatant forms of political horse trading and associated systems of injustice have become legitimized through systems of law that tilt the scales in favor of the politically connected and wealthy.[20]

The contemporary US pattern of corruption can also be viewed in terms of the carefully calibrated, everyday practices of consumption that are evident everywhere in society. These patterns of consumption lock most ordinary people into a grid of nearly identical daily activities. For example, members of the middle class feel compelled to maintain a good credit rating, keep a job, pay a mortgage, own an automobile, possess insurance coverage, and so on. As I illustrate in Chapter 3, it is the orchestrated maintenance of multiple elements of the daily grinds of ordinary people in the United States (as elsewhere) that keeps a vast engine of economic and social order going, which in turn sustains elite networks in politics and big business.[21]

Shared Characteristics of the Three Levels of Corruption

The three levels of corruption—petty, administrative, and grand—are typically linked to one another in the ways I have already stated, but there are greater variations and complexity than these categories may suggest. In some emerging countries, such as India, China, and Nigeria, the three forms seem to form an amalgam, with clear linkages from petty to grand heights of corruption. In advanced economies like Canada, Japan, or the United Kingdom, only political corruption may be in clear evidence, with petty or administrative modes rare or completely missing. In these countries, the situation may be interpreted as representing important political victories for the public for enforcing the rule of law in everyday transactions and preventing malpractice and cheating, especially among government officials. Enforcing the rule of law implies that elected or appointed officials cannot behave with impunity in their interactions with the public. Yet, these countries demonstrate "influence markets," where elite groups in and out of government exchange favors on a colossal scale with each other without the knowledge of ordinary people, but yielding detrimental outcomes for them.

Whatever the particular arrangement in a given society, it is possible to identify two broad trends: (1) an identifiable pattern in the everyday practices of the general public to accommodate corruption and (2) the formation of a discernible tight group of individuals, forming an elite network and gaining varying levels of political authority, money, or both.[22]

Political corruption is therefore a blend of different layers of deceit or extortion, sometimes running through entire segments of society and sometimes only within elite groups. Its connections to organized crime and white-collar crime are well recorded. White-collar crime is itself rarely addressed or even detected in many of its forms, as when executives in private or government establishments violate their own organizational norms, engage in violent crime by themselves or engage others to do so, form partnerships with each other to extort, steal, or otherwise distend rules, and ultimately change the very norms for their actions. When criminality is detected in government, it is sometimes represented as though external elements have somehow contaminated its otherwise good and well-founded laws. Often, however, it is the legal system itself and the very criteria of legitimacy associated with it that have to be questioned in this context. In addition, political parties and the system of government may depend on resources that extend well beyond formal, legal operations.[23]

Rarely, as in Uganda under President Idi Amin, one might encounter conditions where a single individual effectively steers and manages an entire economy of bribes and exchanges of favors. Of course, these conditions beg the question as to exactly what laws are being violated when the entire system rewards just one person and his coterie. More typically, in developing countries, as I suggested earlier, one finds retail forms of baksheesh, money that is extorted by public officials from the public for everyday transactions. There and elsewhere, one finds different modes of clientelism, in which elite networks of bosses, including heads of corporations, other owners of extraordinary wealth, and elected officials, are entangled in deals that usually end up favoring themselves disproportionately.[24]

Despite these intricacies, the view of corruption that has become popularized through media attention is that it results in a scandal involving a central individual and a few of his or her closest allies, simulating the "excitement" of a classic gangster plot. This is a misreading of how corruption operates at different levels as multiple linkages run through broad swaths of society, sometimes covering all of it. A single crooked officer in a sea of righteousness is unheard of; it is more common to find cultures of bribe taking and a gradation of payoffs. More generally, at the scales at which administrative or political corruption operate, a complicated network of relationships, favors, and cultures of deceit is essential to keep the system operating smoothly. Nevertheless, virtually every television drama and popular tale of corruption are about a scheming villain who controls a criminal network and the politicians, only to be foiled by heroes or superheroes like Batman.[25]

The image of a briskly networked and substantially large circle of operators, a veritable den of thieves, like the one revealed in the Panama Papers, is rare in the collective imagination. Moreover, by aligning themselves with the widely propagated "arch-criminal versus superhero" perspective, even many scholarly studies on corruption emphasize particular types of criminal activity involving an individual or group and focus on removing individual incentives for those cheating the government.

Against this mainstream view, which is increasingly seen among corruption scholars as problematic, I next take up a few alternative historical understandings of corruption. I then use contemporary scholarship to help guide me toward a more useful interpretation of corruption.

How Have We Understood Corruption to Date?

Corruption in the Greco-Roman Classical Period

In one form or the other, the danger of corruption has been a central preoccupation of political life since antiquity. Corruption is an old word, but we first hear of it in the chronicles of territorial rule, where potentates had to impose order on vast areas under their dominion. The Babylonian Code of Hammurabi from about 1750 BCE called for punishing someone bearing false witness as if they were convicted for the crime. In the ancient Indian Sanskrit text, the Arthaśāstra—the putative fourth-century BCE mirror-of-princes treatise by Kauṭilya, Chandragupta Maurya's presumed confidant and minister—several passages refer to bribery, embezzlement, bearing false witness, and theft of state property. All are harshly condemned.

Similar descriptions can be seen in two of the earliest Greek and Roman texts dating to the fifth century BCE: *History of the Peloponnesian War* and the *Law of Twelve Tables,* respectively. In 388 BCE, bronze statues of Zeus were put up outside Olympia bearing inscriptions naming and shaming those athletes who were caught cheating, including the boxer Eupolus, who bribed three of his competitors to assure his own victory. Early Roman law was acutely aware that witnesses could be bribed to give false testimony and required that those caught be subjected to extreme penalties. Indeed, most of the early texts that outline legal codes or practice, describe how magistrates and rulers were enjoined to punish the guilty so harshly as to serve as a deterrent for others; yet they say little about other modes of political action needed to stem the rot.[26]

The idea of bribery, as incentives exchanged across individuals or groups to shortchange rules, also has mythical origins. In Greek mythology, the Judgment of Paris is one of the earliest stories of alliances formed across classes and types of power. In the legend, Paris, the child of Queen Hecuba and King Priam of Troy, is prophesied to destroy their kingdom. Predictably, he is not killed but is left in the wilderness to grow up to become the very shepherd who catches the attention of Zeus, ruler of the gods. At that time Zeus must decide to give the golden apple designating who is "the fairest" to one of three goddesses. He gives Paris the responsibility to make that judgment. Paris, turn, treats it as a choice from among three types of bribes. Hera offers him the prize of political power; Athena offers wisdom and bravery; and Aphrodite offers him the hand of Helen, the most beautiful mortal woman in the world but who is already married to King Menelaus of Sparta. Paris choses to elope with Helen and sets off the chain of events dramatized in Homer's *Iliad*.

In ancient Greece, another sense of corruption, *stasis,* was already in use to convey civil strife leading to the degeneration of social order. Stasis was corruption that resembled a form of contamination, causing a loss of health and power. In allied usage, it was self-indulgence, exuberant consumption, loss of integrity, and a situation where people sank to a debased form of behavior.[27]

In classical Greece and Rome, although ordinary people could be corrupted, this was not a prominent theme except in some writings from late in that period. Homer used three words for people—*laos, demos,* and *plethos*—each with different meanings. The *laoi* are the followers of a leader; the *demos* is a group of individuals sharing a name, a common place, and a sense of their identity; and *plethos* is an undifferentiated multitude. In its heroic tradition, the ancient Greek ideal of the *polis* could imply all of these understandings of the "people." A polis's inhabitants had a stronger affinity to the city-region or republic than to the gods. But the symbol of the polis was also the community of *ekklesia* or the assembly, where adult male citizens would jointly gather to develop the good life with joint responsibility and benefits. Females, slaves, and other noncitizens were co-creators of the *polis,* whether it was democratic like Athens or an oligarchy like Sparta. But they had little or no voice or practical intervention in its functioning.[28]

Athenian democracy was prone to corruption when class snobbery, the exchange of favors among elites, and the rise of demagogues distorted the preconditions of free speech and transparency in political operations. Moreover, Athens acted with impunity and imperial power when it annexed nearby lands. In the short but infamous Melian dialogue, we see how Athenian hubris—its belief in its own moral, political, and military superiority—revealed its brutal face in international politics. During the Peloponnesian War, Athenian diplomats went to the tiny island of Melos and, to the bewilderment of their hosts, simply demanded that they surrender to Athens, which they earnestly believed to be a superior society.[29]

Corruption in the classical world was seen as a type of tragedy: the systemic failure to reach the self-professed ideals of justice on which all types of political authority are built. Many scholars have understood the decline of Rome as despair widely felt over several generations. But, as we shall see, certainly many other well-organized territorial powers with legacies of legitimacy and effectiveness have endured centuries of slow decline. Corruption, in its Greek and Roman classical sense, in particular, was thus seen as the formation of a political authority built around the need to structure a just society, but whose very practices could become saturated with the likelihood of failure to achieve it.[30]

As implied in the maxim "power corrupts," the tragedy of politics is that almost any formation can have the tendency to degenerate over time. The political theorist Arlene Saxonhouse writes that corruption in ancient Athens was overlaid with multiple meanings. It could, for instance, be represented in a Sophist's use of the rhetorical tools of flattery and deceit to hide the truth about relations of power. Or it could force a painful reexamination of things as they are or, perhaps tragically, reveal the imperfect union created by social lives:

> To be human . . . requires the examined life. Examining, though, means corrupting what society offers as *given* and engaging others in this process, just as Socrates the corrupter of the young does. . . . Corruption is the *corrective to the unattainable political ideal of eternity.* Both Thucydides through Pericles and Plato through Socrates look for perfection in the city, and both acknowledge the inaccessibility of that perfection. Corruption inevitably occurs.[31]

Socrates rejected the charge that he was a corrupter of youth. He turned the tables on those who promoted smugness, thoughtlessness, and the idea that everyday institutions are part of the natural order. It was they, and not he, who made society corrupt by pitting order against democratic practice, which in turn raised uncomfortable questions relating to the examined life. The tension between promising calm while requiring acquiescence versus allowing questioning but risking chaos remains a recurrent theme in political discourse.[32]

Corruption as Political and Social Decadence: The Machiavellian Insight

In Asia and Europe, throughout much of the first millennium, intimations of corruption came from discourses on its moral elements. In the early Christian era, the emphasis was on one's own role and actions in the world. In other cultures, for much of that period, similar frames of corruption existed but are largely now associated with the personal failings of leaders and their supporters; for example, as elaborated by Augustine, Avicenna/al-farabi, Confucius, and Kauṭilya. Over time, these interpretations also began to be formed around the sovereign claims and duties of kings and princes, which depended usually on the size of their territory and the rival expectations of other groups, including the poor.

By the middle of the second millennium in Italy, multiple powerful city-states had the ability to invest in trade by redirecting some of the surplus produced from farming in the rural hinterland. To enable that trade, small sets of elite landowners and merchants began to support political institutions that had at least a nominal republican form in many locations. In Genoa, for instance, pirates, traders, and landed elites were in bitter competition before seeking to establish the rule of law. Corruption was seemingly hidden in a world of gangsters and conflicts among them, with no bureaucratic or kingly authority to prevent war. One had to look for it in the emergence and development of new syndromes of elite networks and forms resistant to them. By the fifteenth century, a coalition of the *popolo,* or the "popular group," was included among the main rival gangs in forms of representative government all across Italy.[33]

The popolo were simply the non-elite, or ordinary people, all those who did not make the rules or keep the order but were subject to both. The much smaller factions on the other side were grouped into the *patricii,* comprising the priestly, landed, and government classes. In classical Rome, around the beginning of the Common Era, the patricii claimed bloodlines going back to Rome's legendary founder Romulus's first appointed senate of one hundred men, the *patres*. They held control over land and income while also creating for themselves a powerful place in the evolving republican government.

In fifteenth-century Italy, the proper guidance of rulers was deemed essential, given that they and their progeny needed skills to use their substantial resources of power to punish or prevent crimes and to foster well-being. Both the republic ruled by a coalition of popular and patrician representatives and the principality with a single sovereign ruler were in search of jurists, interpreters of the law, and appropriate forms of governing well. Perhaps no other figure from medieval Europe is better known for providing such guidance than Niccolo Machiavelli, although his advice was hardly straightforward. Machiavelli famously wrote *The Prince* from prison to appease one of his former patrons, the wealthy merchant Lorenzo di Piero de Medici, who had incarcerated the erstwhile diplomat after usurping the "throne" of Florence and destroying its para-republican form.

In addition to providing his readers lessons about administrative intrigue, Machiavelli's interpretations of Italian political formations have substantially enhanced our understanding of corruption by associating it with the tendency for degeneration in political societies. Machiavelli taught us to see corruption as being characteristic of the schemes of those in power to hold onto it and to try to amass even more by deploying skills to form lucrative alliances, thereby gaining control over resources and people, political formations, and territory. This corrupting tendency of power arises from the violence imposed on society, evidently enough, by a nexus of wealth and power.

One of the most fascinating features of *The Prince* is that Machiavelli keeps his readers guessing whether he is being ironic about the qualities of the sovereign individual he seems so sincerely to be admiring. The best use of one's *virtù* (valor, fortitude, skill) may sometimes be to be feared rather than loved. The ideal prince can be cruel and even ruthless at times but must always mobilize collective sanction for his actions. Corruption might take the form of tyranny not only among the powerful, as it did with the Caesars, but also among the people themselves—when they are indifferent to singular or oligarchical cruelty or engage in collectively destructive strategies. Sometimes corruption can be a combination of all of these elements. Often, it is luck (*fortuna*) that determines corruption's consequences and sets in play future games of the dominant in relation to each other and to others.

Tyranny is usually expressed in a single figure who usurps absolute power. But that individual is hardly acting alone. Guarding against these various entanglements of corruption requires a vigilant set of counter-strategies. In Milan, at the end of the three-decade tyrannical rule of Duke Filippo Visconti in the fifteenth century, a republic was quickly instituted and the populace mobilized to restore ancient ideals. Yet, Filippo's son-in-law Francesco Sforza betrayed the republic by initially supporting it and then plotting against it. Machiavelli writes,

> I say that no accident, even though grave and violent, could ever make Milan or Naples free because their members are all corrupt. This one may see after the death of Filippo Visconti, for although Milan wished to return to freedom, it could not and did not know how to maintain it. So it was to Rome's great happiness that [their] kings became corrupt quickly, so that they were driven out before their corruption passed into the bowels of that city. This lack of corruption—men having a good end—was the cause that the infinite tumults in Rome did not hurt and indeed helped the republic.[34]

A corrupted people arises in the form of an anti-political, privatized mob composed of individuals who cynically conceive of the political arena in purely instrumental terms as a source of power for advancing their personal interests. For Machiavelli, much like Aristotle nearly two millennia before him, corruption is a process of moral and political disorder that might take various forms and be expressed in different degrees from bad to worse. In the absence of good habits and practices and an alert constituency, even good laws that are introduced by one person or a republic will not suffice, especially if old habits return once that person dies or a republican regime is overturned. But where good institutions are prevalent, "where the matter is not corrupt, tumults and other scandals do not hurt."[35]

In his magisterial account of the social and political context of the Florence of Machiavelli's times, the social historian J. G. A. Pocock writes,

> Corruption [for Machiavelli] appears, initially, as a generalized process of moral decay whose beginnings are hard to foresee and its progress almost impossible to resist. The constitutional order is rooted in the moral order, and it is the latter which corruption affects; on the one hand there cannot be *buoni ordini* [sound institutions] without *buoni costumi* [good morals], but on the other, once *buoni costumi* have been lost there is a very slender chance that *buoni ordini* alone will succeed in restoring them. Institutions are dependent on the moral climate and laws, which work well when the people are not corrupt produce effects the reverse of those desired when they are.[36]

As it turns out, the corruption of the people simply worsens the likelihood of the corruption of the polity ever being discovered and dealt with. The people of Milan were incapable of maintaining justice in their republic for long, unlike those of Rome. The former were corrupted in the sense of being "apolitical": they lacked an urge for social justice along with political order. This may be because they were too concerned with their private worlds to engage impartially in public life. Again, as in classical Greece, corruption inevitably seems to happen as often as the people tragically lose their sense of mutual goodwill and trust. If Socrates famously preferred to take hemlock rather than denounce his own efforts to influence the youth of Athens, he did so in in the hope of creating a more just republic by stirring people out of their complacency generated by their false quest for personal gain and propelling them toward a particular type of social order. And although Plato does not quite suggest it, there is enough in his and others' work of that period to convince us that Greek democracy too, was tragically subject to degeneration.[37]

The strategies of those taking hold of territorial power could be just or unjust, but there is no easy way for an observer of history to make moral distinctions across regimes, other than in terms of their effectiveness and legitimacy—with the latter showing the extent to which the regimes command the fear and respect of the people. Yet, all political societies are constantly at risk of degeneration at multiple levels; this risk affects both those who directly hold power and the general public.

The Managerial Face of Corruption Today

So far, so many varied senses of corruption. In contrast, the contemporary understanding of corruption, at least in policy circles, tends to be far less ambitious and much more "managerial" in its form and purpose.

The term "managerial" can be explained by examining the way many multilateral agencies and governments today define corruption: the abuse of public office for private gain. If a person holding public office or having some obligatory role to a large public gives the appearance of deceiving that constituency, usually by making windfall personal gains through her or his actions, that person is termed "corrupt." Alternatively, corruption has been associated with the violation of the rules of public office by anyone focusing on private (including personal, family, or clique) gains. If the person seems to act in collusion with others, then a larger cartel with shared interests in pooling resources is deemed to be corrupt.

These definitions are prevalent in spite of there being several orders of ambiguity around the meaning of their words: "public," "private," "office," and "gain." Moreover, it is not clear what forms of corruption are included or excluded. Perhaps it is handy to have a simple account of corruption centering on an agent's motivations for private gains because it fits nicely with a market orientation. It is easier to imagine that all parts of society follow a similar and analytically simple microeconomic logic of maximizing welfare for the collectivity of agents in that world. This means that the level of corruption in any given market can be assessed by determining the maximum supply of bribable goods and the total amount of bribes that individuals are willing to pay to obtain them. Scholars of corruption who use this framework often speak of a "corruption equilibrium," the optimal level of corruption to keep an economy on an even keel of development. The managerial response can then be derived as a formal set of incentives to bring corrupt acts to some optimal level.[38]

A rational choice framework—whether involving analytical techniques, such as game theory, which examines so-called principal-agent problems (where a person or "agent" makes decisions that affect another, the "principal"), or empirical accounts of criminalization of political leadership and parties—provides many useful insights into some of the dynamics of corrupt transactions involving key actors. But it frequently misses the forest for the trees by paying more attention to particular acts of bribery than to the social and political conditions that make them possible. By concentrating simply on the incidence or even quantum of bribes paid in a given place or context, we are distracted from viewing the stable elite networks of mutual advantage that are typically represented in relatively small groups of extremely powerful and (generally) rich persons who constitute a special social class as such. But equally important is the way the rest of society seems to readjust itself to accommodate these elite networks, and more often their immediate clients, within a mosaic of power connections.

By bypassing non-aggregable qualities of political corruption and their long-term effects on public trust within societies, many analytical techniques, given their customary biases of atomism or what is termed "methodological individualism," are unable to represent collective forms and their relationships. Similarly, they tend to neglect their legacy and network effects and the emergence of new institutions and social formations, evidence of which is widely available in ethnographies and other reports.[39]

Techniques to diminish managerial corruption remain attractive and can range from giving more straightforward policy instructions to administrators to hiring additional auditors to a combination of training, new rules of compliance, and more reliable monitoring of employees. They are practical and relatively simple ways to implement guidelines that will ostensibly reduce corruption. But they tend to focus solely on the act of taking a bribe or giving a bribe by public officials, seeing in them egregious criminals or at least their actions as morally dubious individual transactions that can be given graded punishments as a remedy. They typically assume that self-interest is at the base of every action among all the players at stake and furthermore that such self-interest is measurable in monetary (or utility) terms. Addressing corruption is logically, then, primarily seen as the work of improving rules for bureaucrats and other government employees both to reduce incentives for their stealing public resources and to make it more attractive for them to become committed to doing their jobs well.

Thus, managerial approaches tend to view corruption as the outcome of badly formulated rules and careless oversight: corrupt practices are the result of certain choices that in turn arise out of distorted incentives. They are then manifested as a certain type of unprofessionalism among government employees. These behavior patterns may be grouped to include nepotism, slacking off, bribery, extortion, and permitting illegal actions or charging personal fees for legal services. What are called for in response are well-designed ladders of hierarchy that bring in a chain of command, assessment of employees' skills, and incentives for noncorrupt actions, transparency, and accountability; in other words, a tightly managed organization within the offices of government. These reforms are expected to improve governance, in the sense of streamlining the activities of the state and making its functioning and delivery of services more efficient.

Clearly what the managerial definition does not cover are fuzzy forms of undue influence enjoyed by elite groups, such as raised by this question: Is it corruption when elected political representatives are more prone to listen to wealthy lobbyists than to other constituents, even if the former only make contributions within the law to their campaigns and not to their personal coffers? This is because it fails to distinguish between time-honored customary connections among elite groups in power and those who seek their undue help; it treats practices arising from those connections as individual failings rather than as societal institutions of inequality and injustice; it may even consider them as "traditions."[40]

Doing *Something*

The managerial view has shaped many contemporary public perceptions of and responses to corruption. In addition to ranking countries on the corruption scale—largely based on perceptions of how often one needs to bribe bureaucrats and politicians or their intermediaries to do business there—the managerial focus of corruption is typically interpreted as finding ways to streamline public sector procurement and other government practices in developing countries. These "cleanup" operations might help reduce line-level or retail corruption, but they often have the detrimental effect of making illicit actions even more clandestine. Instead, the changing relations between the private and public sectors, constituting contrasting poles of wealth and power in many cases, should be the focus of contemporary discourse on corruption. These relations are steadily more multinational in character, and often involve deep pockets and murky networks, as the Panama and Paradise Papers scandals reveal. Elite networks gain control over movements of substantial amounts of capital while reshaping policies in preferred directions through a nexus of military, financial, and political interests. By demanding a greater role for the private sector, they justify the growth of oligopolies having inordinate influence on regulators. They also end up supporting specific patterns of large-scale consumption that help organize our everyday routines and habits on an already ecologically compromised planet.

In 2004, the first UN Convention on Anti-Corruption (UNCAC) went into force, and this was a significant achievement for the international community, requiring all parties to the convention to abide by its principles and guidelines. UNCAC has since become an important element of international law because it has the potential to induce governments to improve their systems of transparency and public accountability. It also sets up many mechanisms to identify and check cross-border crime funded by the proceeds of bribery and extortion. The problem is that UNCAC has little jurisdiction over the more general forms of "grand" corruption, through which political and corporate elites form alliances that create legal structures sanctioning cronyism in different aspects of public life.[41]

In circumstances of rising inequality and worsening poverty, economic "rents" (or undue or windfall profits) are routinely extracted from the general population right under their very noses, with little or no recourse to duly elected governments, which may even authorize such injustices. Consider, for instance, the difficulty of securing campaign finance reform or corporate accountability rules in many parts of the world, even as lobbyists routinely block legislation for protecting citizens from dangerous chemicals, affordable health care and education, and so on. With definitions of corruption that focus on individual managers in government on whom we place immediate responsibility may help stop the bleeding associated with corruption scandals, but consign the more systematic injustices to obscurity and leave many hidden networks unscathed.

This professional focus on a stripped-down version of corruption in the context of the global political economy also provides important clues to understanding its managerial emphasis. In the 1980s, many so-called structural adjustment programs that involved harsh reductions in social welfare measures were imposed on developing countries by the World Bank and International Monetary Fund (IMF) as conditions for debt servicing and new loans. Toward the end of the decade, these international financial institutions (IFIs) were compelled to modify these policies, because it became increasingly clear that they had disastrous impacts, ranging from declining returns on investment to worsening unemployment and poverty. In doing so, the IFIs shifted their perspective of governments of developing countries from being disinterested managers of the "commanding heights of the economy" to being rent-seeking states. A useful term that emerged in this period was "rent-seeking," coined by the economist Anne Krueger, who went on to be chief economist at the World Bank and managing director of the IMF. Krueger argued that the creation of complex layers of bureaucracy by the state—presumably to safeguard economic development and increase accountability—would perversely generate incentives for private sector players to bribe officials to "speed approvals."[42]

Many of these countries, however, were also capitalized by loans and subject to global cost fluctuations under the influence of monopoly firms selected by multilateral and bilateral donors to stimulate investment. In the 1990s, liberalization policies were often interpreted to mean the suspension of state regulation in both developed and developing countries on the recommendation of free-market promoters. This implied that elite cartels could proceed with carte blanche to extract shared rents. It follows, then, that the rules of investment and growth would not by themselves guarantee economic development in a country unless those holding the reins acted responsibly.

In fact, in every instance in which private capital investors received incentives to find new markets, recent history at least shows that capital would have flowed there anyway. In the 1990s, for example, the World Bank, led by economists who were driven to create flexible capital accumulation in the electricity sector, made the assessment that only private capital could resolve the fiscal troubles that prevented the expansion of electricity access in many developing countries. At the same time, electricity markets in Europe, Japan, and North America were significantly drying up for *new* investments because of the oversaturation of supply. The reason was that many of these countries—hit by the oil crisis, the ebb and flow of finance capital, power plant machinery manufacturers, and global banks—were already looking for new markets in emerging economies in Asia and Latin America.[43]

In the 1990s, corruption became an important subject in policy discourse, with a new motivation among scholars, administrators, and international donors to define the term properly in order to address it. This firmness of purpose could be associated with an epiphany in mainstream economics that took place in the 1990s: the importance of placing good governance and institutions at the top of the agenda for economic growth, alongside open markets and access to investment capital. This also led to the understanding that a state's governance or internal rules and modes of implementation—that is, its political institutions—are critical to determining how efficient its economic functioning would be and what circumstances could encourage public officials to act like private entrepreneurs. Those professionals working on anti-corruption programs have operated primarily within this economic paradigm in the past few decades and have duly expressed concern with measuring corruption, ranking countries by their levels of corruption, and developing instruments based on perceptions of investors or on assessments of the performance of institutions.[44]

Donors have been especially interested in these measures and rankings, often using them to make recommendations about international aid and to push reform along particular directions allied with their interests. Yet, it is far from clear whether in actual practice these anti-corruption strategies reduce the sense of what Durkheim calls *anomie*—a breakdown in institutions and the sense of community—which resonates with most narratives of corruption in our times. In fact, some reforms, despite their achievements in reducing corruption as conventionally measured, have had unintended consequences that in themselves are chilling.

For instance, graft-reduction tools in Hong Kong have been executed with such technocratic precision and severity that they have ended up worsening mutual distrust and fear. After a long period characterized by the elite capture of power, allocated between organized crime and the police at least since the early twentieth century, one of the first achievements of Hong Kong's Independent Commission on Anti-Corruption (ICAC; created in 1974 by the then-governor Sir Murray MacLehose) was the abolition of the office of the police superintendent. This was done on the basis of the tough Prevention of Corruption Ordinance of 1971, which placed limits on public officials' assets. The ICAC was duly shifted from being under the auspices of the police and became an independent investigative and forensic agency with its own officers having substantial powers for conducting probes, arresting suspects without warrant, filing criminal charges, and bringing suspects to trial. The organization could prosecute cases quickly and also engage in public campaigns against corruption, with the stated intent of creating a "moral climate . . . of popular disapproval" against bribery.[45]

Throughout its history, ICAC has developed a reputation for the intimidation of suspects, widespread arrests, and swift implementation of sentences, with a relatively slim record of successful prosecution of cases. In an already rigid context of state power that limits rights of expression, "ICAC's powers to search, seize and compel suspects," and "arrest without warrant . . . even for suspected offenses that are not its obligation to investigate," created an unnerving effect on the morale of government workers and their families. Furthermore, judging by social attitude surveys at least, citizens of Hong Kong appear to feel no more secure and content than their peers elsewhere in Asia even if corruption in the territory is perceived to be quite low.[46]

Finding Alternatives to the Managerial Conception of Corruption

In recent years, the serious constraints of the managerial framework of corruption have become apparent for scholars and policy makers in the field. They recognize the irony of rooting out corruption simply meaning having better policing methods, when the worst scandals involve players who direct and control the police and other instruments of administration. Corruption must surely involve more systematic and insidious processes if it produces disparagement and discontent within the general public about something foul going on in their societies. There is a growing consensus among scholars that corruption is notoriously difficult to define but easier to recognize in specific contexts. There have been significant calls to broaden the understanding and identification of corruption, and many questions have arisen about its measurement as used in the rankings of countries. Moreover, in the past two decades, the dominant definition—the abuse of public office for private gain—has been challenged on at least two fronts.[47]

The first challenge, proposed by Michael Johnston, Olivier de Sardan, and others, argues for corruption to be studied in systemic terms of practice, rather than as the attribute of specific actions of "corrupt" individuals. Instead of seeking to locate corruption in the rent-seeking actions of individuals who break the law in one way or the other, corruption should be identified with the manner in which wealth and various types of power are deployed as nearly fungible or mutually interchangeable forms of capital to be exchanged within relatively small elite social networks. This shift in focus generates a more layered, multi-attribute view that brings out "syndromes" or "complexes" of corruption in different national and political contexts.[48]

The second interpretation, offered by Akhil Gupta, John and Jean Comaroff, Veena Das, and other anthropologists, tries to unravel the ambiguous moral ground of corruption, especially in postcolonial societies. Gupta and the Comaroffs, in particular, write stories about people leading ordinary lives in contemporary situations in north India and southern Africa, respectively, and their encounters with government officials and other figures of authority. They find that the exchange of bribes for favors is messily tied to local pathologies of gift-giving and cultures of exchange. Yet that is not as troubling as the growing grid of bureaucratization that subtly intensifies certain power relations and helps consolidate new and more insidious forms of control over human bodies. These forms of control have variously been termed "biopolitics" and structural violence. Again, larger and more legal forms of elite consolidation of power and wealth are unnoticed when the focus turns to petty bribery or individual favors granted by officials to their clients.[49]

In spite of significant differences in approach among both groups of scholars, they have a common interest in understanding the particular social and cultural contexts of what is being termed "corruption," rather than simply considering the decision frameworks of individual interactions. This marks a useful departure for my purposes.

Corruption as a Social Process

Syndromes of Corruption

In *Syndromes of Corruption,* Michael Johnston argues that corruption should be studied in much broader and systemic terms as a social process, rather than as an attribute or outcome of actions of "corrupt" individuals. This changed focus leads to a description of features of a society that seem to generate greater consolidation of resources—if not of wealth, then of power, or both; such features include increasing inequality, a deepening sense of mistrust, and greater collective disorder expressed in social despair and lawlessness. The sustained pain and damage inflicted on societies through the raw power exercised by elite networks acting through, or in collusion with, sections of the polity, result in anomie. This then becomes a source of potentially irredeemable despair and simmering anger across wide swaths of a society.⁵⁰

In multiple contexts, one can identify the emergence of several syndromes—or cultures—of corrupt practices, each of which can be distinguished as being tied to systemic social conditions and patterns of legitimate or unlawful authority. In practical terms, this typically means that when large amounts of money are misappropriated on a regular basis, even if they accrue mostly to particular individuals and their families, something is going on that cannot be attributed simply to the misdeeds of a single person or his or her group. By speaking of syndromes rather than degrees or levels, Johnston complicates corruption by asking us to pay attention to the particular political setting in which it takes root and the contingent historical circumstances that shape its evolution.

As an example of distinctive "flavors" or syndromes of corruption, consider Peru under the regime of Alberto Fujimori, president between 1990 and 2000, compared to Indonesia under Suharto. In 2000, Fujimori was forced to resign and flee the country following a major scandal: his chief of intelligence Vladimiro Montesinos had recorded videos of more than 300 cash transactions Fujimori had with tycoons in domestic and foreign businesses; key figures in Peru's judiciary, legislature, media, military, and NGOs; and members of foreign governments. Montesinos had served as the "bank" through which different players were paid off for favors. These "Vladi-videos," as they came to be known, showed that an extensive corruption network of patronage was necessary to keep the Peruvian economy functioning well; indeed, immediately after Fujimori's ouster, economic growth dipped slightly.⁵¹

Peru's conditions were significantly different from those of Indonesia; most importantly, it had an elected president and a constitutional government as opposed to Indonesia's "benevolent" dictator Suharto. Although the police were dishonest in both countries, in Peru they used routine tactics of harassment and intimidation, whereas in Indonesia, they used violence specifically against potential political opponents of the regime. Indonesian society was fraught with fear of a police force that viciously intruded on the day-to-day lives of those who questioned the "New Order." In Peru the state police frequently hounded the poor, but to not greater extent than in other parts of Latin America.

Despite the countries' great differences, their syndromes of corruption shared common elements. Both brought heartbreak: even if the central characters were manifestly dishonorable, the rest of their societies were forced to make difficult ethical choices around the patterns of everyday life available to them, either as participants and beneficiaries in corrupt regimes or as bystanders having little or no meaningful engagement as citizens. Both countries' strategies of control and maintenance of social order were honed over several decades, made possible by a wide network of spies, and spawning perhaps more lasting forms of mistrust and mutual ill will in Peru after Fujimori's departure. The elaborate oligarchies in both regimes shared an interest in quickly accumulating and defending wealth, comprising both physical capital and signs that could be deployed to control institutions and public practices directly and indirectly.[52]

A considerable literature from both Latin America and Europe attests to similar patterns—whether under fascism, dictatorship, or communism—in which a large public has accommodated its everyday practices to come to terms with living normally with the terrors. The political philosopher Antonio Gramsci wrote that political ends are achieved through two fronts: the state not only uses its legitimate right to be coercive but also relies to a large extent on popular consent within what he called "civil society." The coalescence of force and manufactured consent makes up what Gramsci called "hegemony."[53]

In these processes, force may not be necessary at all, when what the dominant classes seek are the very ends that become desirable to the people themselves. If capitalists' goals are to produce ever-expanding markets for their products and they manage to deploy state power for this purpose, the state makes this possible by creating conditions to ensure that these products become a necessary part of everyday life. For instance, the public clamors for cell phones with 4G services, as spurred by marketing, social media, and the continued use of associated products.

Hegemony is achieved when the state's ability to demonstrate coercive force is combined with the public aligning its interests with those of dominant classes. Both of these forms of power primarily operate through the state, but in almost every case they include a coalition of those with sovereign authority, the rulers, and a small and usually wealthy group working with the rulers. Indonesia and Peru both seemed to have certain forms of hegemony: coercive and consensual elements were working together. But it is probably fair to assert that, in Indonesia, given the duration of the regime, those elements meshed very tightly to form even more complex arrangements that would have reverberating effects throughout that society.

Johnston's key insight is that a myriad of such patterns and symptoms characterize corruption across a variety of social and political milieus. All share this common feature: a small group of people who represent various interests are at the center of control over substantial resources that ought to be made available to a much broader public. As a result, gross inequality is perpetrated, both in economic and political power terms. Yet in both Indonesia and Peru, social stability was maintained even while political power and economic wealth were concentrated in a closely knit elite formation.

Johnston goes on to distinguish four broad types of such alliances formed between wealthy and politically powerful elites, all of which "significantly weaken open, competitive participation and/or economic and political institutions, or delay or prevent their development."[54] Each corruption formation is tied to a different combination of political and economic participation; the four together create a typology of countries with similar institutions. These syndromes can be identified by their taglines that appear as chapter titles in his book: influence markets (influence of rent, decisions for sale); elite cartels (how to buy friends and govern people); oligarchs and clans (we are family and you are not); and official moguls (reach out and squeeze someone). Fujimori's Peru may fit the elite cartels syndrome and Suharto's Indonesia, official moguls, whereas the present-day United States is characterized by influence markets.

These types, from influence markets to official moguls, are ordered along a multidimensional gradation from greater to fewer opportunities for participation and the corresponding weakening of institutions. But Johnston shows us how each is different only in its distinctive pattern of corruption, not in the extent of it. Indeed, influence markets are no "less" corrupt than official moguls; only the types of relationships built between political elites and their wealthy allies may differ.

Because corruption seems to have varied features in different countries, something more than the deviant behavior of individuals and their associates is at its root. If characteristics of influence markets characteristics show up in contemporary Germany, Japan, and the United States, these countries must share a similar culture or pattern of corruption that points to shared features of their societies, rather than just of the crooked individuals who happen to get caught. At the same time, what is most noteworthy is the way resulting gains in wealth and political power are shared among a surprisingly small number of players.[55]

For instance, corruption in influence markets (e.g., Britain, France, Germany, and Japan) may be "grand" in form. Political machines and corporations may be so strongly instituted or have such exclusive arrangements within formal rules and processes as to be revealed as major scandals only when there are embarrassing spillovers into the public scene. In contrast, in official moguls schemes (e.g., Haiti, Indonesia, Ivory Coast, and Kenya), one is likely to see insecure leadership that tries to grab what it can while in power, leading to rapacious "hand-over-fist" corruption. Indeed, the depressing conclusion is that corruption appears to be common to all countries—although each form has characteristic political provisions through which elite power groups find conclaves to run larger and better-entrenched machines, both to extract economic rent and to build on other arrangements of capital and social influence by exploiting privilege.[56]

The Emergence of Corruption

Within the substantial literature on the subject, I find Johnston's characterization of corruption most resonant with my own interpretation and therefore a useful lens for this study. Nevertheless, I need to revise his framework for my purpose, because it has at least two limitations. First, Johnston's focus on the contemporary period drives his data toward questions of political equality and access using language and methods that invoke modern archetypes of states and other recent political forms. My interest in the *longue durée* implies that I need to use concepts that are better fits for types of multilayered polities found in other periods and social locations.

Second, in addition to examining political and economic institutions, I am keen to understand more closely the social processes that generate and maintain these syndromes, especially the way ordinary people end up becoming co-opted into elite agendas. I seek to track, in narratives of political formations and societies over India's long history, the different shapes and ranges in which patterns or syndromes of grand corruption can be discerned and the extent to which some seem to repeat or change over time. Johnston's stylized analytical framework generates an alternative corruption map of contemporary polities compared to conventional rankings of countries as less or more corrupt. But it is not rich enough in its social description to be of precise use in my formulation.

Still, I borrow Johnston's word "syndrome" because it conveys a framework of knowledge concerning corruption that is closely related to mine. Elite formations of power appear different from one another, depending on particular ways in which political and economic spaces are captured by some form of dominance. Moreover, these differing formations suggest particular modes of exclusion, intrigue, and the theft of opportunities from the infelicitous, who have little wealth and no access to comparable people and support systems to smooth their lives. For example, in the ninth-century Tang Dynasty, twelfth-century Kashmir, and fourteenth-century Vatican, a distinctive set of actors and circumstances prevailed, even if there were common elements of political alliance formation and systematic extraction of public resources for the use of club members. Moreover, in some cases the corruption was obvious and systemic; in others it was more protected and limited in its impacts. But they all foreclosed or tried to regulate democratizing possibilities in their times.[57]

Beyond the tight group that one might term the "nobility," there is invariably, or perhaps essentially, a larger concentric circle of support for the elite. This comprises enforcers, administrators, and police in their various forms, as well as the ideologues and spin doctors who justify to the public the actions of those in power. The harm wrought by the workings of this second group of intellectuals, priests, and writers who are at pains to justify elite groupings is perhaps most catastrophic, because as a group they overlap with other complacent spectators, whose silence might be tied to the benefits that they, too, derive from these arrangements. These typically form an additional layer of confidence in the regime for the rest of the people, who could often be persuaded to provide mass shows of support when needed.

Each syndrome of corruption is therefore connected to particular circumstances that one can identify in a given form of elite consolidation of wealth and power and that could generate reasons for generalized societal aversion, even if it is not widely expressed. Corruption may then be seen as a common phenomenon across different contexts in that, in all its manifestations, has similar themes of social and political degeneration that collectively signal a generalized loss in legitimacy. The words "trust" and "democracy" are salient in this formulation; so are the patterns of elite power consolidation that are seen to generate various types of social and political disintegration, even if they are mostly latent.

3

The Corruption of Society

Locating Kernels of Mistrust

Noticing Corruption in Social Practices

In 2015, the Fédération Internationale de Football Association, better known as FIFA, was charged with bribery, fraud, and money laundering involving hundreds of millions of dollars. The charges were about the improper selection or misappropriation of game sites, kickbacks from sportswear franchises, under-the-table payments for television rights, and tax evasion. For at least a decade, the National Football League (NFL) in the United States, which makes tens of billions of dollars in annual revenues, ostensibly spent millions researching the combined health impacts of concussions. Meanwhile it secretly altered the results, funding its own physicians and pressuring sports news entities to suppress their stories about brain damage to players by threatening to withdraw sponsorship. The game of international cricket has been beset with problems of match fixing, calibrated spot-fixing of parts of the game, and the theft of millions of dollars involving high-ranking executives. The list could go on.[1]

These are, of course, the very organizations that produce some of the world's most exhilarating public events. Oddly, many of their fans, from casual watchers to dedicated aficionados, are unfazed by these unending scandals and continue to exalt the industry, generating windfall revenues for televised sports. Perhaps in disregarding the sleaze and refusing to look deeper into systemic forms of collusion, they are telling themselves that they care more about the grace and beauty of the game and the athletic feats of their sporting heroes than the moral sins of their managers.

I suspect, however, that the explanation for many fans' continuing support is even darker. Unbeknownst to them, they and other spectators are complicit in the corruption of sport by allowing the very familiarity of gathering in sports bars and cheering for their beloved teams to color their judgment about the illicit money, sexism, racism, and other forms of violence that are entangled with their viewing habits. The public obsession with watching sports in largely masculinized settings seems to go hand in hand with secret deals involving enormous sums of money. Might there be a connection between the two? Perhaps ardent sports zeal in a society is somehow shaped and cultivated to sustain the very growth of institutions that skillfully hide doping and gambling, that promote arcane rules benefiting managers and owners at the expense of both players and the public, that normalize the exploitation of female bodies, and that perpetuate myths of masculinity and other forms of sexual violence toward women and transgender populations.

It is not that women do not enjoy watching sports. But women's sports do not attract the high payments from television and other media outlets that key men's sporting events do. They seem unlikely to become prominent, no matter the skill level of the players and the competition. As a Danish female fan told a sports sociologist, "Life is too short for women's football." As spectators, women tend to prefer to participate in small groups when they watch men's or women's sports but are mostly backers of their male colleagues and friends. Only recently have female-only fan clubs of substantial size and number become visible. In contrast, billions of male fans watch male sportsmen in ritual performances of bonding.

The large community of white-collar managers and brokers in the sport industry may be under public pressure to be more gender sensitive, but achieving it is an uphill struggle. Behind them are the owners and top regulators of the industry, who have overt or indirect connections with each other and with the agents who help manage the workforce and ensure a growing demand for sports. Their collective interests fuel the sports industry, in which patriarchy, violence, and monetary incentives, such as extraordinarily high salaries and "rewards," both legal and illegal, are par for the course.[2]

As bizarre as my claims may seem, the rise of adrenaline-filled action sports, their high monetary stakes, the distressingly high recurrence of scandals, and the deep involvement in them of sporting and nonsporting personnel and their organizations seem conjointly to trigger unmistakably vile pathologies in the rest of society. For instance, in homes, stadiums, and bars across the world, diehard male sports fans are far more likely than less passionate viewers to engage in predatory abuse of women and transgender populations. In examining different repeated incidents of violence, misogyny, and game frenzy collectively as patterns across similar contexts, sports researchers have uncovered a variety of interactive conditions that relate commercially sponsored sports to harmful practices that affect diverse sections of society. The factory-made popular product constituting the world of professional sport is marketed and sold on behalf of a conglomeration of both anonymous and well-known corporations to line the pockets of an elite minority with windfall profits.[3]

Some of the same business tycoons, politicians, sports stars, and influential representatives of media who are implicated in sporting scandals are known to also participate in other questionable deals involving the education, entertainment, real estate, and similar sectors that generate value (in both material and status terms) in society. Connected to them are methodically engineered—"sponsored"—links among different groups of actors who have significant roles in controlling and promoting a sport yet only occasionally surface and only in the most serious scandals. The corporate sponsors of today's athletes—television conglomerates and sports leagues—tend to be closely associated with the most prominent and wealthiest figures in the world. And although none of these prominent individuals may be plausibly accused of plotting out the details of the conspiracies that unfold in many instances, there is no doubt that, as members of elite groups, they work cooperatively to maintain the status quo by invoking governmental and media complicity to expand private wealth and use violence if necessary to suppress scandals.[4]

What is not fully clear is how such patterns cohere into recognizable types over decades, even generations. In the most enduring configurations of corruption, a closely knit but far-reaching set of linkages among elite actors is formed across several domains. Paying attention to their subterranean linkages may uncover corruption's social implications, a less well-trodden path in the broader literature on the subject. As I have already emphasized, it is not enough to say that a person is corrupt just because he or she demands a bribe or conducts some other clandestine transaction that causes public harm. Focusing on individual events of embezzlement and bribery will not necessarily show how these corrupt practices are linked over long periods.[5]

Sociologists provide a rich understanding of the milieus and collectivities that are meaningful to us in our daily lives, and treating corruption sociologically may help uncover the close-knit arrangements among powerful and wealthy people that are of relevance in political corruption. Such rich individuals connected to others who are able wield physical clout to threaten or inflict bodily violence stand to gain significantly from both clearly nefarious interactions and regular, everyday practices. In sociological terms, elite networks, through their special privileges, seek to reproduce and sustain actions of political and economic power to influence those generalized patterns of human interaction that perpetuate the status quo to their advantage. These processes spawn interactive cultures or syndromes of corruption that both remain unique to a particular geographical and historical context yet are part of other elements of power and action in that given society.[6]

This might seem to be an odd way of understanding corruption, even in its grand form. But what I am restating here, following my argument thus far, is that studying corruption syndromes over the longue durée may reveal useful clues about extensive collective processes that cohere into supportive edifices for elite networks. We usually go about our lives feeling confident that our everyday behaviors are the result of our own preferences, or at least the ones we have at our disposal under a given set of circumstances. We may select these actions consciously from a range of options; for instance, our "choice" of lifestyle may dictate our partners, how we use time, and our eating habits. But it is our families, friends, teachers, coworkers, and various talking heads in the media who have long trained us how to sequence our activities throughout the day. We carry out these movements in a constructed environment around us—in a material ensemble of airports, cars, offices, phones, schools, shrines, and traffic signals—each element telling us what to do next in small and big ways. As the former *New Yorker* copyeditor Mary Norris writes, "We have become our own robots."[7]

The patterns that each of us settle into, especially in early life, appear as already available behaviors by which we as adults conduct our lives smoothly in the everyday, the quotidian. We are mostly unaware that these dispositions serve to consolidate and strengthen social mores. As we mature, we happily engage in socially acceptable parenting and schooling, dress, food, and other habits of consumption, rituals and spaces of the sacred, labor and practices of compensation, and so on. These patterns are easy to adhere to because they seldom generate conflict within or across social classes. Only rarely do we examine the structure, patterns, or molds into which we have fit our lives. And even when we do so, we may fail to see that structure and those patterns as being to the advantage of certain entities at the expense of others. Meanwhile, as we continue to set life goals in a manner that appears to conform to the mutually imagined and rationalized views of our respective places and roles in the world, the pooled actions of the multitude quietly fatten the purses and advance the purposes of a few.

From time to time, we might seek to rediscover "common sense" in our everyday interactions. On occasion, we realize that the most frequent expression of our so-called liberty is our collective echoing of each other's habits (say, as avid consumers of fast fashion)—routines that may in fact be detrimental to the long-term interests of various groups of people, including ourselves. Or, we find individuals doing things that cause awkwardness in a given social context, such as making adult conversation at a child's birthday party or refusing to exchange gifts on occasions when everyone else does so. These instances help expose the implicit rules of group situations, the recipes for acceptable behavior, and the limits to which they can be stretched before the rubrics of social order become apparent in their very banality. While human actions are dependent on preexisting social forms that may seem rigid in their patterns, they are intentional, or subject to change at the will of individuals and groups.[8]

Take, for instance, the mating rituals of contemporary societies. Their broad features seem to be shared across the world, involving similar patterns and rules of courtship in controlled settings, followed by intimacy and vows of commitment. Yet, in any community, and sometimes more so within a diaspora, cultural distinctions seem to separate the ways in which people act out their interpretation of love and romance. For example, arranged marriages in India are expected to lead to love and emotional attachment, and they often do. In contrast, in much of Europe and the United States, romance is meant to precede marriage, which seals the commitment. In each cultural variety, we see the outpourings of mutual affection expressed in a certain manner, a certain combination of undertakings by different human agents who—through their reciprocated interaction and other engagement in a field of social habit and place-based constraints and opportunities—generate recognizable patterns in the form of well-worn rituals of dating, marriage, and so on. Yet, these rituals are also tied up with the widespread phenomenon of patriarchy: the instrumental deployment of women's bodies for sexual domination, labor, and exchange.[9]

All this is not to say that romantic love and love of one's children are not subjectively felt emotions. Most people are fortunate enough to experience the familiar pangs of young love and its transformation to a more mature emotion in later life, with varying levels of intensity, joy, and pain. But what makes these modern forms of courtship and parenting worthy of reflection is that they fall into easily recognizable and typical types of human interaction within the universal categories of romance and family life. Love is experienced in Tokyo and Paris in the twentieth century, in eighteenth-century Suffolk, and in Bollywood, Hollywood, and Kollywood, in all their distinctive styles. Each has a narrative that creates an archetype, but any given culture may draw on a mixture of these and several other "tropes," performances that are remembered, enacted faithfully, and mixed with new forms, each tied to its own location and experiences. Individually, many of us willingly conform to romantic or marriage archetypes by following their rules. People in gay, lesbian, and transgender relationships; who live in communal arrangements; or who stay unattached also end up forming their own "cultures" or accustomed routines. The sociologist Satish Deshpande writes, "There are no untaught skills in the social world, where society teaches us everything we know, except that, sometimes, it also erases the signs of its teaching."[10]

Society, or the social, is therefore best understood not as a thing or entity but as the process that unfolds continuously through the actions and interactions of human agents. Yet we often view society as if it were an object, because collective routines seem already established when we first encounter them. Society is shaped by the relatively stable routines of everyday life—the repetitious rituals of diet, dress styles, prayer, speech, work, and so on—that seem mundane to groups of actors in our midst. When these routines form larger constellations, they give rise to social classes. Social structure thus describes how a society habitually performs itself collectively through each individual's life cycle and interactions in the community and its ecosystem. These form repetitive patterns of "structure" that also pertain to an individual's own comforting habits of structure, which is typically how one relates to the sensibility or feeling of one's culture.

A social class is generally identified with some combination of value-laden adjectives, such as "Brahmin," "Dalit," "foreign-born," "Muslim," "peasant," "poor," "refined," "rich, "sophisticated," "Western-educated," "white," "working-class," and "uncouth." These attributes are combined to describe having shared social practices, generally through a hierarchy of labor and its (varyingly) exploitative deployment. Assemblages of such descriptors serve as markers or mileposts in various transactions. There are, of course, many categories of social class, some that are more fine-grained than the ones described here, others less so. For instance, the Marxist categories of class—aristocracy, bourgeoisie, peasant, and proletariat—provide the basis for exploring a range of power relationships from subtle influence to overt dominance and the unfolding of historical social relations, including revolutions. Social structure—the routines that make up any given social class—is not inborn in the individual men and women who engage in these collective activities. Rather, these routines are learned through observation and instruction; they are talked and written about, reenacted, and sometimes resisted; and they occasionally lead to new patterns of interaction.[11]

As nearly every sociologist since Karl Marx has insisted, the social is not the frozen frame into which we are fit and then aim to stay properly in place. Instead, it is a practiced, interactive game that is built broadly around mutual regard and engagement, with skillful conventions that reinforce trust: it is also a game that disguises implicit hierarchies and patterns of domination. Just as football players effortlessly enter a field and play without having to speak to each other about the game's rules, a group's mutual actions and forms of speech in real-world situations appear organized by both explicit and implicit instructions in their given contexts. But unlike football, where the rules are clearly demarcated and strictly enforced by a referee, societies have more complicated rule-making and rule-enforcing agents.

The sociologist Norbert Elias uses the term "social figuration," a more graphic term than "structure," to describe the interweaving of multiple persons engaging in a common activity together, such as a card or football game.

> Taking football as an example. . . . It becomes quite apparent that two groups of opponents, who have a "we" and "they" relationship to each other, form one single figuration. We can only understand the constant flux in the grouping of players on one side if we see that the grouping of

players on the other side is also in constant flux. If the spectators are to understand and enjoy the game, they must be able to understand how the changing dispositions of each side are interrelated—to follow the fluid figuration of each team.... The atomic view of society is certainly based in part on an inability to see that these structures, be they marriages or parliaments, economic crises or wars, can be neither understood nor explained by reducing them to the behavior of their separate participants.[12]

An Ontology of Society and the Material World

A sociological view of corruption is important because focusing only on the individual criminal would result in being oblivious to entirely different orders and patterns of corruption. It could mean misperceiving existing networks that have a structured, ever-expanding influence across geographical and temporal scales. It could also miss the effects of the enormous growth in the dominance of certain groups of families and partners along with their internal arrangements. In any given society, the coercive power and influence of a relatively small interlocked network, along with high levels of inequality, are frequently revealed, especially over the long term, in the very routines and practices that make up that collective's social experience. It is the common and everyday adjustment of our patterns of ways of living to the conditions presented to us as "normal" that is implicated in the formations of corruption experienced in our society.

Another reason to investigate corruption as a social phenomenon is that doing so might resolve a tricky philosophical challenge in social and political theory. The existence of the individual in relation to society and the material world has always been a puzzle. As an individual agent, I feel sure of the motivation behind most of my words and thoughts, but there are social practices such as schooling and visits to doctors that I engaged in while a child that I had no role in developing. Where did these rules come from, if not as the combined result of individual actions? But if they did, what does this say about my individual agency or will, my ability to define and chart my way of acting in the world? Was I simply trained to adopt certain long-term habits without ever having a chance to examine alternatives? What might those alternative lifestyles have been?

There are additional complications. If I were to assume that the solidity of physical objects like our bodies and our mutual acknowledgment of them give them the quality of being real in some universally reliable way, then what about my individual thoughts and beliefs, our collective actions and speech, and what I define earlier as "the social"? How real are these, because they too produce external events and end up being patterned, predictable, or understandable to some extent?

Many scholars of the humanities and social sciences bypass questions of existence or the reality of the material and social worlds by taking a route opened up initially by the philosopher Immanuel Kant and, later, by Ludwig Wittgenstein among others. The ontological status of the world, the assurance we can have about the existence of something, they would say, is masked by our interpretation of the world through language, that is to say, the way words and their conventional relations are substitutes for meaning and interpretation about things and actions. What we can know about the world at all is shaped by the scaffolding our senses and language put over it in an attempt to make shared meaning, suggested Kant, building on ideas generated by his contemporary David Hume. The connection between how we reason about our perception and the way things really are is broken by this limitation, leading to deep philosophical skepticism about the ability of humans to acquire knowledge.[13]

Laws of physics, chemistry, and biology may seem to govern the natural world, but even they are expressed in mutually unrecognizable ways from time to time. Society, however, is always mediated through our words and other symbols we use to describe human relationships, which are no doubt mutable and subject to strategic (that is, power-laden) modes of interpersonal interpretation. Perhaps the words used to describe the natural or material world are also flawed or, at least, capricious, despite the so-called irrefutable logic of scientific laws. Just as importantly, it matters how our interactions and institutions (rules, practices, norms) influence language; for instance, through the use of metaphor. The social world, however, appears to be far more mutable than material things and processes, and seems particularly contingent on the very ways in which we frame it and derive meaning through language. To put it differently, "what we cannot think we cannot think, therefore we also cannot say what we cannot think."[14]

In this book, I draw different conclusions from those commonly obtained from this antispeculative or nonfoundationalist philosophical position around the limits to knowledge, which the philosopher Margaret Archer terms sociology's "torrid affair with epistemology." I accept that human language—namely, our capacity to give meaning and interpretation to shared phenomena—and our ability to change our minds generate a forest of symbols rather than a mirror of reality. But the natural and human worlds are not so far apart that it is impossible to generate useful knowledge through appropriate framing devices or languages concerning both worlds. Making the assumption that they are incompatible worlds of existence and that we cannot generate any universal, transcultural patterns of knowledge about them creates superficial readings of natural science and also misjudges how social relations and circumstances, including speech and communication, are continuously affected by material and spatial conditions, such as a pandemic or climate change. Instead, one may free up ontology to reconsider the relations between our intuitive and cognitive means of gaining clarity about socio-material processes. To do so, we can invoke our powers of imagination to build speculative but plausible suppositions about the organization of the material and intersubjective world as a combined set of emergent interactions.[15]

I find it useful here to take what would be termed a "critical realist" or, more recently, a "speculative realist" view, a position that assumes that objects and processes in our collective experience have emergent properties that have links to one another. Emergent phenomena appear as new processes that are generated from a combination of components that may not have the features found in the original parts. For instance, water is created when hydrogen and oxygen explosively interact with each other, but it looks and feels nothing like either of its constituent gases. The philosopher-psychiatrist team, Gilles Deleuze and Felix Guattari, have described how, before the invention of stirrups, a man on a horse could not be very useful in battle, because he was always struggling to keep himself secure and upright. With stirrups, riders were able to use a lance, a bow and quiver of arrows, or other weapons, creating a man-horse-stirrup-weapons ensemble that was extremely effective in combat. Allied ensembles also changed farm work and, coincidentally, generated new social structures. The combined outfits (e.g., man-horse-stirrup-lance) were not reducible to any of their components, but were assemblages of human and nonhuman elements and had emergent properties.[16]

Society and its routines can similarly be seen to emerge from human interaction within a given material context and history. But such interaction is not arbitrary or random; it is contingent, that is to say, put together by active agents and materials within that milieu. The interaction has pattern and repeatability, which can be seen as having rough edges across history; it frequently manifests itself in mobilizations of large populations in the name of some collective causes that are associated with the generation and fortification of ordered routines. Socio-material assemblages across varying spatial realms and with different degrees of complexity seem to drive coherent action and processes around us. Many social formations, including the first city-states and early Christianity, evolved into more complex forms over many centuries. Their building blocks were stochastic events that emerged out of, say, small powerful groups seeking to consolidate labor around settled farming in the case of city-states, and a moral social movement against the arbitrary violence of a politically commanding empire around the principle of divine salvation in the case of early Christianity. But the resulting socio-material processes have no universal or ultimate meaning even though they gave rise to patterned social phenomena, patterned by the shapes given to them by the victors of history and justified in languages of economic and social progress.

There are countless ways the natural world is not just around us but part of us. A combined reading of social and material processes is indispensable for detecting corrupt formations and transactions over long time frames: it provides a pragmatic macrosociological framework by which to interpret the patterns and movement in relationships among individuals, social processes, and the material world that yield elite networks and associated socio-ecological structures across landscapes. It also helps interpret emergent forms of rent-seeking (the capture of windfall profits) by a small minority and their justification merely on the grounds of having political control over resources through legacies and other means.[17]

An assemblage view of society and the material world is helpful because it allows us to challenge the false sense of permanence and inevitability that social and ecological processes acquire: it invites us to look, instead, for the ways we got here. It also reaffirms the value of a processual view of social and material engagement. Human relationships with each other and their physical environment thereby constitute the interactions among active agents that change with shifting circumstances. What was earlier seen as redundant for social philosophers, the workings of sticks and bones in contrast to studying human interaction, has become especially conspicuous as an absence caught unawares in the epoch of the Anthropocene. In the vast changes of ecosystems and peoples, especially indigenous communities transitioning from relative isolation from the state, it is as shockingly clear as a pandemic virus that there are limits to current ways of human existence. The proximity of "planetary boundaries," the severe biophysical limits on human and ecological continuance over the next few generations, alongside predatory global capitalism gives a new urgency for reviving natural philosophy.[18]

Writing or describing scientific knowledge, at least since the seventeenth century, has meant building a theory based on observations of allied phenomena, as Isaac Newton did with his experiments on mechanical motion. Instead of directly measuring something he would call "forces" among bodies in motion, Newton conducted a series of experiments to examine the movement of pendulums and collisions between bodies in motion. Through a process of elimination by simplifying mechanical motion to a geometry of forms, he could use mathematics to represent these phenomena. Basing their description on his definitions of abstract entities like mass and velocity, he developed a set of relationships to arrive at and then further explain the concept of force. His approach was based on drawing broad conclusions from a series of carefully selected and identified empirical observations and then building thicker theories, or conceptual frameworks of interpretation, from them.[19]

Social scientists cannot work the way Newton did. Newton conducted controlled experiments and was able to get replicable results. In the humanities and social sciences, it is absurd to expect to use those practices and to achieve those outcomes. All human beings are unlikely to respond to the same inputs in precisely the same way, especially while being observed by others. To interview someone is already to change that person's life in small but definitive ways simply by entering it as a social scientist. Human subjects are also apparently whimsical in other ways, preferring to exhibit individuality, an idiosyncratic outward expression of private experiences. All this is in addition to the ethical questions around conducting experiments on human subjects.

Still, with a nod to Newton's style of reasoning of building hypotheses and proposing empirical ways to give them validity, let me make this hypothesis: across the spectrum of long, historical cases of drawn-out corruption and their revelation, there are recognizable syndromes or idiosyncratic processes of societal decay and dissipation—*dérèglement,* for Durkheim—arising out of different ways in which these arrangements happen to be put together in a given society. For instance, variations of a widespread form of corruption that is, in every sense of the word, engendered by patriarchy have remained with humanity for a very long time. Although certainly manifested in changed forms over time, patriarchy has remained hidden in everyday language and human interaction. Feminist political history and theory have expounded on the systematic exploitation of gendered bodies by networks of power in society. The elites in this instance are interlocked with other nodes of power associated with control over capital and labor at multiple scales, those who have symbolic influence and authority, and those with formal jurisdiction over upholding the law. The shared histories of the violence of capitalism, colonialism, and racism are certainly compounded by patriarchy.

Corruption in the degenerating sense can be seen in the collective despair of societies that have long become accustomed to the everyday characteristics of misogyny, racism, and other forms of humiliation. The embarrassment of knowing that one too has been to blame for being complicit even by being complacent in the face of social violence is a partial recognition of this shame. But whose interests and what institutions is one serving? How can we build empirical studies of these relationships between networks and social processes? As I began this chapter by musing on the relationship between gender violence, the masculinities of sports fandom, and rising fortunes of the few, I might claim in other cases as well, "Follow the money!"

The Political Backdrop of Corruption

The study of politics is perhaps the oldest human science. But it is also a practical rather than theoretical science, a distinction made first by Aristotle. This implies that the real-world lessons learned from looking at societies as they form and stay together are more valuable than abstract models of politics. If the social is viewed metaphorically as the glue or matrix that reveals the structure and patterns of human exchange, politics is the differential strength of that glue in various parts and moments of such interaction. Of course, that metaphor is useful only up to a point, because human relationships are made up of active agents whose interactions are fluid with changing circumstances, which is why the idea of a mutable assemblage makes better sense than the image of a persistent, hardened substance. Differently put, politics is the name given to the effort mobilized by different alliances, including that of a majority of ordinary people, to give shape to a social assemblage by trying to coordinate human action to achieve collective ends.[20]

It is not easy to mobilize large groups to act in coordinated ways, but representations of collective life that are large and flashy and seem otherwise cogent are known to be irresistible reagents for mustering popular support. Still, for such political action to be authoritative and effective at a given spatial and temporal scale, it needs to demonstrate the capacity to use various types of persuasion across a landscape, including the credible threat of violence to generate compliance with a set of institutions or patterns of practice. *Political power* is the term used to describe the general ability to consolidate and mobilize social forces, often over a territory that extends well beyond face-to-face relationships. Such power is typically understood as primarily residing in the state, which could take one of several forms.

The modern state, though of recent vintage in its recognizable institutional form, is enormously varied and fragmented. It nevertheless conveys a fixed and legitimate set of performances, made famous in the giant fixture of the Leviathan in the seventeenth-century political philosopher Thomas Hobbes's frontispiece in his book of that title. Despite its legitimacy or "rightfulness," the state is an invented category whose administrative features loom large in the scholarly and popular imagination. In constitutional republics, the fabricated nature of the state is rarely much of an issue and has only recently received scholarly attention: the focus is usually elsewhere, on its functions and roles. The modern state is also controlled within a constitutionally bound form. And even though the rule of law is meant to diminish the arbitrarily skewed character of political privilege and power in many societies, it routinely serves the very opposite of its purpose.[21]

The route I follow from Charles Tilly and others is to assume that state elites did not only frequently organize themselves to yoke territorial control, but in certain transitions sought to expand their "biopower" by exercising much wider control and discipline over domestic spaces of larger populations to aid the preservation and expansion of wealth. In premodern periods, a more apt term for the state is the *polity*, best understood as a dominant mode of power that effectively steers action over a mostly porous though marked territory, including its various collectivities of individuals, which in turn may constitute a people. I prefer "polity" to "state" because, although they both designate an authority controlling territory and population in a manner that extends beyond face-to-face relations and kinship practice (such as extended family structure), a polity's reach and level of domination may be far less extensive than that assumed by the modern, bureaucratic state. Polities may often extend into what is normally termed "civil" society; that is, their authority may sometimes be embedded within parts of society that are well outside the select group of persons who are typically identified as having legitimate or broadly acknowledged authority. Many such polities have been in existence since antiquity, and I later describe some in the Indian context. A few may be so intricately woven into everyday life—into familiar and proximate practices of power—as to have no recognizable central authority in a single figure or group of figures.[22]

A *territory* is the spatial domain of the polity. But in more general terms, it is a space that any singular site of power seeks to protect. It could cover scales from my personal space to my home and habitat, my "culture" or "cultivation," a landholding, a sovereign dominion, and so on. The multiply interlinked material and symbolic characteristics of territory are worthy of much more deliberation than they are usually subject to, as both "culture wars" and the frequent use of military metaphors in international relations can attest to. Sovereign territory assumes a people is living within the territory of a polity; it constitutes a special locus of authority with spatial and social dominance. The state or polity has the authority, implying the strength and explicit consent—either in silent complicity or more actively as vocal support—of the majority of those under its control within its territory. Political authority itself typically has a limited time span across generations either because of the lack of skills (virtù) or ill luck (fortuna) of the protagonists. The strength of authority is continually tested by subordinate forms of power, although not always through direct confrontation, and often by disrupting some part of existing social relations. In republics there is popular representation in both subordinate and state authority, although its strength lies mainly in the establishment of the rule of law. Machiavelli's explorations of Italian politics are instructive for understanding these multiple dimensions of territorial or sovereign power.[23]

The city-state of Florence went through a major political transformation in 1494: it moved from an oligarchy controlled by the Medici family to one that was decisively republican in form, expelling the Medicis from public office for eighteen years. Lorenzo de Medici, having carefully cultivated his political skills, had built an empire of oligarchs who were members of his family and their business associates. His son Piero was both unlucky and incompetent, failing to secure the support of Florentine elites against the 1494 invasion of Charles VIII of France. His quick military and strategic surrender, especially in light of the subsequently discovered weakness of the French garrison in Florence, infuriated the people, who formed into mobs that raided the family *palazzo* and brought about the establishment of the Florentine Republic. The people were so angered by Piero's submission to French power that they negotiated directly with Charles VIII, who permitted constitutional reforms and the establishment of a republican government. The new government attempted to restore a lottery system for representation and other reforms to keep out the oligarchs. Things took a twist when Giralamo Savonarola, a Dominican preacher, managed to wrest control of the agenda and of the mobs, changing their focus from political to spiritual reform; through his apocalyptic preaching, he involved the mobs in such actions as a "bonfire of the vanities," in which objects tied to vanity, temptation, and sin were burned. Savonarola's efforts to take Florence in a conservative Christian direction were ultimately unsuccessful but nevertheless caused long-term harm to republican efforts. Less than two decades later, in 1512, the Medici used Spanish and papal support to restore themselves to power, abolishing all the institutions of the republic.[24]

The establishment of early modern states in Europe around this time also played a role in Italian history. France and Spain eyed Italy as a site for their expansion, given its fragmented territories and perceived weakness. The need for political conquest beyond one's borders is shown clearly in all the cases in *The Prince* and has at least two objectives for a sovereign: (1) to establish his symbolic, military, and administrative power over a new people and territory he has inherited and (2) to capture rents to maintain his state. Territorial power is also a means of maintaining a close-knit set of elite alliances both within and beyond one's borders. France and Spain saw the powerful geostrategic position of Italy and its wealth as important for their expansion and engaged in a pattern of alliance formation and war where necessary to gain territory. Yet their motivations to gain territory transcended their specific economic interests or rational tactical moves to anticipate key opponents. Added to them was an affective element: the growing sense of separateness of the French and Spanish nations, with distinct kingships. Nationalism created an affective pride in the French and Spanish armies' victories abroad and also increased the motivation of loyal troops to fight for national causes.

Machiavelli s lessons on politics are also helpful because he distinguishes between the *grandi,* the rich and the powerful, and the *popolo* or *plebe,* ordinary people. The former "desidera di essere libera per comandare" (want to stay in control), and the latter "desiderano la liberta per vivere sicuri" (want to live safely). For Machiavelli, the lessons from history are clear. When elites "realize they are unable to hold out against the common people, they begin directing their influence toward one of their own men and make him prince so that they can give free play to their desires in the shadow of his protection. Similarly, when the common people realize they are unable to hold out against the rich, they direct their influence toward some one person and make him prince so that they can be protected by his power." But as I have noted earlier, there are also conditions when the people are corrupted and have little or no capacity to stay alert to the significance of these possibilities.[25]

A state is therefore a *performance* of statehood, displaying a governing elite's effective command over various forces—armies, police, rent collectors—and the symbolic means to display them: flags, anthems, and military insignia. The modern state is deemed to be legitimate and effective when it has a formal separation of powers that help keep the peace between various groups that actually control power and wealth but that act on behalf of the vast majority of citizens in constitutional polities. It must also serve a "public" purpose: to create peace, foster prosperity, and generate the institutional infrastructure that creates these conditions. It is frequently justified by various theories of social contract, constitution making, and the rule of law, but sometimes there are flagrant flaws in both its arguments and practices. Most significantly, in its historical formation the state was often justified in the name of the people but typically comprised a small elite class of propertied business interests with grand ideas. Yet, democratizing claims by broader coalitions of people have also been noteworthy across places and times.[26]

In spite of the richness of the social sciences within the academic world, there is widespread resistance elsewhere to seeing collective phenomena as having independent orders of significance. Instead, there is a tendency to interpret them either as the aggregate effects of multiple rational actors' behavior or to assume mysterious "cultural" reasons for any unexplained collective performances, whether they appear as riots or voter apathy. Even sociologists have only recently paid attention to the nexus between white-collar crime and street crime, the connections among elites, and their entangled relations to multiple forms of corruption, of the sort spawned in Suharto's Indonesia, for instance. The corruption of the people is manifested in their becoming so accustomed to their conditions of life that they often mistake their own ways of living as being desirable lifestyles in themselves.[27]

Social Theories and Corruption

Scholars in social philosophy would correctly point out that my description of corruption is prefigured in several other important terms in social theory, especially ideology, hegemony, and socialization. These terms complement my focus on elite roles by describing social processes that express some enduring and multiscale operations of networks of power. An ideology, for instance, is a collective set of beliefs that a group takes for granted as a form of influence over its practices, even if they are ultimately harmful to the group. An example of the effectiveness of marketing ideology is its ability to make us imagine that buying a new model of a gleaming object every few years is essential, especially when that is objectively not the case. The religious studies scholar Catherine Bell draws on multiple sources to define ideology as "a strategy of power, a process whereby certain social practices or institutions are depicted to be 'natural' and 'right.' . . . It is a strategy intimately connected with legitimation, discourse, and fairly high degrees of social complicity and maneuverability."[28]

Using a different lens, the sociologist Pierre Bourdieu finds the term *habitus*, introduced by his predecessor Marcel Mauss, to be of great significance in interpreting the persistence of social practices or structure. Habitus is (or are) our multiple, regularized senses of our bodies being in control of their movements in space, their fluid "constitutions" and "dispositions," whose sequences adopt sensations and mechanical routines, as well as feelings, that engulf us as soon as we enter cars, classrooms, churches or temples, hospitals, offices, stores, and so on. A person's habitus can also be expressed as the collectivity of "homes" acquired and created for oneself, which may vary in different places and according to multiple daily, weekly, or seasonal customs. It is by no means far-fetched to say that a habitus can be seen in the patterns of even some nonhumans. For example, my adult and somewhat aging cat Kitty is trained to live both indoors and outdoors (mostly out). At home, she seems lazy and sleeps most of the day on the couch, although she is ever alert to any activity near her food sources in the kitchen. Yet, if made to leave, once outside the front door she is vigilant, and her body seems to stiffen up. As she savors the fresh air, her demeanor is transformed. She quickly relaxes and reorients her bodily movements into familiar rhythms of outdoor life—first, by going to her bowl of water and then toward one of her usual resting places.

As individuals, we tend to acquire and internalize a set of responses to everyday and regular encounters with the state, religion, and other forms of social life. These collectively form an internalized set of trained bodily dispositions or habitus that acquires symbolic or cultural significance. The anthropologist Talal Asad writes,

> The concept of *habitus* invites us to analyze the body as an assemblage of embodied aptitudes, not as a medium of symbolic meanings. . . . I think that [the anthropologist Marcel] Mauss wanted to talk, as it were, about the way a professional pianist's practiced hands remember and play the music being performed, not about how the symbolizing mind "clothes a natural bodily tendency" with cultural meaning.[29]

These bodily references provide a clue for understanding why the unraveling of political corruption often appears as visceral discomfort, especially when it occurs at close quarters. The encounter nearly always seems to shake up our habitus and what seem to be our own settled, comfortable pattern of existence. We are more than annoyed when we are forced by a scandal to peer into dark labyrinths of our ordinary daily lives and there discover exploitative routines we are part of, and sometimes, even enjoy. Our irritation only rises as we recognize our multiple deceptions and begin to identify which individuals and entities constitute the network that exploits us.[30]

Our understanding of these socialized routines and their early formations in modern European society has been influenced richly by the philosopher Michel Foucault's "genealogies" of gymnasiums, prisons, hospitals, and schools. He drew our attention to the types of speech, textual interchange, and other symbolic forms of meaning that societies-in-the-making give rise to as these practices become ordinary or "normal." Each of these figuration complexes make up a *dispositif,* or apparatus: "a thoroughly heterogeneous ensemble consisting of discourses, institutions, architectural forms, regulatory decisions, laws, administrative measures, scientific statements, philosophical, moral and philanthropic propositions . . . [altogether having] a dominant *strategic* function."[31] A dispositif is a type of assemblage, a put-together assortment of material and human entities and their dynamic interaction, as Foucault describes it, but one that takes shape collectively and gains coherence through bodily impressions, ideas, habits, skills, and shared language. It also makes up social structure, the patterns of everyday life that we find ourselves conforming to through imitation and practice to near perfection.

What Foucault called "discourse" is a type of order in the formation, collection, regulation, and dissemination of information that justifies and helps reproduce social practice. Foucault analyzed examples of eighteenth- and nineteenth-century forms of education, military training, forms of psychiatric treatment, and punishment to trace the genealogies of these apparatuses that served the purpose of creating and "taming" bodies while producing forms of knowledge and means of regulating populations in a self-styled "modernizing" European society. The birth of the clinic, school, military barrack, and prison, as ordinary and uninteresting as they might seem at first, each took a specific form that has come to be widely understood as an ordinary byproduct of the growth of human progress. Foucault showed how each became linked to systems of what he termed power: "a more-or-less organized, *hierarchical,* coordinated cluster of relations . . . that operate through a juridical form."[32]

An ideology or a belief system—ideas, narratives, and forms of collective imagination making up its dispositif—is extended and becomes hegemonic when there is general consent, rather than coercion, to assimilate habitual attitudes that appear as "normal" or "just the way things are." *Hegemony* is associated with the ability to exercise forms of control over large groups without direct coercion by building a willing collective acquiescence to engage in routines and activities that primarily benefit elites within that society. There is much social science scholarship on ideology and hegemony beginning with Karl Marx's and Friedrich Engels's early writings, which were compiled and published as *The German Ideology*. They pointed out that it is our actions that generate our ideas, not the other way around. How we work, interact with each other, and form patterns of dominance generate our modes of justification for the structure of our societies; we are not basing our actions on our (own) ideals. Under capitalism, the *bourgeoisie* (the class of capitalists, namely, the owners of capital) create mechanisms to extract as much additional value for themselves as possible from the labor of the vast majority of society. The dominant ideas of capitalist society become its ideology, which aim to become hegemonic through the use of coercion, where needed, but mostly through advertising, education, and religious institutions to generate popular consent.[33]

It is certainly wrong to assume that any type of social ordering causes profound social injustice just because it pursues routines and patterns of stability. Forming lines and then waiting in them at bus stops and the grocery checkout counter to streamline the distribution of a shared good such as transit or food are universally accepted as fair, even democratic, ways to allocate resources. The same is true of rules governing elections, legislative systems, traffic, and so on. Similarly, capitalist ideology provides a language of liberty to promote its rules, even if they harm equality and solidarity. The political theorist Gaetano Mosca suggests that the ruling classes have always needed "political formulas." They are by no means quackeries invented by elites. Instead, they "answer a real need in man's social nature; and this need, so universally felt, of governing and knowing that one is governed not on the basis of mere material or intellectual force, but on the basis of a moral principle, has beyond any doubt a practical and a real importance."[34]

Nevertheless, over the medium to long term, and only occasionally, depending on various circumstances, the regularity and legitimacy of certain social routines may become suspect, because they are seen as serving identifiable interests and configurations of hierarchy. Both classical and more recent historians, such as Tilly, have generally identified elite groups as being at the center of these interests. Sometimes, opposition is expressed as collective challenges, whether effective or not, both to the bodily practices of exploitation and to the beliefs being espoused to justify them. Those opposition campaigns that succeed do so because they leverage the sovereign power of the territorial and networked state, which was for a long time made up of a family or families of oligarchs. Tilly writes, describing the last few centuries of European history,

> Since governments themselves commonly simulate, stimulate, or even fabricate threats of external war and since the repressive and extractive activities of governments often constitute the largest current threats to the livelihoods of their own citizens, many governments operate in essentially the same ways as racketeers. There is, of course, a difference: Racketeers, by the conventional definition, operate without the sanctity of governments.[35]

Indeed, elite networks operated like many still do, not dissimilar to protection rackets or gangs. They have clear morphologies, such as a spoke and hub arrangement or a central core with bowtie-like connections to other entities, with weaker interconnections across groups. Whenever there is stiff resistance to reform, elites end up being those with the most to gain from maintaining the status quo. Bourdieu asks, "Who has an interest in the state? Are there state interests? Are there public interests, interests in public service? Are there interests in the universal, and who are their bearers? As soon as you pose the question as I have just done, you are led to describe both the process of state construction and those responsible for this process of production."[36] Assemblages or interlocking networks of interests, in turn, may then join forces to overcome opposition and maintain a long-term territorial order of exploitation that is unbearable only to the worst off, but that is frequently accommodated and upheld through various knotty norms by the majority, the people.

Foucault used the word *governmentality* to refer to two different ways in which power over daily life was manifest in Europe starting in the mid-seventeenth century. One was through the regularization of routines and habits that subject people to a self-imposed discipline. The other, related to sovereign power, was centralized control over police action in a territory. The two modes of power, one that treated the body as a machine by training it in particular techniques, and another that focused on imposing controls on entire populations, were both "productive" in the sense of promoting forms of life, rather than stilling or suppressing them. Governmentality strengthened routines by providing mechanisms for individuals to justify their regularized behavior, as in the cases of automobility and neoliberal markets, to be described later. Deleuze similarly distinguishes between disciplinary societies and societies of control; whereas the former are associated with confinement and prohibitive actions, the latter provide the illusion of freedom but require adherence to specific rules of conduct (for example, societies of car and cell-phone users).[37]

Elsewhere, Foucault wrote of repressive forms of power. Sovereign power is repressive because it attempts to seize bodies into ordered submission and promote regularized routines through education and work. Repressive structures generate restrictions on such activities as diet, movement, and speech through assemblages around prisons, hospitals, and schools. But these same institutions might also result in productive modes of power by contributing to knowledge, pleasure, and discourses, which in turn sustain themselves by seeming positive and desirable for society. Productive forms, which he terms "biopower," are those that serve to organize and multiply life.[38]

There is much in the work of Foucault and of those who follow his path that shows how, in various historical periods and cultures, dominant agents and institutions collaborated in distinct ways, whether it was the confluence of church leaders and royal authority in the eighteenth century in France seeking to create new apparatuses for controlling the population; or the sharpening of techniques of hierarchy, inspection, and punishment by colonial governments; or the nexus of capitalists, bankers, and the welfare state in the late nineteenth and early twentieth centuries in the United States that put together an array of modes of practice to create well-ordered workers and citizens.[39]

The assemblages or dispositifs of power-practice-knowledge that Foucault marked out so evocatively may also be described in terms of networks or chains involving diverse actors. These chains are not just formed of static relationships but are mobile actor-events, constantly changing and influencing material and human substances and memories. The social philosopher Bruno Latour uses such a framework to suggest that as individual agents, we are continuously engaged with "reassembling the collective," much like Elias describes "social figuration." But for Latour, agents could include human and nonhuman entities, such as viruses and carbon dioxide. In human collectives, within intersubjective spaces of discourse, a social "imaginary" is given shape and meaning through symbols, rituals, and rational justification, forming the "ties in which one is entangled."[40] The actor is any entity that is alert to signals of various sorts and responds with different degrees of sophistication, but that in collective behavior constitutes a network: an assemblage displaying purposeful action at various scales but also exhibiting emergent structure and apparent aims as a "society." In the twenty-first century, we are already part of a new type of network society with the emergence of virtual life and growing demands on our time.

According to actor-network theory (ANT), the social is not a fixed entity but an ensemble that is visible only in its change from one configuration to another. Latour writes, "ANT claims that we should simply not believe the question of the connections among heterogeneous actors to be closed, that what is usually meant by 'social' has probably to do with the reassembling of new types of actors." The social then comprises a *reseau*, a web or network of actors forming a set of conditions expressed in intersubjective fields of language, spatial and material relations, and actions. It is a condition that can change with new material, language, and action, and Latour suggests that it is in these very movements that we can actually detect the social.[41]

What Foucault did not pay close attention to—but which is a central preoccupation of this book—are those obscure parts of the actor-network that seem to accumulate some form of wealth through the very means by which our routines become mundane and unremarkable to ourselves. These routines may not always blind us to the forms of power that sustain them; sometimes our very alienation in the workplace, at school, and, at times, even in places of play and worship signals to us the existence of regimes of elite interests and their patterns of influence. The historian Joan Wallach Scott pioneered the idea that historical subjects are driven not just by rational interests but also by desire, fantasies, and contingencies and accidents. These imply multiple motivations, which may seem well articulated but are mysterious to the actors themselves. It is the very co-creation of fantasy through the languages we have learned in dispositifs that seem to motivate us, allowing us to overlook or even defend the injustices we often see around us, while playing the obedient roles of citizens with established cultural habits. These habits generate secondary and tertiary emergent effects, creating other social norms and patterns that typically serve to conceal even more the original sins of elite networks in power.[42]

The study of elites in social theory has a long history. The sociologist C. Wright Mills identified how elite networks in twentieth-century America held the key to maintaining their power. Building on the ideas of other scholars before him, particularly Gaetano Mosca and Max Weber, Mills postulated that elite groups tend to form interconnected networks with each other across domains of operation; these networks in turn help strengthen their power and consolidate their interests. These networks are alliances between the top layers of corporate, political, and military institutional orders that make up the commanding heights of society. These alliances form nodes of local dominance and often expand to control large territories and their populations, usually by maintaining control over resources and groups of people through networks of regulation. They become interlocked when individuals play multiple roles in the network:

> The inner core of the power elite consists, first, of those who interchange commanding roles at the top of one dominant institutional order with those in another: the admiral who is also a banker and a lawyer and who heads up an important federal commission; the corporation executive whose company was one of the two or three leading war material producers who is now the Secretary of Defense; the wartime general who dons civilian clothes to sit on the political directorate and then becomes a member of the board of directors of a leading economic corporation.[43]

Mills also described how the character of the power elite in North America changed from the nineteenth to the twentieth centuries. The dominance of military and political elites in the early 1800s was followed by the emergence of a new political class made up of generations of men holding different types of "high positions" in society—landed gentry, literary figures, the clergy, successful merchants, and the military. But this class's diverse composition led to a subsequent shake-up and eventual consolidation, led by the corporation, whose special rights were guaranteed by the 14th Amendment to the US Constitution, adopted in 1868. Mills showed that from the late nineteenth century through the 1950s, corporate, military, and political elites went through many different arrangements and changes in relative dominance and character with shifting fortunes.[44]

Elite groupings can be elaborate and interlinked across great distances. Terms like "between-ness," "bridging ties," "brokerage," "centrality," and "tie strength" convey the interlinking nature of networks seen today. They are also ways to describe different varieties of corruption syndromes according to the structure of their elite figurations. But the social effects of these elite groupings are far-reaching and equally varied. Depending on how deep they are—how many secondary and tertiary forms of influence they have on far-off connections and how organized they are—social norms, habits, and discourses may be transformed for the long term. As they do, they harden into ideologies, justificatory dispositifs that can be transmitted over several lifetimes.[45]

How are collective forms of habitus maintained and energized across broad swaths of a society, when elite networks are mostly in charge? The political scientist Mattei Dogan shows how different elite configurations often form diverse patterns of "interlocking" as determined by their era and geographical context:

> Elite interlocking takes various forms in time and space. The most famous historical interlocking is the alliance between the throne and the altar in all European countries, and in most Islamic countries (but not in the Buddhist societies). In contemporary Africa, the elite configuration appears as an undifferentiated elite.... In Southeast Asia, the leadership represents a fusion of various roles in the same person.... In the Mexican presidential system, the structure of elites leaves room and freedom to the sector elites.... Even among the Western European countries, the elite configurations mark significant differences.[46]

There are many examples of interlocking processes between elite groups and mechanisms that otherwise influence social practices and have authority over them. Consider corporations that manage databases, credit card companies, banks, and credit rating groups, which collectively share an interest in promoting regulation to enable universal identity cards, credit checks, and so on. These tend to be subtle in their workings but end up tightening constraints over what individuals may or may not do, but usually in the name of expanding freedom. Often, these create engineered types of habitus, as in the case of private cars in some societies, which I describe later, but also mobile phone dependence, expectations of work and vacations, and so on. As the rhythms of everyday life become more interlocked across domains and increasingly habitual, it seems to be in no one's interest to disturb them.

On the basis of Latour's actor-network framework, the geographer Michael Woods suggests that elite structures have their own regenerative logic: they are formed to reinforce the special privileges of their members, whose actions then mobilize resources that keep their institutions secure:

> Rather than as a functionally defined group of 'power holders,' elites might instead be understood as a key element in this process [of habitus-generating assemblages]—as networks of individuals (of varying degrees of integration) which provide a relatively stable matrix of connections enabling the rapid and routine mobilization of human, institutional, material, and discursive resources into networks of action.[47]

Elite privilege within society is clearly of great significance for a sociological view of corruption. But it is the social relations and patterns of rationalization—dispositifs—that have the lasting effect of cementing elite privilege. Much of Foucault's work can be seen as suggesting ways to investigate these forms of rationalization—what he elsewhere termed "governmentality"—and how they help reproduce certain apparatuses of power that emerge with industrialization and geopolitics. Power is transmitted by such so-called truths, but they also implicate the manner in which rules of right (legitimate authority, judicial and other legal conditions) are produced and sustained. These truths form dominant routines we readily fall into by following the rules not only set by larger political regimes like the state but also those that involve specialized knowledge and seem already preexisting to us in spaces such as hospitals, schools, churches, workplaces, and markets. Power, for Foucault, produces our reality for us and, in so doing, maintains a particular form of order in a specific place and time.[48]

Finally, one must ask how the public might respond when confronted with knowledge of these elite networks. At one end of the spectrum, there can be anger on the streets, which has had many types of expression throughout history. Yet often people feel directly intimidated by the shows of power of an authoritarian state or an oligopoly of private organizations that have seemed to take over their society, much like gangs that ruled cities such as Genoa in the fourteenth century or New York City in the nineteenth. If it is too dangerous to have open displays of fury, especially when there is considerable political support to keep elites protected, some groups might resort to more clandestine methods of resistance by developing shared performances of artwork and ways of living that explicitly mock or try to change established and dominant routines. But tragically, even such opposition generally is absent or muted, revealing a "corrupted" public, several of whose most articulate members are content to follow conventions that are somewhat oppressive to them but are far more so to those beneath them in social and economic standing.[49]

Assemblages of Corruption

My treatment of society and corruption may seem incomplete or even wrong to readers who think it discounts the role of the person, the human agent. I later show how individual autonomy—or our ability to change our minds at times, exercise control over our routines, and influence others—need not always be in defiance of social norms. It may even act in support of the set of phenomena I describe as corruption. But when individuals resist corrupt practices, especially by becoming mobilized in sufficient numbers, they are able to expose the long-standing injustices of entrenched social structures, which can lead to large-scale transformation. The Buddha, Jesus, and Gandhi were remarkable examples of individual leaders, but perhaps at least tens of millions of others have also expressed such leadership. In other words, it is misleading to take a bifurcated view of society and individual agency. Rather, one needs to assess how their relations and the emergent processes that ensue—whether they are strong or weak, whether they can be modulated by durable organizations or changing practices, at which scales do they operate, and which external circumstances, including chance events, influence them—can change the course of history.[50]

Let me begin with a straightforward challenge relating to individual agency. The typical readers of this book would seem to have the liberty to live as they would reasonably want to and for as long as physiological conditions allow.

If most of us have managed to achieve these freedoms, why should we not assume that everyone else has the same opportunity, with perhaps a little more effort and personal enterprise needed? On what moral ground does my complaint about grand or political corruption lie?

Success in almost any part of the world is identified with how much money a person either makes in a salaried job or a stable set of "gigs" or has access to, such as income generated from inherited family wealth or from other benefactors. Those who retire early and lead a comfortable life in any part of the world must have saved enough money for this venture. Otherwise, they are doomed to work or beg for a living until the very end without generous state support. On closer inspection, it becomes clear that these few sources of success are entirely dependent on institutions of privilege in various forms—and these institutions are based on the sustenance of privilege over long periods that is typically disguised as ideology.

For instance, inheritance is primarily tied to patriarchy: it is a form of transfer of economic power through exchange of the means of reproduction; that is, female bodies. It is women's unpaid labor doing domestic work that allows men in families—nuclear units of childbearing couples and their children—to accumulate wealth. Such wealth was initially in the form of produce from land, livestock, tools, and so on, which mostly accrued to male heads of families. Over time, rules were developed in most societies for male progeny to be given titles to inheritance. Today, there is evidence from much of India and elsewhere that women were primarily treated as property and, in turn, were not allowed to own any by themselves.[51]

Inheritance is also associated with another type of power relation, because it relies on a weak justification of rights to property and their transfers within families. Property rights depend largely on a view, attributed to the philosopher John Locke, that one's own labor directly contributes to the level and command over a territory, objects, and so on. But even if that property was acquired by such labor, its value is secured only if it grows over time to become "wealth." Such growth in wealth is in turn possible only when property generates surplus through rent—that is, through a gatekeeping fee for its use by others or through additional value generated by the use of others' labor:

The economist Adam Smith provided what is perhaps the earliest definition of rent:

Rent, considered as the price paid for the use of land, is naturally the highest which the tenant can afford to pay in the actual circumstances of the land. In adjusting the terms of the lease, the landlord endeavors to leave him no greater share of the produce than what is sufficient to keep up the stock from which he furnishes the seed, pays the labor, and purchases and maintains the cattle and other instruments of husbandry, together with the ordinary profits of farming stock in the neighborhood. This is evidently the smallest share with which the tenant can content himself without being a loser, and the landlord seldom means to leave him anymore.[52]

Rent is therefore a form of income paid to the landlord from his tenant farmer only because of the territorial power the former exerts over the latter. The landlord is like the proverbial dog in the manger who has no use for his property but charges a fee for others to create value from it. He generates a surplus (or savings) over time by having control over the asset. This surplus is artificial in that it is the difference between what might have been distributed either equally among those who labored to build it or split disproportionately between an identifiable someone (or a group) controlling the labor and the laborers themselves. Typically on the basis of new property rights developed in modernity, shareholders of a corporation collect far more in profits than actual workers who produce the things for sale do as wages. Therefore, because they earlier used some surplus to purchase a piece of "property," they stand to gain disproportionately more than those who built the product or developed the service.[53]

Yet, property itself, in addition to material value, also has symbolic qualities or value, deriving from the guarantee of the sovereign power, the state. For long periods in history, in many parts of the world, a mighty king and—occasionally, a queen—was solely in charge of the state. The ruler was the sovereign owner of an extended territory, commanding an army and exerting control over arms and all economic activity within the kingdom. In turn, taxation was viewed as a secondary guarantee by the state of one's right to property but was evidently another form of a gatekeeping fee (or rent). Over time, many of these elements were continued, in modified form, in democratic societies and were consolidated and streamlined as law. Together, these elements bring about a convergence between those who occupy seats of sovereign power and the wealthy, a feature that is the very hallmark of corruption.

Two present-day examples, relating to automobile use and the economy, may be helpful in explaining my argument. The reader may think that there are more explicit cases of corruption to consider such as shady real estate deals, military purchasing, and Big Pharma. Why pick on driving a car or buying and selling everyday goods, each a functional activity that is a means to an end and that also leads to an expansion of one's choice of goods and autonomy over time and space? What next? Will I find some dark meaning to brushing one's teeth daily? Indeed, some may find this entire line of reasoning to be peevish, especially if they believe that any social process, even if it demonstrates the deployment of power, is the necessary cost of "development" or "progress." But it is surely also the business of a social philosopher to ask what one means by such terms, what or whose interests are thereby being defended, and what modes of systemic exploitation accompany everyday practices and patterns of rationale.

Case 1: The Question of Automobility

In the United States, between 1960 and 2005, car and light-truck ownership rates went up from about 300/1,000 (per thousand people) to about 800/1,000. The 2005 figure represents an ownership rate of about 1.2 automobiles per licensed driver. Most countries in Europe have fewer private vehicles, but even Denmark—which has some of the world's most diversified transportation modes, substantial rapid transit infrastructure, and greatest support given to cycling, walking, and public transport—has a private vehicle ownership rate of about 440/1,000 people, or nearly one in two. If the world were to achieve the same average rate, this would amount to having about 3.5 billion cars in a few decades, when the global human population will be roughly eight billion. This is an unsustainable outcome on many counts.[54]

The automobile industry is vast but is concentrated in enclaves that focus on specific functions. About a dozen manufacturers control the majority of the worldwide market, totaling close to US $2 trillion annually. Similarly, just a few oil companies manage the bulk of the global market, which is also worth around US $2 trillion. Oil companies are remarkably vertically integrated—the same firms manage the product from exploration to refining to final retail sales at the gas station. Along with cars and the associated fueling infrastructure come roads, highways, parking structures, manufacturing and industrial jobs, advertising, drivers, traffic rules, licensing regimes, financing and insurance, road accidents, urban sprawl, air pollution, the destruction of local ecologies, worsening global warming, and so on. Together, these processes constitute the assemblage or dispositif of "automobility," a substantial arrangement of ethico-socio-technical phenomena in motion that lie behind the shiny new car that remains enduringly in the mind's eye. Several of its elements, including in discursive forms, are dominated, if not completely managed, by small groups of elite cartels and the firms under their executive supervision. Importantly, these agents of the global hyper-elite largely know each other in multiple formal and informal settings, building patterns of trust that keep defections to a minimum.[55]

The attentive and purposeful agent-participant wades through several ethical questions while engaging with this assemblage of automobility. Cars provide enormous individual autonomy, making it possible to be mobile, travel long distances, and plan elaborate routes quite easily. That makes their use a special problem from a moral or normative perspective. Do cars enable human freedom? Evidently yes, but if one were to consider equality as another positive aspiration for humanity, automobility ends up causing intolerable collective harm when such liberties are made widely available.[56]

Automobilized cities are characterized as being geographically vast networks that are entirely dependent on automobiles for any meaningful way to move through them. While they do have mass transit, it is generally much more time-consuming and less effective than point-to-point travel in personal automobiles in sprawling city-regions. Atlanta, Los Angeles, and greater Delhi are examples where these conditions hold. As walkability is replaced by automobility, one sees most vividly the formation of a new habitus—our self-image, accumulated responses to routine situations, and social and physical makeup—that generate a specific set of performances. Witness the novelist, Joan Didion, describing the art of driving in Los Angeles in the early 1970s:

> [She was] not somewhere on Hollywood Boulevard, not on her way to the freeway, but actually on the freeway. If she was not she lost the day's rhythm, its precariously imposed momentum. Once she was on the freeway and had maneuvered her way to a fast lane she turned

on the radio at high volume and she drove.... She drove it as a riverman runs a river, every day more attuned to its currents, its deceptions, and just as a riverman feels the pull of the rapids in the lull between sleeping and waking.[57]

What is the allure of the car? It is difficult to describe an inanimate object in affective ways. Yet, it is fair to say that the car is an object of desire both in itself and on the basis of its operation, by virtue both of the spatial and tactile sense of driving it and how it makes one feel. But cars in the plural are also a blot on the landscape; they deeply increase our dependence on one mode of experience and perpetuate bad habits in several spheres. Many decades of urban living have shown that far less environmentally harmful and more socially inclusive outcomes occur in cities that encourage walking and face-to-face interaction than in those that are automobilized, even as several cities in their peri-urban and suburban expansion, from Beijing to Houston, are using Los Angeles of the 1970s as their paradigm. With the prospect of billions of cars in circulation worldwide, there is widespread alarm in many circles about the multiple ways that can harm our societies and our planet. What the psychologist John Platt quite aptly describes as a "social trap" of automobility pervades the planet: individually, I might be ambivalent or even unhappy about having to be car-dependent, but I, and many others like me, seamlessly fall into the pattern of dependency because the alternatives seem onerous. Collectively, we thereby fail to recognize the snares that we have set for ourselves until it is too late.[58]

The social world of an automobilized society is not the result of conscious deliberation. It instead is a continual, constant creation through the actions of human agents, corporations, governments, and other groups who are methodical about achieving their goals and aspirations and whose actions end up constructing social routines and rules. These agents' actions are complemented by the constraints imposed by laws, machines, and the built environment, making up an active assemblage. The historian Cotten Seiler writes,

> More than merely a set of policies or attitudes cohering around cars and roads, automobility comprises a "multilinear ensemble" of commodities, bodies of knowledge, laws, techniques, institutions, environments, nodes of capital, sensibilities, and modes of perception. This apparatus

has channeled power in both the productive and repressive senses of the word: it has regulated, legislated, aided, and compelled the motion of bodies mechanical and human; it has established and delimited a horizon of agency, social relations, political formations, self-knowledge, and desire.[59]

Thus the assemblage should not be read as an accidental or spontaneous result of market forces. Markets are directed by power, as I argue in the subsequent case, and so was automobility. In North America from the 1940s onward, the history of automobiles was shaped by a complicated set of strategies led by vehicle and petroleum companies, real estate developers, members of Congress trying to promote corporate interests and jobs in their districts, and a growing marketing industry promoting "individual freedom" as an idea. The emergent outcome of these strategies was not only the massive growth of automobile sales and the building of highways and other road infrastructure but also a set of bodily dispositions and attitudes toward driving as a "normal" enterprise of everyday life.[60]

I suggest elsewhere that the very practices of automobility, whose habitus appears to reproduce certain bodily and spatial routines of individualism, constrain our ability to treat them critically. Such processes that hide the intentions of background power in its various forms have been termed an "ideology" or the power-laden formation of a value system. In other words, because drivers and other actors in the enormous system are constantly co-creating the apparatus of automobility, the language of the vehicle and of the road itself seems to acquire the status of a metaphor for various liberal values, with individual freedom represented in bodily autonomy over mobility. People often feel good about driving; it strengthens their belief in the value of personal control over their space and time and fuels a greater geographical range of interaction even if it ends up generating a certain type of isolation. Alternatives to driving may be seen as fringe concerns of radical environmentalists, not as opportunities to enhance social solidarity and improve one's quality of life.[61]

Furthermore, even if some of us feel uncomfortable with the advertising industry's manipulation of our symbolic association of cars with happiness— the smiling child, a sunny sky, or an outing with friends—we are still deeply affected by these images and are more often than not willing to be influenced by them. We trust that those forces that manipulate us are ultimately useful to us because they create goods or services that serve us well. As our dependency on automobiles and the system of automobility grows, we end up placing our trust in the hands of a relatively small number of human actors who play a significant role in specifying the habits that dominate our lives. But our own continuing practices in creating and sustaining automobility also generate a certain complacency that stabilizes the dominance of these actors, who repeatedly show themselves to be far more self-serving than we hope: over time those actors' behaviors may deflate our belief in them and the system that sustains them.

We should not, I reassert, just be alert to the scandal of an automobile company that knowingly meddles with emission control software and violates formal rules: we need to pay attention to the entire set of social and spatial relations that automobility spawns, which will direct us toward the formations of a growing framework of grand or political corruption. Just living and working in Los Angeles, one of the most automobile-dependent cities on Earth, does not make a person corrupt. But it is the social practice of automobility that becomes normalized in the repeated name of improved personal autonomy, which one must become suspicious of. What social and spatial conditions have produced this sense of normality? Which networks of power are connected to this formation? How must we investigate their multiple assemblages?[62]

The normative aspects of this mega-assemblage that justify the use of the term "corruption" may be seen only subtly and over the long term in the numerous harmful implications of automobility that go hand in hand with the nexus of a small group of political actors who use terms like "freedom," "mobility," "jobs," and "growth" to protect an oligopoly from being questioned seriously. The discursive apparatus produced by the disciplines of automobile engineering, transportation planning, and urban planning carefully constructs the car-driver-highway assemblage as a fait accompli around which challenges such as traffic accidents, pollution, and access to ordinary services like hospitals, schools, stores, and playgrounds have to be addressed. Even more generally, the large-scale corruption of cities through automobility shows up in the inability of citizen-drivers to form a consciously articulated response to the behemoth that they have helped create. That corruption also points to the less obvious power of global elites in similar and broadly allied sectors, such as finance, militarization, and real estate, whose power typically comes in the form of persuasion to benefit from monopoly rents or windfall profits.[63]

The philosopher Hannah Arendt describes a totalitarian society as one emerging from a type of depoliticization of the public that promotes indifference to public affairs, as well as atomization, individualism, and unbridled competition. If the habitus of automobility, by promoting private travel in closed vehicles, cultivates such indifference even in small ways, it also sadly permits vehicle owners and their users to participate unwittingly in a regime that promotes this ideology. This locked-in practice and its expansion generate harmful impacts on the world at large and the perpetuation of diverse measures of violence and injustice in several pockets of it.[64]

Case 2: Market Fundamentalism and the Corruption of Everyday Life

The global economy is best understood as an assemblage of different elements that vary with historical context and physical location. Each participant in the market is invariably connected through money to a much more extensive network of transactions that creates social groups—not only buyers and sellers but also social classes such as merchants, traders, noblemen, the police, administrators, and so on. It is also separated by sovereign territorial boundaries, which separate countries, each with their own sets of complicated regulations for monetary exchange and corresponding forms of social transaction. Within each given territory and its rules can be found a unique economy. An economy typically entails discourses and pedagogies around economic "laws," for instance, despite repeated evidence challenging their universal application. Individually distinct, economies collectively have emergent properties that give rise to multiple entities and processes, ranging from complicated financial instruments such as derivatives on Wall Street to barter and complementary currencies in the *souk* or bazaar.[65]

Money is perhaps the most perplexing economic product, having both enormous symbolic significance and great material implications. Originally intended to replace simple barter as a medium of exchange, the use of money has become extremely complex, with the involvement of political authority becoming of paramount importance. A piece of currency is worthless without the guarantee of the state (today known as the central bank), and if it fails, so too does the value of its obligations. Together with its uses, money is what the geographer David Harvey calls a "concrete abstraction," something whose properties are symbolic but that nevertheless has tremendous power to move society in very material terms. Still, money is just one component of the economy, which is also swamped by demands for entities known as resources and their converted products, known as commodities.[66]

In the broadest possible terms, an economic problem is a practical or normative approach to finding the best possible way to get the most out of a set of materials and conditions. As individuals, we may exercise choice in determining what we buy and what we do for a living, but these decisions are shaped by our time period and geographical context. Yet, economics collectively is a moral challenge, a choice among possible pathways. How should the household live on what it can forage, steal, create, barter, earn as wages, or inherit from its ancestors? How must communities and nations do this collectively and effectively? Can a given society maximize its rewards to get the most out of the sum of individual circumstances?

Economic problem solving is therefore a means to improve one's life conditions, the circumstances that might help enhance one's ways of living. The particular manner in which resources are allocated is justified as generating shared value in any society. In this sense, it is a "discursively" produced endeavor. As societies grow, they find it necessary to define rules for how labor should be assigned and what commodities should be created in surplus and sold for profit; that is, how to accumulate wealth and reinvest most of it. When these rules are onerous, some relief through the redistribution of resources is usually either demanded or provided anyway to try to cover up elite extravagance; this increased redistribution is often justified by announcing new theories, policy frameworks, histories, and traditions. At most other times, rules are quietly distorted to accommodate elite demands. What this shows is that it is by no means inevitable that the current system of economic activity today, in the form of twenty-first-century global finance and capitalism, will remain dominant in the future. Rather, it is best viewed as a contingent and emergent product of multiple forces and circumstances—but one in which elite networks consistently remain dominant in terms of their symbolic and material wealth and power.[67]

Economic phenomena, like most other assemblages, have multifaceted features because of the unexpected twists and turns of a combination of actions of a network of agents, both human and nonhuman, within changing contexts. These actions often generate volatile processes and have unforeseen long-term consequences. Nevertheless, as Marx and, more recently, the economist Thomas Piketty famously pointed out, there are often identifiable loci of dominant power in the form of specific human actors, who manage to maintain their exclusive advantage over the long run despite periodic economic crises. Frequently, there are also prevailing concepts and terms that are used to justify the continuation of some of these social practices, which makes it even harder to fully discern the structures of power involved. Meanwhile, the market "leaves its mark," says philosopher Michael Sandel and in doing so corrupts social relations by putting a price on everything.[68]

The economic historian Karl Polanyi debunked the notion that free economic activity arose in the nineteenth century and flourished in the twentieth century as a natural outgrowth of favorable conditions: "It was not realized that the gearing of markets into a self-regulating system of tremendous power was not the result of any inherent tendency of markets towards excrescence, but rather the effect of highly artificial stimulants administered to the body social.... The road to the free market was opened and kept open by an enormous increase in continuous, centrally organized and controlled interventionism."[69]

Notice how closely this resonates with the following quote from an interview Foucault gave to the French journal, *Ornicar*. Foucault was describing here industrialization in early nineteenth-century France, where a combination of incentives and rules was used to keep an inchoate working class in place, while

> pressuring people to marry, providing housing, building *cites ouvrieres* [factory towns] practicing that sly system of credit-slavery that Marx talks about, consisting in enforcing advance payment of rents while wages are paid only at the end of the month. Then there are the savings-bank systems, the truck system with grocers and wine merchants who act for the bosses, and so on. Around all this there is formed little by little a discourse, the discourse of philanthropy and the moralization of the working class.[70]

Over time, arrangements emerged to provide schooling for children, jobs for women, childcare, and so on, all of which seem to normalize the aim of ensuring that factories run properly while making workers feel grateful for their conditions, "so that you get a coherent, rational strategy, but one for which it is no longer possible to identify a person who conceived it."[71]

The dominant narrative in economic thought is that it is in the natural order of industrial capitalism to continue and prosper as it is doing in the early twenty-first-century, even when it is clear that particular forms of long-term government intervention or its strategic lapses have been decisive for supporting conglomerates from banking and finance through defense and petrochemicals. These conglomerates, in turn, have been responsible for promoting the extreme concentration of wealth we have today, in which only a few dozen individuals currently own as much as half of the rest of humanity. The ideology underlying this economic system, referred to as *neoliberalism* by its critics, relates to what Michael Johnston describes as "influence markets" (see Chapter 2). It stipulates that personal enterprise in a sea of opportunities is justly compensated; the more daring and ultimately successful the idea, the more outrageously it receives support. Even if one or a few individuals control the market, there is no need to be alarmed by these developments. Instead, the only role for the state is to keep the engine of growth going, both by freeing up barriers to capital accumulation and supplying the infrastructure needed to support it. Influence markets, by design, end up excessively rewarding oligarch rentiers or landlords, who own assets or capital, make them artificially scarce, and then overcharge others for their use.

The ideology by which the markets foster free enterprise, with little role for public support, came from economists such as Friedrich Hayek, Ludwig von Mises, and Milton Friedman. With the end of the Cold War posited as a "triumph" of markets, their theories were used to justify the large-scale privatization of public resources starting in the 1980s in the United States and Britain. In turn, the World Bank and the International Monetary Fund unabashedly promoted their principles as lending policy for the Third World until the early 2000s. Those elite groups and concentration of wealth that emerged were seen as the inevitable outcomes of entrepreneurship. Such a set of enterprises formulated by new entrants, according to the mid-twentieth-century economist Joseph Schumpeter, could be so large and explosive as to take over the world, which scholars should not find alarming.[72]

Neoliberal advocates also typically deploy a particular form of economic science, which can demonstrate that greater competitiveness will bring in newer forms of capital and keep innovation going to maintain a vast consumption economy that will drive demand and output. Although economic practices based on these principles may be unmistakably clear to those schooled in the "church of economism," there are at least two considerations that demonstrate that it is a chimera, a false but uncannily good fit for a selective part of the evidence.[73]

First, the bulk of innovation today—or the successful mass introduction of new products, be they phones, coffee shops, or insurance policies—tends quickly to be controlled by monopolies or oligopolies. These then decide the most profitable means to keep customers in place, rather than improving the best or most socially beneficial products. Second, the government actively supports several of these and other elite producers so they can retain their market share; increasingly, these producers are positioned to serve as arsenal in international trade and its politics. Government itself tends to be less involved with mass consumption and to be more engaged either with corporations that serve a few clients, as in defense, from which they also buy a lot of equipment, or with others that have substantial geopolitical clout, such as petroleum and finance. How the government makes economic decisions regarding powerful companies is a large domain in itself, known as political economy. In some cases, rules are reworked to accommodate business conglomerates, especially in relation to secretive domains, such as military hardware. The more successful a leading monopoly is, the more it either remains secret or penetrates everyday life, both as ideas and languages—in the same the way that consumer objects of various sorts enter our homes, offices, and the places in between.[74]

In the United States, between the 1940s and the 1970s—the decades when progressive labor reforms and social safety nets were most evident—workers in manufacturing jobs improved their lot considerably, and economic growth was robust. It seemed that economic policies had reached their perfect pitch and that it was indeed possible to improve prosperity all around through domestic action. It was also a period characterized as Fordism, the continuation of a regime started by the auto magnate Henry Ford, who decided to produce cars cheaply and increase wages so that workers could afford to buy the products they made.

The higher wages paid to workers in streamlined assembly lines in factories also seemed to secure their acceptance of the new routines of work and everyday life. By the time crises rolled around in the form of rising energy prices, recession, inflation, and substantial foreign competition to US industry, the global economic order had been reorganized and neoliberal ideology had become securely established: it became hegemonic. Of course, all this was helped by an aggressive US foreign policy that controlled the terms of trade with the rest of the world, rising militarism, and the dominance of the dollar in the global economy. With the collapse of the Soviet Union, the "American lifestyle" was entirely vindicated, in spite of repeated economic, political, and social crises domestically and around the world.[75]

Neoliberal politics and policies tend to create influence markets, through which elite networks and social processes are both locked into formal institutions and legislation. For example, the 2008 financial crisis was followed by judicial action on campaign finance reform with the 2010 *Citizens United* decision in the United States. The causes of the 2008 crisis are well documented. A small but extremely influential set of financial firms, political lobbyists, key government staff, and a few elected representatives together manipulated virtually the entire global economic system so it became "hyperfinancialized," with little or no oversight and plenty of opportunities for the powerful to manage the increasingly obtuse financial system. In the second instance, a conservative Supreme Court upheld the right of lobbyists to have no upper limit in their campaign contributions, allowing key elite groups to decide exactly when and how they could grease political machines.[76]

More than being a set of ideas or beliefs, neoliberalism is a standard set of practices, routines that ever-growing numbers of people are ineluctably drawn into and from which they can never escape without undergoing severe and sometimes catastrophic hardship. For instance, university education in the United States turned into a highly priced (and prized) commodity after the 1980s, until which time it had been predominantly viewed as a public good to be subsidized by the state. The annual cost of going to a reputed college currently exceeds the country s median household income. As a result, those not born to wealth or who do not qualify for the limited number of scholarships are compelled to take out large loans, sometimes several times greater than their anticipated earnings. On graduation, they are forced to seek jobs that provide sufficiently high incomes to pay off their loans, even while they are forced by circumstances and social pressure to go into more debt for transportation, housing, and household commodities. What has further complicated the picture since the 1990s is the way in which these debts have become "securitized," converted into financialized entities that are then traded speculatively at multiples of their actual value in global markets. Neoliberal practice, in other words, seems to generate a series of social traps to sustain itself, but it is also driven and supported by key actors in high political office and well-endowed private organizations.[77]

It would be missing the elephant in the room to focus solely on the economic or even biographical dimensions of neoliberal practice. The role of politics has been well characterized recently in the United States and in Western European polities, which have related but distinct features. Both politically liberal and conservative alliances tend to favor the rich in at least two ways. First, elected officials may give direct favors in return for campaign contributions, and several associated trades among intermediaries may follow. Second, politicians may be deeply implicated in the ways in which various forms of docile political subjects are created. That is, neoliberalism has a discourse, a form of justification, and repeated practices that keep the super-rich on a rising trajectory that is predicated on a ready-made set of habits. As the political theorist William Connolly observes,

> Neoliberal ideology must become a machine or engine that infuses economic life as well as a camera that provides a snapshot of it. That means, in turn, that the impersonal processes of regulation work best if courts, churches, schools, the media, music, localities, electoral politics, legislatures, monetary authorities, and corporate organizations internalize and publicize these norms. It also means that active state policies are needed to produce this result. . . . It is a form of biopolitics that seeks to produce a nation of regular individuals, even as its proponents often act as if they are merely describing processes that are automatic and individual behavior that is free.[78]

In 2008, it was quickly recognized that financialization was a shell game without any significant tangible value available to underwrite the gambling and enormous rents being generated from it. The result was a collapse of the bubble economy, but at whose leading edge was the collateral value of hundreds of thousands of physical properties, retirement accounts, and pension funds, along with similar assets affecting life savings and shattering the everyday existence of tens to hundreds of millions around the world. But it was also a jolt to the middle income and the poor living in the Global North, who came to the rude realization that neoliberal agendas and elite interests went together with state power at their behest.

Still, the most significant and enduring outcome has been the maintenance of the myth of the crisis being a "mid-course correction" in a long march toward global prosperity. With financial analysts and commentators in the United States and Britain deploying metaphors such as "getting back on one's feet" and "finding an effective fiscal medicine," governments adopted neoliberalism wholeheartedly as the very framework needed to solve the crisis. This meant that more and more public money was poured in to "rescue" failing banks and other large financial institutions, even while hundreds of thousands of homeowners and others in deep debt became insolvent, lost their assets, and neoliberal ideology prevailed in the end.[79]

In "post-industrial" conditions, which include the gig economy and factories of big data, we can discern a manner of mass exploitation that is just as pervasive as nineteenth-century labor practice. Today, the global middle class can sustain itself only barely through its total dependence on institutions such as insurance, mortgage financing, retirement funds, and college loans, which can only be supported through specific patterns of work and everyday life that may distort, or at least modify, human interaction. A highly financialized world gives people no time or space to form ordinary bonds of community, but rather measures their interaction in terms of monetized transactions. It exacerbates inequality, poverty, and exploitation through value chains of underpaid workforces compelled to function in increasingly vulnerable conditions. Worse yet for the long term, it creates an alternative symbolic universe of commodified language that fills our collective imagination and patterns of speech.

In both automobility and neoliberal economism, corruption may not appear as grand as the fall from glory that occurred in ancient Rome and the Vatican and, to a lesser extent, in places like Indonesia after Suharto, the Philippines after Marcos, or Argentina after the Perons. Indeed, many may not view either of my examples as constituting corruption at all, which makes my task challenging but also exemplifies the quotidian character of grand corruption. These stories illustrate the humdrum of a neoliberal lifestyle:

building the economy, creating prosperity, and advancing autonomy and personal mobility, while cultivating elite power relationships. In both the examples, corruption is somehow obfuscated for long, if not forever, unless brought to light by scandals. The 2008 financial crisis was, along with its excruciating hardships, helpful in removing the public's blinkers concerning the respectability of finance capital. In so doing, it revealed, at least partially, the networks of banks and their political engagements that permitted fraudulent and risky ventures that made enormous rents on the fortunes of ordinary people, to which years of regulation and corporate accommodation had built labyrinthine links. The case of automobility has not produced crises of such scale and brutality, but major scandals around safety and environmental laws have appeared periodically. These have been important enough to catalyze a small but growing social movement around building more compact and less car-dependent communities around the world.

Corruption in Everyday Life

My proposal for a sociological view of corruption can be summarized as follows. In its most elementary form, human interaction takes place as a set of relationships among individual bodies in a spatial and temporal landscape that has both physical and symbolic features. But these are not inert, atomistic relations based on uniform rules and causal interfaces. Rather, they are intentional (or purposeful) engagements, driven as much by the proximate material appetites and aversions of agents as by the collective build-up of memory, affective (emotion-inducing) representations that are sought and interpreted, the deployment of resources and the creation of rents, ecosystem entanglements at multiple scales (in our times extending to the planetary scale), and the creation of new rule-like structures that make up emergent social processes that have further (downward) impacts on individual human motivations and actions. Because these are neither random nor strictly ordered phenomena, it is useful to see each set of arrangements, or dispositifs, regulated by composite grids of power, as well as chance events.

Along with today's criminal networks of the powerful, whose success in some cases has been phenomenal, there are other models of much slower but sustained accumulation that affect deep swaths of society and foster enduring images and ideas about sovereignty and authority. A sociological perspective, which relates corruption to a rich set of themes in social theory such as alienation and anomie, can also illuminate relationships across social phenomena, such as ideologies, habitus, coercion, and hegemony, with elite social forces. It is also possible to relate corruption to longer time frames of hegemony, where a whole pattern of actions has a discourse, making up dispositifs—cultural mores of social forces that last over many generations.

The power complex itself may comprise dominant and subordinate elements, the former of which are somewhat clumsily but still pointedly associated with agents making up elite networks. Still cruder would be to suggest that these agents form a conspiracy, which is not my intention, especially if that word is meant to indicate deliberate forms of conniving with clear long-term goals in mind. Rather, one might find, based on my model, the slow coming to fruition of stable and interlocking arrangements of elite control at multiple scales that end up creating routines of false necessity and a social structure whose underlying fairness is persistently dubious but rarely questioned. These, I have described as patterns of patriarchy, slavery, and the modern capitalist system, which is simply and strategically described as the market system run by autonomous, "natural" laws.

Just as relevant but not something that I can meaningfully explore in this book are the varieties of subordinate power in these material-social assemblages that are made up of other interlocking networks and of accommodative and resistant countercultures. What can, however, be sometimes discerned is the imprint of the entire complex on the long-term social and political systems that seem to cohere in a given region. The narratives in this book identify such patterns or syndromes of corruption across long periods of Indian history. Where possible, I describe them as familiar, everyday social formations by identifying the assemblages that get entrenched into ordinary expectations of order, hierarchy, and patterns of living. Over long time frames, they may slowly generate conditions that highlight some linkages between the humdrum routines that make up societies and the rent-seeking activities of elite networks. The criminal or malicious machinations of these cartels may only rarely become evident to larger publics over the course of generations; when they do, they illuminate particular corruption syndromes ever more distinctly.

Corrupt practices reveal the connection between assemblages of recognizable persons and our familiar routines, providing us new clues about how our societies are formed, through the modes of power and everyday actions they generate. Our interest in studying them need not be sensational; however, by turning our attention to well-respected personalities, communities, or even specific networks, we can express our dismay at not having seen the obvious corrupt practices around us. They might reveal our ideologies to ourselves, the beliefs that we cling to, but that revelation itself may uncover the other shallow foundations on which they rest.

PART II

Tales

4

Early Symptoms of Corruption

Harappan Routines of Bodily Practice

At Mohenjo-daro narrow streets and alleyways branch off of the major streets, leading into more private neighborhoods. Many of the brick houses were two stories high, with thick walls and high ceilings to keep the rooms cool in the hot summer months.... Inside the city to the right of the corbelled drain and gateway is an area of the city that has been identified as a crafts quarter. Large quantities of manufacturing debris have been found in this area indicating the presence of workshops for making stone beads, shell ornaments, glazed faience ornaments, stone tools and possibly even gold working.

Treading Softly

The remarkable material remains from the Harappan civilization in the third and second millennia BCE give us credible accounts of its political geography and society. My ventures in this vast landscape are bound to be tentative and cautious, for I can only speculate on its prehistoric elite networks and corrupt processes. Still, I am intrigued by several themes in Harappa's archaeological record that resonate with patterns found in other syndromes of corruption explored in this book. First, it was a highly regimented society, as reflected in its technically advanced urban form, patterns of craft, and vast networks of trade and political reach. Second, it had an industrial economy that generated surpluses, and these gains were further consolidated through trade. Third, it had a set of elites who inconspicuously (to present-day eyes) managed the economy across a vast region and controlled its revenues for centuries.

These governors and administrators played powerful roles in an entangled web of codependencies across a vast domain. They managed to reproduce a strict social order, which was needed to develop and sustain unique routines and highly formalized city planning. Nevertheless, given the relatively austere lifestyles of the people, it is conceivable that there was no grand deception. Harappa may have been a democratic polity that used procedures and practices unfamiliar to us today. At the same time, its rapid disappearance as a vast urbanizing force was most likely the result of domestic social causes rather than external ones, which favors the explanation that its decline was indeed the result of the breakdown of a syndrome of systemic social exploitation or grand corruption, even if those details are murky.

The Harappan civilization stretched across a half-million square miles from present-day northwestern India, Pakistan, and Afghanistan up to the borders of Iran. There were more than one thousand Harappan cities of varying sizes that were strikingly similar in form and artifacts. Harappa's area was larger than that of the ancient civilizations in Mesopotamia and Egypt combined, which too had elaborate social practices and planned urban features. At its height, Harappa was almost certainly engaged in sea trade with Mesopotamia from the port city of Lothal in the Kutch region of Gujarat, which is on the west coast of India. Moreover, trade originated from many parts of the region, from at least as far away as Mohenjo-daro, some 400 miles inland and perhaps even from the other major city, Harappa, which was 800 miles inland.

The use of the term "civilization" here is intended to represent a large society extending across a vast geographical area and exhibiting forms of practice that display a quantum advance in technology (as demonstrated by their tools) and social structure over previous smaller groups of forager-hunters and scattered pastoral or nomadic farming settlements. The earliest form of civilization is associated with Chalcolithic (involving the use of copper and bronze) or later periods rather than with Paleolithic or Neolithic technology regimes, although the use of stone tools was widespread throughout. Civilizations are also typified by settled farming practices, industries of varying scales, and sometimes extensive trade and military campaigns that characterize regional if not global connections.

Each civilization in Mesopotamia, Egypt, Harappa, and the Mayan peninsula lasted between a few centuries and millennia, suggesting that they were able to endure for several generations of elites and commoners. In the absence of external factors like climate change and other environmental shifts or destruction by invaders, they must have found it possible to produce considerable economic revenue in the form of finished goods, some of which were exchanged across great distances following patterns of trade that lasted considerable lengths of time. These activities meant that they had to have robust institutions of trust networks across many geographies, which were supported by diverse labor practices and possibly tax revenues. The social structure of these early civilizations indicates the formation and entrenchment of distinctive syndromes of elite networks.[1]

There is archaeological evidence that Harappa's networked cities engaged in multiple scales and activities related to ancient industrialization: the production of shell and stone-based jewelry, technologies of construction, water engineering, trade and shipping, and urban planning. These activities were organized into similarly aligned routines in multiple sites across an enormous area, even while they had local variations. At least a few hundred thousand people in each generation enacted the spatial rhythms of the Harappan economy that enabled the maintenance of its cities and its material flows. Equally impressive was the rapidity with which this urban civilization arose and almost as quickly disappeared, after remaining dominant in the region for several centuries. By the second millennium BCE, it was erased from the historical memory of an otherwise prolific Vedic society; it remained unknown until its archaeological discovery in the nineteenth century.[2]

A vast civilization having almost military-like precision in its infrastructure and many of its apparent everyday customs, but with no discernible center, armed forces, or any other recognizable means of enforcement of these activities, is itself a wonder. Its location, life history, and apparent loss from collective memory are added mysteries. For these very reasons, it is here that the story of the social structures of corruption in India must be launched.[3]

Harappa, the Archaeological Enigma

Like other archaeological landscapes in prehistory, Harappa has no written record: a "script" possibly exists, but it has not been interpreted. Still, the lack of a written record is not entirely unfortunate. Archaeologists have for long understood that the academic bias toward writing tends to privilege the accounts of the literate segments of early societies and to overlook material evidence of the actions and lives of the less powerful. The objects and spatial relations identified in a given site are not the unintentional result of aggregate individual actions; they are *produced* through the practices of agents who form a political society, with structures of power whose legitimacy and authority are reproduced through routines of habitus—what I described earlier as bodily dispositions in a given spatial and temporal location. Material evidence—involving animal and human bones, their location, spatial orientation, extent, and state; the design, construction, chemical composition, and layout of tools and other artifacts; and the arrangement of housing, shared infrastructure, and other public spaces—can provide substantial and often cross-corroborated evidence for the shape, origins, and maintenance of political arrangements.[4]

Throughout the subcontinent, there were numerous Paleolithic and Neolithic settlements, which possibly were the temporary abodes of small clan-based societies and other bands of foragers and hunters who created tools and small weapons by sculpting stone, shells, and possibly wood, often alongside rivers or by the coast: these peoples and their lifestyles lasted for a very long time, including through Chalcolithic and later periods. In central India, near the banks of the Narmada River in Bhimbetka, a remarkable set of cave paintings, first made around 30,000 BCE but added on to, with interruptions for tens of millennia, depict changing social formations in a single location. These paintings allow us to make conjectures about patterns of daily life in a landscape with a diversity of flora and fauna; they also give us some insights into possible social formations. By doing so, they provide the opportunity to move away from fixed images of categories like "hunter-gatherer" and "farmer" and to create narratives about more nuanced social relationships. One can make reasonable claims about how such a society reproduced itself, what type of significance painting had for representation and therefore communication, and what some of the hunting episodes and possible raids might imply in terms of clans or groups in conflict or cooperation. Even more boldly for a scholar, the paintings offer a rough portrait of the dynamics of their relationships of power and what such early polities looked like.[5]

The small village settlement of Mehrgarh in southern Baluchistan, west of the Indus Valley, is considered one of the precursors of Harappa. It is also one of the earliest farming and herding communities in South Asia, with origins in approximately 7000 BCE. By 5500 BCE, its inhabitants were growing wheat and barley; herding goats and cattle; making various implements and ornaments out of stone, shell, and bone; and even practicing fine dentistry. Mehrgarh is the only site in the subcontinent to have shown signs of domestication and settled farming and to have maintained these practices in a continuous sequence for several millennia. Barley and wheat were grown in small plots and sheep and goats were the most common pasture animals. Personal ornaments made up of steatite microbeads strung into necklaces of a variety of types were common grave goods.

During the next two millennia or so, the practice of community farming spread farther east to various parts of the Indus Valley and Ghaggar-Hakra or Saraswati River basins. By around 3000 BCE, terracotta figures, including cattle and female figurines, can be discerned in multi-room structures having firepits and clay ovens. Pottery ware was common around this point, some of whose designs and technology endured later in Harappan styles. Between around 3300 and 2600 BCE, farming communities, made up mainly of pastoralists, in the Sindh region began to form settlement patterns such as found in Amri and Kot Diji in the plains, which share some characteristics with later urban forms in Harappa.[6]

After 2600 BCE, however, Harappan sites no longer appear as a continuous transition from earlier settlement patterns. Instead, in a very short period of time, some new sites were created, and old ones were destroyed and rebuilt, but with a far grander construction quality and size. Each settlement had a precisely aligned urban design, with perpendicular streets, bricks everywhere made in the same ratio, nearly identical patterns of housing, the most advanced water and drainage engineering of the time (unmatched, even two millennia later, in ancient Rome), and similar tools, pottery, and other artifacts, implying interconnected forms of daily life. Harappa itself was the first such settlement and among the largest cities discovered in the constellation; it is located in Punjab in present-day Pakistan. The largest site is Mohenjo-daro, 400 miles to the southwest, in the Sindh province.

Recently, Harappan cities of comparable size have been found well outside the fertile, alluvial plain of the Indus Valley, in the Kutch region of Gujarat and in eastern Punjab in India. Harappan sites have also been found in present-day Afghanistan and eastern Iran. East to west, the Harappan civilization stretched from the deserts to the highlands, with at least a half-dozen midsize to large cities of ten thousand residents or more, such as Dholawira, Ganweriwala, Kalibangan, Rakhigarhi, and the port of Lothal in Kutch. There were several hundred smaller cities and numerous small hamlets, most of which were correspondingly well laid-out and planned settlements. Texts and material objects found in Mesopotamia, Oman, and Bahrain reveal contact and trade and that migrants had settled in West Asia from "Meluhha," which most scholars associate with Harappa.

The near uniformity of Harappa's symbols has been the source of great linguistic and cryptographic interest. But it is not just that identical seals and other artifacts of mysterious significance were found throughout a vast region. The spatial architecture, materials, and outputs of all its cities were highly standardized, which indicate that they were part of a correspondingly well-organized pattern of everyday life, constituting a far-reaching habitus. A significant lacuna in interpreting the record is the lack of a definitive analysis of the script (or, at least, repeated symbols), which shows little connection to other or subsequent language forms in the subcontinent. Ancient Harappa is truly one of the great enigmas of archaeology.[7]

The First Urban Revolution

One way to make sense of the archaeological record is to locate it historically and spatially in relation to other developments. Chronologically, Harappa is associated with what is generally termed the first wave of urbanization. This wave swept across western Asia, starting around the eighth millennium BCE and lasting for more than 6,000 years. Beginning with stone age or Neolithic towns like Jericho, Mehrgarh, and Çatalhöyük, and later Chalcolithic (copper or bronze age) settlements such as Eridu, Larsa, and Uruk, this explosive rise of cities appears to constitute what the geographer Edward Soja and others have termed the most significant instances of *synekism*. Derived from the Greek *synoikia* (συνοικία), referring to "neighborhood," synekism denotes the emergence of socio-spatial formations characterized by purposeful clustering and cohabitation in an interdependent system of relatively dense settlements. This closeness implied a set of social relations that were, in turn, associated with the development of particular political patterns around protection of the settlements, order, control, and so on.

The ancient city was different from nomadic bands, including those that combined foraging-hunting with settled agriculture. Even a small city of a few thousand relied substantially on a hinterland of grazing pastures, water sources, and farms, which all played vital roles in its sustenance. For its manufactured products, buildings, and other goods, the city needed materials and organization that were often spatially and ecologically demanding. It was the locus of trade in goods supplied and processed from a vast region beyond its walls—which were built to enable means of control, mark territory, and provide protection from invaders. But the city was also a site of vitality in symbolic ways, where shared patterns of community life were expressed through ritual and sacred performances.[8]

People living in early cities created emergent social forms that were markedly different from nomadic lifestyles. They formed new types of relationship with each other, with evolving rules of interaction around sexual reproduction, clan identity, forms of barter, and types of battle. These new relationships were partly shaped by the increased opportunities for face-to-face contact compared with those available for earlier wandering bands of much smaller size. Many cities emerged out of embryonic exchanges that developed among units of people living in proximity to each other; these exchanges were later consolidated with the development of settled agriculture, incipient patterns of administration that directed a remarkably engineered infrastructure, and new urban political systems.[9]

Çatalhöyük, in south central Anatolia in present-day Turkey, is a case in point. The dense settlement, probably the largest urban area of its time, flourished between 6250 and 5400 BCE, with a population of up to 8,000. People lived in modest houses that were very close together, with no footpaths or streets separating them; holes in the ceilings acted as doors, and there were ladders or stairs into the homes. They initially domesticated sheep and plants and, later, cattle. A variety of ceremonial elements have been found, including human and animal skulls and body parts, motifs of animals and birds, and assorted forms of decoration. In fact, it has been postulated that ritual collective activities, from hunting wild animals together to having genetic and other links across households, including clustered burials and the exchange of skulls and other body parts to remember the dead, might have been crucial for building a sense of community.[10]

Çatalhöyük can be interpreted as an assemblage, a put-together system of parts made up of individuals, social units, housing, water sources, fields, pastures, animals, machines or tools and their associated infrastructure, and the routines of organizing these elements. But any such assemblage, even one with far less entanglement between human and nonhuman elements, creates new emergent phenomena with their own dynamism and patterns of adjustment to changing conditions. In Çatalhöyük and other early cities, the generation of food surpluses was an emergent outcome of synekism, but surpluses also introduced patterns of incipient inequality with respect to access to them. In other words, control over food and managing *scarcity* became a novel feature of early urban societies as a result of an assemblage of proximate ecologies, patterns of coercion and consent to engage in settled farming, and elite control over surpluses.[11]

The political scientist James C. Scott explores why human populations became "sedentarized" relatively recently in human history—in the last few thousand years—compared to the hundreds of thousands of years when they lived as foragers and hunters. This appears to have been true even though people knew about domesticated food plants and livestock long before then. He asks, "Has it been the aim of all states, classical and modern, colonial and independent, populist and authoritarian, communist and neoliberal, to assemble rural people on fixed agricultural fields—to sedentarize them?"[12]

Settled farming is indeed a relatively recent phenomenon, less than about 8,000 years old. Its precedents may, however, be traced to a period following the Younger Dryas, a 1,000-year period of glacial cooling that began around 12,000 years before the present (BP) after a relatively long warm and wet period. The Younger Dryas is named after the flower of the characteristic alpine tundra grass, *Dryas octopetala,* which was suddenly abundant in Europe. In the course of centuries of several harsh winters, populations remained huddled near coastlines, where food sources were limited to fishing rather than forest produce. Constrained by geography, with harsher conditions inland, fixed-plot farming may have emerged as a strategy for survival at first and then as a way for a few powerful groups to create and accumulate agricultural surpluses. During the thaw, especially in some areas near freshwater and at river deltas, increased population pressure on available arable soils may have been the impetus for paying more attention to planting and breeding, leading to the intensification of cultivation practices and possibly the deployment of hired or slave labor. In the beginning of the Holocene (the geological period that followed the Younger Dryas), warm, well-irrigated, rainfed areas were attractive places to plant crops, although there were intermediate periods of cold, dry weather, including around 6200 BCE. Local agents having geographical advantages may have leveraged their positions at multiple scales to behave as fee-collecting gatekeepers for the use of prime land for production, creating the earliest enclosures. They may have charged (presumably in grain) those who produced food and other crops and offered protection from human and animal raiders in return. Thereby, they made petty gains of grain or other exchangeable stock, such as domesticated animals, which in turn created surpluses. Over time, the robust agricultural productivity of grain (e.g., 10 to 1 ratios for harvest to seed for wheat and more than double that for rice) allowed them to consolidate control and accumulate resources.[13]

Scott usefully points out that, although settled farming could have begun early in the Holocene, there is no evidence for it for several thousand years into the geological era. He argues that strong polities—states—first had to take shape in order to shift the course of food production from tubers and legumes that required little or no attention to cereals that had determinate timing and measurable yields, which made their production amenable to controls and taxation. Along the Nile, in Mesopotamia, and in some other silt-rich regions that were otherwise semi-arid, polities emerged to "manage" scarcity, often by controlling key resources and carefully calibrating their deployment along with rising populations. Farm life also brought about new forms of everyday life, and cities became "state-amplified late-Neolithic resettlement camps." Scott describes early practices of settled farming that made up a disciplinary habitus with elites overseeing the operations:

> From field clearing and preparation (by fire, plow, ard, harrow) to sowing, cultivation, and weeding to constant vigilance as the field ripens, the crop organizes much of our timetable. The harvest itself sets in train another sequence of routines: in the case of cereal crops, cutting, bundling, threshing, gleaning, separation of straw, raking, winnowing, sieving, drying, sorting—most of which has historically been coded as women's work. Then, the daily preparation of grains for consumption—pounding, grinding, fire making, cooking, or baking throughout the year—sets the tempo of the domus [hearth]. These meticulous, demanding, interlocked, mandatory annual and daily routines, I would argue, belong at the very center of a comprehensive account of "the civilizing process." They strap us to a minutely choreographed routine of dance steps; *they shape our physical bodies; they shape the architecture of the domus; they insist, as it were, on certain patterns of cooperation and coordination.*[14]

Other modalities of evolving interactions among residents in settlements and human–material interactions in settled farming also gave rise to emergent patterns that are worth noting. The archaeologists Ian Hodder and Angus Mol write,

> A dependency relationship between humans and emmer wheat at the dawn of agriculture led to genetic change in the wheat such that, as a result of a tough non-shattering rachis, wheat could no longer reproduce itself without human intervention. Humans and wheat thus became co-dependent or co-reliant. But as a result, humans were also drawn into harder labor in order to thresh and winnow.... The relationship involved dependency in that humans became both enabled by and constrained by wheat, trapped into pathways involving new forms of labor and new technologies.[15]

Settled farming was therefore a key element in the chain of social transformation: it helped regulate human labor, created a surplus, and paved the way for different forms of redistribution of that surplus. I later describe how rice cultivation is emblematic of settled farming's generation of substantially more produce than that required for consumption by the farmers working the field, but this feature is broadly true for almost any cultivated crop. It is likely that the category of land ownership (in any sense of tenure) very likely coincided with the creation of a category of nontenured farmers, who worked as slaves, tenants, or otherwise bonded labor. Rents of one sort or the other became a logical outcome, thereby creating the first leisure class comprising people who could live off the toil of others. It is easy to forget that all these familiar features of our present system occurred as a result of a major transition that began less than 10,000 years ago and gained shape as a "model" of civilizations a few millennia later. But that may simply be because concepts such as "property" and the private accumulation of "rents" have become so completely naturalized in our minds today.[16]

Kot Diji and other proto-cities may have resulted from the early territorial takeover of places of habitat previously occupied by foragers and occasional farmers and hunters, some of whose niche areas of temporary occupation were repeatedly colonized by larger groups. This resulted in the emergence of dominant polities of group- and clan-based societies, not exceeding about 500 persons each, as compared to earlier ancestor bands made up of 30 people or fewer. Clan-based societies generally required a new type of leadership that asserted control over larger areas than before and played a special role in abetting the consolidation of elites. Moreover, foragers with their variegated nutrition may have been in more robust states of health than their aggressors; therefore, the early "civilizing process" was perhaps more harmful than useful.

Early cities and their precursors provide us a glimpse of emerging mechanisms of sedentism and the elite capture of agricultural surplus. Rather than having centralized authority over a vast area, these polities were localized nodes of power with strong links of trust among specially empowered groups of agents and their affiliates across extended geographies that required many days, even months, to traverse. Archaeological and written evidence from Mesopotamia and many other early civilizations suggests that only a small number of individuals were part of such cosmopolitan networks. They invariably had control over the labor of much larger groups of people whose products were traded across long distances. Because of the advantages they enjoyed, elite agents typically were able to influence the actions of large publics in highly well-coordinated ways.[17]

Attempts to control the surplus of an entire network of rent collectors probably took place much later after the development of settled farming. They were made possible by the birth of the territorial entity, the kingdom: its most spectacular example was ancient Egypt, recorded to have emerged at least 6,000 years into the Holocene. Through a tight syndrome of elite networks centered on the Pharaoh, who was divinity himself, a unique geography of control over a vast captive population trapped along the Nile by the desert, a kingdom and later empire sustained itself over several millennia. In a more positive sense, the regime maintained an elaborate system of dikes and artificially constructed basins and canals, especially in the poorer, upper part of the Nile River, ensuring the people's dependence on that infrastructure for productive farming. In addition, authority was delegated to subordinate administrators stationed across the provinces to ensure control and the extraction of resources. It was this larger, so-called hydraulic strategy of elite network domination and source of revenue that seemed to have been important in keeping the Egyptian state enterprise intact.[18]

It is significant that those polities that developed naval power were also some of the most likely to claim territory; they included not only the Minoans but also the Egyptians, Persians, and later the Romans. This is because trade and control over trade routes, like settled farming, created opportunities for hoarding a surplus or creating scarcity, especially for luxury goods. Both surplus and scarcity were effectively managed by well-networked gatekeepers who also maintained a hierarchy among themselves. These gatekeepers may have included some farmers, but most had economic, military, and religious authority, in some combination, and were successful in building their links with key agents and actors. At the top, stronger nodes of military power and extended spatial influence likely began to form.[19]

Each of these networked polities, coalescing into civilizations, lasted at least a few centuries, if not millennia, suggesting that they were able to support themselves in a relatively stable manner for a considerable length of time. They formed "territories," geographies that they controlled, and often coordinated the fledgling actions of earlier clan and group-based associations into much larger scales. In the absence of external factors like climatic change and other environmental shifts or destruction by invaders, they were able to generate considerable economic revenue, some of which was exchanged across long distances, by following patterns of trade that lasted for long periods of time. These activities meant that they had to have robust institutions of interdependent networks whose influence spanned long distances and whose activities were supported by labor practices and the collection of revenues. These resources were then invested to maintain urban agglomerations over the long term by creating water and sanitation systems, roads, city walls, housing, and so on.

The territorial impulse of elite networks might be explained in a variety of ways, but the most common explanation is the need to hoard enough wealth among a small minority in order to satisfy power-sharing agreements and support hierarchies within elite networks. This might only be possible if sufficient rents can be collected for strategically located groups to have exclusive access to "luxury goods," which provide prestige to a small minority (and add to their symbolic capital) who self-fashion themselves as elites and seek both differentiation from the masses and the ability to control armed groups. The talent to achieve such "sovereign power" rests on the creation of a typical "gang" of physically and materially powerful actors and a spatially dispersed set of gangs dependent on the metropolitan or central gang's largesse. Harnessing such a network successfully over time has meant possessing geographical and technological advantage, that is, having trustworthy connections across a vast space that require technologies such as horses or ships for traversing and also occupying locations that have strategic military importance. The loci of elite power networks and their supporting institutions are typically towns and cities, whose spatial architecture and synekism serve as nodes of amplifying power.

Much earlier, during the millennia after the Younger Dryas, elite networks were perhaps much more disconnected and still seeking successful strategies of control and authority over local populations. The latter, out of conditions of at least partial distress and climate change during the big thaw, were sometimes trapped in place for reasons of terrain and at the mercy of the controlling elite. Over time, for reasons explained above, elites sought greater territorial power and needed to expand their influence in distant locations through alliances or military invasion. Once the consequent networks and their inner circle built coherence around a specific ideology, they turned invisible and spawned civilizing cultures.

Early urban civilizations were likely bound together by an ideology that kept their routines and practices going; in turn, this meant that there was some sort of dominant power, which having the authority to enforce policies, must have sought popular consent. There is simply no evidence in global history of any regime having stayed in power for centuries without obtaining broad and willing participation in the daily business and activities of government early on. One way this participation was achieved was through the creation of urban services; another was through the creation and maintenance of interlocking networks of trust, first in clans with firm kinship rules and, later, through guilds and other clubs of interdependency. A third way was the creation of rituals of social practice around a common set of ideas of the sacred or the otherworldly, which frequently involved the mediation of a unique elite grouping or social class known as priests.

Material Culture of the Ancient City

Cities were made, occupied, and governed as specific ways of living in spatially confined societies, each having their own modes of production and reproduction in a given region, each with an associated habitus of a given landscape, each generating social routines that served to sustain economies extending beyond subsistence and local areas. Archaeologists who identify and study physical objects as elements of towns and cities often refer to them as part of "material and landscape culture." Examining these traces gives us clues into the forms of power that directed the organization and social order of cities.

As mentioned earlier, although most Harappan towns and cities were situated along the floodplain of the Indus Valley in present-day Pakistan, several important sites were found to the south and east—in Gujarat, northern Rajasthan, Haryana, and western Uttar Pradesh in India, as well as in the Helmand Province in Afghanistan to the northwest. In contrast to Mesopotamia, the broader region was known not just for its rich alluvium but also for its minerals, including bitumen, copper, steatite, various gems, and small amounts of gold. The earliest settlements were small farming communities and pastoral holding posts that were transformed into larger areas by around 3800 BCE and expanded in size and number across the region. Over the course of the next millennium, these village cultures began to become increasingly urbanized, as evidenced by the specialization of craft, the erection of flood defenses, denser and more populated settlements, and trade with neighbors.

The period between 2600 and 1900 BCE marks what is sometimes called the "urban" or Harappan phase. It is during these seven centuries that urban sites seem to have proliferated, displaying remarkable feats of engineering; mining and industry, forming an elaborate supply chain for bead production and other artifacts in clearly identified workshops and factories oriented to export trade; and clearly organized and planned spatial units. Around 2600 BCE, several new developments delineated the beginning of the urban phase. Across the entire region a major transition took place, involving the abandonment of nearly two-thirds of the original sites, the destruction by fire of many others, and the rise (often in the same locations) of a far more complex and organized society. In the span of decades, new and larger planned cities appeared, several with cardinally oriented streets perpendicular to each other; carefully laid-out brick-lined wells, tanks, and drainage networks; neighborhood grain silos and other public facilities; industrial-scale production involving new styles of crafts; and inscriptions found on seals and buttons symbolizing wealth and status. The most impressive structures, artifacts, and design elements were seen in the large cities (ranging in size from about

100–600 acres) of Mohenjo-daro, Harappa, and Dholavira, but similar configurations existed even in the smallest sites that were smaller than 10 acres in size.

The archaeologist Gregory Possehl, describing the beginning of the Harappan phase as a "paroxysm of change," identifies these four characteristics:

1. sudden emergence of writing
2. development of a wide variety of features associated with Harappan town planning, such as the construction of massive brick platforms, well digging, drainage systems, and grid plans
3. appearance of a widely used system of calibrated weights and measures
4. changes in a wide variety of more subtle features such as the Harappan ceramic corpus indicating craft and career status and social and political stratification[20]

The transition was abrupt in some locations. Possehl cites the investigator, F. A. Khan, who notes that "the prominent and clearly marked burnt layer strongly suggests that the last occupation level of the early settlers (that is the Kot Diji) was violently disturbed, probably totally burnt and destroyed."[21] Yet, there is no other evidence—either of weaponry or funerary remains—to support the notion that warfare or violence was the cause of this destruction. Furthermore, there is some evidence from other sites that there was not a uniform "break" in social patterns but instead an evolution of them. The archaeologist B. B. Lal writes,

> The combined evidence from sites like Kot Diji in Sindh, Harappa itself in Punjab, Kalibangan in Rajasthan and Banawali and Kunal in Haryana shows that many of the characteristic features of the Mature Harappan civilization had begun to manifest themselves by about 3000 BCE. For example, the houses were oriented along the cardinal directions, with the streets naturally following suit. The typical Harappan brick-size ratio of 4:2:1 had also come into being. Some of the settlements, like Kot Diji, Kalibangan, and Banawali were also fortified.[22]

It might be easier to understand the birth of the urban phase as the launch of a region-wide Harappan urban "style," a carefully designed and engineered set of urban structures that prompted a new way of living, modeled on elements that had been in the making in Kot Diji and elsewhere in the vicinity. If the development of Harappan culture in some locations of the alluvial plains of the Indus Valley and Ghaggar-Hakra was gradual, away to the southeast, in Gujarat, it was abrupt: after 2600 BCE, Dholavira, a sprawling city of fifty hectares, arose in accordance with a mathematically precise plan and monumental architecture, with a citadel, middle town, lower town, and reservoirs and stadia. Dholavira was encircled by massive walls and housed a major workshop for craft production: bead making, pottery, shell artifacts, and metalworking. The city had perennially low rainfall and depended on enormous reservoirs for water. It relied for its food and timber on a largely pastoral hinterland. There is evidence to suggest that Dholavira's urban structure became more complex over time, particularly in the area of the citadel.[23]

Around 1900 BCE, Dholavira and the towns surrounding it were abruptly abandoned, but were resettled within a few decades with smaller groups of people with less sophisticated technologies. The transformation, if not collapse, of Harappan society close to the beginning of the second millennium BCE is a mystery that has potential implications for the study of corruption. But that narrative can only be properly constructed through a fuller material history.

Unearthing the Harappan Phase

Many, though not all, Harappan sites had well-organized industrial processes for pottery; agate, carnelian, faience, shell-based, and terracotta jewelry production; and construction, which complemented farming and trade as occupations. In almost all the major cities, there is evidence for factories solely organized for bead production.

Recent explorations in Lothal in Gujarat indicate the clear presence of a dock and a massive bead factory, suggesting that it was also a major hub of trade along the Arabian Sea. The manufacturing of carnelite, faience, and steatite beads required considerable skill, advanced tools, and several days, if not weeks, of labor. Some materials had to be brought from hundreds of miles away to factories where they were crushed, melted, and dyed; to make beads from other materials, stone fragments had to be sawed or chipped and ground.

Most of the 30,000 or so beads found in Harappa were drilled with copper or stone drills that had sophisticated designs. So intensive were some of the techniques that one necklace may have required more than a year of full-time labor. Given the widespread distribution of some of the beads, it is likely that the trade in beads, not farming, constituted the primary source of revenue.[24] The archaeologist Norman Yoffee notes that in early civilizations, a

> major source of economic power is through mercantile activity. Long-distance, regular networks of exchange are generally found to accompany the first inequalities in access to production in early agricultural societies. Not only does the acquisition of preciosities represent burgeoning economic status, but the process of acquisition also becomes an institution requiring organization and thus a means through which status is produced. Long-distance trade, when coupled with other instances of inequality, becomes a particularly important and visible institution in ancient societies precisely because economic "action at a distance" produces wealth and status outside the moral economy of sharing usually imposed by kinship systems.[25]

It is hard to draw clear conclusions about the characteristics of the elite groups that gained windfall profits (rents) through arbitrage, made possible by their control of trade. But that only makes the engines of such diligent economic activity in Harappa ever so intriguing. Internally, a seeming obsession with managing water and drainage characterized most cities, which had wells, tanks, networks of reservoirs, baths, drainage pipes, and inspection holes for the maintenance of sanitation drains: all these engineering systems were unprecedented. Virtually every house had its own water supply, toilet, and bathtub, with drains to carry away the dirty water, flowing in deep brick-lined sewers under the streets that had manholes to allow regular cleaning.[26]

Equally of interest, the Harappans fashioned and used a remarkable collection of artifacts, including toys and sophisticated metal and flint tools, fishhooks, razors, knives, cooking utensils, and shovels. The archaeological analysis has focused on the large collection of seals, stamps, and coins made of steatite and other materials. The artifacts, which uniformly seem to have a "competent dullness," are so strikingly similar across sites that the style and other elements of craftsmanship across all of them must have had a single origin.[27]

Although the sizes of Harappan cities varied widely, there were no palatial residences and hardly any special luxury products, in contrast to those found in other civilizations of the time. Instead, an uninteresting but standardized design characterized almost every city. Each had two sections: a well-planned residential complex and a smaller site, the citadel to the west or north, which served as an administrative or priestly center. Streets in both areas were frequently at right angles to each other. Enormous tanks in the lower city were found in both Mohenjo-daro and Harappa, presumably for public ritual bathing purposes. Other cities also had such tanks, but they were generally of much smaller size. The houses were relatively similar, between 500 and 1,500 square feet in Mohenjo-daro and larger in some other cities; each typically had a courtyard and two or more rooms. Most strikingly perhaps, virtually every Harappan building was constructed with bricks in a constant ratio (1:2:4), some of which were produced in kilns at very high temperatures. One estimate, following the logic of archaeologist Shereen Ratnagar, is that several hundred person-years of labor would have been required to manufacture all the bricks found in any of the major cities.[28]

Standardized cubic weights and microweights in denominations of a binary system (1, 2, 4, 8, 16, 32), stamp seals, and signs making up the writing system also confirm that the Harappans were active traders. Button seals with floral designs first appeared in Mehrgarh around 3300 BCE and continued to be used to various extents for the next two millennia. Around 2800 BCE, seals with animal symbols and script made their appearance in proto-urban settlements and were in wide use in cities until late Harappan times, largely disappearing, along with the Indus script, by the first millennium BCE. Factories for producing seals, however, have only been found in the city of Harappa, suggesting that seals constituted some type of currency and were produced at a central mint. These seals have been discovered in faraway places, indicating widespread trade across the region and beyond. Indeed, as mentioned, there is compelling evidence that trade constituted the most important element of the Harappan economy, especially given the timing of the abandonment of many cities by 1900 BCE and the substantial fall in trade with Mesopotamia that had occurred a century or so earlier.[29]

The post-urban phase began in 1900 BCE, after which a period of de-urbanization seems to have taken place until about 1400 BCE. The largest sites, including Mohenjo-daro and Harappa, along with several others, were effectively abandoned. During this phase, Harappa had a much reduced population in a location famously termed "Cemetery H," which had almost no resemblance in its material culture to the glory days of the Indus Valley civilization, except for a few continuing Harappan motifs in its pottery. After this period, there is almost no sign of an urbanized society and polity, although many Harappan artifacts—in particular, its pottery ware—were found in later periods in Gujarat and elsewhere east of the Indus and Ghaggar-Hakra Valleys, suggesting some continuity to the identities of the original inhabitants.[30]

About the change after 1900 BCE, the archaeologist Jane McIntosh writes,

> At Mohenjo-daro, the last period of occupation of the city shows a serious decline in civic standards, with poorly constructed houses, pottery kilns in what had previously been residential areas, the neglect of civic amenities such as drains, and corpses thrown into abandoned houses or streets instead of being buried with due rites. Important public buildings such as the Great Bath went out of use. Some stone sculptures were deliberately broken. A similar situation is known in many cities and towns, and others were abandoned altogether.[31]

Whatever remained in the major cities for at least a generation afterward was either destroyed or ruined, or they were settled by new inhabitants who had very few of the characteristics of the people living during the mature phase of Harappan society. Although there was some variation in these developments, particularly in the borderlands where some of the earlier cultural practices may have continued, the earlier urban planning and standardization of production were certainly forsaken in the early centuries of the second millennium BCE. In Gujarat, the hamlet of Kuntasi and the much larger port city of Lothal—both of which had been centers of manufacturing and trade—became reduced to squatter settlements with rundown housing, probably as infrastructures—factories and trade routes—more inland in the Indus and Ghaggar-Hakra Valleys began to be abandoned.

The abandonment of major Harappan cities and the near-complete transformation of the civilization have spawned many hypotheses in the archaeological literature. Tectonic changes may have caused flooding in the lower part of the Indus Valley, and a combination of reduced rainfall and fluvial changes in the Ghaggar (or Sarasvati) River basin may have caused it to dry up. But it is unlikely that environmental changes were the sole drivers of the transformation. Given the vastness of the region and the sophistication of its engineering systems, Harappan society would, in all likelihood, have had the resilience to adapt to the natural disasters of the period. Similarly, earlier theories about an Āryan invasion having destroyed or overrun the Harappans have been refuted by more credible ones suggesting the cause of decline was mostly endogenously produced, with some environmental and geopolitical events complementing this process. It is quite likely that major social change was accompanied by crippling losses (possibly to elites) caused by environmental damage and the breakup of trade networks, resulting in the decline of the earlier regulated institutional arrangements.[32]

B. B. Lal suggests that over six hundred years the human impact on Harappa would have been profound. Overexploitation of land and consequent loss of soil fertility, together with the cutting down of forests and firing of billions of bricks, completely changed the landscape. All this might have been exacerbated by tectonic activity that reduced the mighty Saraswati to a stream. Lal writes,

> With the drying up of the Sarasvati, the impoverished folks of the Harappan settlements in its valley were obliged to move eastwards where they could get reasonable water-supply, to sites like Hulas and Alamgirpur in the upper Gangā–Yamunā Valley. Perhaps a change of climate to aridity may have also added to the troubles of the Harappans. And the final blow to the prosperity of the Harappans seems to have been delivered by the snapping of the trade with Western Asia.[33]

Overall, with dwindling resources, it became increasingly difficult to sustain the painstaking planning, construction, and maintenance of these finely crafted towns and cities. Given that trade and access to political power were closely tied together, making possible the maintenance of a healthy market of products generated by a vast network of cities, most likely some nodes of power had to have kept the vast enterprise moving. Most likely, a far-reaching trader guild managed to keep a substantial number of workers employed in the production of goods for trade. Sometime around 1900 BCE, this network may have been forced to disband or otherwise lost its moorings, especially with the concurrent decline of the Assyrian kingdom in Mesopotamia.[34]

If trade was such a significant part of the Harappan civilization, what its people got back in return for so carefully maintaining a strong industrial base and a vigorous trading pattern is a mystery, unless slaves and forced labor were used to minimize the costs of maintaining the enterprise. But there is no evidence of Mesopotamian goods or people in Harappa, nor do DNA evidence and human remains reveal any apparent signs of the presence of outside populations. It is possible that luxury goods such as fabrics or other perishable items were the primary imports, but if so, these were enjoyed in small quantities, given the paucity of written records from exporters in West Asia. Certainly, the division of labor and its vast deployment in the manufacture of beads, necklaces, and seals implied an economy that had a hierarchy and elements of social control. These considerations suggest a formation, unique in Indian and perhaps global history, of a corruption enclave built through an elite network that was maintained by a substantially decentralized and out-of-sight power that nimbly and efficiently made a much larger public conform to its interests for several centuries. Yet the character and operations of this power remain cryptic. In the rest of this chapter, I shed some light on this mystery.

Toward a Social Theory of Corruption in Harappa

It is in the Harappan phase that we see a very clearly patterned life in its cities' spatial layout and society. This required a division of labor and engineering practice, organized forms of production, prearranged social interactions, including possibly well-defined gender roles, and trade. These, in turn, signal resilient arrangements of power that kept these operations and habitus going for several centuries. Harappan society, like any other, was possibly held together with a discourse around its collective purposes, which articulated reasons for its practices. These practices may have been cemented through law or formal rules that spelled out forms of overt administrative power. At the same time, it is important not to view the day-to-day activities of Harappan life as done by soulless, automatons in an early stage of the evolution of human beings. Harappans may have been well regulated through coherently organized political forces that were part of either a single or a polycentric process. But in their everyday performances as human agents forming assemblages of variously patterned social rituals, their existence and actions certainly expressed, just like for ourselves, definite subjectively formed conceptions and experiences of satisfaction, joy, happiness, or grief, and most likely an active sense of purpose.[35]

Describing the prevalence of clay artifacts in two small Harappan towns near the Kutch region of Gujarat, beyond the alluvial heartland of Harappa, the archaeologist Brad Chase and his collaborators postulate,

> Cross-culturally, domestic life is rife with ritual great and small, from the taking of meals to the celebration of holidays and life events, and many of these involve the creation of objects that may be recognized as toys. In small communities with active pottery traditions such as Bagasra and Shikarpur, it is expected that the clay forms of some such objects occasionally would have been fired, preserving them for posterity.[36]

It is also possible that there was a spiritual and political center in Mohenjo-daro or Harappa that directed administrative control over a wide region. The presence of citadels in each of the towns certainly indicates stratification operating at a dispersed level, which may be interpreted as autonomous points of control over local populations. The evidence for an organized center that coordinated these local authorities is thin, except for rare artifacts that suggest an elite concentration of some sort. The art historian Massimo Vidale, for instance, describes an enigmatic terracotta figure that represents high status. What appears to be a throne, but also has features of a cow and a boat, is significant, both because it is an exquisite object dissimilar to any other found in the entire region and because it symbolizes a regal procession of some sort.[37]

Regardless of what we may eventually learn about the identity and seat of Harappan elite power in relation to the rest of society, we are left with the phenomenal *absence* of evidence of an emperor or of lavish satraps in the different cities or of rulers; no material evidence of their propensity to assert their power has yet been found. There are no signs of them living in palaces, sponsoring extravagant ceremonies, building temples or shrines, or being venerated through prominent funerary rites on their death. Certainly, not all ceremonial pride would have been marked in stone. But a society that was proud of its civic engineering, as its docks, drains, streets, and baths show, would also be expected to have architectures designating social differences or hierarchy in its cities. The lack of evidence for such spatial and architectural differences between the nobility and the peasantry is therefore unusual.

The archetype of an early polity is a centralized state that deploys grand symbols, such as temples, palaces, ceremonial burials, and sacrifice, which "naturalize" authority and create elite centers of power as guardians of these symbols and their associated rituals. The ideologies of such spectacles of power are quite familiar across history. Most forms of state power—the types of political authority that usually accompany control over large territory—are characterized by pomp and circumstance of some sort, as reflected in both elite kingly and ordinary household life. This is true of monarchies as well as other forms of government, ranging from the Roman republic to Yoruba leadership councils in West Africa. Harappa was by no means an equal society: its seals and jewelry indicate gradations in status, control over labor and resources, subtle differences in funerary rites, and an extensive ideology of conformist practice. Then why did its society not display these differences in its material culture?[38]

The anthropologist Daniel Miller provides what I find to be the most useful framework for developing a social theory of Harappan order and its relation to elite power, both of which I associate with corruption. I draw on Miller's structural integration of three observations—the absence of grand demonstrations of power, the homogeneity of the decentralization of power, and social transformation—as a launchpad to promote my still hazy theory of Harappan corruption.

No Grand Demonstrations of Power

First, rather than being similar to other social and spatial patterns of contemporary civilizations such as Mesopotamia or Egypt, Harappa represents a "check, reversal, and systematic suppression" of their elements, resulting in a "more idiosyncratic form of social control and social organization."[39] What Miller is pointing to here is the absence of grandiose demonstrations of power. In other places, the existence of spectacular monuments and funerary arrangements for high-level officials, priests and kings, and wealthy protectors and their representatives was corroborated in inscriptions, thereby establishing the presence of well-marked hierarchical societies. Instead, in Harappa, housing, drab jewelry, and utilitarian everyday objects indicate a sameness rather than difference, for the most part.

At the same time, the presence of power and dominance seems all too evident, although it may be characterized more through powerful organizing symbols than by singular sites of authority. Seals were especially important and evidently had great symbolic value. A seal not only bore the inscription and motif representing its origin but also had the ability to replicate that code on another object or spatial symbol. In doing so, it marked territory and had the collective force of an authority behind it. Moreover, because it was also used as an ornament, it created another demonstration of such authority on the person wearing it.

Seals came in a wide variety of motifs, but after 2600 BCE they started to be produced in a small number of workshops along with molded faience tablets. Jonathan Kenoyer proposes that animal symbols were used along with a written inscription to ensure that both literate and illiterate Harappans could understand their meaning. The animal most often represented on the seals was the mythical unicorn, which completely disappeared from later Indian figuration. Interestingly, although there was a small but thriving community in the post-urban phase of Harappa and many of the earlier cultural practices continued at least until about 1700 BCE, neither seals nor formal inscriptions of any kind were used after 1900 BCE.[40] According to McIntosh, "seals were not personal possessions but objects related to some official role, disposed of when the holder left office.... While some seals show signs of considerable wear, others were almost pristine, suggesting that the seals also served another function, most probably to identify the holder and to authorize certain activities that he (or she?) undertook."[41]

Seal bearers clearly had an official status and were certainly elite members with political power in Harappan society. Yet we have no reason to assume that they had some connection with what we might call a state, a sovereign authority with centralized control over territory. And yet, it is clear that only a polity with sovereign authority would have had the power to implement the specific set of coherent social arrangements that emerged across the Harappan landscape and lasted for centuries. How did a spatial ideology of rigidly planned surfaces, directionality, and material deployment become organized against the natural, but uniform, order across locations? What constituted such a polity, if it existed, and how did it exert its authority across large distances in the apparent absence of weapons or armies, but with occasional fortification? One possible explanation is that

> the deliberate destruction of old settlements and the creation of new ones following certain principles, such as the cardinal orientation of streets and the emphasis on water supply and sanitation, reflect the widespread adoption of a new ideology, which was to underlie the unity and considerable uniformity of the Indus civilization. In this scenario, rather than reflecting enemy action, the destruction by fire of the settlements was an act of ritual or ideological purification. Indeed, some scholars suggest that the Indus civilization was not a single state but a collection of smaller independent polities unified by this shared ideology, a hypothesis that has its attractions.[42]

The notion of a shared ideology across fractured polities is an intriguing one that requires some clarity about how to describe early political systems without invoking the archetype of the modern state. Present-day views are obviously colored by recent experience with state forms perfected in Europe and the United States in the eighteenth century; such forms involve bureaucracies, police forces and judiciaries, standing armies, and contemporary means of taxation. For the ancient polity, one needs instead to consider different modes in which authority, coercive power, and legitimacy are claimed and made available to different segments in a given society.

Key to the potential for coherent political action in such a multi-nodal form of power is a shared habitus of members of that society. To be both effective and legitimate, these multiple sites of authority must eventually align themselves around a disciplinary set of strategies that generate similar habits and routines. As discussed in earlier chapters, ideology is not transmitted as a set of abstract beliefs by hidden conspirators to the populace through some sort of metaphorical lobotomy or brainwashing; it is best understood as entering into individuals' lives through their everyday practices that are somehow concurrently deemed functionally important and appealing. That multiple formations of power might have generated such an ordered society as seemed to have existed in Harappa is itself a grand mystery.

In a review of various theories on the Harappan polity, Possehl cites the archaeologist Fairservis's portrayal of it as 'a "great tradition" marked by both urban and rural elements evolving out of hybrid "little communities," with interrelated elements that were perhaps "transformed into an indigenous or 'primary' civilization in which village and city alike shared a common culture" during the Harappan phase. Possehl goes on to propose that as a "faceless culture," with no cult of personality or aggrandizement of the individual, it is possible to surmise that the Harappan polity was nothing like the centralized archaic state common among other civilizations of the time. Yet its centralizing institutions could nevertheless have been formed through strong temporary alliances among several groups. Mohenjo-daro may have been the original archetype for all other settlements to follow; its landscape and habitus created the ideal city on the hill that others could aspire toward building elsewhere. The Harappan polity could then be seen as a "heterarchy," with sites of power that were spatially and hierarchically decentralized but with political elites nevertheless coherently capable of reproducing authority and order.[43]

The archaeologist Adam T. Smith's concept of an early complex polity is useful here. Smith is critical of the category of the state and the founding story of its natural formation into a central power with a monopoly over violence, a narrative that seems to conceal the astonishing variety of local and regional forms of authority that have territorial power. States in this monolithic conception tend to be placed within an evolutionary framework, so that sovereign authority, an administration, police, and armies constitute the natural next step after the chiefdom, whose limited face-to-face authority within small groups and kinship-based hierarchy and rules of succession give it less control. This tidy account obscures the actual complexity of political space and creates the superstition that societies are always subject to lawlike forces or simply that typology suffices as explanation.[44]

In its place, Smith proposes a model of early urban forms: dense settlements with multiple sites of authority that may forge agreements over time. Such consolidation would result in coherently organized modes of power shared among a small set of elites, each exerting influence on grassroots social groups organized by kinship or occupation. Thus, decision-making power around daily practices and the longer-term spatial planning and revenue generation needed to implement it might devolve to different social agents, who would negotiate their roles and distribute among themselves symbolic and physical capital as rewards for such cooperation.

In this model, the locus of authority lies along a particular confluence of interests among different elite groups that sustain, with ritual but loose and transitory control, a set of asymmetrical relationships that maintain "the proper order of things."[45] In Harappa, such devolution may have taken a radically decentralized dimension, but one that generated practices expressing a strong and shared ideology whose precise form remains mysterious. Nevertheless, it also delivered, in very practical and everyday terms, a faceless though *sovereign* authority for the Harappan people.[46]

Material and Landscape Precision as Ideology

Miller's second point is that it is the very homogeneity of decentralized production that constitutes Harappa's specific ideological expression of elite power: this feature may indeed describe the Harappan syndrome of corruption. The production of various unadorned artifacts and buildings, with a sameness in their forms, across an enormous area would suggest centralized production by a large factory-like system. Yet, within the largest cities, the evidence points to most manufacturing activity taking place primarily within houses and small workshops, with only a few larger specialized workshops. In smaller sites such as Lothal and Chanhu-daro, however, one does find workshops with high levels of production involving metalworking, bead making, and the manufacture of seals, stone weights, and shell jewelry. Also made conspicuous by their absence, and in striking contrast to Mesopotamia or Egypt, are expensive, exotic, or exclusive "art" objects. Luxury goods as such—in the form of bronze mirrors, metal vessels, and necklaces—were simple and plain; gold and silver were rarely used. Similarly, although there was extensive trade in raw materials, not even border sites in the Kandahar region, such as Mundigak and Shahr-i-Sokhta, had any Mesopotamian material, suggesting an embargo of sorts on the import of artifacts.[47]

A related feature of Harappan craft production is its spatial location with respect to other elements of Harappan practice. Based on an analysis of the different types of manufacturing processes in Harappa, the archaeologist Heather M.-L. Miller suggests that craft production of pottery and metalworking that required high temperatures were located separately from those involving lithic and shell working. Yet there is no evidence for any form of active control over these sites by elite nonproducers.

In other words, decisions about locating (or collocating) different types of production appear to have followed common sense and entrepreneurial preference rather than systematic planning by elites. In contrast, decisions about the volume and type of production, their designs, and their uses may have been made by specific members and levels of the hierarchy, which led to the development of elite centers of authority. If an "invisible hand" of producers and consumers of remarkably similar and plain goods seemed to rule Harappa, then present-day narratives about the division of labor and the marketplace of free exchange clearly have little explanatory power regarding the drab appearance of its landscape and material culture across virtually every sector of its extensive economy.[48]

Daniel Miller also points out that the formalization of the physical landscape—the standardization of bricks, the orientation of the roads, and so on—and the material regularity and drabness did not manifest directly as an imposition of strict control over social life. There was evidence of individual variation within the well-designed grid. One finds significant differences in housing size and structure across towns and cities that indicate that the order as such was not intended to subsume all domains of life in Harappa. Rather, Miller explains the drabness as a type of aesthetic formalism showing a "style," in which composition took precedence over iconography, much like in modern art today. What distinguishes various modern art movements since the twentieth century is the absence of a single reference, including perspective: each genre—cubism, Dadaism, abstract expressionism, and pop art—tries to remain indifferent to obvious references to place or individuals and focuses instead on a signature form. Harappan architecture and planning may have represented a single such movement, corresponding to the International Style in architecture, in which standard materials, radical simplification of lines, and mass production of construction were the hallmarks.

In standardizing the objects, artifacts, and architecture of everyday experience, an ascetic ritual element seemed to have formed a dominant habitus, mirroring in the spatial landscape of each person an internalized sense of leading an ordered life. The discovery of fire altars in Kalibangan and other sites, along with the enormous attention paid to water management and use, provides some evidence for the claim that public and private ritual must have played a significant role in Harappan society. Indeed, it must also have been a form of ritual that paid far less attention to material objects such as idols and far more to texts (which were in all likelihood oral). Ritual itself may have been intended to emphasize purity, order, asceticism, and hard work. Some type of authority would have regulated it, ensuring means to organize practices that reordered and reiterated a broad range of power relationships.[49]

What was the nature of this authority? It probably operated on two registers that complemented each other. The first was through some, as yet unknown, set of rituals involving water and perhaps fire too, based on the very limited number of altars that were found. Harappan rituals constituted a highly regulated set of practices guided by the authorizing voice of moral, innate, eternal, and inescapable power. Authority was also exercised through the well-adapted routines of everyday life, especially the production of standardized objects and the patterned structures in well-ordered cities—and perhaps the exemplar simplicity of a priestly class.

Sometime between its pre-urban and Harappan phases, evidence points to the emergence of an elite configuration asserting its influence and authority across Harappan society in a decisive though disaggregated manner. This political power was perhaps dispensed in the very terms of an ordered material landscape and in the strict discipline of monks' ritual practices. Their authority appears then to have been performed by diffuse social agents, who fashioned a broader habitus in a manner that generated not only loyalty and consent but potentially also fear and coercive power, as evidenced by the extensive industrial enterprise of bead and craft making.

As we have seen, in Harappa, in contrast to other civilizations of the time, there is no manifest symbolic representation of sovereign authority as spectacle. Rather, its singular locus of power seems to have emerged through the very routines that characterized its society, which were regular, self-reinforcing, perhaps reassuring to many, and extended over multiple sites in a strangely similar fashion. Harappan commitment to collective action, its faith, was expressed in its mundane everyday practices that nevertheless generated a strictly specified spatial order and large-scale participation in the organized production of a material culture relying on standardized designs and processes. In the Harappan phase, these practices appeared to have become embodied habits, sensibilities, and dispositions that varied only with the capacities of participant-performers in the social routines that developed. Miller writes,

> The so-called barracks are more likely to have contained monks than slaves. In such a culture there is a gradation from the formalized abstraction of the guiding principles and values through to the direct involvement in the everyday world.... There is no reason either why the complex bureaucracy that must have existed or the use of ritual forms need have been restricted to a separate class or group. *Control may have been the more effective through being highly dispersed.*[50]

Emergences and Folds

Miller's third observation relating to the problematic emergence and disappearance of Harappan society provides a final linchpin for formulating a fuller theory addressing these quandaries. Using the idea of "epigenetic" change—like the development from germ to organ—Miller suggests that social transformation emerges from both stochastic, or chance, events and more discernible developmental elements that generate processes that could either stabilize structures of power relations or unsettle them, leading to unpredictable effects.[51]

The emergence of the Harappan civilization in its mature form was perhaps the consequence of an assemblage of different human and nonhuman elements coming together across the vast region of northwest India in the third millennium BCE. These included the synekism of early towns and proto-cities such as Mehrgarh and Kot Diji generating new technologies for bead making and other crafts. The appearance of "philosopher-kings" or lawmakers may have helped create new institutions characterized by rigid discipline, precision engineering, detailed rules concerning the use and management of water, and new opportunities for industrial-scale production and trade. It is also likely that contact with Mesopotamia had already begun, but that conditions for vastly expanding trade relations were just being established.

In the early period around 3400 BCE, patterns of trade and political organization likely began to take largely new and autonomous forms, while a shared set of practices started to develop simultaneously. A small group of elites may have acquired control over resources and established a set of networked dependencies for access to these resources. Those who had jurisdiction, if not ownership in the modern sense, over land would likely have been different from those who actually worked on it. In the subsequent millennium, an elite class, possibly formed through kinship, specialized training, or nomination by elders, may have found persuasive means to completely re-order the social ecology of the cities so that all their structures, plans, and forms of enterprise were aligned a particular way, as characterized by the Harappan phase. Trade may have been a singular route to generating economic surplus, but this was likely accompanied by a further differentiation of roles and control.[52]

At the beginning of the Harappan phase, the small but increasingly powerful group of traders may have made strategic moves to initiate systematic forms of urban planning, organize labor for industrial-scale production of items of trade (presumably dominated not only by gemstones, beads and necklaces but also by goods that have long since perished, including crops such as indigo and turmeric, textiles, rosewood, and furniture), and gathered influence through forms of worship. Together, this assemblage may have ended up creating fetishized or ritual patterns that solidified into social structures such as kinship rules, primogeniture, forms of capital, relations of production and exchange, and possibly, conditions to establish sovereign right, sacred spaces, and so on. These practices would have comprised an ideology of "ceremonial complexes" that reinforced elite authority.

Harappan social order could then be imagined as having a powerful normative force with strict rules forbidding the import of luxury goods and strong organizational forms that were nonhierarchical, in the sense in which one typically understands hierarchy. That is, elites (seal bearers and possibly residents of the citadel) had significantly re-created a habitus of asceticism by emulation in the lives of others and, through that practice, acquired the sovereign ability to mobilize resources. Altogether, Harappan society was not ordered with military precision after all, but its systematic material culture and landscape generated a collective habitus that may have implied a sense of considerable individual choice and variation. This may well have been a prehistoric version of individualism that I described in the context of automobility in Chapter 3: it may have been the personal expression of a style.[53]

After maintaining a fairly stable set of institutions for more than 700 years, it is possible that new events and processes were folded into the assemblage of Harappan society, generating completely changed conditions. A series of environmental disasters such as river flooding or drought may have affected farming or industrial processes, leading to cascading economic crises in certain parts of the region. These may have weakened key political structures in dominant cities, such as Mohenjo-daro and Harappa, leading to a loss of continuity in everyday social practices of production, religious rituals, or both. If there were latent resistances to the legitimacy of Harappan social order at the same time as there were a declining demand for goods in Mesopotamia and competing trading partners in the Mediterranean, it is likely that the larger edifice was at catastrophic risk of collapse by around 1900 BCE, at least in the major cities and some of the adjoining regions. A group of ordered, decentralized polities thus experienced fracturing of a material habitus of transregional conformity, even though some elements of it continued around borderlands in Punjab and Gujarat.

A more likely possibility is that the exceedingly rigorous social order generated, over time, a crisis in which local administrators had systematic incentives to misreport key information on the production of various goods or on crop patterns and yields. Such misreporting periodically took place during the Great Leap Forward in China, when peasants would surreptitiously reallocate time from collective tasks to private ones. Scott writes, "When all these petty acts were aggregated, however, their consequence was, by 1978, a procurement stalemate between the state and rural producers.... [T]he persistence [of such tacit conspiracies] contributed greatly to an abrupt reversal of economic policy."[54]

Rigid discipline may have been a political ideology essential to keeping Harappan society from fragmenting or being "contaminated" by outside influences. But events occurring around 1900 BCE that changed the social order would have exposed vulnerabilities in the system. Perhaps change was initiated by people in one or more of the larger cities, who exploited fragile environmental conditions and revealed that what was promoted as the concerted collective action of vast publics to maintain good social order was actually enriching sites of privilege for elite groups while exploiting many.

It is well-nigh impossible to say any more about the character of Harappan social order and its transformation, but already we see a plausible hypothesis for corruption in that society: the unraveling of a set of justifications for maintaining disciplinary strategies, in Foucault's sense of the term. In later chapters, I argue that there is a recurrent theme of re-appropriation, if not resistance, to the imposition of social order by consent and coercion. The collective recognition by at least a segment of a polity that all is not well with the prevailing order is indeed the moment that the corrupting influence of that order is sometimes acknowledged. How that might be acted on or what changes could take place in the polity vary by context.

5

The Vedic Period

The Esoteric Rhythm of Sacrifice

Take the notion of tradition: it is intended to give a special temporal status to a group of phenomena that are both successive and identical (or at least similar); it makes it possible to rethink the dispersion of history in the form of the same; it allows a reduction of the difference proper to every beginning, in order to pursue without discontinuity the endless search for the origin; tradition enables us to isolate the new against a background of permanence, and to transfer its merit to originality, to genius, to the decisions proper to individuals.

Antecedents of Hinduism

For hundreds of millions of Hindus around the world, the rhythmic drone of Vedic chants is a familiar and comforting sound, even if their meaning is obscure to most. The innumerable modes of worship that go by the designation "Hindu" are dominated by ecclesial rules whose provenance and rituals are quite diverse. But it would be fair to say that most of these practices claim their sanctity today from the Vedās. No sacred books of Hindus are considered more hallowed than the Vedās, which for at least two millennia were only orally recited as occult texts and transmitted by men within highly select clans after a rigorous initiation. Nevertheless, there is evidence that many faiths in India, including early Śaivism and Vaishnavism, challenged or did not observe Vedic rituals for several centuries and were only later appropriated into what is now considered Hinduism.[1]

The word *veda* refers to "knowledge," both in its conceptual form and in a specific practical sense of ritual or repetition as tacit bodily knowledge. But it also has a deeper meaning in terms of a quest for *bráhman*, which the historian and philologist Frits Staal handily translates as "sublime language." It is a language capable of uncovering the principle underlying all reality that can only be transmitted from father to son, teacher to pupil, by *brāhmanas* (associated today with the endogamous caste groups of Brahmins), or learned men. The Vedic universe was built around homologies, between the cosmic reality and the personal realm, united in esoteric ritual sacrifice. The universal principle revealed as bráhman to initiated ones required a sublime language, namely, the sounds (*vāc*) of the Vedas that were part and parcel of the *ācāra* (habitus) of sacrifice and thereby layered with meaning.[2]

Vedic literature is conventionally associated with the four Vedās (Rigveda, Samaveda, Atharvaveda, and Yajurveda), which are mostly made up of hymns of varying length; their prose commentary in the Brāhmanas; the Śrauta Sutras, which explain public sacrifice or *yajna*; the Aranyakas, which describe and speculate on ritual; the Upaniśads, which are philosophical commentaries; and the Grhya Sutras, which deal with domestic rituals relating to rites of passage, such as birth, puberty, and marriage. The four named texts of the Vedās and all the accompanying commentaries and interpretations up to the early Upaniśads constitute what is known as the Vedic corpus.

The hymns and prose elements that make up most of this corpus were composed, refined, and consolidated into a closed canon from about 1500–500 BCE. The earliest composition, the Rigveda, is an enchanting mix of poetic elegies and rhythmic verses to be recited when making oblations to divine entities symbolized by fire, wind, and the mysterious *soma* plant, among a number of other *devas* or gods. Vedic literature is denoted by its *śruti*, a special word suggesting both revelation and tonal depth. As if to emphasize that tonal depth, parts of the Samaveda consist of pure sound, with no semantic content as such. Many verses were treated as *mantras*, spiritual chants having the magical power to transform circumstances, and as sacred speech, vāc, containing secrets of creation and the cosmos. The Atharvaveda and the Yajurveda either reproduce or draw on many existing verses of the Rigveda, but include several additional mantras in prose or verse and are mostly meant as ritual aids for priests.[3]

The Vedās are considered by the faithful to have been divulged by divine inspiration (as śruti) to a few families of wise men in ancient times who, on hearing them in sacred moments, composed verses set to perfect patterns. These few hundred poet-sages wrote the Vedās and, with the help of powerful patrons, perpetuated a line of kinship-based connections of extraordinary influence across generations.[4]

The Vedās were initially transmitted through more than a hundred of these *śakhas*—family branches, recensions, or schools—of which only a handful remain. Almost all present-day Brahmin families make lineage claims to one or more of these śakhas, which likely developed in the early post-Rigvedic age, perhaps by the eighth century BCE. Each śakha belonged to a particular chieftainship whose Brahmin community and landscape were part of a particular tribe or subtribe. Each one's hymns, prose aphorisms, instructions, and invocations were ultimately consolidated into a finite set of editions maintained by the śakhas, numbering anywhere from about a half-dozen redactions for some texts to more than a hundred for others. The oral rendering of the Vedās preserved both their exact wording and the accents that otherwise disappeared in later usages of Sanskrit, which emerged in its literary or *kāvya* form only in the early part of the first millennium. Each recitation had to be performed with the right intonation and accompanied by ritual prayer involving specific bodily routines.

Although they are called texts, the Vedās have been transmitted to the present day entirely through oral recitation. They are therefore best understood as a form of aural memory. Their carefully preserved ancient and highly arcane chants are recited in flawless meter, with tonal variants—syllabic and nonsyllabic sounds that have been ritually transmitted without a trace of change in intonation or cadence. To the best of our current understanding, the Vedās and their corollary commentaries and affiliated materials were not made available in written form before the end of the first millennium CE, because there were strict prohibitions against writing them down or copying them.[5]

The fact that Vedic texts were only transmitted orally does not, however, raise doubt as to the authenticity of their present-day renditions. As the philologist Michael Witzel describes them, Vedic texts were chanted as if in a continuous tape recording for nearly three millennia. Although it is not known how accurate these transmissions were before authoritative versions appeared around 600 BCE, their recitation has been kept intact by a carefully preserved practice, with a large number of stipulations maintained by and constituting the lifeworlds of priests (*hotrs*) and sacrificers (*yajamānas*). The stringency of Vedic practice seems far more significant than its beliefs as such, leading to the conclusion that Vedic religion is better characterized as an ortho*praxy* (straight or ordered practice) than an orthodoxy (strict belief).

Yet it is important to distinguish the Vedās and the ritual sacrifice they were chanted to from the collective liturgical memory of what was later called the Hindu religion. In contrast with other religions relying on canonical religious texts, the manifold Hindu faiths deriving from the Vedās are different from the divinities and forms of devotion described in the Vedic canon. Although some Vedic hymns are de rigueur in present-day Hindu rituals officiated by Brahmin priests, both the rituals and beliefs of the composers of the Vedās and their immediate descendants over the next millennium or so were distinct from those of present-day Hindus. As the philologists Stephanie Jamison and Michael Witzel write, "'Vedic Hinduism' is a *contradictio in terminis* since Vedic religion is very different from what we generally call 'Hindu religion,' at least as much Old Hebrew religion is from medieval and modern Christian religion. However, Vedic religion is treatable as a predecessor of Hinduism." The practices of Vedic society are indeed distinct from major Hindu practices as they emerged during the first millennium of the Common Era and evolved thereafter.[6]

At the beginning of the Common Era, Sanskrit poetry and drama began a flourishing life as an art form in courts across the subcontinent. It was by then both a language of high art as well as ritual practice. In its kāvya or art form, Sanskrit only flourished among the cultured and educated. But although the script was well established by this period and other philosophical and liturgical writing arose, the Rigveda did not appear in written form before the fourteenth century, to the best of current knowledge. The strict parameters of communal sacrifices (yajna) in the Vedic period (1500–500 BCE) reflected the strict, austere institutions governing much of the rest of society, or at least this is what the texts seem to suggest.

What I refer to as Brahmanism is more of an unbroken thread over several millennia. It is the expanding system of practice that developed over centuries around increasingly more elaborate Vedic rituals and forms of social organization, in conjunction with orthodox beliefs around their efficacy in reaching bráhman, sublime language. Male Brahmins, as a clan abiding by strict rules of worship and endogamy, were leading protagonists in these developments, primarily responsible for setting the rules that preserved kinship structures in privileged sections of society. During substantial lengths of time, including under non-Hindu rule by Buddhists, Jains, and Muslims, Brahmin priests were either directly supported by dominant political classes or formed other reciprocal connections with them across changing contexts. In any event, Brahmanism spawned a mode of long-term social exchange and interaction across distinct groups, a pattern that is unique in world history. These modes were laced with power, to be sure, but probably went through many changes before getting transformed to something resembling the present-day caste system only in the colonial period.[7]

As an aside, it must be noted that invoking the authority of the Vedās—or constituting a "Vedic imagination"—has gained profound significance in recent Indian political discourse, particularly for those who affiliate themselves with Hindu revivalism. Whatever the origins of the Vedic people, it is fairly evident that the Vedās were composed in an ancient Indo-European language in the Indian subcontinent. But in twenty-first-century India, controversy over the meaning of these verses also motivates some Hindus to deem themselves rightful "sons of the soil" with exclusive territorial claims over the land of Vedic origin. Thus, the terms of political debate are increasingly framed around themes of recovery, collective memory and *parampara*, a term implying heritage and tradition conveyed through successive generations' transmission of sacred practice and learning. One might describe this as a contemporary emergent form of Brahmanism, an ideology seeking hegemonic status.

It is, of course, impossible to draw lines of connection between the small groups of Vedic sages and their patrons who originated in northwest India sometime in the second millennium BCE and generations of elite networks that operated over much larger areas and longer time frames. Some genetic heritage is certainly conceivable. Far more significantly, Brahmanism changed shape considerably and its dominance has waxed and waned since then. Across generations, families and their kin may have risen or declined in status. There is historical evidence that Brahmins and a few militarily strong and wealthy elites had powerful ties to each other and their alliances gave rise to territorial polities having extended reach and the growth of various types of capital for a privileged few. By the end of the Vedic period, the most prominent Brahmin men and their kin formed alliances with families of other wealthy clans and those with military power. In subsequent millennia, some generations of these elite networks in turn developed multilayered connections with trade and merchant networks, local administrators and police forces, criminal syndicates, and political elites in other locations.

Together, the religious and the political elite networks formed cartels of patronage and exchange. The rest of Vedic society, including possibly the majority of Brahmin families, consisted of small pastoralists, along with petty tradesmen, foragers, and peasants, all of whose relationships to power were diverse but of a subordinate order.

Members of early elite networks may have been Vedic poets, tribal chieftains, or clan leaders. Others may have been their subsidiaries, clients, spies, and other connected individuals who occupied key roles in usurping power. Beyond the Vedic age, at crucial points around the turn of the first millennium CE, the joint political strategies of Brahmin families and warrior clans constituted one of the defining centers of power with sets of overlapping interests and strategies in a web of linkages that unfolded in the subcontinent. During the Vedic age, however, conditions were simpler and more ephemeral. Changing forms of influence generated relatively small but militant and technologically advanced pastoral communities of mutual privilege that managed to shape the fates of larger populations, primarily by having decisive roles in influencing their idioms and ways of living. By studying the longue durée we can see how the seeds of such sharply nucleated nodes of elite power sprouted and later became entrenched in much broader social routines and habits in Vedic India and later, thereby helping constitute certain enduring cultures of Indian society. The long view also brings into relief challenges to elite power and even occasional democratic rebellions that achieved transformative change, sometimes breaching practices that seemed as if they were permanently established habitus of domination and control.

Understanding these histories exhaustively would require both delving into the meanings of the texts and of the ideas themselves and paying attention to implied bodily arrangements and activities, or habitus, and their collective expressions in everyday practices. From the early formations of Vedic authority in its specific, socially constitutive customs that bring about the cultivation of individual behavior and the associated implications of *tapas* (ascetic endurance), *śrama* (ascetic endeavor), and yajna (sacrifice), we may be able to see the emergence and operations of power in a given social context. In what follows, I take deliberate shortcuts to gather rough clues from others' work about the formation of ideologies and associated elite networks of power.[8]

Continuity or Change?

Among the most controversial questions concerning ancient India is whether the poets and chieftains associated with Vedic culture in its earliest phases migrated from across Central Asia or whether they represented a continuation of earlier social formations, most notably, in the Harappan phase. The lack of a clear archaeological signature for the Vedic people heightens the difficulties in resolving the debate. Still, there are strong indications of difference, if not discontinuity, between Harappan culture and Vedic society in both textual readings of the Vedās and the material record. There is convincing linguistic, genetic, and other material evidence to suggest that many of the protagonists of the Vedās and, therefore, potentially their composers, were migrants or descendants of migrants from Central Asia and Iran who had access to chariots and horses, both hitherto unknown in India. For my purposes, however, the question of Vedic origins is not of great significance, other than to establish a rough starting point for understanding the trajectory of Vedic culture's indubitable influence in the subcontinent.[9]

The earliest iron artifacts in the subcontinent were found in the eastern regions of the Indo-Gangetic plain, around 1800–1400 BCE. They were typically used as weapons, for cooking and other daily activities, and as tools for hunting. Iron was also in fairly widespread use in the Deccan and farther south in societies associated with megalithic cultures around 1200 BCE. These discoveries possibly reflect autonomous innovations in different regions, but they were far from the areas described in the earliest Vedic texts: the northern Indus and Doab region between the Ganga and Yamuna Rivers. The Rigveda was probably composed before the Iron Age, given that it mentions other metals but not iron. When the Vedic people independently discovered or acquired iron and moved eastward, they were able to master its use fairly early. Indeed, there are indications that smaller clans that consolidated after 1000 BCE used the productive and emergent possibilities of iron to transform themselves into a powerful if federated territorial entity.

Not much is known about who the Vedic poets were, other than that they called themselves āryas (nobles) and composed hymns describing heavenly deeds and creatures as eloquently and familiarly as they did earthly ones. Early Vedic society, circa 1500–1200 BCE, probably comprised a numerically small but dominant group of pastoral armed āryas and a larger, motley population of peasants, servants, and slaves. Subsequently, their societies became more complex, with merchants and traders, as well as an upper strata of clan leaders and sanctified ritualists. They were a seminomadic people who raised cattle and cultivated crops; performed yajna through Vedic stanzas to divinities of fire, plants, and the cosmic order; and developed a social order around particular forms of patriarchy and clan identities.[10]

At certain times, it is clear that the Vedic people settled down in and around river valleys, but mostly in small cattle-herding groups organized as tribal units. There were several times when tribes were in conflict before their consolidation as a sort of federation. The earliest Vedic texts refer to the *sapta sindvah*, the seven streams making up the northwestern region and the Punjab; later texts include other features further east, down the Gangetic valley. The Vedic tribes shared a few striking similarities with other Indo-European clans about whom more is known, notably the ancient Avestan peoples of Persia, although they developed entirely distinct rituals and forms of life.[11]

One of the earliest significant archaeological finds is the Gandhara mound in northwest Afghanistan, which is dated to around 1400–800 BCE. There, in the Swat Valley—called "Suvastu" in the Rigveda and lying along long-established routes of armies, migrants, and traders that led through the mountains to northern Iran and Central Asia—remains have been found of a three-fire ritual site, horse burials, horse bits and trappings, representations of horses on pottery, cremated human bones, and a chariot.[12]

Until about 500 BCE, Vedic society was largely pastoral, its peace interrupted by warring clans possibly using horses. By then, with the help of iron implements and armor, tribes were able to expand and consolidate their pastures and farmland in the north Indus region and farther west in the Ganges basin in the foothills of the Himalayas at Uttarakhand. Vedic texts describe settlements of mud, straw and wood construction, having none of the striking urban forms or engineering associated with the Harappan civilization. Clan members were likely spread thin in rural hamlets, with denser settlements appearing south and east in areas like Mithila, Mathura, and Hastinapura after 800 BCE.[13]

Indeed, Harappa, whose dominant phase was from 2600–1900 BCE, was substantially different—and it developed more than a millennium earlier—than the lifeworld described in the Rigveda. The absence of the horse in

Harappa—and its powerful symbolic value and widespread use in Central Asian and Vedic societies—is generally seen as the clearest sign of the difference between the two civilizations. But perhaps more significantly, dissimilarities in settlement patterns, the sanitation system, habitat, crops and food habits, trade routes, and funerary practices strengthen the notion that we are speaking of distinct cultures (though not necessarily of different ethnicities) having a few overlapping locations but whose areas of influence were far apart and also separated by many centuries. Theories of invasion and occupation are largely discredited in the scholarly literature, and much of the emphasis now is on the possible in-migration of small groups of people from Central and West Asia in waves beginning around 1500 BCE; their multiple forms of exchange with locals helped spawn new cultural practices and language systems across a wide region.[14]

Farther east, representing a very different pattern of settlement and social formation, new urban centers probably developed first around 800 BCE in Kaushambi and in the sacred or "luminous" city variously known as Kashi, Benares, or Varanasi, and a few centuries later in Pataliputra (Patna); they were soon followed by a series of smaller towns. By the fifth century BCE, this development was identifiably part of the second wave of urbanization in India, which had mostly Buddhist and Jain roots but later was key to transforming Vedic society and increasing its prominence.[15]

We also have evidence of several other, presumably non-Vedic, societies contemporaneous with these developments: in the megalithic cultures that had large stone dwellings, as well as other ritual and storage structures in the Vindhyas, and in several sites along riverbanks in peninsular India and the northeast that had iron implements with varying uses and high degrees of sophistication as early as the fifteenth to twelfth century BCE. Unfortunately, little further material or textual record is available to tell us much more about these and other cultures. Some may have had state-like structures, but most would have resembled forager-hunter societies that did not involve capture of labor power to generate surplus wealth for elite networks.[16]

One fixed date marking the transformation of Vedic society is the fourth century BCE, when there is evidence for a strict formulation of rules of Sanskrit grammar by the ancient linguist Pāṇini and the appearance of the literature of *smriti*, or "recollections," both of which led to a tradition of codified practice. There is no clear evidence of when and how quickly literacy first

The Vedic Period

became part of daily life in India; most likely the first written words were inscribed on rock. There may, of course, have been less permanent writing on bark or leaves, but even the presence of Harappan symbols on seals need not be taken as evidence of widespread literacy in that society. Still, judging by the sophistication of the composition of the Vedās, it is clear that their poets, custodians, and interpreters over several generations were highly skilled in crafting and responding to aural verse. Around this time, the Vedic age gave way to a Sanskrit culture that marked a new phase of linguistic and cultural expression.[17]

The Electric Sounds of the Vedās

The Rigveda is the primary source of the other Vedās. It is believed to be composed by more than a hundred male *rishis*, or sages, from ten distinct families. As mentioned earlier, it largely contains hymns to various deities, each invoked through *agni*, or fire, and the extraction of divine essences from the mysterious soma plant, which appears to have had hallucinogenic effects. Its 1,028 hymns are found in ten books or *mandalas*. Books 2–7, called the family books, are the oldest. It is generally acknowledged that Book 10 was an especially late addition, completed perhaps around 800–700 BCE.

Of the many rishis, a half-dozen or so stand out for the scope and significance of their hymns. A single hymn was usually attributed to one rishi, and each family book is ascribed to a single clan across a few generations. The final redaction of the Rigveda may have taken place by the fifth century BCE, which was before or perhaps at the same time as the composition of the Pratiśakhyas (500–150 BCE), instructional manuals that laid out the proper means of recitation using the right sound and diction. Before the Pratiśakhyas were composed, all knowledge of the Rigveda and Yajurveda was restricted to a small group of priests known to belong to select śakhas.[18]

Humans connected to the gods through smoky offerings of animals and plant extracts, accompanied by a suitable chant of praise. The Rigveda pays primary attention to the deities *Agni, Indra, Soma,* and *Varuna,* representing fire, thunder, the soma plant, and divine order, respectively. Although principally a collection of tributes to divinities in song, the Rigveda is also a representation of nature as an expressive force in itself, as a form of consciousness. Vedic knowledge is regarded as divine and bears the entire weight of spiritual and moral authority. For this reason, the language of the Vedās may have been constructed in a manner that was deliberately obscure. The Vedās thus uniquely combine many abstract philosophical concepts with sacred, spiritual affects or sentiments, practical instructions, and ribald jokes. In Vedic times, the exhortation to conduct rituals of sacrifice to appease the devas was paramount, and was subsequently used as means to mobilize peoples. Still, it is primarily the interpretations of the sacred that make the Vedās a fount of great metaphysical and ethical thought, much of which occurs within the wider Vedic corpus and is termed "Vedanta"—literally, the divine knowledge and questioning that come at the "end of the Vedās."[19]

Vedic literature is distinguished from subsequent works such as the Dharmasutras, which are collections of aphorisms on how to conduct a proper social and political life, and the various *śāstras,* or treatises, around domains such as political activity, the Arthaśāstra; moral life, the Dharmaśāstra; and art, the Natyaśāstra. Other literatures composed primarily in the "high" language of Sanskrit until the first few centuries of the Common Era included stories and mythology, such as the major Puranas, the Rāmāyana, and the Mahābhārata. Vedic literature up to the Upaniṣads, which were supposed to have been divinely revealed as śruti, is distinguished from later materials that were composed solely by humans and memorized and termed "smriti."[20]

The Upaniṣads, which are full of aphorisms, riddles, stories, and Socratic dialogues, were of profound significance to later spiritual leaders and saints, particularly Śankara and Ramanuja, whose sects are still prominent. But their philosophical skepticism makes them stand apart from other Vedic texts and subsequent Hindu narratives and commentaries that focused on the proper means of engaging in household and communal ceremonial practices. As the historian Romila Thapar writes, the Upaniṣads represent "a shift from the acceptance of the Vedās as revealed and as controlled by ritual to the possibility that knowledge could derive from intuition, observation and analysis."[21]

Yet, there is little or no indication even in those texts that such knowledge could replace sacrifice; rather the Upaniṣads' aim is to impart secret, superior knowledge of the *ātman,* or universal life force, but only for certain select initiates *(dvija)* having undergone the sacred thread ritual of *upanāyana.* Over subsequent millennia, a prodigious scholarship has appeared largely in the form of interpretation, codification, and responses to Vedic stanzas and has resulted in distinct philosophies and practice. Altogether, this material helps reconstruct a plausible narrative of Vedic poets and their changing social and geographical conditions.

A stanza of lasting impact known as the Purusha Sukta, a eulogy to the cosmic body or primeval man (*purusha*), was perhaps inserted late within the tenth mandala of the Rigveda. It describes the ordered universe as originating in dismembered parts. It is also the earliest account of a division of labor based on birth: four classes are said to emerge from purusha:

> The brahmin was his mouth. The ruler (Kshatriya, mentioned here as *rājanya*, kinsman as well as establishment of the *rājā* or ruler) was made [of] his two arms.
> As to his thighs—that is what the freeman (Vaishya) was. From his two feet the servant (Śudra) was born.
> The moon was born from his mind. From his eye the sun was born. From his mouth Indra and Agni, from his breath Vāyu was born.
> From his navel was the midspace. From his head the heaven developed.
> From his two feet the earth, and the directions from his ear. Thus they arranged the worlds.[22]

The Purusha Sukta speaks of positions in the social world as emerging from separate parts of bráhman, interpreted here as the eternal body and ultimate reality, as well as its divine self revealed to the sacrifice through the correct recitation and sacrifice associated with the very mantra, the Purusha Sukta. This expressive and recursive treatment of bráhman as a bodily metaphor induced a visceral connection to a community of the chosen for those hearing it and practicing strictly supervised and appropriate ritual oblations. At least, this would be the expectation, and perhaps experience, of the poets who composed the Purusha Sukta.

Each member of the *varnāśrama*—the confederation of Vedic people with presumably a pure clan heritage—is supposed to feel various levels of freedom and possibility. Presumably, those from Purusha's head and arms have the greatest choice, in addition to helping harmonize thoughts and actions with each other. The belly, although an important part of the body, allows for less autonomy, guided largely by external and involuntary muscular and nerve action. The feet carry the burden of the rest of the body and may be least privileged to do what they please. The Purusha Sukta thus expresses through its cosmology a set of existential justifications, an ontology, for the persistence of hierarchy and class division that became ascendant and established as Hindu law in succeeding centuries. Those who had power to conduct yajna were supreme; others were the common people and members of the working classes. Sexual contact across social classes was forbidden, and any subsequent progeny was stipulated as having the lowest possible social status.[23]

The four Vedās represent the ideas and practices of what was clearly a narrow segment of religious life within Vedic society. Centering around hymn and ritual, they say little about politics and other aspects of human relations. They also do not provide much evidence of the overarching social stratification that appeared later in the form of the caste system. The four *varnas* (segments of society) mentioned in the Purusha Sukta may have become meaningful categories only late in the Vedic age, although priests (Brahmins) and lords (Kshatriyas) also appear briefly, if somewhat obliquely, in the eighth mandala (VIII.36 and VIII.37).

In other parts of Vedic literature and later commentaries and instructional texts, adherence to the separation of the varnas appears to be of paramount importance. This came to be represented as *varṇāśramadharma,* or strict observance of the rules of endogamy, which became the very basis of what later came to be known as Hindu law. But the roots of these rules can be found in Vedic sacrifice. Throughout their development and beyond, the content and use of these all-important hymns and rituals remained a closely guarded secret within relatively small endogamous communities that were a significant chapter in the story of elite networks in ancient India.

Unearthing Vedic Society

The composers and guardians of Vedic texts moved from present-day Afghanistan and the Swat Valley in Pakistan to occupy a vast region across the Indo-Gangetic plain by around 800 BCE. Most of the Rigveda describes Vedic society as seminomadic, pastoral, and clan based, with horse- and chariot-riding nobles or warriors. The āryas encountered various other nomadic tribes: some, the *dāsas,* they vanquished, but others—the *dasyus*— required divine intervention to defeat. In due course, as a result of intermarriage with locals, the consolidation of clans into larger tribes, and the subsequent federation of several clans into the Kuru and Panchala dynasties over present-day Punjab and farther into Uttar Pradesh, distinct power centers were created that might be described as proto-kingships of uncertain and possibly mixed form. The "kings" making up the Kuru and Panchala *mahājanapādas* constituted clan leaders from greater configurations, *desas* or countries, which were either monarchies or oligarchies.[24]

The household or *grha* was the basic unit in Vedic society, although it became prominent only during the late period, beginning around 800 BCE. As mentioned, the earliest clans of the Vedās were probably part of larger pastoral tribes, spreading out from around Taxila and farther south. A few had access to horses and chariots and were thereby able to bring many local communities that were initially rivals into the Vedic fold. They were likely organized as *kulas,* extended family units, which shared fluid blood ties over several generations, but were subsequently bonded around common ritual experiences. As families of cattle owners and their kin expanded their numbers and landholdings through liaison with each other, possibly involving exchange of daughters and cattle, they also built out their pastures over ever-larger landscapes.

Early Vedic society was probably organized in small hamlets and villages of no more than a few hundred, in mostly kin-based groups. Individuals typically inhabited familial households, occupied by patriarchs and their brood of perhaps more than one generation. Because the archaeological evidence is weak, it is difficult to speculate much on the occupation and political organization of larger units, even as village societies. It is likely that the tribesmen were mostly pastoralists, although others also grew barley and wheat in the early years and, around 1100 BCE, moved to rice cultivation in the middle Ganga Valley.[25]

Clans, generically comprising the *viś* or the "people," grew wealthy by raiding neighbors' cattle and, less frequently, their horses. The chief or rājā was the one who led these raids, with the booty then distributed among leaders and priests. Clan leaders, known as rājanyas and later as lords (Kshatriyas), were frequently compared with gods, especially Indra, who smote enemies and captured their cattle. Indra's hyper-virility and overt sexual prowess were often highlighted to invoke one's power to procreate and expand one's own tribe. Modeling themselves on the valor of gods by destroying their rivals and stealing their cattle, the clan members obsessively conducted ritual sacrifice to devas to seek their favors. In every household, daily oblations became mandatory, but grander sacrifices on behalf of clans slowly grew in size, sponsored by those who occupied nodes of ritual or military authority and, later, by monarchs who controlled land and cattle.[26]

Some clans may have sought consolidation with others: the eighth mandala of the Rigveda tells of a shakeout of sorts in which the Bharata clan emerges victorious. Two hymns report a "Battle of the Ten Kings" by the River Ravi in the Punjab, which King Sudās of the Bharatas wins with the support of Indra. As they descended from mountain passes and valleys of the Indus and Ganga tributaries, the Vedic clans, perhaps led by the Bharatas, established themselves in the northern parts of the Indo-Gangetic plain on the banks of the Yamuna River. There, they increased their pastoral wealth and adopted more settled forms of agriculture by cultivating rice. Some of their land-clearing and sedentary agricultural practices may have been made easier by the discovery and use of iron tools such as axes and plowshares.

The shift to growing rice, probably around 1100 BCE, marks an important event in the history of Vedic society. Cultivating rice is generally much more complicated and labor intensive than growing barley or wheat but yields more than twice the number of calories per unit of land. Productivity increases considerably when rice is grown in irrigated fields.[27]

In particular, the move to cultivate wet rice (with flooded fields) typically involves a quantum change in social relations. It requires the establishment of sedentary forms of farming and the deployment of sharecroppers and other peasant workers typically encamped for the purposes of seed selection, land preparation, water management, and harvesting. Wet-rice cultivation is often conducted using workers in forced or bonded conditions of labor, controlled by middlemen and human traffickers. When rice fields are irrigated, all adjoining fields are flooded simultaneously, and water is controlled not by the farmers themselves but usually by those with access to irrigation systems that redirect water resources from rivers and lakes.[28] When done successfully, rice cultivation generates a substantial surplus that is typically shared on the basis of an asymmetrical division of labor and compensation.

Worldwide, the earliest instances of settled rice farming can be found in the lower Yangtze region of China around 6000 BCE, with practices involving irrigation becoming established by 4000 BCE. Even when rice was grown in these prehistoric times, there were other sources of food, primarily wild gathered foods, which were plentiful. The earliest systems based on wet paddy field systems developed after 4000 BCE and were associated with the separation of cultivated or domesticated strains of rice from wild varieties to reduce cross-pollination. Between 4000 and 2200 BCE, enormous social changes—increased population density, the formation of elite groups, more intensive cultivation and harvesting methods, and the mobilization of larger workforces for managing water systems—occurred in the Yangtze region. Those who captured the surplus, either through taxation or the deployment of slave labor, were also likely to benefit the most from trade, which led to the development of other parallel forms of social organization and of a protostate that administered these arrangements.[29]

In South Asia, the earliest rice finds date to 6400 BCE in Lahuradewa in the northeastern reaches of the Gangetic plain in present-day Uttar Pradesh, but there is little or no evidence to determine whether it was wild or cultivated. By the second millennium BCE, rice was being harvested regularly in some parts of Harappa and the northern Indus Valley by both settled and nomadic groups, although there is little indication of surpluses (of rice as opposed to other grains like barley) being generated for trade or storage. It is also not clear at what point the Vedic people deployed wet-rice techniques, because the Rigveda does not mention rice cultivation or its use. Evidence of domesticated (as opposed to wild gathered) rice cultivation appears only after 1400 BCE in the middle Ganga. In the Śatapata Brāhmana (eighth to sixth centuries BCE), there are several references to rice as food and as part of ritual offerings, and there are a few mentions of it as a cultivated grain.

Other evidence suggests that it was not until sometime in the first millennium BCE that larger clans of Vedic society, with their great cattle wealth and the additional surplus provided from some settled rice agriculture, may have joined forces and exercised control over large stretches across the Indo-Gangetic plain.[30] On the basis of comparative prehistoric evidence, the social historian Michael Mann provides an explanation for how nomadic pastoral and agricultural tribes might form more territorially established societies: "Where a group invests labor in creating tools, stores, fields, dams, and so forth, whose economic returns are delayed, a long-term and in some respects a centralized organization [becomes] necessary to manage the labor, protect the investment, and apportion its yields."[31]

In the middle Ganga Valley, settled agriculture also brought about increased social stratification:

> The use of land and irrigation in itself required not only intensive labor but the organization of labor on lines of cooperative interaction.... With the increase in the size of effective holdings, a hierarchy of control over the resources and their working became necessary since there was more than a single resource-base and the interlinking of these required a coordinating group invested with authority. It would seem that the rich *grhapatis* [household / clan heads] were noticeably richer and this would have made for greater stratification.[32]

Alongside these developments possibly came the organization of markets and storehouses, as well as a growth in military power to protect these investments made possible by the use of bronze and, later, iron weapons; using those weapons effectively required the development of specialized roles and hierarchies within armies.

Thus, initially small nomadic groups came together to form tribes that spread out over the land but were connected by social practices of control and by kinship relations. Gaining access to raw materials like water, pastures, or other groups' livestock may have been an important impetus to the consolidation and strengthening of these small groups. This access may, in turn, have led to tighter rules of kin exchange through marriage across growing distances, as dominant groups sought more territorial authority and influence.

It also seems likely that, as hierarchies developed, their gears needed to be "lubricated" by favors dispensed across networks. Favors were made possible by elite access to capital so that various modes of support—formations of capital, the income derived from it, its material and symbolic legacies, and so on—could be guaranteed across distances and over time and be rewarded at different class levels. What today would be termed "financial capital" had its proxies in Vedic times—most likely, the stock of pasture animals and grain left over from the previous year's harvest—that were possibly initially controlled by a small group of tribal chieftains but later by "kings" and their closest allies.

During a period of expansion and maturation, which began around 800 BCE, an aristocracy was formed in Vedic polities that controlled large areas.

Over the course of several centuries, the Vedic people—those who called themselves āryas, along with their slaves and servants—found more strategic locations to invest their surpluses, such as places with favorable ecological niches near Kaushambi or present-day Allahabad (recently renamed Prayagraj) at the confluence of the Ganga and Yamuna Rivers. Much of the land in this flood plain had been naturally fertilized through silting, which also gave access to minerals, as well as water. This fertile land provided support for permanent conditions of farming and herding and thereby led to the protection and accumulation of property. Long-term investment was made possible by the forging of a tightly shared culture among several generations—even between the living and the yet-to-be-born. Villages and kin groups like clans developed, with the help of these bonds, into societies with temporal continuity.[33]

By 500 BCE, these motley groups, which had earlier been dispersed in nomadic clans connected by language and cultural practices, were consolidated into large kingdoms stretching across a thousand miles from Gandhara up to around Videha in the Doab region near the meeting point of the Ganga and Yamuna Rivers. The Kuru and Panchala kingdoms were established in present-day Punjab and Western Uttar Pradesh, respectively. They had a powerful neighbor to the west, the Achaemenid Empire in Iran; to the east there was the mighty kingdom of Magadha with its capital in Pataliputra, presently Patna. During this period, the Vedic people may have comprised a small but powerful minority in the subcontinent.[34]

In addition to their territorial dominance, the Vedic people probably gained a liturgical influence over neighboring regions by providing services in the form of ritual sacrifice. This is borne out in later Buddhist and Jaina texts, but it appears likely that Brahmins performed ritual for local chieftains in the eastern parts of the Doab for centuries earlier.

That Vedic practice was ordered and maintained by tightly knit priestly communities is itself a fascinating story. It tells the tale of embryonic elite structures of power generating emergent social phenomena that began to be manifested in relatively small and slow-moving populations. Over the course of nearly a millennium, these priestly groups advanced their liturgical and, thereby, political influence across the Indian landscape.[35] As Mann suggests, "emergent regularities of economic, military, and political cooperation were conceived of as a *nomos,* a sense of the ultimate order and meaning of the cosmos. The gods were now located within, in a privileged relationship to the clan, lineage, village, or tribe. The divine was domesticated by the society."[36]

By 300 BCE, Magadha had risen to become a powerful rival to Brahmanical authority by claiming control over an enormous territory extending across contemporary India and Pakistan. But by then, the growth and consolidation of Brahmanical power may itself have been substantial. In the whole subcontinent, nevertheless, there were many groups that had learned the "art of not being governed" by state authority; that is, they provided little or no contributions to centralized powers, unlike others whose members were coerced into agricultural labor and conscripted to fight battles.[37]

Elite Formation in Vedic Society

Sacrifice and the Vedic Corpus

Vedic texts provided the exclusive knowledge of how to conduct yajna, sacrifices, endowing those supervising the ritual with a special set of skills—and it was those skills that enabled later rulers to maintain authority and control while pleasing the gods and their ancestors. Yajna was conducted by yajamānas, worshippers who performed rituals pertaining to plant and animal offerings under the guidance of specialist brāhmana priests, who knew each of the physical and temporal elements of sacrifice and recited the appropriate Vedic verses.

In the early period, it is not known whether those with the knowledge of how to make sacrifices enjoyed a special status in society. Yajna likely became a much more solemn and high-stakes affair for the sponsors and officiating priests (hotrs) only in the later period, when regulations pertaining to the precise organization of the ritual space were fully described in the Brāhmanas and Śrauta Sutras. Entry to that space was restricted to three distinct social classes: "Not everyone may enter it [a specially constructed shed or hall on the sacrificial ground] but only a Brahmin, or a Rājanya, or a Vaishya, for these are able to sacrifice."[38]

Yajna, performed as a means to maintain order, $ṛtá$, is the central motif of the Rigveda. In addition, the Purusha Sukta's central doctrine, seen in its entirety, is that the cosmic body needs to be reconstructed and maintained through yajna. According to the historian Silvain Lévi, "the sacrifice is not made, it is prolonged, it is continued; the sacrifice must be prevented from ceasing to be." Yajna was therefore the core activity for maintaining cosmic order and, in doing so, provided the route to immortality for humans. The rājā, or supreme sacrificer, was at the center of this activity, like the Purusha or cosmic man himself, and the daily offerings within households became the obligation of all members of Vedic society. Brahmin hotrs were, in turn, "human gods" (*manusya devas*) and required subsidiary offerings after the needs of heavenly gods were met.[39]

The household sacrificial fire had to be maintained and rekindled every day by men initiated into the practice. Wives were essential partners in yajna but could only play subservient roles. Sexual activity was itself likened to yajna, just as procreation was an obligation, a debt to previous generations. These duties were increasingly represented as the necessary elements of a householder's life cycle. Thus, yajna was not only a way to appeal to divinities for worldly support but it was also a perpetual requirement to maintain the universe, because it represented the founding act of creation. It was a type of consecration whose every episode permitted the sacrificer to be reborn and thereby not only sustain the order within his own dominion but also harmonize the cosmic order.

Conducting these processes correctly, together with the proper recitation of Vedic hymns, took rigorous bodily effort, memorization, and vocal and aural training that enabled the suitable elocution, perfect repetition, and tonal quality even of long passages. Brahmins, according to the later śāstras at least, were required to undergo very precise forms of ascetic bodily conditioning to remain within the fold. There were rules regarding various forms of contact with other men and female sexual partners, as well as about the distinct order and types of touch and taste at different times of the day and even the year; a discourse developed about yajna's esoteric sacred forms during particular divine mantras and associated rituals.[40]

Boys from the Brahmins, Kshatriya (lords), and Vaishyas (tradesmen) were ritually identified as members of their respective groups following the upanāyana, a ritual ceremony marking an ārya's true Vedic birth, according to later lawmakers. Those who grew up without having done the ceremony lost their status and degenerated to become Śudras. Furthermore, the varna-based ordering of initiated men as participants in Brahmanical ritual created its own circle of continuity and strength. The classification of those initiated through Vedic study and the daily practice of fire sacrifice produced a regimented structure guided by endogamy rules and other requirements for status: it was completely arranged hierarchically around knowledge and authority with respect to ritual practices.

The appeal of an ordered social life to dominant classes in any society is understandable. The wealthy and powerful want stability and regularity for themselves and among the masses, so that they can go about their business without trouble or disruption. Conveniently, for those who need to toil for a living, order can be also predictable and soothing, even when it seems tedious and forces them to exhaustively compromise their autonomy. Evidence from around the world reveals that the formation of order by states and other "legitimate" social arrangements has never been automatic but is the result of political engagement across various elite networks—gangs, to put it simply—and of finding those rules that enable the most effective compromises for the consolidation of political strength across a shared territory. It may never be known whether this consolidation always creates syndromes of corruption over the long term, in which a deeply embedded ideology is repeatedly constructed through punishing social practices and the ensuing rewards that are generated are pocketed by the tiny few. But that process happened often.

For early Vedic society, the will to create insider and outsider rules and thereby develop a collective alignment as a closed society—the ideology of Brahmanism—was clearly powerful among elites. Movement toward this closed society came first through battles among clans for dominance. Over time, there was more convergence around elite groups, even though each one maintained clan purity. The *dāśarājna,* or the "Battle of the Ten Kings," was likely told from the standpoint of the victors, the Bharatas, a tribe that rose to prominence around the River Ravi after 1500 BCE and subsequently fought against many rivals. In addition to defeating the confederacy of kings, the Bharatas were also victorious against their chief rival, dāsa chief Śambara and the Panis.

The Kuru clan was presumably formed from the consolidation of several smaller sects, tribes, or clans, including the Bharatas and the Puru. Their family books were collected in the Rigveda. They then joined with the Panchala, representing tribes farther east, in the lower Doab. At this point, the center of Vedic society moved to the settled alluvial plain at the confluence of the Ganga and Yamuna Rivers. A late Vedic urban settlement, Kaushambi, was also the seat of the rājā, to whom the viś were expected to pay tribute.[41]

In the Vedic period, by creating at least two mutually exclusive groups of significance, the Śudras and nonconformists among the dvijas on one side and the initiated men on the other, Brahmanism came to acquire for itself a habitus—an ordered life around ritual purity and pollution, rules of yajna, and eventually a hierarchical society whose directives classified men, women, and children; priests and scholars; kings; and peasants and outsiders into multiple statuses with distinct roles through emerging rules of endogamy.

The development of Vedic society very likely took the following form. In the early period, say around 1500–1000 BCE, when they composed the Rigvedic canon, the poets and ritual generators began instituting—that is, putting into wider practice and habituating—a set of household and tribal activities. Of these, yajna became the most important, with fire and oblations made to various divinities on the basis of proper and secret chants. These habits had the social effect of creating community and sacred communion, to varying degrees, and forming kulas, extended family units; strictly regulated ritual practices—first for priests maintaining the catechism but later for lay specialists—by identifying societal or clan-wide or tribal acts, distinguished between what was pure or in place and what was defiling and impure.

Over centuries, as rājās grew in power and wealth, a new social order was established in which the relationship between kings and Brahmins was represented, especially in the early Upaniṣads, as one of mutual respect and equal exchange. Rājās may even have taught Brahmins, but always received the latter as guests in their presence and honored them with food and lodging. The defense of the material wealth of rājās became intertwined with the promotion and sustenance of Vedic ritual and its secrets, but it was only much later, perhaps well into a subsequent era I term the Age of Dharma (see Chapter 6), that justification for these practices became strictly codified as a social law with rules specified to excess just to isolate elite bloodlines.[42]

Brahmanism and Its Expanding Territoriality

Brahmanical power refers to the authority of Vedic ritual established through the alliance of priests and kings, with the support of the viś, or common people, a grouping that included artisans, farmers, and tradesmen (the last are commonly associated with Vaishyas). The Brahmins were members of a varna, or a kin-based social group, associated with priests and scholars, and Brahmin priests were the protagonists who perpetuated Brahmanical rituals, particularly sacrifice. Yet it is useful to remember that the sponsors of sacrifice, the most prominent of whom were later kings belonging to the Kshatriya varna, played at least as central roles, if not even larger ones, because of their wealth, access to political resources, and consequent ability to expand the scope of sacrifice.

During the Vedic age, Brahmanism was still in formation as an ideology, having created dispositifs (discursive apparatuses and forms of practice) to justify a Brahmanical lifestyle and the practices that reproduced it, but not yet establishing customs that were in wide use across society. Especially in the early period, the viś, most of whom were organized into clans, were most likely bystanders in arcane exercises of sacrifice and most of the cattle raids described in the Rigveda. The dasyus were rival clans who also perhaps raided the āryas' cattle, but there were probably many other outsiders who did not possess such means.

Clan leaders were those who had the physical strength and the ability to garner supplementary advantages (such as chariots and horses) to gain power over rival clans. Likely they tried various strategies to aggrandize their material and symbolic resources in a manner that helped distinguish them from their peers. The archaeologist Brian Hayden lists several such schemes that have been discovered in other ancient societies with emergent forms of political hierarchy. They include making special claims to ownership, organizing feasts and rituals, profiting from trade networks, setting bride prices, and hoarding prestige items. Rising elites may also make claims to privileged access to supernatural and worldly power.[43]

Historians of this period are hard-pressed to come up with dates or even a distinct sequence of alliances of the Vedic peoples, but the Kuru-Panchala kingdoms represented a more consolidated phase of Vedic society. But what drove the need for consolidation? The frequent raids among rival clans may have been one of the factors. Clan leaders in the Vedic age were frequently seeking periods of settled peace when they lived in in temporary but fixed locations. When needs arose, they went on the move again either to gain new lands or to raid cattle from other clans or tribes.[44]

Clan leaders may have been motivated to amass increasing entitlements to cattle and pastoral resources and thereby gain dominance over their peers. A shift in social relations brought about by a consolidation of political assets or, rather, territorial power, began when clans started to get organized beyond the point of poets praising sacrifice. Clan leaders' aggrandizement of resources—controlling pastures and gaining access to chariots and horses—and passing on esoteric knowledge and cultural status to their children along with these material assets were ways of accumulating prestige and wealth in families. In the late Vedic Age and thereafter, patrilineal bonds were ritually strengthened to ensure the accrual of wealth and status across generations. Important positions in society were held by an alliance of Brahmins and Kshatriyas (*brahmakṣatra*), but only the high-ranked among them were allowed to conduct elaborate ritual sacrifices.[45]

The word *rājā*, loosely translated as king, is scattered throughout the Rigveda, but its meaning as sovereign authority over a demarcated territory—the figure who manages to consolidate his authority beyond face-to-face relationships, as opposed to clan or tribal leader—emerged only later, perhaps after 800 BCE, in the course of the formation of the Kuru-Panchala federation. The changing character of the rājā's role in Vedic society is difficult to trace directly, but at least three efforts to do so stand out in the scholarly literature. Usefully, they complement each other, while emphasizing different features of Vedic history. Thapar describes the transition from lineage to state as taking place over several centuries and becoming consolidated only in the late Vedic age, around 800–600 BCE. In the early phase, whose dates are unknown, there were men who led cattle raids. One such was Prithu Vainya who, although expelled to the forest as a hunter and gatherer, began to rear cattle and plow the fields, thus earning the name of "earth" (*prithu*) from the goddess Prithvi. With this development, land became recognized as something to be accumulated as wealth, in addition to cattle, but its usefulness would also increase around that time because of the supplementary use of technology in the form of iron implements and the horse and chariot. But gaining any significant control over the land, such as a settlement, required the consent the viś.[46]

The formation of the state that was personified in the body of the (newly consecrated) rājā thus resulted in a new relationship between government, land and society. The Kuru-Panchala regime was likely a network of alliances among victorious chieftains and had lines of ascendant rājās, including Pariskhit and his son Janemajaya. Over time, several other compound *janapādas,* or territories—making up a confederacy of rule over pastoral communities—were formed, with a discourse on territorial polities and sovereign rājās appearing in texts like the Rigveda, Atharvaveda, and Brāhmanas. By around the beginning of the Common Era, more than 200 janapādas were cited, including those in the Mahābhārata and the Puranas.[47]

Thapar also points out that in the Buddhist tradition, *ganasanghās* were prominent in the latter half of the first millennium BCE in the foothills of the Himalayas and elsewhere in the periphery of the Vedic alluvial plain; they largely eschewed Vedic orthopraxy. A ganasanghā is an assembly of the equal, which could be interpreted either as a republic or oligarchy. But virtually nothing about its actual functioning is available in either Buddhist or post-Vedic texts such as the Mahābhārata, which mentions it only as a polity from an earlier time with diffuse power, perhaps with limited or no social stratification, and little or no coercive authority.[48]

By 800 BCE, conditions may have facilitated the consolidation and expansion of tribes. This, in turn, demanded explicit Vedic justification for an emerging social order that saw the rapid generation of surplus wealth and its use to harness political power over large tracts of land. The Brāhmanas and subsequent instructional books are supposed to have their origins around the time of the formation of the earliest states, which had instruments of power recognized to have the authority to enforce order. They are dated to around 800 BCE, at least three to four centuries earlier than the formal law books, the Dharmasutras. It is conceivable that Brahmin initiates who were trained to perform ritual sacrifice were also required to generate lawbooks, beginning with these instruction books, in order to help maintain order in the janapādas.[49]

As different types of viś began to be recognized, attempts were made to widen the influence of particular rājās. Grand rituals like the *aśwamedha* (horse sacrifice), *agnicayana* (creation rite), and *rājasuya* (consecration of the king and his elevation to divine status) represented systematic attempts to incorporate larger groups of viś into the rāja's realm. The aśwamedha, in particular, was a ritual replete with symbolism. Before its ceremonial slaughter, a sacrificial horse was allowed to wander for a year, guarded by warriors, and if it trotted far from its ruler's dominion, the rājā was permitted to make claims on whatever land it wandered to. The rājā, the principal sacrificer, then became *digvijaya* (victorious in conquest in all directions). This military element of ritual sacrifice thus gave the rājā a new status as sovereign over remote lands, as compared with his predecessor chieftains and clan leaders. In the middle to late Vedic period, more complicated ritual forms became significant, ones that could only be conducted on a grand scale by the rājā.[50]

In a similar vein, the historian Kumkum Roy places emphasis on the manner in which sacrificial rituals became increasingly grander as well as more somber, culminating in the *agnistoma* and other performances described in the Śrauta Sutras, which required more than a dozen priests and lasted several days. She writes,

> The association of creation with the sacrifice had certain important implications. On the one hand it envisaged a role for human protagonists in creating or restoring the cosmic order. At the same time, the fact that this function was associated with ritual activities suggests that certain specific humans, viz., those who were qualified to perform the sacrifice or get it performed, probably exploited this notion to assert their claims to a unique status.[51]

The philologist Theodore Proferes takes a singular approach, reading between the lines to depict yajna as having principal symbolic significance by creating vital social connections of power and collective meaning through bodily reenactments around ritual fires. By describing fires at the household (grhya) and larger community (śrauta) scales, the Vedās emphasize both their unitary character and their separate spheres of existence. Fire can exist at multiple places at once but stems from the same source. Jointly the priest and the sacrificer kindle the tribal fire, whose control by the rājā or tribal leader "is the equivalent of control over all levels of society." During periods of seasonal migration, Indra might be summoned to solemnize the collective practice of domestic and śrauta yajna, with him leading the tribes. Typically these communal sacrifices could produce conflict with peoples in occupied lands, the dāsas and dasyus.[52]

Proferes also points out that some of the non-Rigvedic verses found in the larger yajna sections of the Brāhmanas, which describe śrauta rituals, were distinctly in the Kuru dialect. In particular, these pertain to the gathering of materials for the agnicayana: a complex, twelve-day ritual that could only be carried out by yajamānas with considerable organizing capacity and convening power. The agnicayana was designed by one or more priests in a Kuru court to glorify a leader who was especially powerful. It took place, as has been well described in the literature, including in modern times, on a site shaped like a bird, which symbolized the sun. The king was ritually reborn as the sun, just as Agni itself was once a "child in the waters," *Apām Napāt*, whose latent potency is quickly kindled and, once nourished with ghee and other fuel, grows in size. Almost oversaturated with symbolism in this way, the ritual of yajna normalized the symmetry and relevance of central authority to forge clan unity, kinship, and tribal ascendancy.

Proferes pays close attention to multiple symbolic elements of different yajna rites, including their spatial geometry, solar imagery, and the idealized picture of the formation of Five Peoples representing four cardinal directions and the center. Just as the sun shines over each unit or clan, the rājā acquires the cosmic right to rule, and his fire is both greater than and drawn from the same source as individual fires. Furthermore, a threefold hierarchy is evident in the maintenance of fires: the *grhapati* is a single domestic fire, a "hearth fire"; the *viśpati* is the "courtier fire"; and the *samrāj* is the "king's fire," all of which are fused as Agni.[53]

The Rigveda and the Brāhmanas are filled with such homologies between earthly and divine entities, and the liturgy provides insights into the development of a cosmology with complexity and an internal coherence. The various subtle variations in sound, intonation, and meter of different parts of the Vedic corpus seem to provide substantial value and metaphysical order to those who have the skills to construe it. At the same time, their rituals are transparently about creating a habitus of Brahmanical order, with a hierarchy of place organized around birth and gender.[54]

In these multiple descriptions of a world rife with signification and its systems of representation in carefully articulated ritual sacrifice, it is useful to recall the sociologist Stuart Hall's definition of culture as a set of practices that are "concerned with the production and the exchange of meanings—the 'giving and taking of meaning'—between the members of a society or group. To say that two people belong to the same culture is to say that they interpret the world in roughly the same ways and can express themselves, their thoughts and feelings about the world in ways which will be understood by each other."[55]

Hall proposes that meaning, language, and representation are closely tied to each other in the formation and sustenance of cultures, in which "members of the same culture must share concepts, images and ideas which enable them to think and feel about the world, and thus to interpret the world, in roughly similar ways." The complex institutions of sacrifice and their changing character from early through late Vedic society can be understood as culture-making processes whose rules and evolution were strongly influenced by the growing "metaphor generating" power of Brahmanism. Making kingship divine was a vivid and extraordinarily detailed activity of culture making articulated in the Vedās. Undoubtedly, that was an endeavor that expended significant rents from the symbolic and material capital of elite groups and their networked descendants. Along with these ideological props for a new type of *rājanya* (kingship), Vedic Brahmanical culture remarkably also served to perpetuate two related systems of mass domination—patriarchy and slavery—that I explore briefly in the next section. Perhaps the props and the forms of domination were related to each other in still-to-be-explored ways.[56]

Patriarchy and Slavery

Two key relationships of power in Vedic social structure may be construed from the śruti literature and were even more clearly expressed in later texts. The first has to do with the structure of gender relations and the position of women. With few exceptions, women were treated as a propertied group of bodies serving male sexual and domestic needs, to be penetrated largely at will; they were required to procreate and uphold domestic order by being good spouses and mothers and to stay mostly in the background during cardinal ritual moments of their men's lives. The second key relationship is that of the self-styled superiority of the āryas over the dāsas and dasyus, who were abhorred or merely tolerated as servants, slaves, and enemies. Both relationships together formed a complex of overlapping and dissimilar patterns of subjugation making up the social backdrop of Vedic corruption.[57]

The contrast is noteworthy between the high register of the language used in typical verses in the Rigveda, when they refer to the pressing of the soma plant or sing hymns to various gods, and that used in the lower register of frequent slangy references to women, playing dice, and breeding cattle. A distinct social place for women was carved out, first as a separate class from the original triad of varnas, the brāhmanas, kshatriyas, and viś, but also one having its own hierarchy and ritual practices around menstruation, marriage, procreation, and being supportive partners of a patriarchy built around wealth and symbolic power. Indra was the paragon of masculinity: a "bull or stallion and surrounded by female mothers, sisters and daughters and Heaven and Earth as well as by the fingers of the one who prepares the draft" of "life and the continuance of life." Indra's valor in the battlefield and his lustfully represented sexual appetite provided representative actions for earthly male leaders to follow.[58]

Indeed, ideals of manhood were somewhat of an obsession in virtually every Vedic context. Martial strength and prowess, the ability to conduct cattle raids and also compose liturgical poetry, and license to dominate women sexually, sometimes forcefully, were associated with *vira,* or manliness. Both men and gods shared these attributes in equal measure, the latter only having additional special powers to cause celestial trouble. The performance of Vedic ritual may have helped reinforce the poets' metaphors of masculinity and habituate the way men were supposed to understand their bodies in relation to animals and women. Gender, in general, was sharply understood in distinct roles of masculine identities expressing physical superiority and capacity for violence and divine control over elements vis-à-vis their complementary regenerative female identities of birth (e.g., Uśas for dawn), rivers and waters (e.g., the river Sarasvati), and the earth (Prithvi), representing forces of reconciliation and renovation. In the end, all men in Vedic society appear to have benefited collectively from patriarchy, although it served elite warriors and priests the most.[59]

Masculinities are widely deployed dispositifs whose institutions and varieties of justification for resource allocation, interpersonal relationships, and sexuality are typically organized around a single logic: an ideology that justifies the creation and sustenance of dominant and subordinate gender roles. In Vedic society, that logic was absolutely central to sacrifice, and the elaborate differentiation that could be also made across age and varna lines defined the appropriate roles in the yajna for each individual. For boys and men, as for girls and women, fitting into their appropriate roles would have meant creating the right body reflexes that aligned their habitus with the larger social goal of keeping intact all the precise elements of the sacrifice. Models of masculinity were sustained in everyday life as patriarchy in the household and mirrored in kingship at the level of territorial control; in both cases, it was ritually reproduced through yajna.[60]

Sometimes, controlling sexual desire was seen as a condition of yajna and was itself expressed as a form of male austerity. For instance, an excerpt from Chandogya Upaniśad states, "Now, what people normally call a sacrifice (*yajna*) is, in reality, the life of a celibate student, for it is by the life of a celibate student that one finds him who (*yah*) is the knower (*jnata*). And what people normally call an offering (*ista*) is, in reality, the life of a celibate student, for it is by seeking (*istva*) through the life of a celibate student that one finds the self."[61]

Just as men's bodies were shaped to support Vedic practice, women's identities were constituted largely through a male fantasy of ideals of femininity involving childbearing, hospitality toward guests, and being junior silent partners during rituals. A woman's presence at the yajna site was essential, but only if she occupied a specific background role that was prescribed for her. Moreover, women were frequently pictured as being erratic ("the mind of woman is not to be instructed, and her will is fickle"; RV VIII.34.17) or untrustworthy ("there exist no partnerships with women: they are hyenas' hearts"; RV X.95.15). The levirate practice, or *niyoga,* in which a brother-in-law is allowed to have sex with a woman whose husband (his brother) was either dead or impotent, was legitimized on the basis of producing sons. Some women poets are mentioned in the Upaniśads, but only as exceptions that serve to highlight the rule. Although women were allowed to receive Vedic instruction in the Grhya Sutras, throughout the Vedic period, they were definitively excluded from initiation or Vedic study.[62]

Female goddesses, however, were numerous and powerful in their own right: Aditi (Innocence), Indrani (Indra's consort), Prithvi (Earth), Sri (Fortune), Uśas (Dawn), and Vac (Speech) were variously described as eternal and timeless; having an elemental force; and being munificent, gentle and caring, or vain. There was, in contrast, the goddess (demoness?) Nirrti (Dissolution) who could destroy order and upend control in a person's life. Demonic women could threaten men and disrupt rituals, but they were sometimes treated with awe and fear, because they represented women's secret powers. In the same way, women's sexual independence was a source of great anxiety. By the late Vedic period, women who had sex with men from lower social classes were to be punished in proportion to the distance between the classes. In post-Vedic society, these strictures were formalized as codified law.[63]

Thus, in the Vedic context, it seems safe to assume that the dominant images of male virility and female sexual submissiveness were not accidental byproducts of the poetic imagination run wild but instead played a powerful role in creating and embodying habits and patterns of speech (dispositifs); in turn, these dispositifs justified distinctive modes of masculinity and their associated forms of sanctioned domination over women and transgendered persons.

In the early Vedic period, patriarchy may have been reflected in yajna within households and clans belonging to face-to-face spaces. During this period, one might reasonably claim that it largely followed the customary patriarchal politics of an extended family and tribe, having clearly marked roles linked to age, gender, and relationship, and headed by a single male figure of authority or a small clutch of men. It is also likely that some of the more heroic āryas became clan leaders in the pastoral communities they formed.

Dāsas were enemies who had been destroyed by the divine Indra but reappeared as vanquished peoples. The word *dāsa* could mean both "servant" and "slave," as indicated in such hymns as one describing the ārya who "leads the Dāsa as he wishes." In contrast, dasyus were ongoing enemies of the āryas, according to the Rigveda, and the poets would repeatedly ask for the gods' help against them. They also had several attributes: as people who did not perform sacrificial rites, they lacked Vedic knowledge, disobeyed the gods, and therefore did not belong to Vedic society. They were considered ill-omened, with the ability to be wily by creating illusions and therefore dangerous and not to be trusted.[64]

In a few passages, dāsa and dasyu appear as suffixes to the names of kings, as in Sudāsa, Divodāsa, and Trasadasyu. These identifiers further add to their ambiguity. Asko Parpola proposes that some dāsas and dasyus were (linguistically, if not ethnically) pre-Vedic Indo-Europeans in Bactria, some of whom had strayed from the earlier ways of their ancestors and cultural allies in south central Asia. In encountering them, Vedic Āryans found both partners and enemies. As Vedic society expanded, its ordinary people may have mixed with lower orders of earlier societies in the regions that they began to occupy, while priests and warriors absorbed upper classes into their fold. Over time, any memory of their migration and different origins may have been lost, not only because of intermixing with native populations but also through consolidation of clans and tribes and the transformation of Vedic society.

Both dāsas and dasyus were occasionally described as being dark-skinned and having flat noses and curly hair. Although the Rigveda makes a distinction between dāsas and dasyus, the two terms were associated with humans (and occasionally nonhumans) who shared the characteristics of being outsiders. Over the course of centuries, dāsas in the upper reaches of sapta sindhva (or seven rivers) in the Punjab and northern Indus valleys appear to have been integrated into Vedic society. This was also the early spatial extent of Vedic society.

It seems plausible that clan leaders among the new migrants self-styled as āryas began to emphasize the purity of descent to distinguish themselves from those dāsas who had inserted themselves into Vedic society through sexual contact. However, some dāsas and their female version, dāsis, later were clearly taken as slaves, although this reference only appears late in the Rigveda. There is evidence for strong enmity against the dāsas. By vanquishing the darker and inferior dāsas, Indra increases the might of the āryas.

In early Vedic society, dasyus and others who were not amenable to the Vedic lifestyle (*vratá*) were eventually treated as a separate social class, the Śudras. Other terms refer to artisans, chariot makers, and other "helpers" of the rājanya. The social order was not always clear-cut, and many were considered Śudra. In fact, R. S. Sharma argues that there may have been many Śudra groups that had ārya origins, and just as many who had been outside the fold but were later brought in to serve āryas. In the early to mid-Vedic periods, strict endogamy may not have been enforced, but this seems to have changed after around 500 BCE.[65]

After being conquered, either through slavery or other form of subjection, dāsas became part of the viś, but it is unclear whether some of them were in the late Vedic period included among the dvija of three Chosen lines, the Brahmins, Kshatriyas, and Vaishyas, or were all designated Śudras, who were now the undifferentiated non-dvija.[66]

The introduction of Śudras in the Purusha Sukta may create the impression that there was not only an informal consensus for enabling designated social classes and actions but also divine sanction for an extensive division of labor along kinship lines. Importantly, however, there is no evidence of social distinctions in other passages of the Rigveda, although such divisions had unmistakable significance in the ritual texts, especially the Atharvaveda, the Brāhmanas, and the Śrauta Sutras. There, social class or hierarchy was very strongly expressed and reinforced in the many symbolic elements related to the sacrificial fire and other ritual features. Was social class a late Vedic innovation? We do not fully know, but it seems likely.

Vedic Authority

Brahmanism was not a proselytizing religion. In fact, Brahmins provided services to sponsors—later, the kings—who did not even have to accept various claims made in Vedic texts or care much about the rites. They simply had to consent to Brahmins' ability to carry out the necessary tasks needed to create propitious conditions for their own advancement. This often meant, especially in later periods, that even non-Hindu kings would turn to Brahmins to conduct the suitable rituals needed for appeasing the gods. By the end of the Vedic period, with the creation of the Grhya Sutras and Dharmasutras—rules of the household and social practices, respectively—subtle transformations likely had already taken place in Brahmanical society.[67]

Similarly, slavery—or at least the impoverishment of conquered peoples and their growing subjection to Brahmanical ideology—created a hierarchy of social class that was organized around bloodlines and male lineages of practice such as the upanāyana and regular yajna, which together conveyed a culture of austerity and strong discipline. Consanguinity, unification through the maintenance of fires, and the growing consolidation of sovereign power by rājās helped maintain elite hierarchies along rigid and elaborately safeguarded lines. Subsequently, these social structures changed form to become law, thereby gaining a psychologically remote but legitimated power, with sanctions against infractions committed by those who were not necessarily connected to a single point of authority. In practice, however, a tight network of men in warrior-king and high priestly positions oversaw the law. In other words, gender roles and institutions were formalized in the late Vedic period only after the formation and exercise of sovereign power.[68]

The Vedic texts serve as powerful clues to an intended, and perhaps self-reinforced, rigid order within small communities. The significant and widespread prevalence of yajna emerged over time to form clear patterns of hierarchy and a type of territorial power. Specially designated Brahmin priests knowledgeable in the Vedās and capable of conducting sacrifice came to be of primary importance, but equally central were the Kshatriya kings and lords who sponsored grand sacrifices. Everyday family routines and rituals too played a major role in organizing and systematizing social life, which was largely driven by pastoral lifestyles and worlds of training for organizing sacrifice. A synoptic view of Vedic society-in-the-making therefore reveals the emergence of a new form of authority.

Any type of authority can be described as a set of processes that are capable of generating and reproducing the social effect of dominant and subordinate roles. This effect is typically expressed in an audience that is both coerced and persuaded by authorized speech and practice. That audience itself may have internal relationships and practices—stations of power—that display patterns of re-appropriation and in-house coercion and persuasion. It may also seem cowed into silence, but it also has ways of speaking to itself without affecting the agency of the speaker. The religious studies scholar Bruce Lincoln points out that the endurance of social patterns reveals a certain level of trust in authority; hence, authorizing—giving sanction to and approving. In the long run, the instruments of coercion and persuasion really need to be deployed only as that trust wanes. The net effect is to sustain authorized practices and maintain the status quo through speech and practice organized by elite interests.[69]

Vedic authority can best be seen as a set or practices that built up a rhythm of carefully organized order. Across a range of cyclical actions, from the sounds of incantations for yajna throughout the daily and seasonal calendar, the design of the fire altar, and the life stages of the twice-born to the practices of social hierarchy, there was ṛtá, a universal natural, moral, and institutional order that could only be maintained through ritual. By the time of Kuru sovereignty, the proper incantation of mantras and other meticulously observed rites of everyday life expressed in the Grhya Sutras and the Śrauta Sutras had turned into an obsession. It was a totem led by Brahmin priests, upheld by Kshatriya kings, and observed by the viś. Outsiders were turned into slaves unless they were outside their sphere of influence as foragers and hunters in the forest or were in non-Brahmanical janapādas elsewhere.

The legitimating authority of the Vedās lies in its symbolic power around claims to extraordinary knowledge, which is not derived through human reasoning but is a transcendent, infinite knowledge of ultimate reality. This knowledge is accessible only through Vedic practice and the vocal elocution of mantras by those authorized as legitimate speakers. In the Vedic age, all dvija householders and rājās were to participate in this practice. In addition to consanguinity, whose justification might be to enable the selection of excellence through breeding, the accumulation of symbolic property of high value within the śakhas was another outcome of these practices. They also gave rise to territorial power in the form of rājanya, which protected physical and symbolic wealth across a large domain. By the time of the aśwamedha (horse sacrifice) in the first millennium BCE, laying claim to land and borders was another product of Vedic social development.

In the second half of the first millennium BCE, to the east, in Magadha, a parallel territorial power grew in size, gaining significance and marking the center of the next phase of political change and elite reorganization. Almost simultaneously, as iron weapons, horses, elephants, and chariots began to strengthen the artillery wing of armies, a variety of geographically significant powers emerged on the subcontinent and beyond. A new phase of modest globalization and expansion of trading and territorial interests began to change the face of elite power and its expression in multiple societies.

A Corruption Syndrome in the Vedic Period?

The drive to consolidate territorial power in the mid- to late Vedic period is an important verification of my theory of political corruption. The reordering of social life grew in scale and intensity after 1000 BCE, manifested in the final canonization of the Rigveda; the rhythmic aural and other bodily patterns of daily, seasonal, and occasion-specific yajnas; and the formation of well-coordinated calendars among newly identified dvija clans for whom rules of endogamy became increasingly strict. In this social order, a new pattern of overlapping and hierarchical networks of power emerged, but in the process, so did the rājanya, or that which belongs to the rājā, the physical seat

The Vedic Period   183

of courtly power, a domain of political consolidation of territory that would gain distinct forms and legitimacy over the next millennium or so.

Outside these intersecting sets of elites was the emergence of two social classes having complex but subordinate positions. Patrick Olivelle characterizes the conditions of women, notably non-Śudra women in relation to Śudras:

> Uninitiated and barred from studying the Veda, women are only marginally superior to Śudras. The twice-born status of non-Śudra women comes merely from their group affiliation, not from their ritual rebirth through Vedic initiation. Their low theological status corresponds to the widely shared view that women are by nature prone to evil. . . .
>
> There is also ample evidence that at least in the early period women participated in major Brahmanical institutions, such as vedic initiation. On the other hand, Brahmanical theology considers women never to be independent agents; in many respects their status is similar to that of children and Śudras. The history of Brahmanical theology is a constant movement in the direction of an ever-increasing restrictive ideology regarding the status and role of women.[70]

One of the great difficulties in trying to describe hegemonic Brahmanical power in Vedic society is that there is a serious danger of viewing it through the lens of the present-day caste conflict, which is a complex conglomeration of affirmative action claims by different caste groups, the ongoing oppression of Dalits (Buddhists, Christians, and Muslims among them), and widespread identity-based violence around intercommunal sexual relations. Although some parallels may exist, the Vedic conditions of social interaction, belief, and motivation were vastly different from those today. Whatever conclusions we are able to draw regarding the character and formation of Vedic authority have to do with the regularity and sanctity of yajna, the symbolic importance of sacrificial fires, and the surplus generated from systematic masculine domination and slavery. Our evidence for the conditions of yajna is entirely based on Vedic literature, but these sacrificial ritual practices clearly established a pattern of social life that served a tightly knit set of elites, as well as other groups in subordinate positions of power.

Beyond this, it is difficult to assert that distinct crimes of the powerful resulted, except that much harm ensued to women and Śudras. But insofar as the formation of rājanya was associated with territorial violence, it is clear that some shake-ups among multiple lineages were responsible for geographical consolidation, even in a form of sovereignty that still remains mysterious. The primeval sacrifice created the warrior class, whose leader would offer the same protection as Prajāpati, the protector of all life on earth. The elaborate rituals of yajna and the potential gift of accessing true knowledge for those who truly followed the Vedic code, even if they were occasionally outside the fold, helped seal the ideology.[71]

A critical turn occurred toward the end of the Vedic period: east of the Doab and gaining substantial territorial power for several centuries thereafter, Buddhism and Jainism developed greater political favor than Vedic Brahmanism. This is today magnificently manifested in the Mauryan, Kushana, and Satavahana monuments, sculptures, commentaries, and epigraphs. The rise of Magadha in influence and territorial power over the rest of India after the fifth century BCE—and extending through the beginning of the Common Era and for a few centuries beyond—is the first direct sign of territorial authority: it was the earliest polity to resemble modern conceptions of a state, with the capacity to mobilize resources of scale and generate organizational structures of control.

What, then, is a Vedic age syndrome of corruption? I argue that it begins with the Vedic habitus. Gavin Flood's notion of "bodily entextualisation" is relevant here: he proposes that the disciplined body in Yoga and Tantra a millennium or so later, through the cultivation of their practices, is itself the text that is written by individual action in the world. For Yoga, the instructional texts were simply the patterns to be followed, but the practices themselves were encoded in the body and transmitted as such. In the Vedic period, in contrast, the strict spatial and purity-danger dichotomy of Brahmanical instruction was inscribed into the body as such. Indeed, as we shall see, tantrism was later overtly rebellious against Vedic tradition by citing its own texts of secret lore, the tantra-śāstra. Some inkling of this element is present in Brahmanical principles of maintaining a certain physical distance from impure objects or bodies, such as dogs, untouchables, and menstruating women. These principles, first recorded in the fourth-century Dharmasutras, are even stricter, if not shocking in their harshness, in the Manava Dharmaśāstra several centuries later, about which I say more in Chapter 6.

To pollute the dvija body was then to require ritual ablutions to cleanse the body. Significantly, water was often used to wash the entire body, rather than in ceremonially small amounts that might be intended to symbolize the act of purifying the body after it was "contaminated" by some impure contact. The Brahmin who encountered an untouchable would have to bathe himself or herself again so as to wash away the effect of the encounter, especially through touch but typically also through looking. An obsession with bodily purity and pollution is common to many societies and is typically associated with corresponding patterns of separation of clans and genders. In the Vedic case, it was made more austere by creating a special esoteric class of authorizing figures for the society's supreme actions, namely, sacrifice.

The peculiar ordering of Vedic society into dvija and non-dvija members and the creation of a special Brahmanical habitus were perhaps unintentional at first. But in their development, we start to see the hoarding of wealth, in the form of cattle at first and later with territorial control. Both of these provided means to generate rents, so that elite wealth increased, far exceeding the assets of the average person. In the rājanya, then, one sees the first creation of the proto-state; the elite network of claimants to territorial power who aligned themselves for sacrifice with the Brahmins, who in turn instituted the bodily rigor of Vedic dvija society and the use of dāsas as slave labor. The rājās and their entourage, including hotrs who led the sacrifice, made up the inner circle of mid- to late Vedic society rājanyas. How they conducted themselves is mysterious, but we have had room to speculate in several directions.

6

Dharma Yuga

Contentions over Justice

"Brahmins united with Kshatriyas," it is stated, "uphold the gods, ancestors, and human beings." The word "punishment" (*danda*), they say, is derived from "restraint" (*damana*); therefore, He [the king] should restrain those who are unrestrained.

Dharma Yuga

Dharma is an indispensable word in Indian political philosophy. It refers to many overlapping concepts: customary practice, duty, ethical rules of living, law, precept, and support or undergirding—and these are just the major definitions. These various understandings are also a sign of the word's long and checkered history. Between the death of the Buddha (480 BCE?) and the end of the Gupta reign in about 550 CE, one can identify the most significant debates in the history of dharma around its meaning and uses. That period, which I interpret through the lens of elite networks in this chapter, is properly designated as *Dharma Yuga*, the Age of Dharma.[1]

Almost everything about India's material and symbolic landscape changed dramatically in Dharma Yuga. Settled farming (involving plant and animal domestication on a widespread scale) came into prominence only after 500 BCE. The Harappan civilization did produce food but only for local consumption and from crops that were not cultivated in fixed-field agriculture requiring irrigation or substantial care; in addition, there is no evidence for granaries or the creation of grain surpluses. As discussed in Chapter 4, Harappan wealth likely accrued through trade surpluses. In Vedic pastoral societies, barley, wheat, and millet were largely grown in wild landscapes without much field clearing or preparation, again producing little surplus. The material capital accumulated in Vedic times was primarily cattle: its symbolic capital and command of substantial political resources were perhaps more significant.

In the late Vedic period, around the time of the formation of *mahājanapādas* (large polities) in north and northwestern India, cities began to develop as seats of power. Settled forms of agriculture were also becoming common, although wet rice cultivation most likely developed in the eastern Ganges and Orissa around 800 BCE and became widespread in the subcontinent only over the next half millennium. The transition to India's second urban age was well underway after 600 BCE, when much of the subcontinent saw increases in population and spatial clustering, the cultivation of grains in formerly forested areas, the increasing use of iron implements for clearing and tilling land, new trade routes and monetary exchange, and the emergence of writing. Until then, territorial control had only a few fledgling forms; it was mainly a matter of clans in federations controlling pasture lands and occasionally making grand border claims. These clans probably found ways to fence their settlements for protection from the nearby forest dwellers, who were known to be daunting raiders of grain and cattle.[2]

In Dharma Yuga, sedentarism became more firmly established. The early institutions of sedentarism, to recall James C. Scott's argument, had achieved transformative change by gaining territorial control or dominion over land. In its more advanced form, territorial control was shared among a tight but significant minority: kingship was an almost universal institution that was able to create stability through the managed reproduction of material and symbolic capital. At this time there developed a plethora of pastoral and urban societies, in which agricultural fields were scattered across a large hinterland that had earlier been mostly under forest cover. Elites and non-elites disputed the proper means of living sedentary lives, but some of these discourses provide clues to the varied forms and shifting authority of elite networks.[3]

Clearly, these processes did not take place on the head of a pin but had large-scale effects: they reshaped landscapes; altered the living arrangements of animals and people; and led to the establishment of cities, trading routes, and armies. Internal differentiation and stratification of societies into elites, commoners, and slaves took place through the reorganization of labor for sedentarism and a new leadership ideology that emerged from its practices. The archaeologist Norman Yoffee writes about how urban agglomerations provided the unique opportunity for early elites to gain power over populations by exercising control of economic, societal or ideological, and political resources. This power comprised "economic productivity—the control over the resources and distribution of subsistence and wealth, [ideological resources,] the segregation and maintenance of the symbols of community boundary, and [political power,] the ability to impose obedience with force."[4]

Urban centers, serving as repositories and distribution hubs of capital, were the sites of concentration of those controlling wealth and wielding administrative authority. These centers—notably, Kaushambi, Mathura, Pataliputra, and Taxila—were scattered across the region. The Greek historian Strabo described Pataliputra, near present-day Patna, around the turn of the Common Era:

> It is said that Palibothra [Pataliputra] lies at the confluence of the Ganges and the other river, a city eighty stadia [10 miles] in length and fifteen [1.9 miles] in breadth, in the shape of a parallelogram, and surrounded by a wooden wall that is perforated so that arrows can be shot through the holes; and that in front of the wall lies a trench used both for defense and as a receptacle of the sewage that flows from the city; and that the tribe of people amongst whom this city is situated is called the Prasii and is far superior to all the rest; and that the reigning king must be surnamed after the city, being called Palibothrus in addition to his own family name, as, for example, King Sandrocottus [Chandragupta Maurya?] to whom Megasthenes was sent on an embassy.[5]

In contrast to the vast, decentralized, and yet fully structured and well-coordinated urban societies of the Harappan civilization, Dharma Yuga was marked by sweeping change in forms of territorial control made possible by the use of iron farm implements and weapons. Its urban settlements were typically of high density and polycentric, both spatially and in terms of elite order. In several distinct territories made up of networked urban centers from Taxila in the far northwest to Hastinapur, Mathura, Kaushambi, Varanasi, and Pataliputra in the Gangetic heartland, Indian polities were thus fabricated and consolidated into forms that had metropolitan or centralized state-like qualities. Magadha, Kosala, Videha, Anga, and Kalinga made up these substantial territories, in addition to the grand Kuru-Panchala federation. In the fourth and third centuries BCE, the Mauryas, India's first emperors, made expansive territorial claims (that they could not possibly have enforced as prevailing law) throughout their territory. It was only with the later Guptas in the fifth century CE that strong administrative forms of government were able to function as state systems that effectively collected revenue and tribute across a relatively well-demarcated territory with urban centers and interlinked elites.

In Dharma Yuga there developed a uniquely Indian form of kingship, one that was reproduced as a social institution that could promise public order over territories of varying size by using dynastic rule to make and enforce legal structures. Territorial kingship operates with a certain Hobbesian logic: it assumes that, to maintain social order, a monitor who creates and enforces rules is essential and that person (or group of persons) must have supreme dominion over the land and its people. To the king is given the responsibility and the right to impose punishment on the guilty for small crimes and large. But the king needs a network of support that has to be put together through trial, error, and imitation. It is the elite network made up of the king and his entourage that typically creates the necessary conditions to organize, consolidate, and extract a material and symbolic surplus across a vast territory, thereby creating the institution of the kingdom: a territorial state with a monarch at its helm.

In Chapter 5, I drew attention to how several historians characterized the transition from lineage societies to incipient forms of kingship and territorial power. Their focus was primarily on how patterns of surplus capital formation changed over time, how exchanges of luxury goods among elites built up cultures of tribute and mutual expectations, and the formation and cultivation of a nucleus of wealth and political power sharing that extended outward to secure ever-larger areas of commercial and agricultural advantage. Sometimes, this consolidation was accomplished through coalition building; at other times, through conquest.

In the late Vedic period around the sixth century BCE, this consolidation led to the establishment of the Kuru-Panchala kingdoms and the growing importance, scale, and scope of many forms of yajna—including the aśwamedha, which made a grandiose ritual point of marking out sovereign territory, and the *rājasuya*, which was the coronation sacrifice.[6] This occurred across the Indus Valley and Indo-Gangetic plain, spreading even to a few forest areas and mountainous areas. As the Kuru-Panchala and other territorial interests expanded, they formed sixteen mahājanapādas (large territorial polities). Each mahājanapāda had one or two principal urban centers, with a ruler and his entourage (rājanya) or ceremonial clan-based oligarchy (*gana-sangha*), together with a vast hinterland. The value of such land may have been determined initially by the presence of water bodies, pastures, and soil fertility and later for its suitability for cultivating crops and engaging in settled agriculture. By the fifth century BCE, each mahājanapāda also controlled ports and watercourses for trade, which justified the expansion of territorial control for geopolitical ends.[7]

By the end of Dharma Yuga, elites had come to rely on multiple sources of (material and symbolic) capital formation: agricultural surpluses, mercantile wealth through arbitrage in long-distance commerce, and administrative rents collected by sovereign rulers and their courts, as well as ritual practice and the evangelism of karma, reincarnation, and the promise of liberation. Some of these sources of capital, including spiritual knowledge, which I discuss further below, were pitted against each other, and sometimes combined, reflecting the intense competition for territorial control and for strategic alliances that generated new social processes and cultural archetypes. The expansion of territory using military power was also meant to ward off marauders, and those factions with the biggest and most effective campaigns emerged victorious and powerful.

The rule of law was a timely invention that provided a common basis for the legal justification of coercive and noncoercive patterns of social order. As it happened, the first popular and widespread use of dharma as law appeared in Emperor Aśoka's remarkable edicts on pillars and rocks across the subcontinent (268–232 BCE) with no mention of dharma's Vedic associations. Dharma played a minor or even insignificant role until quite late in Vedic literature although, by the end of Dharma Yuga, it became a central concept guiding Brahmanical practice, constituting the rules that governed a civil—an orderly and ethically viable—society. Nevertheless, Brahmanical orthodox and heterodox actors, along with Buddhist and Jaina ones, demonstrated that there was more than one way to define these rules. For more than a millennium after the Buddha, these efforts had mixed outcomes but were also transformed by the influence of both proximate and distant social forces.[8]

Until quite late in Dharma Yuga—and some may argue never—despite the consolidation of such forms of power across many settlements, no single set of social practices or beliefs around dharma became hegemonic in northern India from Afghanistan to the eastern Ganga plain. Still, there were rules and customs relating to *artha,* or legitimate political authority, that did become hegemonic. In some regions and clans, Brahmanical traditions drew justification for gaining territorial power primarily from Vedic literature. In others, typically around emerging urban centers dominated by traders, the ideas and practices of ascetic leaders of Ājivikism, Buddhism, and Jainism held sway among large groups of followers. Away from cities and perhaps even at their fringes were foragers and hunters living outside the dominion of centralized polities. In between and beyond, judging from the traces that remain today, there were many heterodox regimes of practice. But it is clear that, throughout the period, centrally located urban elites developed vast networks of influence across a mosaic of areas well beyond their immediate neighborhoods, and these networks formed the very basis of territorial domination. Dharma Yuga could thus be called the age of the birth of territory in India, manifest in multiple treatises and pronouncements of sovereignty, authority over land, and other rules of territorial power across the subcontinent.[9]

At the other, personal end of the scale, a common and vital question across multiple traditions related to the individual's own dharma and what was the proper lifestyle needed to maintain social order and promote the good life. The answer involved the cultivation of particular bodily and interactive practices, along with the formation of a social structure and habitus, collectively expressed as a particular culture. In Dharma Yuga, attempts to amalgamate dharma into a unified concept were complicated by the difficult political question of how to lead proper lives in sedentary societies of growing complexity.

I claim that, some two millennia ago, dharma turned into an ideological *prop*: it acquired the power to influence people to become "territorialized," even while it spawned a divergent set of heterodox lifestyles. In other words, it became a means to validate certain sorts of political strategies that elite networks used to govern large and spatially dispersed populations. At the same time, the rise of heterodox interpretations of dharma also meant that there were counter-hegemonic resistances that sometimes solidified into new patterns of consent and coercion that benefited elites.

Dharma as Law

In Vedic society, arcane practices around communal and household fires were fiercely followed and deemed to be of vital importance for establishing social order. Knowledge of yajna was instrumental, the Vedās suggesting that knowing one's place and actions would result in an ordered world and please the gods because that knowledge formed the basis of appropriately designed oblations. Sometime in the middle of the first millennium BCE, starting with the Grhya Sutras, but reaching its zenith centuries later in the Dharmaśāstra, or classical Hindu law, Brahmin scholars began—initially in aphorisms and then in meticulously metered Sanskrit commentaries—to propose a grander universal purpose to guide collective human action.

Within roughly the same time frame, Buddhist scholars described a practice in commonly spoken languages to introduce the central significance of *dhamma*, the ethical way of living according to the Buddha. By doing so, these scholars appropriated a word from Vedic literature, one that hitherto had relatively minor significance. Certainly, this seemed to raise the stakes considerably for Brahmanical scholars and, in due course, there were numerous public debates on dharma within and across traditions, providing the very rationale for calling the entire millennium Dharma Yuga. What mattered in each polity was how a particular meaning of dharma—Buddhist, Brahmanical, or other—was enacted as law.

Law can be understood broadly as what a large collective may associate with coded reasoning and rules of justice. To be bound by "official" rules in a given society is so readily taken for granted today that few feel the need to locate law's philosophical underpinning. Jurisprudence is the use of reasoning to validate patterns of dispute between parties, to find fair or just outcomes. It is expected to apply equally to everyone within a given jurisdiction, a word that is perhaps not unintentionally associated with territory. What is commonly left unexplained is why a specific system of law and its jurisprudence should be given validation as being legitimate, or righteously authorized, in a given territorial polity. The ability of a set of actors to claim to be unbiased and therefore serve as appropriate arbiters of a dominant interpretation of the law—indeed, to have jurisdiction over the law—determines the success of the polity in achieving state-like authority. Complementary to this of course is consent, the popular belief that the law is unbiased and is enforced in an unbiased manner. This might also be termed the "constituent power" of that polity or state, its internal sovereignty.[10]

The majority of modern states are constitutional republics where the rule of law implies the presence of institutions designed to safeguard the republic from excessive control by any one group; there is a separation of powers that provides some checks on absolutism. Almost none of the constitutional elements of the modern state, however, were present in antiquity. Whereas a population or its representatives explicitly define the republic as being a popular sovereignty, most regimes in antiquity placed authority in a person who was crowned as leader; less frequently authority was assumed openly by a group of persons. But even those polities created frameworks of territorial authority around law. For this reason, as well as others, I find important similarities between the powerful territorial polities of Dharma Yuga and a more generous definition of the state system adopted by the political theorist Bob Jessop. According to Jessop, a state has these features: (1) a set of discursive devices and associated political institutions involving coercive, administrative, and juridical elements—a dispositif, (2) a territorial character with claims about the spatial extent of its jurisdiction, and (3) a people over whom decisions are made. By the beginning of the Common Era, these features were unmistakable in many parts of the subcontinent, and it is more than likely that elite constructions to generate dominant understandings of dharma were decisively used to assert territorial rule.[11]

In the Harappan civilization, the absence of coercive military power in material or symbolic forms may suggest that its complex polities did not fully constitute a state in Jessop's sense of the term. Yet, legal institutions must have existed in some yet to be discovered and interpreted form and violence to enforce it (or the potential for it) was also present. This is evident from the remarkably well-ordered society that regulated itself in a sharply defined dispositif, an ordering language, which established rules governing the creation of customs and a resulting habitus. Civil and criminal procedures of social justice were enforced, despite the lack of firm evidence of policing power over both the city region and expanding areas. Operating in a completely different register, the mahājanapādas in the first millennium BCE may best be described as monarchies or oligarchies in formation, but possibly without the ability to develop legal institutions across a widespread territory. As the sanctification and code-making ability of ritual sacrifice increased, status and the symbolic visage took on greater significance and greater differentiation took place to create elite dominance and consent for sovereign authority. Ritual slowly enlarged in scope, becoming the lavish public sacrifices of clan leaders, who eventually formed complex territorial polities. This process was complemented by the proliferation of private ritual within dvija households, creating layered distinctions across a larger public, who saw similar logics in their home life and that of the sovereign representative of their elite networks. Over time a complex habitus emerged within bloodlines and clans, reinforced by pedigrees of practice that were consolidated and formalized over time, with networks of those having ritual knowledge interlocked with clan authority.

For Talal Asad, ritual is a process of establishing what he terms "authorizing discourse" in a community through its practices. He proposes a move from approaching ritual as a universal category, preferring to focus on its technologies of power in each case, rather than its symbols. Asad submits that a symbolic view of the disciplinary apparatuses or assemblages of religious power commits the same mistake made by an earlier paradigm, which constructed a false dichotomy between cognition or mental states, on the one hand, and feelings or sentiments associated with religious practice, on the other.

Asad also explores how ritual (or religion, more generally) has both a regulative power—that is, the power to induce others to follow social rules of, say, going to the temple and making offerings—and the constitutive power of law, which takes on the very category "religion" and, in so doing, creates religious "subjects" through its practices. The latter form of power is what interests him most, because it helps locate both coercive force and the "authoritative discourse" in religious training. Constitutive power helps generate consent by creating knowledge and self-understandings about religious practice; for example, it saves my soul, it gives me happiness, it brings me in contact with ultimate Truth.[12]

The voice of tradition to which one responds through ritual practice may be operating to create docile subjects, but such "docility" can also be seen as the cultivation of self-consciousness that allows one to achieve certain collective practices of salvation, as well as freedom from personal suffering and that of the world. This understanding puts a wrench in any framework that attempts to neatly separate social groups that make up their own deliberative and unforced ways of living from those that are lemming-like in their imitation of dominant traditions. The political subject of any time self-fashions themselves in accordance with their habitus. This habitus tends to become hegemonic and expresses itself as the very basis on which sovereign claims too become normalized.

In older polities, dispositifs comprising ritual practices and spatial order, as in Harappan and Vedic territories, sustained certain complexes of elite sovereignty, yet legally constituted state power did not emerge until later. Like most other social dispositifs of importance, a tradition of law is formed within the context of its particular ancestry and evolution. The principal point of reference in jurisprudence is Roman law, the oldest known form of the very regulatory pattern that is now generally called "law." Although law is associated with a set of restrictions on elite power that were extracted by plebeians, the principles of a fair trial, torts, and so on were likely drafted by the patricians themselves in an attempt to forestall foment.[13]

In its codified and stabilized classical form, Roman law by 130 CE comprised the rules that were in widespread effect and backed by military force. They were wielded over a vast territory centered in Rome, with a regimented administrative structure that was replicated in different parts of the empire. Law's original legitimacy was patrician: Romulus lay down the laws according to tradition. Machiavelli explains why good laws may have emerged from a military order. By educating the public that the disorder would make it difficult to have peaceful and prosperous societies, ancient Roman law created the new subject of the citizen who was also relatively free. The firm hand of Roman law was constructed and implemented by specialists, themselves drawn from elite networks: initially networks of priests and, later, of secular jurists.[14]

The philosopher Jacques Derrida asks whether law is necessarily associated with justice; that is, whether the rules one follows in a particular legal regime can at all be properly justified. He associates law with "aporia," meaning something that is doubtful, ambiguous, or impossibly difficult. Enforcing the law has invariably required the use of force, whether direct or indirect, physical or symbolic, coercive or regulative, and in multiple combinations thereof. Less overt forms of force include illocution, performance, and rhetoric, and interrogating their patterns is valuable if we need to engage meaningfully with law in particular circumstances. These features of "speech acts" by dominant actors can contain warnings, threats, and entrapments that potentially generate harm. The foundations of law are deemed critical, but they "can't by definition rest on anything but themselves, they are themselves a violence without ground. Which is not to say that they are themselves unjust.... The same 'mystical' limit will reappear at the supposed origin of said conditions, rules or conventions at the origin of their dominant interpretation." Indeed, they could be based on "decorum, the law of the strongest, or the equitable law of democracy."[15] That is to say, a system of law may rest on flimsy foundational principles, but habitual legal practices seem automatically to give that system its familiarity as well as its own acquired force of legitimacy. Almost every system of law contains its own logjam of foundations (the "aporia"), and yet the tantalizing possibility that people can appeal to the law and obtain a just resolution.

In Dharma Yuga, there were many attempts to carve out a singular constituent power as the normative basis for law and to create forms of authority that could become commonly acceptable to their subjects. Where state power directly promoted dharma, as under the rule of Emperor Aśoka, it was mostly in the form not of legal strictures but as a set of aphorisms and advice to act correctly and to follow the righteous way. There is also no evidence that even Brahmin rulers, such as the Shungas in the second century BCE, tried to impose rules of dharma as codified in the Dharmasutras, nor is there any indication that the later Dharmaśāstras were widely enforced in subsequent regimes. Nevertheless, dharma can be loosely translated as law because its principal function is to serve as instructions for many arenas of social life, especially in the later Dharma Yuga. Then dharma meant both the express right of sovereigns to pass administrative decrees and the regulatory power of priestly orders to sustain community life on the basis of everyday do's and don'ts.

The legal historian Donald R. Davis Jr. also treats dharma as a form of law, which he understands expansively as socially determined rules backed by an authority that enforce sanctions. The primary location of dharma was the community of households, in contrast to the larger republic or political community, where ancient Roman conceptions of law and their enforcement or laws on transgression were placed. In earlier periods, dharma was rarely, if ever, enforced with the *danda* (military stick or punishment), and never systematically. Dharma, then, was the "theology of ordinary life," with religious logics motivating rules of everyday practice: a set of regulatory practices around the exposition of sacred mysteries. In later periods, however, Davis writes, "Hindu law viewed protection of the people and the promotion of the system of castes and life-stages as the ruler's main duties. Punishment is the root and the means of such protection and promotion."[16] But it was not just ritual life that Hindu law dominated in its many manifestations. Persons, things, and land were also the concern of dharma. Davis points out that they were treated not in possessive terms nor as properties of objects, but as relationships. These interactions were flexible, changing shape in different contexts, so that in colonial and postcolonial times, for dharma as household law, categories such as caste began to be reproduced as life-creating dispositifs whose discourses had entirely new meanings.

At the end of the Vedic age, especially during Brahmanism's encounter with the many urban centers that had sprung up by the early sixth century BCE, new and unlikely circumstances of risk to ācāra, or custom, arose. One recurrent anxiety was that the Vedic dispositif, its ideological apparatus, was weakening within the ranks, which may have been the impetus to introduce an increasingly orthodox tone within the social habitus. A few counternarratives arose as well. Indeed, the entire millennium of Dharma Yuga is replete with instructional material from a consolidated Vedic Brahmanism, together with seditious takes from multiple sources.[17]

After the second century CE, the Dharmaśāstra laid out severe penalties for digressions from varna endogamy in traditions later associated with varnāśramadharma, birth- and gender-based duties by life stages. But it is unclear how strictly these sanctions were imposed, other than in the patriarchal clans belonging to the dvija varnas. Perhaps because no single state form or legal structure was hegemonic across India for a long time, unlike in ancient Egypt, Rome and China, law itself was also plural and differently interpreted during this period and later. Broad regional heterodoxies went hand in hand with community-bound enclaves of orthopraxy. Not only may distinct elite groupings be discerned but also contesting social forces suggesting domination, realignments and crossfires, appropriation of cultural resources by subordinate client groups, and other political arrangements and their dharmas.[18]

Compared to the Vedic age, in Dharma Yuga there was not only continuity with earlier practices but also distinct new patterns of consolidation and strengthening of elite networks. These included a king-priest nexus, with many variations, including the creation of new rājanās (sovereignties) and rājyas (sovereign territories). A class of the nobility made up of propertied elites was emerging in new lands, possibly with what may be described as "extraversions" of some members of forest people with territorial elites, generating exchanges of favors to quickly add territory and new labor from among forest peoples. The Dharma Yuga can thereby be designated as an early pattern of colonization through domestication in India.

A Kaleidoscope of Elite Networks

In geopolitical terms, events from about 500 BCE onward created a sharp challenge to Vedic ideas of rājanya, or kingship, as well as the ācāra or habitus of household and public sacrifice. Much of the new development occurred around trading towns along the Ganga, at many other strategic points along rivers, and at natural seaports in different parts of the country (befitting a second urban age). In central and eastern India, iron ore conferred strategic advantages on some of these locations, nowhere more importantly than in southern Bihar and Jharkhand, at the center of the Magadhan territory, in Pataliputra and Rājagriha. The wealth generated at these urban centers was likely controlled by coteries who sought to consolidate larger realms. Where did they derive their surplus from, and how was it sustained? We do not know for sure. But there is evidence of granaries, settled cultivation, and increasingly, trading networks, which I discuss in the next chapter. Wet-rice cultivation may have been common by the end of the second millennium BCE in regions north of the Ganges that flooded often, but it was certainly more widespread in the Iron Age after around 800 BCE.[19]

As described earlier, in the late Vedic period, the Kuru-Panchala kings and their social practices of sovereignty constituted an early configuration of territorial power in the subcontinent. Importantly, the end of the Vedic age heralded no supreme territorial ruler but rather loose claims of authority from urban centers in sixteen mahājanapādas of roughly equal order. By the fourth century BCE, however, Magadha became an exceptional territorial power, annexing nearby kingdoms and rising in importance to build an extraordinary legacy. Magadha's strategic access to iron ores in the Chhota Nagpur plateau gave its rulers control over the production of superior armaments and boosted its economic productivity through the use of agricultural technology.

Around 480 BCE, Ajatashatru claimed his father Bimbisara's kingdom, which was a relatively small province centered in Magadha. Bimbisara was heir to the Haryankas, whose founder Haryanka (or Harydnga) set up rule in Rājagriha. Ajatashatru imprisoned his father and went on to use military might to annex the Licchāvi republic (assumed to be a form of collective rule by several thousand rājās) of Vrijji near present-day Nepal. Over time, he managed to defeat other mahājanapādas and claimed sovereignty over an empire extending as far west as the Indus Valley while fortifying its capital in Pataliputra (Patna).[20]

Ajatashatru's reign seems to have created a template for an Indian mode of sovereignty that later became the basis for statecraft or the art of territorial political administration, as articulated later in the Arthaśāstra (composed possibly in stages from the fourth century BCE onward). Ajatashatru's successors met with violent ends, including Shishunaga, a former minister who was reportedly placed on the throne with popular support. Mahāpadma Nanda usurped his seat and then turned out to be another empire builder. Mahāpadma's elevation appears to have rankled the Brahmanical authors of the later Puranas, because not only was his mother a Śudra—flouting the rules by which one was eligible to be king—but also he is described as having destroyed Kshatriyas.

Bimbisara and his son Ajatashatru were contemporaries of Jina Mahāvira (who established Jainism), Gautama Buddha, and Gośāla (the founder of Ājivikism). These and other city-based teachers in Magadha and its surroundings explicitly or implicitly criticized Brahmanical sacrifice and other rituals, while promising that alternative ways of living would generate personal happiness and community life. Buddhist and Jaina stories relate tales of verbal jousts with Brahmins whom these teachers met in Magadha and in other mahājanapādas. Yet by and large these encounters are reported to have been respectful, peaceful, and without incident.

The rising power in the eastern Gangetic region of greater Magadha made possible the expansion of formidable networks of Ājivika, Buddhist, and Jaina teaching and practices across the subcontinent. The growth of these apostate beliefs well beyond settlements in forested areas meant that, despite its influence within the Kuru-Panchala territory and beyond, Brahmanism was suddenly compelled to guard its interests. In particular, the incursions from Magadha up the Ganges valley potentially meant a declining need for Brahmin priests to conduct sacrifices, including animal sacrifice, to which Buddhists and Jainas were vehemently opposed.

Vedic societies were sedentarist, characterized by several strata of territorial and connected networks bound by interpersonal trust. Before the

Kuru-Panchala mahājanapādas, having a chieftain or proto-king was a strategic choice made by elite groups, a usurper to a seat of control, a patriarch, or wealthy man. From about 500 BCE, it is difficult to characterize the demographic composition and mobility of Brahmins, because their numbers, occupations, networks, and territorial extent remain a mystery. But they were likely to have been few in number, a minority in the emerging cities beyond the Kuru-Panchala territories. Despite their minority status, they were highly respected for their scholarship and ritual skills, which provided them modest means of support. At least some of their principal priests were key participants in kingly ceremony, wherever it was needed. Brahmin scholars, who first rose to dominance in the Kuru-Panchala territories in the northern and western parts of the Gangetic plain, soon found that they could be mobile and that Vedic knowledge was something they could use even in areas outside the Doab and north Indus valleys. In the Iron Age, with the development of new farming implements and weapons, the production of rice and other foods and possibly also cotton and yarn led to the accumulation of wealth through rising surpluses. In Magadha, strategic resources, such as iron ore, were also of growing importance. With rising wealth in the Iron Age, the king's role was principally that of maintaining security for a growing surplus of food and other resources that could fetch arbitrage for controlling local elites. In the centuries that followed the birth of the Buddha and Mahāvira, however, Brahmin priests found that rulers were increasingly uninterested in conducting sacrifices.

Some had learned through travel eastward and later southward beyond the Vindhya mountains that their skills were indeed portable and gave them special advantages in other areas. Where they were successful in gaining access to royal networks, Brahmins were primarily employed in courts to conduct rites but also served as advisers, law producers, and instructors for young princes. The philologist Johannes Bronkhorst writes, "When Brahmins offered their services to kings, they did not only offer their worldly expertise, or their learning, but also their access to occult powers. The Arthaśāstra, which may be looked upon as a manual for Brahmins who made a career in and around the royal court, confirms this abundantly. It is full of indications that magic and sorcery were accepted facts of life."[21]

The Brahmanical system of organization of ritual was based on a certain stable order between chieftains, kings, and priests around sacrifice that had operated within village-centric institutions of public sacrifice. Yet towns and cities had new and strange institutions such as market centers, guilds, financiers, and various associated political structures. In changing times, Brahmins of all occupations were compelled to adapt to the new and fast-growing economic and political power elite from Magadha whose territorial extent, especially along trade routes and at strategic locations, was increasing.

Both in the Doab and in greater Magadha, a secondary strand of Brahmanical practice arose as śrauta yajna declined at the clan or larger levels. Cleansing the body within individual households began to take on greater importance, and not just in the families of hotrs and their allied Brahmin and Kshatriya supporters. This practice and the associated concept of dvija, or twice-born, may have been consolidated around the sixth to the fourth century BCE; from this point forward, three superior varnas were constituted by clearly defined rules that separated them from *mlecchas* (outsiders) and Śudras. Although many of their services may have been provided in certain areas within greater Magadha where Brahmins were known to have lived, none of its rulers performed the śrauta rites: probably they would have been considered ineligible to do so anyway, given their lack of noble (ārya) lines of Vedic kinship. Magadhan kingly elites were also untouched by other forms of Vedic influence. For instance, Ajatashatru was associated with the Ājivika ("Follower of the Way of Life") practices of its founder Gośāla, a wandering ascetic whose central tenets have since been lost.

What we do know about Ājivika philosophy are its overarching rule of order or destiny controlling future events (*niyati*) and very precise cosmology about how many trillions of repeated births as atonement for past and present actions would have to be completed before reaching nirvana. The last stages of one's existence on earth are as an ascetic but are nearly impossible to reach because the individual faces an existential problem of rebirth, activities of everyday life, and karmic redistribution that generate no redemption over nearly endless cycles. Buddhism and Jainism also shared ideas of karma and reincarnation, but each had different solutions to this problem. The Buddha proposed the Middle Way (achieved through the Eightfold Path), whereas Mahāvira advocated the cessation of any human action that could have an adverse impact on other creatures.[22]

The Kuru-Panchala kingdoms and other mahājanapādas could not have foreseen the rise of Magadha from 500 BCE onward and its continuing dominance through the height of power of the Mauryans, India's first emperors. In Magadhan dynastic rule, we can see the dominance of the political—that is, elite power networks commandeering vast territory and in so doing legitimizing a collection of substantial physical and symbolic capital for a small court. How that sociological process of creating consent and coercion to sway a large group of people spread out over long distances from a small elite network would of course be a riveting story, but also one about which too little is known to tell fully.

In 326 BCE, Alexander of Macedon captured Gandhara and moved his army towards the Punjab, thereby shaking the foundations of Brahmin control over many aspects of social life in that region. In a probably unrelated event, the Mauryan Empire, whose capital was in Pataliputra in Magadha, expanded its territory to encompass former mahājanapādas under Brahmanical influence, effectively transforming the ideological landscape and further limiting whatever authority ritual sacrifice used to have. Still later, in the second and first centuries BCE, "invading armies of Greeks and Scythians (Śaka) destroyed much of what was left of the existing Brahmanical order of society, so much so that *Yugapurāna* described how the complete breakdown of society and end of the world expected would come very soon."[23]

Historians attribute the rise of the Mauryan state in Magadha to two major developments. The first was the expansion of the agricultural economy. Wet rice grown under state sponsorship perhaps originated in the eastern Ganga Valley, although the techniques may have come from elsewhere. Other forms of farming also developed around the same time. Sources suggest that farm rents for fertile lands in particular were very high: the sovereign took as much as three-quarters of the produce, leaving only one-quarter for the cultivator. The second development was the use of iron, both as implements in agriculture and as weapons.[24]

The polity centered in Magadha was at first like every other territorial entity in its neighborhood, but having made effective use of military strategy and armaments, empire building provided it with several advantages. Its newly instituted taxation policy, military strength, agrarian support mechanisms, and sponsorship of religious practices constituted novel features of government, which in turn aligned social structures with interlinked local elites having courtly power. We do not have accurate accounts of the Magadhan state's means of coercion and consent, but we know that the latter was established morally, at least in the time of Aśoka, through the invocation of dharma as a moral law. Where consent had been based on practices centered around yajna, now it was subject to a radical re-description based on the outright rejection of sacrifice.

Brahmanism's most stringent rules were becoming entrenched into the uppermost strata of dvija society, primarily for clans of hotrs and rājās, but also as a requirement for maintaining dvija membership. All men born into dvija bloodlines had to take on personal vows to follow clearly demarcated life patterns (preparation for manhood, married life, a period of withdrawal, and lastly, renunciation). Each phase was traversed through motivation and effort (aśrama). Those who failed to do so were relegated to mleccha or outsider status, which later gained multiple meanings.[25] These strict rules may have initially been attempts to close the ranks of kinship more strictly than ever and to make claims to purity on the basis of ethical living, family lines, and traditions. But they also sanctified—at the domestic level more than anywhere else—a continuity and collective memory of clan rituals and the ashrama, the stages of life to restore social order. It was this sense of dharma as natural law as preordained in the Vedās and the s that was rendered suspect in Pali uses of the word "dhamma."

What Does It Mean to Be *Chakravartin* (World Ruler)?

In a letter to his friend Friedrich Niethammer in October 1806, written when Napoleon was battling Prussian troops just outside his home in Jena, the philosopher Georg W. Hegel wrote, "I saw the Emperor—this world-soul [*Weltseele*]—riding out of the city on reconnaissance. It is indeed a wonderful sensation to see such an individual, who, concentrated here at a single point, astride a horse, reaches out over the world and masters it."[26]

When the sovereign makes a physical appearance out in the world, he inexplicably seems both magical and unremarkable. The king has two bodies, says the historian Ernst Kantorowicz, citing the medieval English jurist Edmund Plowden, which are made up of two different substances. One body is mortal and can become frail and die; the other—the body politic—is symbolic, spectacular, and eternal. Even during the stirrings of the European Enlightenment, this doctrine helped maintain the legitimacy of royal rule, while still explaining why that particular imbecile on the throne continued to deserve office. But how did the sovereign acquire his or her predominance in a society? And why have there been so many kings all around the world and throughout history?[27]

The earliest monarchs known to control vast territory over extended periods were the Egyptian pharaohs (*c.* 3200–30 BCE), whose lands were replete with powerful symbols, especially during the Middle Kingdom (2050 BCE onward). Pharaohs were depicted as having a divine and immortal double, their *ka*, which characterized their link to the gods and to all their predecessors. To the extent that ka stayed vital in the public imagination, it provided a remarkable ideological vestment that gave the king supreme power. Even though the pharaoh was born with ka, it was really its representation through imagery and the continuation of such metaphors throughout his life and beyond that established the legendary figurative power of divine kingship.[28]

Kingship survived in ancient Egypt for such a long time in part because of the region's unique geography of deserts bordering the Nile, which created a captive, immobile agriculture-dependent population that could not easily flee tax collectors. Royalty in all its grandeur may have had its earliest and most expansive stint in ancient Egypt, but it flourished independently in several other parts of the world. In China, starting around 1600 BCE, the Shang Dynasty used an elaborate system of bronze vessels of special significance, which were handed down through generations as markers of elite power. These vessels were shared within members of the royal family and the local governor and were used on ritual occasions to serve grain and wine. Only the select few were permitted to cast and use these vessels, which were supposed to be linked directly through ancestors to the god *Di*. The Shang case also demonstrates how urban centers were dominated by an inner circle of elites who succeeded in creating political landscapes that maintained cultural order well beyond their household establishments or courts. This was achieved through political alliances with local leaders in distant areas, exchanges of gifts among elites, and the continuous negotiation of power with extended networks through kinship ties, warfare, ritual, and select control over bronze production and symbolic objects.[29]

Dynasties all over the world enjoyed similar types of sovereign control over economic surpluses (through agriculture or trade); they had a tightly knit but geographically separate inner circle of elites who, in turn, built interlocking networks with managers and workers dependent on the protection provided by surplus-generating establishments. In addition, their symbolic power legitimized social structures in contexts that extended well beyond face-to-face relationships. The existence of an inner circle constituting the regime also acted to project force and benign order with the support of the military and administration, which in turn helped maintain political control within territorial limits. Often, existing networks of power beyond the inner circle stayed intact, especially when their clan-cultivated skills of military command and state-making were successful in successive regimes.[30]

The ruler's magical powers as a paternal protector of the people is a common trope in the literature of all regions, including early India. Kingship was constructed as an essential and familiar figurative template for reinforcing certain social practices, including settled farming and the generation of surpluses that were the source of wealth for the ruler and his entourage. In *Politics,* Aristotle associates rule over children in the household with the word "royal" (*basilikoi*), but he also says that to earn that description as opposed to "tyrant" (*aesymneta*), one had to rule over willing subjects according to law. Paternal linkages have been surprisingly abundant in both monarchies and divinities across contexts, perhaps because bodily metaphors around sexual power, control, domination—and consent—within patriarchal societies were amenable to being translated to much larger territorial collectives. What precise roles these mechanisms of social modeling and transference served may be difficult to discern in each instance. Yet, it is obvious that the stakes must have been quite high for so many elite orders to sustain such strong and persistent visceral associations between sexual politics and territorial control.[31]

One way to understand how these associations may have worked *affectively* is to note that magic is frequently associated with an aura or presence, which for royalty was typically established in the form of elaborate crown jewelry, along with actions that expressed the king's munificence and power to command obedience. Well before the turn of the Common Era, palaces, festivities, "grants" (typically awards of land) to the people, and other majestic performances of the royal family became common occurrences in India—along with the need for acts of war to expand the king's territory so he could collect tribute, sometimes in addition to special taxes on agricultural produce. No lineage of kings endured for more than a few centuries in ancient India, regardless of the size of their territories. In contrast, dynasties in China, Egypt, and the Holy Roman Empire had millennial-length reigns. Yet, there is evidence that, even before 500 BCE, a distinct, dynastic syndrome of kingship was identifiable in Magadha and within the Kuru-Panchala territory. A millennium later, in the Gupta period, the emperor gave formal control over territory to select representatives of defeated forest peoples in the form of numerous imperial land grants inscribed on copperplates. Similar acts of grant-making took place among the Pallavas in the south and the Vakatakas in the Deccan. These local lineages of nobility (rājās) grew in size and covered vast areas of what used to be unsettled land. By the sixth century CE, a rājā's sovereignty over his rājya (kingdom) was completely normalized across the subcontinent.[32]

The king in India, as much as in other parts of the world, was therefore greater than the particular person who at any given time may have held office as monarch: he was an historical subject, a collectively remembered luminary. The very act of constituting sovereignty in the body of the king—through treatises, epics, and other stories retold—involved the balancing of interconnected elite networks so as to capture symbolic and material control over multiple channels of his territory. Sustaining sovereign power rested on a widely asserted, but collectively remembered "good king" or perhaps one with god-like qualities. This memory need not be construed as some mystical group mind, but one made up of individually repeated utterances and metaphors, whose broad contours were socially constructed using a shared symbolic language—collectively, its habitus. Thus, in various parts of the subcontinent, perhaps starting in the Vedic age, monarchs were tied to *itihasa-purana*, mythologies of origins from gods or sacred rishis and their progeny.[33]

Despite his otherworldly symbolic power, or perhaps because of it, the king was a relatively minor or often even a captive character in what Elias terms a "social figuration" of interdependencies making up his court. Indeed, the aura of the king emerged out of a series of performances of his entourage in a palatial theater of opulent solemnity. These became so entrenched over many generations that they coalesced into immutable social forms. Each was identified with a recognizable set of networked relationships, with identifiable social distinctions that hardened into roles as diverse as *dutaka* (messenger), *kancukin* (doorman or chamberlain), *mahāmatra* (high-ranking official), and *rājādhirājā* (emperor) himself. Each had associated customs and mannerisms appropriate to the role, which sometimes became essential but onerous routines that had to be kept up for the show to go on. By the turn of the millennium, courtly cultures, especially in Magadha and the Chola territory in the south, were extravagant, giving rise to new genres of literature, mainly poetry and drama. These literary arts were, in turn, formative crucibles of interpretive communities, elite subcultures of those who consumed such art and thereby created assorted categories of refinement.[34]

The historian Daud Ali describes some of the processes through which cultures arising within the palace served to develop social classes in the outside world through the patronage of art and literature. By the time of the Guptas, courtly ways had become so well developed as to serve as a potent engine of broader societal change. By acting as "a great barrier" between the "high" and the "low," between the lives of "good people" and the "vast laboring populations which supported them, . . . the ways of the court formed an acculturative mechanism through which aspiring men and local elites entered into the pale of 'good society.'" Ali suggests that, during the longue durée of the first millennium of the Common Era, a well-established set of bodily dispositions, ethical norms, and aesthetics evolved to form a courtly ethos that played a critical role, along with other changing features of the dispositif, such as religious ritual and economic relationships, in creating new social structures in dominant layers of Indian society.[35]

In the Gupta court, the men of the court were dvija and were expected to conduct their lives around dharma, artha (wealth creation), and kama (pleasure). Around this time there developed śāstras (detailed rules of practice) and sutras (aphorisms that were generally less well codified than śāstras) on these subjects. These rules were collated into practical, normative treatises, aptly termed Dharmaśāstra, Arthaśāstra, and Kamasutra. The refined man and his less presumptuous but elegant female partner could thereby display a distinctive expression of privilege, often within a public social space. Courtly society constructed a formal aesthetic style for elites to flaunt and for others to admire and hope to emulate. This style was represented in palace architecture, exclusive jewelry, clothing, refined food, and gardens, as well as in the oddly formal manners and customs of the nobility. Ali describes how texts began to appear by the sixth century that specified various aspects of the palace complex: the proper sizes of palaces for different types of vassals and rājās; the proliferation of titles and categories of privileges for members of the retinue, comprising wives, courtesans and dancers, attendants and companions, relatives of the king, bodyguards, counselors, and teachers; how the members of the retinue should conduct themselves, down to the appropriate spatial relations and the need to speak in soft voices and calm tones; and an entire aesthetic and skill-development program for royals, in particular.

The king was the divine embodiment, but his sacral character was void without the larger figuration, or dispositif, that made up a given courtly habitus. Collectively, the king, his cortège, and the aura that surrounded them constituted a spectacle for others to revere and about which to form expressions of wonder, including in art and legends, all of which were woven deeper into the dispositif. The sociologist Maurice Halbwachs describes how, in medieval France, everyday discourses on events in one's own past helped connect ideas and opinions that eventually formed networks of meaning across time, creating an enduring sense of "collective memory." Every significant occasion was marked by the enumeration of places, symbols, and figures (human or divine), so that each such assemblage became associated with a particular narrative and moral truth:

> Behind the fields, forests, and fertile lands the personal face of the lord is perceived. The voice of the laborers answering the question of to whom these lands belong with "This belongs to the Marquis de Carabas" is the voice of the land itself. Such an assemblage of lands, forests, hills, and prairies has a personal physiognomy arising from the fact that it reflects the figure and history of the noble family that hunts in its forests, walks through its lands, builds castles on its hills, supervises its roads—the noble family that brought together its lands acquired through conquest, royal gift, inheritance, or alliance. . . . [This deference] depends on the idea that the owner of a title to a property cannot be replaced by anyone else: he exercises his right of possession by virtue of the qualities that are his alone or that belong solely to his family or blood.[36]

The Aśokan Moment: A Brief Social History of Empire

The Mauryas were India's first emperors, distinguishable from less magnificent monarchs because of the dizzying stretches of territory across which they claimed to exercise control through their military generals and other agents. That the body of a person could be perceived as standing at the helm of a vast empire was an emperor's most significant source of symbolic power, as indicated by the quotation from Hegel opening the previous section. Accordingly, the Mauryas left behind an enduring legacy. From their own records and the changes in other textual traditions within post-Vedic societies, it is possible to ascertain a powerful impulse to create ordered societies across vast landscapes. Of Mauryan relics, none are more remarkable than the collection left behind by Emperor Aśoka.

Aśoka's edicts constitute a singular phenomenon in Indian history in several ways: their geographic expanse; their strategic use of writing, including the language and location of the inscriptions; and undoubtedly their content. The earliest edict is the Kandahar rock engraving in both Greek and Aramaic dating to around 260 BCE. In it, Aśoka declares that ten years of his reign have been completed and that his message of *eusebia* (right conduct in relation to divinity) has changed his people and himself and caused them to abstain from killing other living things, become more temperate, and live more harmoniously. *Eusebia* may well be a mistranslation of dharma, just as the Aramaic word *qysht,* or "truth" seems to be. But perhaps the implicit goal of the apparent mistranslation was to reintroduce, in imperial handwriting, ethical messages on toleration and the golden rule, which were already somewhat familiar to locals.[37]

The remaining three dozen or so rock and pillar edicts are scattered across numerous sites throughout the subcontinent and are mostly in Brahmi and Kharoshthi script, though some are in Greek. In remote locations, the inscription was sometimes both in the local language and Magadhi, suggesting that imperial administrators were an important segment of the intended readership. As a way of organizing these texts, Romila Thapar suggests reading them as part of a threefold imperial strategy involving the metropolitan court, the core areas, and the periphery. At the metropolitan center, in greater Magadha, Aśoka's edicts in Brahmi are similar to those found in the cluster of rock sites just south of the Vindhyas in Andhra and central Karnataka. Even before they were annexed by the Mauryas, core areas such as Gandhara already had statelike qualities. The northwestern periphery near the Khyber Pass was a strategic area of military control, and the Greek inscriptions may have had an intended audience of frontier Yonas and others with Hellenistic influence. But no matter where they were placed, almost every edict referred to the emperor as *Devanampiya* and *Piyadasi* ("beloved servant of the gods"—which ones?—and "one who is looked at amiably," respectively).[38]

Aśoka's primary goal from the start was to be perceived as the paragon of the good king. Citing no other prophet than himself, but also in alignment with what later came to be known as Buddhist *madhyamāpratipad,* the Middle Way, Aśoka first described his own good deeds in his early edicts. These were his claims to meet the health care, water, and other service needs of people and animals on his land, while spreading the message of dharma along the way. Brahmins and ascetics were collectively referred to as embodying high levels of dharma in the form of virtue and piety, but these virtues were never associated with their ritual roles. Dharma was accordingly associated with good action, almsgiving, truth, and purity of deeds. It was promoted both through laws forbidding killing and also through various types of persuasion resulting in personal change, which proved more effective than prohibitions and penalties.[39]

Major Rock Edict XIII is a prime exemplar of Aśoka's inscriptions. It is found in several locations, including Andhra Pradesh, Kandahar, Karnataka, Gujarat, the Peshawar Valley, and Uttarakhand. This edict is often cited because it is a very personal expression of the emperor's remorse felt after his military triumph in Kalinga (modern-day Odisha) eight years after his coronation; notably, it is not found in Kalinga, although others are. Aśoka laments the hundreds of thousands who were slaughtered, killed, or deported as a result of war. Even if a small fraction of these people had been harmed, it would still weigh heavily in the mind of Piyadasi. The calamity obviously made a powerful impact on the emperor and resulted in his epiphanic love of morality.

> What is even more deplorable to the Beloved of the Gods is that those who dwell there, whether *brāhmanas* or *śramanas* [mendicants], or those of other sects or householders who show obedience to their superiors, obedience to mother and father, obedience to their teachers and behave well and devotedly towards their friends, acquaintances, colleagues, relatives, slaves and servants—all suffer violence, murder and separation from their loved ones.[40]

Furthermore, there is "no country where these (two) classes, (viz.) the Brāhmanas and the Śramanas, do not exist, except among the Yona [Greeks]; and there is no (place) in any country where men are not indeed attached to some sect." At that point Aśoka chose to insert a remark on the extent of his empire, having also claimed that he is Devanampriya ("Beloved of the gods"), indeed, *dhammavijaye,* or conqueror of dharma, which Upinder Singh says "is not a conquest but a victory consisting of effectively propagating dharma everywhere."⁴¹ The edict then makes a point of issuing a warning to *ātavikas,* the forest people:

> Even the inhabitants of the forests, which are in the dominions of Beloved-of-the-gods, even those he pacifies and converts. And they are told of the power which Beloved-of-the-gods (possesses) in spite of (his) repentance, in order that they may be ashamed (of their crimes) and may not be killed.⁴²

These three societal categories—the Brahmins, śramanas (or ascetics), and the forest people—were significant in Aśoka's time. Both the ascetics and the forest inhabitants were outside the dominion of the state, but the forest dwellers presented a special threat to its very existence by showing that it was possible and even desirable to be a forager-hunter who did not have to contend with the struggles of sedentarism. Both were also associated with the *nāstika,* the naysayer who rejects the Vedās.

The edict's somewhat uptight message was thus that the emperor was still powerful and that his statement of remorse should not be seen as diminishing or relinquishing his sovereignty, especially in remote and underexplored forests. Instead, as if to reemphasize this point, the edict listed the vast areas that marked his territory and the numerous peoples who received and lived by his message of dharma—the Andhras, Bhojas, Codas, Khambojas, Nabhakas, Nabhitis, Pandyas, Pulindas, and so on. Moreover, the content is very similar to sections of the Arthaśāstra, which conveyed a similar anxiety about those who lived in the spaces in between: the ātavikas.⁴³

Major Rock Edict XIII deals both with a military and a moral victory. In relation to dhammavijaye, the historian Namita Sugandhi poses this question: How was the moral victory organized administratively? She points to other edicts that signal the presence of mahāmatras (high officials of the sovereign), including *ithijhakamahāmata* (officer who keeps an eye on women) and, more prominently, *dhammamahāmata* (dharma officers) who, with other provincial support, established and propagated dharma throughout the territory. In Dharma Yuga, Aśoka's transition to Buddhism served as a model for a state religion in India, demonstrating that it could be a powerful way of maintaining symbolic and material control over rents and territory. Rents, in turn, could be carefully dispersed and therefore create a cadre of loyal servants to the elite agents who most benefited from these arrangements.[44]

Aśoka's regime may have engaged in some of the same type of palace intrigues and kingly strategies that had involved his grandfather Chandragupta (who may well have had a minister who formulated the principles of the Arthaśāstra) and father, Bindusara. But it is also clear that Aśoka sought to create an alternative template that formulated new rules for the legitimacy of the sovereign. His edicts were simultaneously the expression of moral obligation based on the down-to-earth ethics of mutual coexistence, the personal confession of an emperor, and the strategic geopolitical markings of a vast territory.

Since its inception, the expanding Mauryan state managed its empire through elite networks that were ordered in a complex and spatially organized manner: the state provided incentives for increasing agricultural production, appropriated trade networks that connected markets, generated rents through the extraction of raw materials, and created more extensive and reliable networks of communication. Building and operating these structures across a large territory required a system of imperial law and order, which was handily available in the language of dharma. In her thoughtful biography of Aśoka, the historian Nayanjot Lahiri notes, "The writ of the state is not written down, but the emperor takes trouble to elucidate the spiritual basis for his political interventions." In other words, Aśoka was at pains to communicate a new message to the world, but that very act of proselytization was itself an innovation in imperial strategy, serving to construct the long-term collective memory of the "good king."[45]

Within three decades of Aśoka's death, signs of the Mauryan Empire disappeared. Aśoka's prohibition of sacrifice likely displaced the very rationale for the Brahmin class—whose ritual focus had to be refocused elsewhere, toward the rules of the household and the king. In 185 BCE, Pushyamitra Shunga, an army general, assassinated Brihadartha Maurya and usurped the throne in Pataliputra. Pushyamitra was a Brahmin who revived the aśwamedha sacrifice and persecuted Buddhists, but little more is known about the Shunga Dynasty, which lasted for about a century. Then, or soon thereafter, a new set of alliances formed states, but their borders had little or no bearing on the sixteen original mahājanapādas of the sixth century BCE. Elsewhere in peninsular India and across the Deccan, the Satavahanas emerged as a new imperial power in the first century BCE. Even though they were familiar with the Brahmi script found in many Aśokan edicts, the Satavahanas made no written references to the Mauryas. Instead, their material remains referenced Vedic rituals and varna rules and showed evidence of a thriving coin economy controlled by royal sanction, along with land grants to both Brahmin communities and Buddhist monks.[46]

Lastly, how much freedom does an emperor have to reflect on the legacies he has inherited and the stakes he claims subsequently? Does power indeed inevitably corrupt those who rule or are there conditions for autonomy, especially when elite agents pause and take stock of their actions? Here then is the stuff of tragedy. Aśoka's remorse-filled Major Rock Edict XIII is paradigmatic of his split identity: he invented a new moral code for himself and his successors to follow, but he was still an emperor who had to reassert the territorial expanse of this law to other pretenders, warning disbelievers such as forest peoples that they, in particular, had better conform to his rule.[47]

Beginning primarily with the Mauryas, sovereignty and territorial law became refined to become the very exemplar of empire, operationalized as a series of linked networks involving appropriate delegates at various urban power centers. Over time this was transformed into a familiar Indian syndrome of political domination as manifested in the courts of *mahārājās* and *bādshāhs* (emperors). But even within their territories, alternative modes of elite political strategy were also in evidence, some of which fused their cultural practices with princely rule.[48]

Post-Vedic Sights on Dharma

Although Aśoka broadcast the Buddhist interpretation of dharma to the world in a most dramatic manner, the term "dharma" was probably already in fairly wide use by the early third century BCE, before his inscriptions were emblazoned across the subcontinent. But whereas dharma was one of the cornerstones of Buddhist thought, it did not have a prominent place in Vedic literature. In the entire Rigveda, the root *dhr* appears fewer than 100 times, mostly as *dharman*, which bears the meaning of "support" or "foundation." Brereton points out that the most frequent occurrences of dharman are in books 1, 9, and 10 (forty-five times) versus only nineteen times in the remaining seven mandalas (the older family books and book 8) of the Rigveda. Indeed, dharman was used differently from ṛtá, or universal law: the former referring to the process or actions of buttressing the world and the latter associated with a more abstract order or natural law. It is also what Brereton calls a "developing term" in the Rigveda that was not found in Indo-Iranian texts; it is a neologism in the early Vedic period.[49]

In Chapter 5, I described how sacrifice was the central institution that maintained a stable relationship between Vedic āryas and devas—between nobles and gods—with Brahmin priests acting as the mediators to ensure that the ritual acts were properly conducted. Dharman, in the few passages where it appears in the Rigveda, is used to describe sacrifice as playing such a support or foundational role: the object of such support could be the gods, heaven, or *soma* (3.17.1,5). Other verses refer to dharman more metaphorically or even symbolically as implying "holding firm," "maintaining order," or "staying resolute" (3.38.2). Elsewhere, in verses 1.134.5, 9.35.6, and 10.63.13, the term suggests foundational authority, and indeed royal authority, hinting at later connections with the formal basis for law, both earthly and heavenly. The philological shifts across these verses also reflect the passage of historical time.[50]

In the Upaniṣads, the word "dharma" appears rarely and, when it does, it has little to do with living a righteous life. Dharma might be expected to have a prominent place in the Grhya Sutras (around 500 BCE), which are devoted to household life and ritual (habitual bodily tendencies: *śarira samskāras*). Yet there were only six uses of the word there; in one intriguing instance it is proposed, with no explanation, that an offering had to be made to dharma and adharma (the antithesis of dharma) before entering the home. In three other places, dharma seems to come closest to denoting habits, customs, and norms, signifying the only links to later Dharmaśāstric texts. In the Śrauta Sutras—texts associated with ritual sacrifice and probably composed in their earliest forms after 800 BCE—dharma took on its more familiar meaning of law, but only in a single passage and obliquely: "How does one know a defiled obalation? What āryas who know dharma and who love dharma consider unfit to be eaten, with that he should not make an offering to the gods."[51]

To make unorthodox use of a dominant society's language or ways of living and to do so effectively at a grand scale accomplishes several things at once. First, it is a type of rearguard action that signals the parvenu's subsidiary position in trying to mimic the first, rather than being original. Second, in a more adversarial role, it is also a way of mocking the original innovator by, say, changing the meaning of key terms. Third, it creates a new language and proposes an alternative lifestyle that may seem more deliberative and therefore reasonable. Early Christianity adopted some of these strategies and, as a result, became such a powerful social force in the Levant that the Roman Empire was compelled to make it a state religion and take over the reins of its political arrangements.

The powerful new religious practices that grew in strength with sovereign elite sponsorship from Magadha propagated a complete disavowal of Brahmanical sacrifice. As a consequence, the elaborate and Brahmin-mediated instructions of Vedic sacrifice came under threat, the imperial message pointing instead toward practical and straightforward rules of ethical living. It was a force comparable to Lutheranism in northern Europe during the Reformation, although it was even larger in size and scope, with a legacy that extended all across Asia. But, as in Europe in the second millennium, a counter-Reformation of sorts also developed in India during Dharma Yuga.

This attempt to congeal Brahmanism into a more structured and internally guarded bulwark of dvija practice took the shape of a vigorous dharma discourse that began with the Dharmasutras in the middle of the third century BCE, roughly coinciding with the edicts of Aśoka. Sutras (threads) are aphorisms strung like pearls. First seen in late Vedic texts such as the Aranyakas and Brāhmanas, they were often arcane and required commentary by scholars in the Upaniśads and various other texts that were mostly composed in the Common Era. The Dharmasutras also came in different "flavors," reflecting their diverse authorship. They include Apastamba, Baudaranya, and Gautama, the first two of which may have been composed in a region south of the Vindhyas.[52]

Although the Grhya Sutras did not mention dharma, they were the forebears of the Dharmasutras, because they established the basic structure of codes for the ārya habitus. The Grhya Sutras were an elaborate set of instructions for the minutiae of everyday household (*grhya*—members of the household, belonging to a house, domestic) activities and for life-cycle events as aśramas (life stages), marked through rites of passage and strictly organized by gender, age, and varna.[53]

The household instructions of the Dharmasutras closely followed similarly strict ones in the Grhya Sutras, cementing the bond between them. But dharma also took on a special technical meaning in the Dharmasutras: it was nothing other than the proper enactment of model rituals, which were elevated to five household *mahāyajnas* (great sacrifices). These five household sacrifices were previously highlighted in the Grhya Sutras: food offerings to Beings (e.g., crows); food offerings to guests; the use of wood as a fire offering to gods with the word *svāhā*; offering water to ancestors with the word *svādhā* (both words assumed to have esoteric reference to divine feminine entities); and conveying the householder's connection with cosmic order through the practice of bodily endeavor and Vedic recitation (*svādhāya*).

The king was the primary figure on behalf of whom the authors of the Dharmasutras sought to legislate dharma over a larger society:

> The king rules over all except Brahmins. He should correct his actions and speech, and [be] trained in the triple Veda and logic. . . . He should be impartial to all his subjects and improve their welfare. As he sits on a high seat, all except Brahmins should pay him homage, . . . and even Brahmins should honor him. He should watch over the social classes and the orders of life in conformity with their rules, and those who stray should guide back to their respective duties.[54]

An innovation in the Dharmasutras was a near-obsession with maintaining varna bloodlines, with strict rules concerning agnate and levirate relationships, along with graded punishments in relation to sexual intercourse with non-dvija men and women.[55] The exhaustive directives in these texts, often involving mantras (formulas delivered through chants), served to translate this obsession into rules of everyday life. When widely practiced within patriarchal dvija households, they established a regularity of action, a sense of order and routine that was self-perpetuating and bolstered by hierarchies of enforcement. Second, they marked out boundaries of everyday practices—

between men and women, across varna, age, and so on. Third, they gave Brahmin priests special roles and responsibilities—officiating at ceremonies, learning and safeguarding mantras, and reproducing the memory of Vedic chants for domestic (*grhya*) ritual—to compensate for the decline in the occurrence of śrauta yajna. Fourth, they produced Śudras, those who were marked as prohibited from engaging in numerous activities of the ārya (dvija) household, including initiation, "the consecration of a person seeking vedic knowledge carried out according to vedic rules," preparing food for āryas or having any form of physical contact with them.[56] An ārya woman who had sexual intercourse with a Śudra was made filthy and impure (*asuci*), resulting in the loss of her social class.[57]

In the subsequent evolution of Sanskrit literature, the sutra gave rise to the *śloka*, an elegant thirty-two-syllabic verse form that reached its apogee in Classical Sanskrit poetry. The Dharmaśāstras were composed in śloka form in the early centuries of the Common Era and took on the status of law books of high gravitas after receiving solemn endorsements from later commentators. A śāstra in the Indic tradition was the systematic and organized form of a set of rules that had been cited among scattered forms of knowledge earlier; it thereby became a standard reference. It was produced out of an expert tradition and was interpreted by experts (*sista*) who received instruction at a young age and thereafter engaged in a lifetime of learning and reflection on the tradition. The Brahmin experts (*dharmapathaka*) in the Dharmaśāstra were most likely to be consulted to interpret the right ways to settle a dispute based on the śāstras and also preexisting laws and customs in a particular societal context, which often played a significant role in arbitration.[58]

What was new in the Dharmaśāstra was its author Manu's attitude toward Śudras, displaying a virulence that was absent in the Dharmasutras. How could the lowest class pose such a threat to Brahmanical hegemony? Perhaps collective memory was at work, because Śudra kings and emperors (mainly, the Nandas and the Mauryas) had once possessed awesome power and could always regain it. These very sovereigns had severely limited the Brahmins' access to political capital, even within the Punjab and Doab regions, where Kuru-Panchala kings had previously sponsored sacrifice and kept Kshatriya-Brahmin networks intact. Those networks were rendered superfluous with Nandan and Mauryan territorial expansion, along with the proliferation of practices that eschewed faith in the supernatural, such as Buddhism and Jainism.⁵⁹

There is an additional interpretation of this perception of threat. Along with mlecchas, "outsiders" whose uncouth speech contaminated Brahmin rites, Śudras within the confines of ārya society were a geographically confined marginalized group that served as a reminder of the distinctions of that society. Pierre Bourdieu famously explores this use of signs and other markers of habits. In *Distinction: A Social Critique of the Judgment of Taste*, he proposes that social distance is created through a series of badges around forms of speech, habitual bodily dispositions, lifestyles, and presentations of wealth. The construction of a symbolic landscape in social space enables the creation of hierarchies and patterns of power based around "cultural competences," which are built by acquiring and deploying cultural and material capital. People reflect their relative positions by calibrating their modes of speech, objects owned, and practices that they believe belong to members of various groups that they assume to be above or below their own. The distance between dominant classes and others is as distinctly marked as that between middle orders and the lowest class through a variety of everyday practices and physical spaces that different groups place themselves in. In the contemporary context, this would mean that a junior executive in a department store, for example, would know precisely where on a multidimensional scale janitorial staff, nouveau-riche shoppers, peasants, senior executives, and university professors would stand in relation to her own position.⁶⁰

Until the late Vedic period, Śudras may have been a cultural category to be merely tolerated and employed as primary providers of services to āryas. With urbanization and the advent of Buddhists, Jains, and other non-Brahmanical ascetic sects, which gained patent dominance across the subcontinent, a recalibration of social space was necessary. Dharma texts that further codified the varna system served the purpose of defending Brahmanical society from these new threats to its elite structures. The meaning of Śudras expanded to designate Buddhists and others considered outside the fold, in addition to slaves and others serving āryas.⁶¹

Three points are worth reiterating about post-Vedic uses of dharma. First, the Brahmin male subject became the primary focus of attention, along with Kshatriya and Vaishya males, although the latter two were clearly on lower rungs. The purpose of this attention was to enable the maintenance and reproduction of Brahmanical patriarchy. Second, this was accomplished through the self-disciplining of boys and men to consciously enter into different life stages (*aśramas*) with specific rituals to initiate their commencement, progress, and termination. These rites of passage also reaffirmed varna rules that became known as a compounded term, varnāśramadharma. Together, these two elements, along with an emerging ideology, seemed to provide the practical leverage to manifest a third: political domination over and exclusion of Śudras and forest peoples (*mlecchajātis*).[62]

Olivelle postulates that the reactivation of dharma in the later Brahmanical literature resulted from it becoming a central feature of Buddhist religious discourse. It is in this setting that the sardonic uses in Pali (dhamma) of an obscure Vedic word might be understood as the dialectic of contestation between the āryas of the Doab region and their powerful Śudra detractors in the Mauryan Empire in the east.[63]

Court Manuals and Epic Poetry

Perhaps the most eminent text of the time that describes the full extent and role of kingship is the Arthaśāstra, which loosely translated, means the "rules for achieving material status and political power." There is some doubt as to whether its author was really an adviser to Chandragupta Maurya, Aśoka's grandfather. But Kautilya, or Chanakya—the Intelligent One—was evidently a careful observer of existing political arrangements in Magadha and was able to define ideal extensions to create the perfect kingdom. In its final redacted form (*c.* 175–300 CE), the text contains a long list of aphorisms for managing a breathtaking expanse of social practices, such as herding, marriage and inheritance, various gradations of punishment for caste incursions and other forms of public behavior deemed antisocial, the many roles of the Brahmin, and countless patterns of surveillance and strategies of war and alliance. But its intended readership was elite court society and its central aim was to create and maintain the conditions possible for an effective and legitimate ruler and his regime.[64]

In an ideal kingdom, the king would rely on his counselor-chaplain and an elaborate network of spies and informants, maintain tributary relations with vassals and subordinate governors, and hold collectors responsible for reliable revenue collection from distant lands. How the king should police and manage his large administrative staff was a principal theme of the text and was to always be accomplished through networks of spies and secret agents, for whom many technical terms were used. Local magistrates came under the direct control of collectors and maintained order by punishing petty crime. City law was maintained by the city manager, who also collected an income tax. Dealing with oligarchies or confederacies (*gana-sanghas*) was a tricky matter; they had weaknesses and strengths, but Kautilya devotes an entire book in Arthaśāstra to how to sow dissension within them so that they could be eventually replaced by monarchies.

It is instructive to note that, like Aśoka in his edicts, the Arthaśāstra uses the term *mahāmatras* for the king's main officers and describes their various duties. It proposes, however, that the king should hedge his bets by engaging spies to monitor them:

> The king should employ them [roving spies]—according to devotion and capabilities and with credible disguises in terms of region, attire, craft, language and birth—to spy on these [mahāmatras]: Counselor-Chaplain, Chief of the Armed Forces, Crown Prince, Chief Gate Guard, Head of the Palace Guard, Administrator, Collector, Treasurer, Magistrate, Commander, City Overseer, Director of Factories, Council of Counselors, Superintendent, Army Commander, Commander of the Fort, Frontier Commander, and Tribal Chief.[65]

According to Kautilya, the king and his sphere are constituted by the "lord, minister, countryside, fort, treasury, army, and ally." The countryside must be "free of mud, stones, brackish soil, rugged land, criminals, gangs, vicious animals, wild animals, and forest tribes" and must be "populated mainly by the lower social classes." Āryas—Brahmins, Kshatriyas, and Vaishyas—cannot be sold as slaves, whereas Śudras and mlecchas can. But even slaves are not as impure as untouchables (Chandalas), relegated to the outskirts of the cemetery, beyond city walls.[66]

In the height of Dharma Yuga, which the Arthaśāstra describes, the typical city at the seat of the mahājanapāda was densely populated, heavily fortified, and designed into sectors organized by varna status, with the king's palace and temples near the center. On the outskirts was the forest—remote, dark, and a threat to political society. Both in legend and the rulebooks, the forest was outside the scope of ordinary politics, a mysterious world that designated danger, defiance, exile, and mystery. The ātavikas or forest tribes were treated as wholesale criminals; captured members were to be taken as slaves in the king's palace. *Mlecchajāti* was a term of contempt associated with outsider status that was used for forest people. Kauṭilya, however, advocated establishing contact with them as a means for the king to pacify them and then take their land, on which he could create settlements.

But this would not be easy because the forest dwellers had their own agendas and advantages over the king and his men. The historian Sumit Guha writes, "Forest communities would be at an advantage because of their familiarity with the woodlands, and the possibility of flight into them, evading the ponderous retribution of lords of the land. The ability to disrupt agriculture and trade was the major sanction the forest peoples could deploy, and agrarian gentry were well aware of it."[67]

Yet, despite these advantages, the takeover and social transformation of the ātavikas were well underway by the second half of the first millennium. The historian B. D. Chattopadhyaya writes that titles of rājā were then created in the forest lands, creating local nodes of elite power that were networked to the central palace through tribute and the commandeering of newly settled agricultural lands. This "transformation of forest spaces into spaces as nuclei of rājyas (kingdoms) had profound implications for local landscape, community and structure of ideology."[68]

Chattopadhyaya describes several instances in which powerful rājās attempted to reorganize forest space to conform to *rājadharma*, which by then included implementing the Brahmanical order as specified in its dharma codebooks. In one copperplate grant from the sixth century, Mahārājā Samkshobha of the Parivrajaka Dynasty, a vassal of the Guptas and a Brahmin belonging to the Bharadwaja *gotra* (lineage), dedicates a temple to a local hill goddess. Accompanying this concessionary gesture, which is actually a proclamation of sovereignty and royal munificence, the plate declares that varnāśramadharma prevails in the forest region and cites the Mahābhārata to validate this claim.

Chattopadhyaya describes this as an instance of "Sanskritization" from above, a process of transforming hill tribes (which the Parivrajakas claimed sovereignty over) so that they would emulate the social practices of dvija peoples by invoking legend as scripture.[69]

The better-known part of the Arthaśāstra relates to foreign policy, preparing for war, techniques of war, and conquest. Military success was dependent on domestic order and the strength of the treasury, but the relationship went both ways. As Mark McClish and Patrick Olivelle write, "If conquest provides one logic for kingship in the Arthaśāstra, another is provided by the general purpose of statecraft: acquiring greater wealth, protecting that wealth, growing that wealth, and spending it on worthy people and projects. This model emphasizes the enrichment of one's inherited kingdom and bequeathing it to one's heirs in a better condition than received."[70]

In this manner, Arthaśāstra created a complex but detailed symbolic map of statehood and its leadership, thereby inviting all future kings and ministers to craft territorial polities in its mold. There is evidence, at least after the decline of the Mauryan Empire, that dynasties endured for a dozen or more generations within networked families of kings, courts, wealthy merchants and financiers, and the military. That continuity is a good indication of the practical effectiveness of the Arthaśāstric codes of courtly practice, which were subsequently enriched by numerous interlinked chains of stories of princely valor told mostly by Brahmin instructors and poets to their flock.[71]

In the Arthaśastra and the epics, the Mahābhārata and the Rāmāyana, both composed between the fifth century BCE and fourth century CE, the king was branded as the ideal (divine) *purusha* (man) with a correspondingly flawless physical body: he had to be trained in the military arts toward perfection. It is worthy of note that in both the Mahābhārata and the Rāmāyana, the sitting sovereigns had weak control over the unjust and tragic events that transpired in their long-winded tales. In the Mahābhārata, King Dhritarashtra was also visually impaired. But the restoring to sovereignty the best possible candidates for the job was not always simple or clear. Even Yudhishthira, the very paragon of justice, lied and was deceitful as a means to make gains in battle, and Rāma was wildly jealous and suspicious of his wife on more than one occasion. They both point to the king-in-waiting's frailty even as he upholds his right to rule.[72]

The Mahābhārata tells a profoundly insightful story about how a group of princes and nobles in the court, the 100 Kauravas, succeeded in wresting territorial control from their cousins, the Pāndavas. Importantly, their "right" by birth and heritage are never much in doubt. The Pāndavas, toward whom the narrative is sympathetic and who constitute the human heroes of the Mahābhārata, or at least those favored by the Lord Krishna, are promised land that they gamble away to their shame and despair. Ultimately, as the narrative proceeds with many twists and turns involving the divine Krishna (who is not a Vedic god but is identifiable as an avatar of Vishnu), the reader realizes that this is not the story of good ousting evil but is a darker saga about the very meanings of dharma—here compassionately, though tortuously, rendered as *justice* rather than merely law. Later in this chapter, I return to the epic's mixed messages of political control and social justice. Importantly, to the extent that the epics, the Arthaśāstra and other dharma literature, and the Puranas point to palace intrigues as the central site of territorial power, they reveal mechanisms of control over long-term social actions. Altogether they demonstrate that kingship plays the role of drawing attention away from the actual operation of far less auric and benign elites, the ruling classes who were part of complex networks across vast geographies of empire.[73]

Three Challenges to the Elite Capture of Social Practice

The austere asceticism of the Grhya Sutras signals to us the regulatory schemes of the body that were already actively promulgated in the mid- to late Vedic period. These forms of body austerity were intended to delineate patterns of practice within dvija bloodlines and also to establish their differentiation from Śudras and mlecchas. The association of Brahmins and Kshatriyas with sovereign power was also thereby justified on the basis of their strict upbringing in addition to their well-preserved bloodlines. In Dharma Yuga, these claims did not go unchallenged. In this section I trace three mostly independent and typically corporeal countercultures, each later becoming at least partially appropriated within new Brahmanical liturgical traditions. All three presented the pursuit of alternative bodily practices or ways of living. One of these "countercultures" actually followed *āstika* (orthodox) traditions, and recognized the source authority of the Vedās, the limit beyond which no reasoning is possible; this was therefore a complex form of resistance, which I can only gesture toward. The main sources of evidence for this tradition are the epics—the Mahābhārata and the Rāmāyana—but echoes of the skepticism latent in them were prominent both in the earlier Upaniṣads and in later poetry and drama.

The other two challenges came from nāstika (heterodox) traditions: systems that denied (or bypassed the question of) the authority of the Vedās. The primary counterculture was Buddhism, but there was also a whole body of other heterodox forms lumped together under the Śaiva Age, including early Śaivism, the Caravakas, Yoga, Tantra, and many other local practices. Most of those who followed nāstika traditions belonged to the fringes of Vedic society and lived in the forests, in Magadha, or in urbanizing and forest societies south of the Vindhyas.[74]

Early Buddhist Practice

The stark simplicity of Buddhist philosophy, much like in early Christianity, gave it widespread and shared emancipatory appeal to the vast masses who may have been practicing homegrown spiritual traditions but had no roles in Vedic sacrifice and Grhya Sutras. Buddhism's simplicity of practice and zero barriers to entry or exit were its hallmarks. Those on the fringes of the Brahmanical order and who may have been forced to be servile to dvija groups on contact now had an alternative set of practices that they could call their own. The esoteric sounds recited by the Brahmin priests in an unknown language perhaps meant little to the Śudras and mlecchajātis. Buddhism, even in its earliest days, during the life of the Buddha, was unusual in its doctrine, with practices and teachings that seemed at the same time both more radical and yet more accessible than any other belief system. In contrast to Brahmanism, its followers were simply instructed to abstain from killing, stealing, engaging in sexual misconduct, making false speech, and drinking intoxicants. Mendicants were not subject to any stricter rules and were only penalized mildly by the lead members of their order for violating any of these precepts. Even later, with the formation of the Buddhist *sangha* (monastic order) with its stricter rules for monks (*vinaya*), only trespassing a special class of them would result in expulsion from the order. In this way it was primarily a voluntary practice, with no restrictions on who could take on vows of renunciation and practice the monastic life or simply follow the sensible Middle Way between strict austerity and wanton pleasure. Meanwhile, in greater Magadha during the time of the Buddha, sovereign power belonged with those who were outside the ritual confines of Brahmanical society.

Buddhism also differed from Ājivikism, whose mind-numbing fatalism allowed for no salvation in this world. Instead, Buddhism, through its promotion of simple, nonviolent values and modest lifestyles, identified the roots of sorrow and promised liberation through the eightfold path to enlightenment. It was relatively far-reaching in its transformation of patriarchy, first, by having no restrictions on the entry of nuns into the order (in many recorded instances, they exceeded the numbers of monks) and, second, by engendering a modest reorientation of dominant patterns of masculinity by implicitly devaluing its violent habitus.

Before Aśoka, only a small group of mendicants in central India made up the Buddhist order. But through the efforts of its peripatetic monks and nuns who established a geographically vast network of proselytizers, Buddhism became a social force of great influence among ordinary people. But Aśoka's imperial mission to proselytize Buddhist doctrine was unquestionably one of the most dramatic religious moments in ancient India. It was arguably more significant than the variously effective territorial formations of the Harappan and Kuru-Panchala regimes, which were examples of early complex polities that lacked the state-like features of the Mauryan Empire. What made Aśoka's edicts different and notable were their missionary zeal, which had the backing of a powerful military whose far-flung exploits were legion. And yet, as I described earlier, only the edicts against committing acts of violence on living beings were issued as imperial injunctions. For the most part, his edicts served as announcements of personal renunciation by Piyadasi and efforts undertaken by his own officers (*dhammamahāmatas*) to spread the message and practice of dhamma, or ethical living according to the Buddha. The edicts were unkingly gestures, and yet their symbolism and strategic locations were signaling something else: the newfound power of a significant religious event across space and time.[75] Aśoka's edicts, in both subtle and glaring ways and whether intended or not, reinforced the very conditions of subjection of his subjects by reminding them of the protective role of the emperor in spreading this alternative practice across the vast extent of his territory.[76]

The Buddhist sangha was the community of practitioners of the Middle Path (*majjhimāpaṭipada* in Pali; *madhyamāpratipad* in Sanskrit). It was vital in spreading a message that resonated widely and quickly in regions well beyond where the Buddha had lived and preached. Within a few years after the Buddha's death, his attendant and perhaps most famous disciple Ananda took Buddhism to Kaushambi in the west and in the process influenced many learned Brahmins there. Some of them and their disciples took the message to Sanchi and farther west and south. Even though the Buddhist order had a schism early on—between Theravada, a conservative sect, and a more ecumenical school, the Mahāsanghika (which later formed Mahāyana Buddhism)—the Buddhist order spread by making opportunistic use of the rapid changes in the Indian landscape—from being a mostly forested, sparsely populated area with pastoral and agrarian settlements of janapādas into powerful urban networks with growing populations, expanding state structures, and thriving economies built on trade and agricultural surplus. Expanding widely across the subcontinent and rapidly into the rest of Asia, through direct and indirect indictments of Brahmanism and other orthodoxies, Buddhism became a surprisingly formidable power at the turn of the millennium.

Evidence of Buddhism's appeal and reach, especially after Aśoka but even before his time, can be found in the accounts of Brahmins who were "converts" to Buddhism. But such a term may be inappropriate to describe Buddhism's unique point of reference, which began with radical theological skepticism and invoking no extraterrestrial salvation. Without an iconic Abrahamic God or a mythology that sustained nonhuman powers, early Buddhist practice was also a lay practice and, in some ways analogous to Lutheranism, offered opportunities for spiritual salvation for both ordinary people and the more austere mendicants (śramana), who survived only on alms while devoting themselves to leading lives of dharma. For the second-century CE monk and biographer Ashwagosha, the Buddha's new message of "true dharma" was irrefutable:

With the irresistible supreme blow
of the true *dharma,* he will burst open
The door whose bolt is thirst and whose panels
are delusion and torpor,

so that creatures may escape.
Gaining full Awakening, this king of dharma
will release the world from bondage,
A world bound with the snares of its own delusion,
a world overcome by grief,
a world that has no refuge.[77]

Ashwagosha, who was one of those Brahmins who turned apostate, was able to describe the appeal of the Buddha in an idiom understandable by other readers of Sanskrit, likely generating turmoil and harsh reaction within their clans. But it is wrong to attribute responsibility solely to Brahmin networks for ending Buddhism in India by the seventh century. The Guptas played a strategic role in sponsoring Brahmanism by creating hybrids of native forms but with a strict core, which expanded their influence. In addition, trade networks were taking monks to parts of Central Asia and into China, which changed the center of gravity of Buddhism by the end of the millennium.[78]

It is also possible to interpret both early and late Buddhism as having the ability to cultivate a pacified and calm public through its minimalist practice that seemed to quell both individual suffering, through the experience of existential truth, and dissent. This would imply that the very openness of Buddhism made it liable to become allied with the interests of ruling elites, who might have enlisted the heads of monastic orders as a buffer against the mantra-wielding power of Brahmins who insisted on maintaining strict endogamous regimes of hierarchy and separateness. The Aśokan moment may even be emblematic of this political role of Buddhism, which arguably continued in altered forms in other parts of the world as it suited the needs of rulers in Sri Lanka, China and Japan. Still, much of early Buddhist practice and teaching, including Aśoka's edicts, can best be construed as a critique of both Brahmanical orthopraxis and of the pursuit of violence and greed that accompanies the neglect of the spiritual life of madhyamāpratipad on Earth.[79]

Buddhist philosophy and practice were characterized by two qualities that were compatible with each other. Buddhist ontology, its construction of how the world exists and operates, was based on human bodily being-in-the-world, a description of the reality or truth of one's own experience based on interpersonal existence in everyday life. The other feature was practical: instructions to follow a clear-headed but modest Middle Way. Both assumed that everyone, regardless of birth or status, could achieve transformation. What happened in operation may have been a different matter, but the Buddha had thrown down the gauntlet, to which a variety of social groups with symbolic and material stakes to protect had to respond.

Epic Rebellion?

The Rāmāyana and the Mahābhārata are epics of magnificent style with multiple subplots involving both divine and human characters of noble birth who connect across several generations and sometimes eons. Most of the male heroes have a military upbringing, preparing them for blockbuster wars that form dramatic climaxes in their respective tales. Although similar to Homeric epics in their long-term societal impact as stories enshrining collective ideals transmitted on a continental scale, these Indian epics are grander in scope when they describe vignettes of tragedy as jealousy and separation, long-standing and pointless rivalries, and love lost and reunited. They also have stories within stories, the Mahābhārata being the far more nested and recursive of the two.

Dharma is a leitmotif in both epics but is handled quite differently in each. The religious studies scholar Alf Hiltebeitel points out that, in the Mahābhārata, dharma is always in question; the Rāmāyana tries to fix it in the ideal of the perfect man; namely, the divine king Rāma:

> Whereas the Mahābhārata gives us a king [Yudhishthira] who questions *dharma* and is questioned in turn by Dharma—his father in various disguises, the Rāmāyana gives us a king whose apparent perfection in *dharma* includes a decisive feel for it even in circumstances where questioning it might seem morally appropriate (such as the killing of Valin; the two ordeals of Sita; the killing of Salambuka). With these differences in mind, one might say that in tone, at least, the Mahābhārata is closer to the pluralistic, flexible, and "broad" *dharma* of the early Dharmasutras, which first define *agama* (tradition, or "what comes down") and the cultural wisdom of learned *sistas* as among the sources of *dharma* (whenever it is "subtle," so to speak), whereas the Rāmāyana is closer to the legislative and "codifying" clean-up operation type of *dharma* that one finds in Manu.[80]

The Mahābhārata is bookended by tales of ruin and despair. It begins with a lament about the decline of utopia and the start of Kaliyuga, the age of wretchedness, within which the entire saga of the family quarrel is said to take place. At its conclusion are long narratives in which Yudhishthira is still repentant about the great war that produced great suffering. He also sees the death of all his family members before he dies himself, and even after that, he is subject to further frustrating tests to prove his mettle. In the twelfth book of eighteen, the Śāntiparvan deals with *āpaddharma*, the rules of dharma during a time of distress. Here, as elsewhere in the text, exceptions apply only to the nobility, for the sake of long-term political order. In one sense, even the most famous part of the Mahābhārata, the Bhagavad Gita—the "Song Sublime"—can be construed as an exhortation to the prince to commit fratricide for the sake of the greater good of the territory and the lineage. Yet, that would be a particularly narrow and unimaginative reading, because it clearly has a much loftier scope—seeking to reopen questions about existence and human agents' ethical dilemmas, thereby reworking the dimensions of dharma to occupy a bigger stage than just the duties of śāstric law.

Interpretations of the Gita have had a long "biography," but some of the most philosophically significant ones have come from the ninth-century philosopher Adi Śankara. Śankara's commentary draws on his particular Vedantic ontology: (1) the phenomenal world is mediated through flawed ideas of the bráhman; (2) humans have the capacity to gain the insight to recognize this monumental epistemological error of misrecognition; (3) the Vedic corpus, particularly the Brahmasutras and the Upaniśads, already contain all this understanding; and (4) the Bhagavad Gita's central message concerns this very intuition, untangling the self from the illusory material world through the epiphanic awareness of its transcendent being. Śankara followed the Mimāmsā tradition, which emphasized the study of the Vedās as the source of all human instruction, notwithstanding the fact that only male Brahmins would have access to such knowledge, with a few notable exceptions who all met tragic ends. He and his philosophical peers and interlocutors marked the end of Dharma Yuga and the replacement of Buddhism with multiple forms that were consolidating under the rubric of Hinduism, though not yet by that name. They and the rest of the Brahmanical social and political order did so by reviving a robust, if metaphysically grounded, rebuttal to the Buddhist critique of Vedic sacrifice.[81]

Setting aside the Gita and its interpretation, dharma talk in the Mahābhārata is often ambivalent and cautious in making judgment, especially when one reads between the lines of Yudhishthira's many travails. Yet the epic's indecisiveness on the efficacy of dharma explains in large part why it is such a rich lode of scholarship. Human frailty, accidental circumstances, and layers of deception continually thwart ethical behavior. The handed-down rules of dharma are helpful only up to a point, and even the acknowledged experts (Bhishma, the Kauravas's and Pāndavas's great-uncle and warrior-scholar, and Yudhishthira, who is known by the moniker *Dharmarāj*, the king of Dharma) are stumped at various junctures. The meanings of dharma cannot therefore be based simply on the mechanical application of the scriptural codes assigned to varnāśramadharma. At two points in the epic, Yudhishthira associates dharma with non-injury (*anrishamsya*), a word similar to *ahimsa* or nonviolence, which is abundantly found in Jaina and Buddhist literature. Elsewhere, dharma takes on other meanings, including that of one's duty to follow the rules of the scriptures; yet for Yudhishthira, it is frequently a bootstrapping exercise, where the struggle to do the right thing has to be addressed from within.[82]

For Yudhishthira, as for Aśoka, one's moral relationship to retribution, or *dandaniti*, is key: "since men are led (to the acquisition of the object of their existence) by dandaniti, this governs everything." But he considers retribution to be a travesty of the imagination and finds solace in the tradition of renouncers:

> If we had been mendicants in the city of the Vrishnis and Andhakas, we would not have suffered this misfortune, depriving our relatives of men.... Goodness, equanimity, self-restraint, purity, absence of enmity, absence of passion, non-violence, truthful speech, these always exist in those who live in the forest. But, greedy and obsessive, clinging to arrogance and pride, we have fallen into this situation *due to our desire for a mere kingdom.*[83]

In the most important part of his coronation, Yudhishthira performs the rājasuya, an oblation made to Varuna, the god of dharma, who then confers sovereign power on the king, compelling all mortals in his dominion to note that he is the sole arbiter of the law. But for the despondent king, this power only heightens the distance between the violent and deceptive events that have led him up to this point and his own perception of dharma. Tellingly, he confesses to the poet-sage Vyasa, "Acting lawfully and ruling are always opposed—this confuses me though I think about it constantly."[84]

Escape is not an option, and neither is compromise, despite the entreaties of others, such as his valiant brother, Arjuna, who argues, "Dharma was promulgated here for the purpose of the maintenance of the world. The best conception of dharma is an absence of violence and good violence. No one is absolutely full of merit or absolutely devoid of merit. Both good and bad are evident in all activities."[85]

If Mahābhārata and Rāmāyana have a similar theme, it is because virtually all their protagonists are troubled by earthly questions of behavior in relation to the law, social order, and political faith—and almost never about their commitment to fulfilling their ritual duties to the gods or the ill that follows from even minor dereliction. The writers of the epics and their courtly transmission revealed largely their own anxieties and forms of remorse with regard to their roles in elite networks. At the same time, a completely different set of perspectives "from below" was available across the subcontinent and beyond. Not surprisingly, numerous folk versions of Mahābhārata and Rāmāyana stories have persisted, many with alternative moral twists and social arrangements. Many of these re-enplotments were passed on through peasant-soldier orders, lower courtly traditions, goddess societies, and later in Rajput and Muslim variations and syncretisms, including in Ismaili and Sufi cults. That the high culture of Sanskrit was re-appropriated in cultures of orality and asceticism may also be seen as a claim by subaltern classes for their own forms of hierophany in addition to, yet distinct, from elite religious authority.[86]

The Śaiva Age: Śaivism, Tantra, and Yoga

The Śaiva Age was from the fifth to the thirteenth centuries CE, when a series of modes of worship proliferated and were adopted by many rulers even while they supported and upheld the Brahmanical order. These other forms of worship included not only Buddhism and Jainism but also devotion to Śiva, Vishnu, Surya, and the goddess Shakti in various forms; worship of Śiva was the most common among these heterodox practices. By the eleventh century, also joining the mix was Sufism, characterized by community forms of worship with song and poetry known collectively as *bhakti*.[87]

If Buddhism, Jainism, and Ājivikism were largely Magadhan traditions, Śaivism's origins are a mystery. The Lord Śiva might have been a later reconstruction of various local deities that were united with the divine Rudra of Vedic lore. One possibility is that it emerged in Harappa in an early form, as the austere god that all Harappans emulated in their commitment to a type of physical asceticism. Indeed, it may have been that very self-discipline that helped create an ordered urban life that was able to build up a substantial material and symbolic surplus from trade. But it is also conceivable that Śaivism's earliest practices were found in southern India and amalgamated with phallic worship in various other parts of the subcontinent.[88]

There were numerous Śaiva sects, with each one typically derived from an ascetic guru who had the divine power of mantra to make a ritual connection between his followers and either Śiva or his consort Śakti. These sects were formed on the basis of learning mantra at the feet of the guru, through various grades of initiation and access to texts called Tantra. But Brahmin devotees also worshipped Śiva; they traced this tradition to the form of Rudra-Śiva, which appeared in the Shvetashvatara Upaniśad, a fifth-century BCE text associated with the Yajurveda. Although it is useful to see how Śaivism can be interpreted as both an insider and outsider practice in relation to Brahmanism, there is little doubt that its established form in Brahmin sects can only be traced to the Gupta period (third to sixth century CE) with the development of the Puranas, a set of sectarian texts on the mythical reconstruction of particular cosmogenetically derived traditions of worship. The Śiva Purana not only tells stories about Śiva but also instructs devotees on where they should worship.[89]

Whereas Brahmin Śaivites followed the practices of varnāśramadharma through their formation and validation in Puranic literature, their non-Puranic counterparts had a longer and perhaps more colorful existence. In the Pashupata sect, strange behaviors were expected from initiates who passed through the first stage of initiation: "These include pretending to be asleep in public places, making his limbs tremble as though he were paralyzed, limping, acting as if mad, and making lewd gestures to young women." These actions were expected to draw the ire of the public and so needed to be followed by a stage of isolated asceticism. Tantra appeared in the early centuries of the Common Era in both Buddhist and Śaivite practices. Tantra, which comes from the word "loom," was built around secret societies that created stages of initiation involving heterodox practices, as in the Pashupata example given earlier. Over time, a separate Tantric identity was created within Buddhist and Śaivite communities; its adherents lived in exclusive communities, mirroring the secret and codified ritual lives of dvija men but having entirely different practices. Some practitioners (*tantrikas*) were ritually obliged to partake in the Five Forbidden Things: alcohol, fish, meat, parched grain, and sexual intercourse. By violating ordinary social norms, Tantric sects created alternative rules to follow but also demanded the cultivation of the yogi (one who has mastered discipline—yoking) by using bodily practices to unify the subtle elements of the self with Śiva and Śakti.[90]

There were a large number of Tantric sects, many of which denying the authority of the Vedās and others drawing direct lineages from them. Those Tantric practices claiming roots in the Vedās were integrated into the Brahmanical canon by the eighth century, but usually with state sponsorship. In eastern India, during the eighth to the twelfth centuries, many Buddhist Tantric texts emerged that were sponsored by Pala kings of the region. Buddhist and Śaiva bodily rituals had remarkable overlap in some instances, suggesting earlier common influences on both practices. Just as likely, Śiva worshippers and Buddhist Tantric practitioners simply borrowed rituals from each other while keeping their iconography separate. In all instances, these borrowed practices were rituals of bodily self-awareness that could simultaneously promote prevailing forms of social and political order and build unknown and therefore risky explorations of the world that could antagonize these forms of power.[91]

When kings adopted Tantric Śaivism or Buddhism, it is helpful to ask what modes of accommodation were in fact sought or made. The religious studies scholar Alexis Sanderson points out that the early royal patronage of Śaivism had several motivations, but it was facilitated by the way Śaivism refashioned itself to constitute a "body of rituals and theory that *legitimated, empowered, or promoted* key elements of the social, political and economic process that characterize[d] the early medieval period."[92] These elements included the system of monarchy that was spreading across the land, the proliferation of landowning temples tied to the royal household and to lesser nobles, the growth of commercial urban centers that sheltered rulers and also in turn were protected by their entourage, the expansion of the agrarian base and systems of irrigation, and the need for greater cultural and religious assimilation. Dominant Śaivite sects molded their ways to be adaptable to Brahmanical codes, with Śaiva Brahmin gurus often playing key liturgical roles in initiating the king (in abbreviated and less onerous forms) and thereby legitimating his rule. This happened not just throughout the subcontinent but also in Southeast Asia by the second half of the millennium. Judging from later practices at least, these and other hybrid sects exemplified strategies of non-elite displacement and mimicry that served as subtle arts of resistance but without yielding much redemption.

Śaivite kingship rituals in the post-Gupta period were not simply modifications of śrauta rituals but, in fact, completely replaced them while still remarkably retaining Brahmanical legitimacy. Did Śaivite practice transform Vedic Brahmanism, or was it the other way around? There may not be a straightforward way to answer this question, except to say that a large and entirely new set of languages of liturgical practice were operative, often in serious conflict with each other, for several centuries, even while Buddhism lost its royal shine. Political contestation, when it did arise in these volatile conditions that were subject to many global changes over the millennium, typically surfaced as conflict within elites, between elites and mobilized groups of people, or across mixed alliances of elites and public collectivities. The identification of elite networks, their status, and operations across these different practices in relation to royalty is only possible on the basis of more detailed analysis of specific sites and characters that grew in importance during this time, which had marked differences across geographies. These included the king, the court, the temple, irrigation systems and the farm, the forest, the itinerant merchant, and the marketplace. These intersecting actor-networks, in turn, shaped emergent syndromes of corruption.[93]

Syndromes of Dharma Yuga Corruption

If the plot in this chapter has been especially confounding, at least some of the blame lies in the complexity of the period itself. The birth of territory in India was characterized by competing elite groupings, out of which emerged a singular plotline of monarchy and its entourage, putting in place the constituent territorial state. That this happened to follow and coincide with similar developments across the globe need not be considered fortuitous, but neither was it the outcome of some grand conspiracy hatched outside India. Instead, the kingship model may have emerged independently in India, but as it matured, different territorial elites learned tricks of the trade from each other, which the Arthaśāstra, in particular, tried to consolidate into a single manual, a model endorsed elsewhere in other courtly literature.

One of the characteristic narratives of Indian kingship in both its Brahmanical and Buddhist variants was that royalty itself was not divine, with very few exceptions, but had to be blessed and cherished by gods. The king was all too human, but dharma was the linchpin of his actions. That the king was the prime exemplar of the dharmic human simply gave him absolute right to make sovereign claims to territory. But that was also the principal element in the elite network that sustained the order of the rājanya.

An associated feature with that of territorial sovereignty was that bloodlines mattered for determining who was permitted to rule, even if that succession came at the cost of violence. Yet some kings, most notably Chakravartin (Emperor) Aśoka and the legendary Yudhishthira, derided violence. The challenge for them was that their court societies were already composed of interlocking elites increasingly tied to long-distance trade and arbitrage who could not afford to have the edifice of kingship and territoriality collapse. Instead, elaborate mythologies were developed and bolstered during Dharma Yuga around the ideal forms of kingship to keep Brahmanical order intact, thereby consolidating the practices of rājanya and its associated rituals.

What might forays into or from the forest have looked like in Dharma Yuga? What we understand is that sometimes the forest people were managed in stealth through strategic alliances with the leaders among them; these alliances had the aim of asserting territorial power over the forest people thereby colonizing them. Territorial control appears to have given rulers and their courts control over large publics principally through symbolic acts, but wild borders were especially dangerous.

There were probably also myriad ways in which Brahmanical, Buddhist, and other urban lives were strategically linked to the growing elites and to several layers of subservient groups. All these interactions in cities and their hinterland made up the very societies of ordinary life in urban landscapes and farmland in Dharma Yuga. What we do know is that these societies were in flux from Aśoka's epiphany onward, which was undoubtedly a radical self-critique of territorial power itself. But even Aśoka was unable to free his own life from that of his courtly elite power. A queen bee might be queen, but she can hardly escape the hive.

7

Trade Winds

Building Global Connections of Corruption

The law locks up the man or woman
Who steals the goose from off the common
But leaves the greater villain loose
Who steals the common from off the goose.

Elite Networks of Arbitrage

From the third millennium BCE, there is written evidence in Mesopotamia of trade with Meluhha or Harappa. One of these pieces of evidence is an inscription of the ruler Gudea (*c.* 2144–2124 BCE) in the kingdom of Lagash in southern Mesopotamia stating that "the Meluhhans came up (or down) from their country" with timber and other materials for the construction of the main temple in the capital.[1] Much later, around the beginning of the fifth century BCE, numerous Chinese, Greek, and Roman visitors (as well as "armchair travelers") wrote about India; later still, many more such accounts came from Arabs, Central Asians, the Dutch, Italians, Portuguese, and other Europeans. Some of these texts conveyed a commercial perspective and intention, describing parts of the land and its riches in a tone of admiration tinged with envy. Early stories of gold and splendor referred to the naiveté of Indians and their casual attitude toward profits. Yet, at least a few Indians were undoubtedly active in the sale and purchase of merchandise for gain across vast distances. They and their overseas associates also established elaborate actor-networks that created long-lasting lingering legacies.[2]

Matching the dearth of conventional histories on the subcontinent, no chronicles survive of itinerants leaving India to seek fortunes elsewhere. But there must have been many travelers even as early as the mature Harappan period, judging by the rich evidence of Meluhhans (widely assumed to be from Harappa) having long-term contact with Mesopotamia. They exported raw materials and artifacts such as decorated carnelian beads, gold, ivory, shell, and wood to Mesopotamia. They also transported perishable items such as barley, cotton, textiles, and vegetable dyes and even set up a trading settlement along the Persian Gulf. There is no knowledge of what goods, if any, the Harappans got in return, but their exports might simply have been a form of tribute for strategic protection from the Mesopotamians. Other early long-distance trade networks likely waxed and waned with the changing global demand for luxury and prestige goods—but it is fairly certain that there was abundant exchange across sea and land in all the periods that followed.[3]

One theme of this chapter is that the political power of elite networks in the subcontinent, and elsewhere, rarely depended solely on internal factors. Across the world, state power in its many forms has for millennia been primarily in the hands of kings and oligarchs, who deployed the apparatus of government to maintain control. They also had to find ways to deploy the fiction of their vital and sole authority over a region. The concept of a territory and its people, as if they formed some sort of natural unity, was a hard-won fabrication that needed to be reestablished frequently to keep the political system well entrenched. The invention of kingship or sovereignty also required oligarchies to generate and capture surpluses in ever more expansive ways, even as pressures intensified to accumulate and protect resources while continuing to hold onto territory.

The domestic generation of surplus through control over revenues from agriculture and the capture of cultural capital in the form of religious sponsorship is often not sufficient means to keep the sovereign firmly in command over people in an extended region. The people must, after all, part with hard-earned taxes or fees of one sort or another to the sovereign, who may or may not keep his promise to offer protection from raiders and infrastructure in return. Ancient Egypt's hydraulic society, described in the previous chapter, was its archetype. But that also deployed a particularly ingenious mode of keeping the people captive to rhythmic processes operating from the court of the Pharaoh and depended critically on the geography of the Nile delta.

In an environment of competing elite claims on territoriality, an emergent outcome was increasing globalization, which required domestic elites to maintain relationships with other territorial powers, both to form alliances and to thwart rivals before they attacked. To sustain themselves over generations, locally significant elite networks needed to tap into and form alliances that had a global reach. As early as the Middle Kingdom, around 1800 BCE, exchange across the Mediterranean and over land were vital points of control to keep the regime secure. The proliferation of trade since then is a historical wonder. It turns out that not only can the sovereign add to his wealth, but the social processes generated by trade in merchandise can supplement the territorial ties of the sovereign to his people through patronage of certain groups and thereby help to enhance mutual regional and global connectivities and allied opportunities.[4]

Well into the Common Era in India, these developments were important not in the modern ideological sense of "nationhood" or "land"; many states were fluid, and their borders changed frequently, much like individual dynasties. But the *creed* of kingship—its symbolic power and its rules of succession and government—had to be firmly established, and so it was, to a degree, during the Dharma Yuga. At that time, the primary source of legitimacy for Indian modes of kingship was textual law, the arguments and discourses that justified a particular structure for the performances of kings, nobility, courts, and territorial rule. The Arthaśāstra generated the formal political structures of statehood and its law. The Dharmaśāstra established the civil code of household and societal law, having at its heart the varna system that fashioned enduring patterns of endogamy and hierarchy. That system undoubtedly took on different forms in different locations and social contexts. But it nevertheless legitimated the category of *jāti,* or birth name, the clan-based association that morphed into caste categories at a much later time.[5]

For several centuries, Buddhism and its allied nāstika or atheist religious practices remained a major disruption to the Brahmanical order, for which the increasingly strong system of clan-based separation had provided distinct advantages to dvija varna bloodlines. It was a disruption of tradition and not in the sense of direct attacks on the still inchoate kingdoms of Kuru-Panchala. In response, Brahmanism revamped itself as a territorial order by appropriating the rules of empire that were originally designed and developed out of Maurya successes, including the empire's Buddhist proselytism and administrative strategies. For Brahmanism, these conditions constituted an entirely new dispositif that became an extraordinarily powerful socializing force. This reorganization took place around the same time as the emergent production of Hinduism as a tradition through the Puranas, epics, and various legal texts: together they created the characteristic dual image of (1) dharmarājā (rightful kingship), following its proper rules, and (2) household harmony for the rest of humanity, which was to follow Grhya codes in the form of āśramas, or life stages.[6]

Along the way, non-Vedic traditions had also influenced and reshaped Brahmanism, and elite interlocking across these forms created new political alliances in urban centers around kings and their courts. But some of these included itinerant traditions with far less hierarchical and smaller groups of vagrants whose lyrical and expressive moments produced new forms of sociality around *bhakti* or devotion, which begat a far more personal and less officiated set of modes within Brahmanical societies. Together, both elite and popular alliances created social orders that were flexible and differently adapted in places as varied as Kanchipuram, Kaushambi, Madurai, Pataliputra, Taxila, and Ujjain. By extending their territorial influence and appropriating some of other traditions' practices, all the while becoming an extremely well-harmonized, mobile diasporic network, Brahmanism—frequently in some type of coalition or contestation with Buddhism, Jainism, Śaivism, and other heterodox practices—melded new political identities. As future kings sponsored sites of worship and thereby symbols of divine power, the old alliances between Kshatriya and Brahmin took on new forms that could invoke both historical and mythical partnerships.[7]

In conjunction with kingship and the household as sites of authority, trade functioned as a critical third leg that maintained the stability of elite networks by adding substantial new resources to them. Trade, as I point out, strengthened the sovereignty or territorial power of the king and his court by providing them tribute in the form of luxury goods with enormous symbolic value. But trade also promoted the exchange of mass goods that imitated luxuries, particularly in high demand during the latter part of the Roman Empire and about a millennium later in Europe.

Traders, as a group, were small groups of actors who created elite nodes built on geographical goods arbitrage. A note on the phrase "geographical goods arbitrage" is relevant here. Arbitrage is the use of price differences across relatively insulated markets for financial gain. It can also be thought of as a way to establish comparative value across dissimilar objects to form an appropriate basis for exchange. For instance, geographical arbitrage would describe a medieval merchant displaying Chinese silks in a market in Italy. In an arbitrage situation, at least one set of objects is typically unfamiliar to a local community of buyers, with whom the trader might want to exchange articles that they possess. The mediating figure in the trade is the merchant, who presents the novel entities to the buyer. The trader would be best positioned to know about both sets of artifacts, because only he or she has been in contact with sellers on the two sides.[8]

From their inception, trade groups and other commercial entities mainly peddled luxury and prestige goods, which helped create culturally recognizable patterns of distinction between the nobility and commoners. Over time, these patterns evolved into hierarchies by increasing the power and wealth of trading clans and their families who could build up their resources by controlling trade. Traders publicly flattered those in symbolic centers of power, mahārājās and bādshāhs, both meaning "great kings," in Sanskrit and Persian, respectively, and referred admiringly to their cosmopolitan grandeur. In so doing, they raised the profile of those individuals and profited from their pride and self-fashioning as having elevated status and right to might. But just as importantly, and also perhaps as early as in Harappa, they were connected to other local elite clusters of power: some were large and spread out, in the form of artisanal networks and landed gentry, and others were concentrated among money people and, potentially, those with access to means of violence. The resulting assemblages ended up generating various types of active services that captured rents, thereby bolstering elite networks in different ways.

It should be remembered that a large fraction of the subcontinent's population managed to escape the state's reach until very recently. Defections from the city and the farm would have been common (as they may have been in Harappa in the third millennium BCE), along with several other interruptions in the captive labor supply caused by drought, war, and political turmoil. In addition, territoriality did not always mean singular control in terms of having a monopoly over violence in every part of the land that was claimed as a rājya. Elite networks in this period may instead have found it useful to operate through a multiplicity of internally connected forms that crossed conventional militarily defended borders but were also linked in spatially noncontiguous but otherwise coupled units, usually involving urban centers. Sometime around the start of the Common Era, with increasing competition from other territorial powers and barbarians at the gate, these long-distance and mobile interactions became just as important as the land that elite networks claimed as territory.[9]

Exchange with groups that exceeded a face-to-face distance probably existed for a very long time. Initially, long-distance commerce was the unorganized, autonomous activity of individual travelers who mostly exchanged gifts with their kin in distant locations. Over time, these became time-honored informal arrangements for sharing items of prestige across communities; they then evolved into networks of trust. As routes lengthened and the volumes of transported material increased, merchant groups were established; they sought, or were forced to accept, protection from sovereign rulers and their military commanders for safe passage. Eventually, rulers worked with leaders among merchants and traders to build mutually beneficial institutions such as purchase guarantees and credit, which slowly evolved to form the modern trading system. The surplus generated from economic exchange that took place across extended geographies may have first been used to purchase luxury goods for elites, which they used to create both symbolic and material distinction from others. These embryonic processes may have had similar beginnings but yielded different effects in different parts of the world.

In India, adventurous merchant groups in Harappa in the third millennium BCE and those in post-Vedic societies two millennia later, during the second wave of urbanization, took early advantage of opportunities for arbitrage. Those merchants created a close-knit organizational structure of their investors and long-distance partners. In the Dharma Yuga and later, these groups were likely to be organized according to kin or endogamous jāti units. Windfall economic gains, particularly those secured by specific families within dominant jātis, had social impacts—emergent effects—that effectively built up institutions of secrecy, exclusive lines of credit, and the disbursement of protection funds. An elaborate patronage system developed to the detriment of those who were unconnected or poorly networked to corridors of power and highest prestige. This distinction between the unconnected and the connected deepened with elite trade networks and metamorphized into distinct syndromes that changed course over centuries.[10]

Trade as a Social Process

Perhaps no other traded good has had as transformative an impact on modern global social processes as cotton. The earliest evidence of the production of cotton appears in the form of traces of thread in copper beads in a bracelet in Mehrgarh from around 5000 BCE. In Mohenjo-daro and Harappa, cotton cloth was used along with wool and leather to make textiles. Independently in East Africa and Peru, cotton fishing nets and textile fragments from the third millennium BCE have been discovered. There is little evidence, however, that cotton fiber or cloth were traded in any significant volumes before the Common Era.

In the first millennium CE, cotton production and processing were virtually absent in Europe and the Americas, but were common in India, elsewhere in Southeast Asia, and in West Africa in small, peasant households whose output were very likely controlled by larger territorial powers. Arab merchants brought cotton fabrics and yarn to Europe before the birth of the second millennium, and several hundred years later, merchant companies were created to sustain a growing demand for this most useful of trade goods. Rents from cotton cultivation and cloth trade financed the African slave trade, which profited from the exchange of fiber as well as trade in cloths, with returns used by capitalists to fuel their growing industrialization. In the seventeenth and eighteenth centuries, slave traders sold volumes of Indian and British-made cotton cloth amounting to several million pounds sterling. Through processes of "extraversion," West African elites deployed themselves to pay for, and profit from, slaves transported across the Atlantic.

The political scientist Jean-Francois Bayart uses the term "extraversion" to interpret these emergent processes of local elite formation through interlocking across cultures that have unequal macrolevel power relations. He identifies strategies deployed by those who tried to secure power in the global metropolis. Agents in colonial African societies participated in multiple ways with external elites, creating a range of social effects in their own milieu as well as beyond. Nimble locals used coercion, deceit, and negotiation skills in their dealings with these outside actors, securing them positions of prestige and other advantages of entry into the broader world. In early colonial history, these alliances captured significant nodes of privilege, maintaining local satraps in power through a combination of violence and persuasion.

Over time, and across diverse societies, these groups developed into extensive networks of influence and exchange, often negotiated over large distances, bound by formal and informal contracts so obscure that the actual operations of political authority and control could be nearly impossible to detect.[11]

Extraversion, in more general terms, involves the maturation and practices of elites in different situations, as they reach across their own positions and localities of power to other levels and political scales to secure additional resources and thereby bolster their hold over domestic groups. Similar conditions prevail in many contexts, revealing complex deals among a dizzying array of political constituencies, party representatives, and other elites, which often involve local leaders exchanging favors with groups elsewhere. These alliances tend to have a variety of emergent forms of elite consolidation both in the colonies and the metropolis, where the interests of particular inner-circle social agents in control at different sites tend to dominate.[12]

In the early eighteenth century in Britain, which was beginning to shape itself as a global state power in conjunction with merchant and military elites, a domestic war broke out between textile interests and upstart elite networks of merchants and traders. This led to the Calico Act of 1720, in which the British government banned textile imports. It spawned the Industrial Revolution, an emergent assemblage with entirely new social forces that elite interests adapted to, seeking new rents from state and local "protection rackets," which demanded control and compensation for more than safe passage, but also changes in legislation for elite customers and special dispensation for violence when necessary.[13]

In the eighteenth century, European colonial expansion was fueled by a "war capitalist" class of elites, comprising a mix of sovereign courts, merchants and bankers, planters and cultivators, and shipbuilders. Together, they saw the opportunity for windfall wealth and income generation, finding it in their strategic interest to collaborate and create elaborate global protection networks, first through coercion and then by generating consent. Much like rice and other grain cultivation gave an opportunity for elite networks to invent the territorial state, the political ecology of cotton—its web of power relations with land and ecosystems, surplus formation and labor, and law, its dispositif—too may have first established the global reach of what the historian Sven Beckert terms "war" or "empire's" capital: "War capitalism flourished not in the factory but in the field; it was not mechanized but land- and labor-intensive, resting on the violent expropriation of land and labor in Africa and the Americas.... At its core was slavery."[14]

The modern state and especially the newly minted limited corporation were the first set of interlocking oligarchies that created stability for sovereign power and rents through protectionism for special classes of merchants. In return for military protection, property rights were ensured even while territorial power found new routes to expand its empire's capital through trade networks and proxies before formally annexing other lands. These processes of capitalism gained momentum, with the elite's creation of rents increasing proportionately with the expansion of slavery until it peaked in 1860, when the US Census tabulated nearly four million slaves in two thirds of its counties. These sudden and dramatic changes were made possible by unleashing violence on the laboring masses; these very institutions made up some of the new forces of the changing face of capitalism.[15] Significantly, this was also the emergence of a new paradigm, what the political theorist George Kateb and others have termed a revolutionary democratic ethic of "American individuality," a paradigm marked by naturalists and other solo ruminations over freedom and equality but also deep separateness.[16]

Over the longue durée, similarly mobile and long-distance assemblages in formation have characterized other types of trade. Anthropologists and historians studying trading practices generally agree that the exchange of material goods across communities is a complex phenomenon that has multiple meanings across time and place. Most forms of consensual exchange seem to fall into two distinct patterns: gift-giving or trade. Exchange of gifts is usually not reciprocal in a formal sense but instead builds up a culture of meanings around solidarity, community, and status. Gift-giving is replete with the symbolism of power and hierarchy, with implicit meanings of what the appropriate size and quality a gift is allowed to be before it becomes an insult to give or accept it, how frequently it should be exchanged or on what occasions it should not be given, what objects can be regifted, when it disrupts social distinctions and when it maintains them, and so on.[17]

When viewed from a contemporary market lens, long-distance trade seems much more straightforward, because it implies exchange principally on the basis of geographical arbitrage—and traveling merchants would always be at an advantage because they would "know the price of lemons." George Akerlof, Joseph Stiglitz, and other economists studying informational asymmetry have pointed out that market distortions, collapse, and windfall profits are all possible outcomes when sellers of goods have substantially more knowledge about their products than do the buyers. In used-car markets, for example, sellers seem to want to push "lemons," or cars known by their previous owners to be beset with particular problems. In a similar way, traders might, initially at least, have the bad reputation of being shady travelers who routinely rip off customers of exotic goods, such as Chinese silks, Persian carpets, and Scottish wool, whose "true" value would always be in question. Over time and through repeated transactions, the likelihood of lemons persisting in the market may decline, but sellers thrive on benefiting from having superior knowledge of their wares.[18]

According to archaeological evidence, different exchange strategies may have been at work in a given site, and sometimes a given culture engaged in several forms. In Neolithic and Chalcolithic contexts, physical space was generally not set aside in urban settings for marketplaces, which probably became routine only in later periods. One of the earliest forms of evidence for large volumes of trade in prehistory comes from ancient Egypt and the Levant. Around 2300 BCE, the port of Byblos in present-day Lebanon, at that time an Egyptian colony, harbored large ships more than 100 feet in length carrying goods such as papyrus, cedar, glass, and silver, gold, and other jewelry. Egyptian trade was initially with the Canaanites, people living along the Levantine coast. Whereas Egyptian trade was centralized and controlled directly by the pharaoh, the Canaanites were organized as networked or independent family businesses. Significantly, all three modes—controlled directly by the inner circle in the state or kingdom, multiple elite interlocking networks, or loosely disconnected, small-volume traders—but especially the last two, involved forms of tribute, in the form of material luxury goods, that helped establish (symbolic) prestige and thereby differentiated elites from commoners. As the rarity and prestige of the transported goods increased, the need for sovereign protection along vulnerable points of the goods' routes also grew.[19]

In Chapter 4, I drew attention to the importance of trade in Harappa. The bulk of Harappan trade was, in fact, domestic, with raw materials such as stones and metals, including copper and tin, being transported long distances to factories in urban centers. Most of these materials were obtained within the vast Harappan region. Sometimes, however, they were also sourced from farther away: jade came from Tibet, tin from Afghanistan and Uzbekistan, and bronze from Iran. The Harappan case suggests that elite dominance in trade networks—their ability to control the exchange of goods across long distances—was essential for maintaining domestic order. But premodern systems of trade had to rely on generating substantial value from multiple relationships across long distances, which were expensive to maintain. Shereen Ratnagar points to the use of Harappan microweights in Mesopotamia, which is possibly an indication that there was high-value trade whose revenues (possibly in perishable items, since no other evidence of goods from Mesopotamia has survived) were sufficient to offset the costs of maintaining the vast enterprise.[20]

It is helpful to characterize early forms of exchange of goods, especially across long distances, as operating in at least three registers. In one, wandering artisans developed new connections in foreign lands that grew into enduring relationships over time. These patterns of trade were often diffuse, without authoritative forms of organization, and sometimes had the ritual qualities of the reciprocal exchange of gift-giving. Gifts of this form were treated as tribute to elites in some circumstances and were transformed into tariffs and customs duties in early imperial states. Another mode of exchange emerged with the accumulation of economic surpluses and the rise of elite groups that controlled the redistribution of objects. Such exchange has generally operated under contracts and prestige, with relatively neutral ports of trade not under the control of any particular group. Until the present day, an important supplemental feature of this mode of exchange has been the exchange of women and slaves across long distances, with dowries disguised as gift-giving. Altogether, these practices built and sealed relationships among family elders, the propertied patriarchs in the polity. A third set of transactions has been the organized and familiar form of systemic movement of goods across established trade routes, such as the famed Silk Road. In this mode, ports also acquired some sort of neutrality among competing interests; in many cases these ports became the loci of some of the well-known independent city-states of the ancient and medieval world.

The movement of these social processes can be interpreted as a series of epigenetic processes involving transitions over millennia. The shifts from small group societies engaging in artisanal exchange, even over relatively long distances, to the more organized Egyptian and Harappan styles of systematized trade networks may have taken place across different junctures in their respective locations. Early social structures of foragers, forest-farmers, and hunters were mostly egalitarian, but as big men and chiefs found it productive to capture rents and form capital by accumulating them, urbanization and intensification of agriculture created their own dynamics after around 8000 BCE.

The earliest dynasties of large territorial extent were in Egypt and China, roughly simultaneously in the third millennium BCE. The template of "emperor" and his (or, very rarely, "her") entourage and rules of succession was remarkably stable and widely replicated across the world for another five millennia or so, until just a century or so ago. Courtly elites established marriage alliances over greater distances, carried out ritual feasting, and eventually created stable elite networks to institute secondary settlements, city-states, property relations, and so on. Irrigation, including rights over water in water-scarce regions, reduced the number of women and men needed for farming; those workers made redundant became specialized craftworkers for making textiles, precious stone jewelry, and later metal implements, including armaments. Rivers not only were used as shipping channels but also provided water for irrigation. Long-distance trade mostly involved raw materials and luxury goods, whereas over medium distances, the exchange of animals, cloths, and grain for consumption by commoners was the norm.[21]

The formation of states created both problematic and supportive conditions for merchant and trade actors. First through systems of tribute with sovereign elites, itinerant traders found opportunities to expand their business. But these were fraught with dangers, since rival interlocking elite networks eventually developed to mobilize resources or to capture territory through piracy on the high seas or raids on neighbors. In doing so, sovereign power was consolidated to leverage resources to conduct trade on its own terms (as was the case in its earliest known instance during the Egyptian Middle Kingdom).

In each region and period, a variety of factors drove the pace of these epigenetic processes. Climatological evidence, for instance, suggests that unusual flooding or riverways that dried up forced trade networks to reroute their transports, shrink, or even collapse. Sometimes, innovation took place as a result of technological change, war, or demographic shifts that helped expand trade volumes while creating vastly unequal advantages across groups. Strategic positions in prime agricultural land or along navigable rivers and natural ports could create similar conditions, providing occupiers what in present-day terms would be called "property rights" but were in fact protection rents. With rising surpluses, official governmental positions were created and generated territorial law. Resolution of conflicts among rivals around piracy also reinforced territorial stability. Traders accumulated rents, formed levels of prominence, and gained internal connectivity. In India and elsewhere in Eurasia, when organized into guilds, traders and merchants tended to remain independent of polities but clearly were also codependent on both rulers in strategic urban centers and market towns and monastic complexes that had the advantages of having local connections in faraway places. Buddhist monasteries were important rest houses for travelers, at least since the time of Aśoka. Over time, bazaars grew around them and became reputable centers of commerce.[22]

Trade in the late Vedic period may have been modest, involving the transport of salt and iron along water routes or on land along river valleys. The rise of Magadha brought about the imperial control of trade routes not only for strategic materials, such as iron implements and armaments, but also for other goods along major rivers to the coast. By the first century CE, trade was fairly extensive, with the transport of manufactured goods and people crisscrossing vast parts of Eurasia by land and sea. Arab sailors had long understood the importance of the seasonal reversal of winds in the Arabian Sea. The word "monsoon" comes from the Arabic *mawsim*, which means "season" but was also used to indicate a "sailing season": the period from July to September when winds are favorable to making quick progress sailing toward the West Coast of India, while the remaining months favored travel in the opposite direction.

In addition to manufactured goods and raw materials, trade in animals, bullion, and slaves began to take on importance, with ports becoming active markets for trade across various territorial entities. In India, there were five major exporting regions having a substantial hinterland—the Indus delta; Gujarat and Kutch and parts of Madhya Pradesh; the Malabar coast; the Coromandel coast; and the Ganges delta. The prominent luxury goods from India around the beginning of the Common Era were cinnamon and pepper, although the latter was imported in such large qualities that it almost became a staple among respectable Roman households. In addition to spices, aromatic substances, drugs, and ointments were in high demand. Trade with Rome became so significant in this period that several ambassadors from both northern and southern India showed up at the court of Emperor Augustus to negotiate prices and protection for safe passage.[23]

This period was also marked by increasingly rigid Brahmanical strictures on varna purity that came into conflict with trade practices, primarily commensality, the act of eating together, an indispensable habit for merchants and travelers. Buddhist and Jain travelers were not affected by this concern with rules against commensality, or contact through sitting with non-dvijas or mlecchas, even if they both refrained from eating meat. Many merchant communities consisted of Jains, whose vegetarianism was tied to their strictures against violence to life forms. Early Brahmanical texts nevertheless gave trade a sanctioned place in occupations, which provided some jātis at least partial relief from restrictions on travel and contact with others without violating rules of purity. Initially merchants provided only modest patronage for monasteries and temple complexes, but that changed later in the millennium, when economic rents were substantially reinvested in their upkeep and expansion. These guilds (*shreni*) had roots at least as early as the Mauryan period and were possibly linked to networks of Buddhist monasteries along the Silk Road. The Gupta period favored the growth of shreni of artisans, bankers, and traders, who collectively acted as agents—or important nodes of networked elite power—managing towns far from the imperial capitals.[24]

In the third century, Roman commercial activity in Asia was in decline, but Arab merchants expanded Red Sea routes along which to trade spices from southern India, even as Southeast Asian and Chinese traders also increased their activity. As a consequence, the Bay of Bengal and the southern ports of Arikamedu, Cranganore, Mantai, and Muziris gained prominence. Overland trade across the Hindu Kush into the Indus Valley was also on the rise because of the growing importance of the Silk Road trade with China. Indians too had discovered Southeast Asia as a site for pepper supplies to be sent to Rome. When Indian merchants moved into Southeast Asian chiefdoms, which showed remarkable similarities to those in India, those polities with reciprocal systems of exchange were radically transformed. The new elites in the region became clients for agate, carnelian, bronze jewelry, cotton fabrics, and pepper, as well as Buddhist and Hindu idols. Over time, it was the enormous surpluses created from the Bay of Bengal trade that bolstered Chola kingdoms for several centuries in South India. Malay sailors were also adept in using monsoon winds to navigate their way to the Indian subcontinent, carrying cinnamon as far as the East African coast.[25]

Trade as Courtesy: The Rise of the Mercantile Bourgeoisie

Cotton fabrics from India were highly valued in China in the sixth century CE. Exchange with China had taken place at least since the start of the Common Era, but there is evidence that a Gupta king (most likely, Narasimhagupta) sent his emissaries from Magadha to the court of the Liang emperor Wu in 503, presenting him with cotton textiles, incense, and perfume. China's strategic significance from the first millennium in the Common Era onward stemmed from its becoming a power pole at a sufficient distance from Rome and yet having relatively stable land and sea trade routes with it.

These advantages allowed sovereign elites charting trade routes to China to demand protection rents from monetary exchanges, enhance their accumulation of symbolic capital through the acquisition of symbolic luxury goods, and create a complex hierarchy of patrimonial connections. India's central location, its own production of prestige items, and its burgeoning urban economies were soon to become critical resources for interlocking elite networks. The opening up of trade both to the east and west provided royal families and their urbanizing hinterlands unique opportunities to make global connections and hoard economic and cultural capital. It also generated a growing demand for luxury goods from courtiers, wealthy landholders, administrative elites, and the merchants themselves, while leading to the establishment of trading towns and ports.[26]

In the first millennium of the Common Era, the political and cultural map of India was quite variegated, with rājyas emerging in all parts of the subcontinent: in contrast to earlier periods, these states were centered around cities that played strategic roles in long-distance trade. Social relations were influenced by spatial networks beyond face-to-face interaction through production and trade involving the exchange of goods and also of women, although the latter frequently followed strict jāti bloodlines. In due course, the expansion of marine routes, particularly in south India, produced new sources of wealth and prestige.

Toward the end of the first millennium, Buddhism waned as a state religion everywhere and soon disappeared from view as a religious practice outside of some monasteries and followers. The last elite patron of Buddhism was Dharampala in the eighth and ninth centuries CE, who ruled over the Pala territory in eastern India. Among the Palas as well as the neighboring Raśtrakutas, Hoysalas, Chalukyas, and several other dynasties, religious patronage was typically inclusive across different traditions. Throughout the first millennium and for much of the second, patron kings also had shifting alliances with Jainism, Saivism, and Vaishnavism, evidenced in the same shrines at times. Jainism prospered in Karnataka, but elsewhere in the southern peninsula, it declined drastically and sometimes violently through battles waged by Pallava and Pandya kings. Islam arrived on the west coast of India through Arab traders and elsewhere in the second millennium after the conquest of lands by Mahmud of Ghazni and other Turkic successors from Central Asia.[27]

Patronage, the superior ability to bestow goods across a populace, was a key element in the growth of trade. It was typically organized in a syndicated way to extract and exchange favors. Wealthy merchants were able to consolidate territorial claims through their networks in strategic places. Often, this meant engaging violently with competing groups and local peoples. Between the seventh and thirteenth centuries, landed groups in the large river basins of south India were supported by Pallava and Chola regimes to form sizable rural settlements around agriculture. Artisans were initially subservient to the agriculturalists, but as trade expanded under the Cholas, their power and prestige grew substantially. They organized into merchant guilds, which became monopolies within their territories and gained control over landholdings, temple finances, the collection of taxes for the king, and local administration.

Under the Chalukyas of Badami, the Ayyavolu Lords, known initially as a group of 500 traders, made substantial endowments to temples between the ninth and fourteenth centuries and extolled in writing their own good qualities and trading successes in flamboyant style. Other itinerant merchants and their guilds left similarly potent messages for posterity. Traders were increasingly cosmopolitan in their outlook, many leaving inscriptions in multiple languages, including Arabic, Hebrew, and Persian.[28]

So influential did some merchant and trading groups in South India become that even the powerful Chola kings could not control them directly. In the Pallava period, before Chola rule, administrative units called *nagarams* formed around spatial clusters, each denoting both a place and its assembly of administrators. Mostly these units were made up of groups of artisans, farmers, fishermen, and local merchants. Over time, merchant groups (*vyaparigal*) grew in prestige and had increasing control over the nagarams, which became the principal redistribution centers for prestige and luxury goods secured by long-distance trade. The sites of Kanchipuram and Māmallaparam were *mahanagarams* (grand nagarams), the latter becoming a major port for trade with Southeast Asia. Temple endowments grew as a result of multiple sources of funding; initially only the king had provided grants but later temples were supported by members of the laity. Most *vyapari nagarams* (mercantile organizations) gained control of their finances, both collecting revenue and disbursing loans to artisans and merchants. Artisanal groups, particularly weavers, grew in strength and size in south India, and a special class of cloth merchants, *saliya-nagattar,* formed their own professional organizations.[29]

Traders and merchant groups were also ascendant in other parts of India, especially around Gujarat and Rajasthan. Kanchipuram, Kashi, Mathura, Pataliputra, and Taxila had been centers of commerce since antiquity, but many more, such as Bhuj, Kozhikode, Madurai, and Surat, became prominent commercial centers as well. Urban cultures became more important in the Gupta period: by this time south Indian cities of great glory, such as Madurai and Kanchipuram, were taking center stage for temple construction and commerce. The rise of trading towns across the subcontinent may have created a shift in the occupations of local populations, who became more dependent on trade. Meanwhile, the increased surpluses accumulated by merchants and traders drew new groups of marauders, pillagers, and pirates whose regulation required the intervention of the state.[30]

By the end of the first millennium, shipowners and large merchant groups were busily trading all along the shores of the Indian Ocean. In the southern Mediterranean and on the east coast of Africa and Yemen, major business conglomerates were formed with counterparts in Gujarat and South India.

The so-called Geniza papers located in an old Cairo synagogue illustrate the internal structure of hundreds of merchant families and their trading relationships. Shipping involved making high and risky initial investments, which only few government officials and wealthy businessmen could afford. The Joseph Lebdi family near Tripoli amassed enormous wealth, beginning in the eleventh century, after making several arduous trips to India carrying copper and corals and returning with spices and textiles. Similarly, a twelfth-century Jewish merchant known as Mamdun was the representative of merchants in Aden, as well as being the official head of Yemenite Jewry. The archivists S. D. Gotein and Mordechai Friedman write, "Mamdun was further styled 'confidant of the lords of the seas and the deserts,' which means that he had made agreements with the various rulers and pirates who controlled the sea routes between Egypt, Arabia, Africa and India, as well as those chieftains who held sway over the hinterland of the south-Arabian ports."[31]

On the eastern side of the Indian Ocean, Arab vessels and ships from the Cholas in South India were plying the islands of Malaya and Indonesia, transporting timber, ivory, and other raw materials as luxuries from the east coast of Africa and spices and cloth from the coasts of India, in return for silk from China. Guarding the straits of Malacca and collecting tolls for passage was the powerful kingdom of Srivijaya, which was defeated by Rājendra Chola in 1025, who along with his son, Rājādhirāja Chola, controlled critical ports in the Bay of Bengal and Southeast Asia. In subsequent centuries, Chinese ships were larger and faster; they also had improved technologies, including devices such as magnetic compasses and watertight compartments. From 1405 to 1433, the Ming emperor sent seven massive maritime expeditions, some with as many as 25,000 men, to Aden and elsewhere in East Africa. The voyages stopped in 1433 possibly because of political rivalry in the court of the emperor after his death in 1424. The rise of rival Confucian groups may have led to opposition to overseas trade because of the defeated faction's enormous wealth generated by disreputable dealings. Future emperors did not favor overseas trade for several centuries; the Qing court of Shunzi suspended it altogether in 1655. Meanwhile, European powers, particularly Portugal and Spain, improved their naval capabilities substantially and began sponsoring long-distance expeditions.[32]

In the fifteenth century, Gujarati ships were already leaving Surat on regular voyages to the Spice Islands and had robust trade networks in Malacca and other ports. Trading agents, who were collectively termed *banias,* were active in many roles. Banias belonged to different jāti lines and played a critical brokerage role while also engaging in their own long-distance trading activity. Those banias who belonged to dvija birth lines were active as financiers and brokers but were prevented by dharma rules against commensality (eating together in groups) from boarding Muslim ships at will. Instead, they mostly pursued moneylending; banking; and trading in commodities such as clothing, ghee, grain, grocery, jewelry, and spices while carefully avoiding polluting substances. Still, they built arrangements with merchants extending well into Hainan in South China, and many received permission from their jāti leaders to conduct business overseas without violating commensal rules. Ships frequently carried a cosmopolitan crew of Muslim Arabs, Gujaratis, and Turks, transporting—to Malacca and the vicinity—Gujarati cloths along with carpets, seeds and grains, incense, and opium sourced locally or elsewhere on the subcontinent. Returning ships mainly carried cloves, nutmeg, and mace, along with camphor, gold, and sandalwood. Surat became a prosperous entrepôt and was an attractive site of territorial interest. In 1664, the Maratha king, Shivaji, raided Surat, which was a part of Mughal territory, but did not occupy it. Instead, his army simply carried back substantial loot to its base in the Deccan, inviting the ire and retaliation of Emperor Aurangzeb. In a few decades, Surat's importance waned significantly when merchants were offered protection from Mughal and Maratha interference by the newly formed East India Company, then headquartered in Bombay.

By the sixteenth and seventeenth centuries, the total volume of trade in the Indian Ocean had increased substantially, benefiting Portuguese, Arab, Jewish, Indian, and Southeast Asian traders. The bulk of the commodities were sourced from India and China by this time. Because Chinese foreign trade was limited due to its anticommercial domestic policy, Indian traders dominated the textile business, amassing substantial fortunes and also becoming powerful enough to manage domestic political interests. The historians Christopher Bayly and Sanjay Subrahmanyam use the term "portfolio capitalists" to describe a special type of merchant, not dissimilar from Lebdi and Mamdun mentioned earlier, who mobilized substantial financial and military resources, diversified their fortunes geographically, and maintained effective control over vast territory and mobile networks. One such portfolio capitalist, the seventeenth-century merchant prince Muhammad Sayyid, had direct contact with both the Mughal prince Aurangzeb and the Safayid Shah in Isfahan; he also served as vizier in the court of the sultan of Golconda in the Deccan until he defected to join the Mughal emperor.[33]

The "salt spray" of marine trade landed concurrently in the East and West Indies, with new commercial enterprises and forms of farming that were directly or indirectly managed by the increasingly sophisticated elite networks involving colonizer and colonized, each operating at multiple registers and involving varied agents of material and symbolic life. Once the growth in the intensity and volume of Eurasian and American trade began to quicken, sometime at the end of the seventeenth century but most pronounced in the late eighteenth and beyond, it began to be clear that European naval power had attained global ascendance. This resulted in a proliferation of ports, trading networks, and newly organized forms of production of tradable goods in specialized sectors in the colonies. But there were not only European actors in these elite networks. In the subcontinent, shipowners and big merchants started collaborating in the sixteenth century under the patronage and protection of the Mughal court. In 1700, Asia was a leading global center of artisanship and associated manufactures, and it dominated world trade, befitting its holding more than two-thirds of the global population and its elites earning the bulk of global silver bullion in circulation.

By the late eighteenth and early nineteenth centuries, European military and strategic territorial supremacy enabled it to become the dominant trade network, displacing inter-Asian trade, even as it became institutionalized as colonial governments thereafter. Entirely new cultures of "coloniality" were established, which were dispositifs of instrumental knowledge creation, extractive capitalism, disciplinary patterns of government, and ideologies of racial and cultural dominance. These syndromes of elite network power changed the course of human and material interchange forever. If their beginnings were modest, the enmeshed expansion of the corporation and the trading colony was soon unprecedented. For instance, in the Caribbean, where industrial-scale sugarcane production achieved early success, complex elite actor-networks were formed of sovereign officials, merchants, slave traders, church leaders, and plantation owners, among others. Collectively, they sought and garnered high rents in both material and symbolic terms, fueled by a steady stream of forced migrant and slave labor working in grueling conditions. Such tales took on different forms across the globe, while changing conditions within Europe itself.

It is therefore useful to review briefly the longue durée of Europe to understand the formation of the new economic regime that we now term "mercantile capitalism." With the development of the Christian-sovereign nexus of the Roman Empire by the fifth century CE, a distributed elite network of papal and kingly power began to take shape across Western Europe. Despite several internal skirmishes between the Vatican and courts in England, France, and Germany, a stable legal regime made up of sovereign and disciplinary power was built up across the continent. Feudal institutions providing privileged legal status for aristocracies were an important part of this regime. A huge gulf was thereby created between peasants and the few men endowed with political authority and power to appropriate surplus, even though the former could make certain historical claims to the land. But what really accelerated trade volumes and began to change the character of elite networks forever was a new set of rules around the enclosure of commons, which started to become prominent in England in the sixteenth century.[34]

Peri-Cene: The Extended Urbanization of Planetary Elites

Between 1500 and 2000, there was a dramatic increase in cropland, pasture, and built-up land, occupying more than half the total area of the land mass on earth and complemented by a loss of more than one-fourth of all forests.[35] Agriculture alone took up more than 30 percent of land cover, with increasing discussion around the turn of the third millennium that even that might not be sufficient to feed everyone. Population increases in the twentieth century were rapid enough to warrant such a concern, rising from 1.6 billion people in 1900 to more than 6 billion in 2000. Urban areas covered more than one-quarter of the total land and influenced areas well beyond cityscapes through telecommunication and roads.[36]

These changes were accompanied by the intensification of capital and labor flows across the world; the extraction of enormous volumes of minerals, timber, and other primary commodities from the face of the earth; and the construction, particularly in the twentieth century, of tens of millions of miles of transportation networks. Perhaps most significant among these changes was the extraction of fossil fuels, or trapped hydrocarbon resources, from the bowels of the earth and their combustion in engines, which released hundreds of billions of tons of carbon dioxide into the atmosphere. Between around 1870 and 2020, the average atmospheric concentration of carbon dioxide increased from about 280–415 parts per million. Most of the increase came from those regions of the world that had the highest levels of industrial activity during this period. It is important to note that the finance capital to kick-start industrialization came from rents from land, both domestic and overseas, combined with arbitrage gains from trade.

Enclosures were created centuries before the birth of capitalism, as part of an inchoate interest in providing philosophical justification or a jurisprudence for the institution of private property. Manorial enclosure began in the thirteenth century in England, through the Statute of Merton, a charter that allowed the lord of the manor to name, mark out, and keep track of various parts of his fluid and hitherto uncharted lands as bogs, common fields, forests, heaths, and woods and enclose them if needed. The claimed purpose was that this provided non-enclosed lands as common pasture for the village. Manorial land, also called estates, had at least three designations. *Demesne* land was the best land, which was attached to the manor and controlled by the lord; "customary" tenants, or bondmen or serfs of the lord, operated *villein* land; and *free* land was available for cultivators to use after providing the lord a fee (later called rent).[37]

This situation was about to change even further. By the fourteenth century, *villein* land was termed a "copyhold," acknowledging the customary continuation of tenant families, and so a notional view of property was born, even though it was still under the lord's will. Estates began pushing out those peasants who farmed on strips of land, replacing them with sheep. The initial process began through Tudor enclosures. With the growing demand for wool, the common pasture land created by manorial enclosures was carved up and kept away from commoners for farming or pasture. "Improvement" was the justification, and the lord could invoke the Statute of Merton to that effect.

Although enclosures caused greater hardship in some areas than in others, a growing demand for land meant a rise in food prices because more land was being diverted to pasture, even as wool cloth exports to Europe were on the rise. Enclosures caused widespread pain to the peasantry in other ways as well. In 1611, when 200 peasants in a few villages of Buckinghamshire were threatened with the loss of their commons by its enclosure, they lamented they would "be utterly undone and have small or no means to relieve themselves."[38] Peasants sometimes squatted on forestlands and formed motley communities, thereby becoming "villains" (derived from *villein*) feared and despised for their disorderly behavior, crime, and utter poverty. With rising social tensions and a growing population, Parliament enacted laws both to limit enclosures and at the same time to criminalize as vagrants those peasants who were rendered homeless.

Crown lands under the Tudors in the sixteenth century were larger than they had ever been and needed a complex administrative apparatus to survey and manage them: the office of surveyors and its allied agencies that collected revenues were the basis of later bureaucratic machinery. As the Crown and duchies vastly expanded the lands under their jurisdiction, they also grew their wealth to extraordinary levels, although much of it was used up to finance costly wars with Scotland and France. The combination of the increasing concentration of wealth in the hands of the aristocracy and the growing centralization of state power had several outcomes. First, tenants, rather than smallholding peasants, were primarily the ones working the land. Second, tenant farmers had to engage in intense competition with each other to ensure they got the highest possible prices for their produce in the market and thereby would be able to pay their leases. In the late seventeenth century, the philosopher John Locke could justify enclosures by referring to the former common lands as waste, which had been improved on through labor and their productivity thereby increased (measured in output per unit of work). Exclusionary rights over land helped clear up disputes over common and customary rights and yet could be defended as adding more value to the common stock than it removed.[39]

In the seventeenth and eighteenth centuries, the development of private property law led to the creation of new forms of ownership. The provision of charters to regulated and joint stock corporations created legal rights not just for individuals but also for constituted entities to hold onto property in perpetuity. Each of the rising powers in Europe took different routes to expanding trade. Until the late sixteenth century, the Portuguese and French Crown directly financed and operated trading ventures and also took the profits. The Spanish Crown used the Council of the Indies and the monopoly of Seville merchants to control trade in the Americas. English ventures were crown-sanctioned acts of piracy, before the growing elite interest in trade led to the formation of the East India Company in 1600, around the same time as the Dutch formed a similar joint stock corporation. Because labor was deemed a form of property around this time, slavery was thereby absolved of its moral problem. A slave became someone dependent solely on his or her "owner" for protection. As the sociologist Orlando Patterson writes, "The slave was a slave, not because he was the object of property, but because he could not be the subject of property."[40] The very institution of slavery was coeval with a regime of personhood and rights (including those over property), even as it took away those same legal attributes from a certain class of persons on the basis of their defined or perceived characteristics.

When the East India Company was formed, Akbar was ruling over a vast Mughal Empire in India. The emperor had recently annexed a powerful rival in Gujarat, which provided his regime with both massive agricultural revenues and control over the sea trade that had recently been established with the Portuguese. India became a net importer of precious metals, in exchange for trade in spices and textiles, among various other products that were being sought as luxury goods in Europe. Akbar's court was famous for its cosmopolitan outlook, which established just the right conditions for building a close circle of trust with the Hindu and Muslim nobility, while employing a large number of Europeans. A non-inheritable system of ranks (*mansab*) was used to give officers of the military and administration a source of remuneration based on how much revenue they collected from assigned areas of land. A large part of this revenue went into maintaining armed forces. Sometimes, rājās were designated as these rank holders (*mansabdar*) and continued their hereditary practice, but as a social class, they formed the landed nobility. Akbar's efforts to professionalize state administration paralleled those that were taking place in Europe, but the system of tribute that the Mughal Empire's satraps and junior nobles had to pay the emperor was quite distinct. It involved accurate measurement of fields and assessment of returns over ten years. In addition, new markets for agricultural produce were encouraged, and a single currency economy was introduced into the subcontinent. In other ways, Akbar's ecumenical regime resembled his predecessor of nearly two millennia earlier, Aśoka: their fusion of views and practices appeared both to build broader coalitions promulgating syncretic views and creating secure commitments for their empires.[41]

The East India Company was founded by about two hundred men, most of whom were merchants and aldermen, and it began quite small. It was chartered as a joint stock company to enjoy monopoly trade over the Indian Ocean, with half the proceeds guaranteed to the English Crown. Its initial efforts in South Asia focused on the pepper trade from the Spice Islands (Malaku) in the Indonesian archipelago. The turbulent regime of Charles I and the ensuing English civil war was a difficult period for the company, but it grew rapidly in the late seventeenth century after it renewed its charter with the protectorate of Cromwell, which was ratified by Charles II. By the mid-eighteenth century, it had vastly increased in power and enlarged its stockholders to include several members of Parliament; it imported spices, teas, textiles, and other goods worth nearly a million pounds, while posing hardly any threat to local powers. Textile trading stations and factories expanded to cover vast parts of the subcontinent, with administrative clusters known as presidencies emerging in Madras, Bombay, and Calcutta. In the colonies, each presidency had its own hierarchy, with wealth accumulation growing dramatically up the ladder.[42] Twenty-four men in London known as the Court of Directors wrote and implemented the company's rules on finances, operations, and membership in the Court, which was passed from father to son.

By the end of the seventeenth century, the power of the Mughals had diminished relative to regional states, in part because Akbar's mansab system had expanded its ranks and the influx of silver from the Americas had reduced the value of bullion. As a result, the actual income of the rank holders fell substantially. A perception of greater uncertainty in India caused many rājās and former mansab rank holders to realign their fates with the East India Company's strategies. In parallel, to mitigate its risk, the Company began to develop new relations with regional powers, as well as the home government in London. Yet, even before this time, Muslim, Parsi, Hindu, and Jain merchants in Bombay and Surat, as well as Marwari groups in Calcutta, had served as agents for the company. In Madras, *dubashis* (or translators) became the prominent agents for the company; they also came from a variety of backgrounds in the area, but soon consolidated their positions to maintain their brokerage privileges within their families. Over time, some dubashis rose to great prominence, like Ananda Ranga Pillai, dubash to Joseph Francois Dupleix, the French governor general of India, and Venkata

Rama Rao, dubash to Robert Hughes, the collector of Guntur. Both were of high social standing, the first from a Vellalar jāti merchant family in Madras and the second a Deśasth Brahmin of Marathi origin.[43]

In some ways, the East India Company's rent-seeking ventures in India fit right into prevailing patterns of exchange and accumulation in the Indian Ocean. Yet, its expansionist practices, Enlightenment reasoning, and heavily instrumental vision of commerce were at odds with established forms of exchange, tribute, and associated power relations. Those differences resulted as much in conflict as in re-appropriation and amalgamation among distinct elite cultures. But in the final analysis, these assemblages took shape through their interlocking with elite networks of company officials, local rājās, trading groups and merchants, priestly classes, and the Mughal court. In broad schematic terms, one might call these developments the rise of the Indian bourgeoisie. Much of the driving force came from an aggressive company-led regime that became increasingly compelled to generate a "permanent settlement" around a colonial vision of economism replacing more syncretic exchange relations. Nevertheless, and this is the key point to note, local elite networks refashioned their own institutions to conform with this vision and join forces with the colonialists, making remarkable gains for themselves that were almost at par with those of company leaders.[44]

Christopher Bayly describes eighteenth-century northern India after the annexation of Bengal as characterized by distinct modes of conflict and social transformation centering on emerging opportunities for extraversion; at the same time local elites moved to extricate themselves from relations of traditional patronage with declining though still grand territorial Islamic empires, alongside the parallel and violent rise of mercantilist European power. The Mughal nobility, which for more than a century had built up great influence over merchant groups, administrators, and local satraps, was losing control in part because of the dilution of patronage from the court in Delhi with the rise of new merchant entrepreneurs, even as local landed interests were expanding their own power in exchange for support from the Mughal emperor to ward off territorial invasions from the Marathas and the Sikhs. By the 1780s, "burgeoning private trade and the ruthless creation of monopolies in tropical produce by the East India Companies had bitten deep into the wealth of coastal India. . . . In a sense Indian capital and expertise was drawn inexorably into a partnership with the alien invader."[45]

After the 1780s, when the East India Company defeated local rulers or made arrangements with them to gain administrative control over substantial areas of land in Bengal and Madras, the English government began paying closer attention to some of the company's employees' efforts to enrich themselves. Company officials had been engaging in private trade and making windfall profits from official transactions, much to the alarm of Parliament back home. A century earlier, in 1695, Parliament had initiated investigations of corruption regarding bribes at various levels, including to the attorney general and the solicitor general, regarding renewal of the company charter, as well as fraudulent contracts involving a large number of peers. In 1757, Robert Clive, the commander-in-chief of the company's forces, defeated the Nawab of Bengal and proceeded to loot vast amounts from the treasury, extort large amounts of private donations from the Bengal nobility, and engage in insider trading—practices that made him enormously rich along with several of his fellow company officers. It was primarily because of the peerage's snobbery and jealousy that a merchant was suddenly the richest man in the world that Parliament began hearings into his dealings in India, which finally vindicated him. At the end of the eighteenth century, Warren Hastings, the governor general of India was impeached on grounds of corruption but was also acquitted and made privy counselor.

In the big history I have attempted so far, the nineteenth century and the "Gandhian moment" form a remarkable cluster of concentrated events that I cannot do justice to in a few short lines. Let me at least mention my reason for calling the next century and a half, between the 1800s and India's founding of its democratic constitution, the "Gandhian moment." I draw on J. G. A. Pocock's insight in his *Machiavellian Moment* that a turning point in political discourses or patterns of historical understanding can take place when intellectuals of the time recognize the limitation of their very vocabulary for describing their crises of political legitimacy and articulate a new democratic consciousness. In sixteenth-century Italy, the idioms of custom, grace, and fortune were woefully inept, which is partly why Machiavelli erupts with questions about the place of virtù or civic power, as well as luck, in all politics and the challenges around corruption. In a similar way, Gandhi's deep insight was that the norms that were being created through colonialism's dispositif were contingent and arbitrary and concealed their violence through the force of colonial law. And yet, they also contained seeds for articulating resistance through the language and practices of freedom, equality, and the commonality of the nation.[46]

This recognition of the deep violence of colonialism may long continue being explored in what is termed "postcolonial theory" and in everyday democratizing practice, as well as in more cautious and rank-closing forms. On one register is nationalism, which was articulately expressed in the late nineteenth and early twentieth centuries through many types of leader, of whom Gandhi was iconic. Nationalism, by definition, is an attempt to forge an identity while reconciling that with a variety of cultural identities and histories of violence. Modernity too has several internal contradictions and resource-based challenges. The struggles to keep these complex democratizing ideals alive amidst a changing cultural, ecological, and political environment still constitute the current predicament.[47]

In the succeeding moment, another set of conditions of elite consolidation and democratizing social forces may be in evidence, but this time it has become complexly woven onto global movements of finance and geopolitical power. The change also involved a technological revolution that is familiar to us. Corporations and capital can now relocate resources and finances in new ways to deploy labor globally. This has resulted in at least three decades of stagnant real wages. Capital may be overproduced, but rentiers rule and generate class relations, in a way that is remarkably similar to how Karl Marx described these conditions.[48]

8

Conclusions

Corporate Power and Its Dissolution, or The Future of Corruption

"From the Pentagon to the private sector."

"Nigeria's former oil minister, Diezani Allison-Madueke, lost $20 billion on her watch."

"How industry transforms our 'scientific' understanding of risk."

"How Interpol got into bed with FIFA."

"The offshore activities of . . . the world's most powerful people."

"Whopping 70% of Trump property buyers are utilizing shell companies to keep their identities secret."

Seeking Closure

This book did not demonstrate clearly which regime-specific networks played elite and dominant roles in Indian history. Nor did it intend to or hope to spell them out unambiguously. Some monarchs, priestly communities, and merchants or traders were no doubt significant, but there are almost certainly many actors and groups missing from the picture. Over time, they would have surely metamorphosed into even less recognizable groups and networks, but ones that still established routines that left a major imprint: creating and sustaining advantages not just for themselves and their descendants but also more deliberately for the restricted few and their successors in other elite networks, by normalizing extreme inequality.

For other reasons too, it is difficult to provide a singular ending to this journey. My meanderings may have been far too varied to generate any significant "discovery" concerning corruption. The only eye-opener for some readers may be that these accounts of elite networks in India's past are not so disconnected from our current planetary crises of democracy and ecology. But I also sadly suspect that more than a few may remain mystified about the very bounds of my argument, which I recapitulate in this chapter.

According to the way I interpreted grand or political corruption, every major (territorial) regime of history since the agricultural revolution was the outcome of small, privileged, and influential formations that created different material and symbolic forms of exclusive exchange and embedded connections. These, in turn, forged elaborate and evolving power relations that burrowed deep into geographies and social units to stay resilient over time. Their strategic interests were the principal engines that created a panoply of social structures and cultural varieties. They took on various elite actor-network arrangements, but the most enduring and familiar ones evolved into monarchies or oligarchies that arose from origin myths; entire social formations were built around them through hegemonic social practices that then evolved into relatively stable long-term institutions. Even democracies, such as that in ancient Athens, were not immune from elite and expansionist territorial power.[1]

Throughout this development, their mythologies at various times attracted widespread suspicion, changed shape, or lingered for long in full view of the people. Although it is the occasional discovery of the extractive modes of particular elite networks that is best associated with the word "corruption," my focus in this book was on the morphogenesis of these syndromes over very long time frames in India. My aim was to understand how institutions and socioecological structures might create the conditions for actors (using networked strategies) to take unfair advantage of circumstances—all the while realizing it is impossible to determine exactly how these institutions and structures managed to have disproportionately instrumental roles in shaping societal cultures.

The most powerful of these nested complexes I termed "elite networks," whose human actors were unusually well connected through patronage, had substantial clout in public affairs, and bestowed their collective advantages on future generations of their kinsmen as well as on others. They spawned durable institutions, such as the churches and education systems and, later, capitalist markets, banking, property rights, and so on. These generated vast benefits and accommodated some forms of equality. But they also created roles for multiple actors, whose regulation and habitus kept buried the alliances and elite coalitions. And these were the very coalitions that created the political forces of social coercion and consent for the new order. They built up entire social formations whose multiple entanglements helped stabilize them. The identities and family legacies of the human agents in these elite networks are extremely difficult to uncover, although it is possible to tell that they existed in the past and continue to do so. But even that is not the main point. Just as dynasties of royalty were often not very long-lived and yet remained paramount as the state itself or as the abstract character of kingship, other types of elite structures too were normalized throughout history.[2]

The king was a splendid human representation of the interlocking elite groups that supported him, giving rise to a small variety of courtly "figurations" of monarchy, in Norbert Elias's rendering, just as they did for other regime types in different periods and places. Over long historical time—the longue durée—such practices and the cultures that emerged and endured became hegemonic; that is, they maintained routines of "false necessity" and gave rise to what are familiarly termed "ideologies" of consent with disparately harsh forms of coercion.

How might one tie the sometimes unmindful but still dissembling roles of such elite networks to culpability? What reparation is conceivable through shaming and equalizing access to wealth and power? Such questions, let alone remedies, may never have arisen as the elites did their work, and therefore histories were rarely written to identify them as elite networks in power that must be overcome. When they were identified, whatever the means through which the injustice was interpreted and resisted, the resulting social change sometimes led to revolutions, such as those associated with anti- and decolonial movements. But for the most part, a longer-term pattern of systemic exploitation and its justification remained intact, especially in relation to patriarchy and other forms of forced labor.

The Marxist argument that sounds just like mine takes a different route, leading to an interpretation of more generalized assemblages in history, such as the proletariat, the peasantry, and the bourgeoisie, and positing emergent outcomes of the interaction of social forces that then define trajectories for revolutionary change. My interest here, instead, is to see if these social processes can be seen in their multiscale interactions, beginning with individuals and small coteries of actors who seem to generate conditions that mobilize the deployment of state or territorial power to achieve larger goals. Might the processes spawned by these elite networks then activate other emergent structures, such as social classes, that serve to stabilize the preferred institutions of elite power? What might prevail over them? These are unanswered questions in my investigation, but I hope I have made the case for further inquiry.

The character (or syndrome) of many elite networks and their emergent social effects did in fact change over time, sometimes adapting to external conditions, at other times becoming enmeshed with other elite interests that strengthened their hegemony. The linkages between privilege and social injustice were also hazy in the past because of deception; misdirection as a result of war, drought, or other external circumstances; or their indirect and delayed effects. Perceived over longer global histories, however, the secret relationships that are typical of most forms of corruption are usually detectable and fall into types or syndromes (see Table 1). These syndromes, in turn, emerge out of the specific circumstances in which elite strategies that serve to reinforce very particular personal bodily routines metamorphose into longer-term social structures. That these routines and their hardening over time were based on deceptions has become evident only by observing the nonhistory of markedly larger peoples and ecologies outside both grand and not-so-grand polities. Reassuringly for the future, a surprisingly vast majority had command over the arts of not being governed.[3]

When processes that can be identified as corruption do become manifest, they typically appear when societies experience long periods of forms of anomie, dissolution, and wasting—deep social and economic malaise—accompanied by the extraordinary accumulation of material and symbolic wealth by the few. Only rarely are connections made between the growing aloofness of elite networks in their luxury, even in the midst of internecine war, and the mounting despair of the majority. Worsening chaos, mutual suspicion and fragmentation, and the growth of separate identity or clan-based groups may increase when matters do not sufficiently escalate to engender political transformation. Blatant exploitation and large-scale complicity are complemented by collective indifference and reciprocal dishonesty. Social trust and reciprocity—the basic elements of creating a people—decline in the midst of the elite' accumulation of symbolic and material goods. In chapter 1, I gave examples of ancient Rome and medieval Christianity, both falling from grace over several centuries, without proper resolution or social remedy.

Table 1. Elite networks and their social impacts in different periods in India

Period	Elite Groups (confidence: High, Medium, Low)	Extent of Territorial Influence	Type of Surplus Accumulation	Dominant Ideology/Habitus	Direct Social Consequences	What Else Was Going on in India?
2600 BCE–1900 BCE	Harappan elites, possibly on the smaller mound in the northwest sections of Harappan cities, whose makeup and modes of operation remain mysterious (M)	Large swath of north-western India, operating through networked cities	Possibly a form of prestige generated through an ascetic aesthetic, but bolstered through elite trade networks within the region and with Mesopotamia; evidence for massive production of beads—necklaces as money?	Unknown ideology but strong patterns of spatial habitus that created codependency and helped maintain the social order	An emergent aesthetic of austere spatial asceticism and high engineering skill, possibly deployed as an ethic and ideology to shape substantial labor pools for producing tradable goods of some sort	Possibly no other territorial power but mostly Neolithic communities in small forager-hunter groups
1500 BCE–500 BCE	Patriarchs, possibly Vedic pastoralists having large herds, initially living in separate clans at war against each other, eventually forming coalitions with territorial control (H) Again, there is little or no information on the character of elites, but we surmise their existence substantially from the Rigveda (L)	From the Swat Valley to Punjab and the Doab region, extending eventually farther east toward Varanasi. Initially clan based, but by 1000 BCE, possible contact with local populations and bringing them into ārya and viś folds. In later periods, the influence of Brahmins was more extensive through mobile networks in far-off cities	Potentially in two forms: control over cattle and pastures, and exclusive right to knowledge of sacrifice, whose symbolic importance grew substantially in the period and beyond. Symbolic power was the power to perform yajna and control territory, which was still in formation in the Kuru-Panchala regime, but possibly changed into a more familiar form farther east and late in the period	For the officiating priests and the sacrificers, the ritual process was the end itself, its exactness in form and arcane character lending the necessary solemnity. This ortho-praxis was ideologically significant only insofar as the justification for sacrifice was to make offerings to the gods. No widespread habitus beyond small priest and wealthy communities until late in the period where quasi-royal formations were significant	The formation of a small but increasingly influential and somewhat territorially significant set of clans, but also producing generations of Brahmin priestly communities and other dvija rules in the formalizing process	Significant forest peoples, who may have successfully carried raids on cattle and possibly crops in Vedic territory

(continued)

Table 1. (*continued*)

Period	Elite Groups (confidence: High, Medium, Low)	Extent of Territorial Influence	Type of Surplus Accumulation	Dominant Ideology/Habitus	Direct Social Consequences	What Else Was Going on in India?
500 BCE–500 CE	This period is the consolidation of territory in the grand form of law, so the "royal court" is the significant elite entity, announced as such; it laid claim to sufficient primary wealth and strategic alliances in society to exercise influence and dominance (H)	Nominally everywhere in the vicinity of urban agglomerations but networked across them through tribute exchange and trade, together with the resources of considerable military force	Same two centers of priestly and kingly power as in previous period, but also evolving through the development of divergence in the law, one strand energized to codify varṇāśramadharma, the other taking a decidedly heterodox and radical tone in making no promises; in early Buddhism, including in Emperor Aśoka's time	Diverse but possibly craft and skill-based deployment of labor for agriculture and allied trades, with a small but evolving elite leisure class. The śramana and āśrama lifestyles were also creating their sometimes dominant subcultures as alternatives to Brahmanism, which varied in size and scope throughout this period	A diversity of trades that are almost all directly or indirectly dependent on the court. This included the ability to conscript them to battle as much as extract taxes from them, which varied in size. The court is a special place of cultivation of manner and distinction between elites and the public	Not much change in forestland and forest people, although the end of the period was associated with Gupta campaigns to take over forest as territory and with local satraps making strategic partnerships with forest people
500 CE–1500 CE	Farm oligarchs muscling out rivals; trade elite networks arise; the court has become a major source of patronage and key partnerships with others across a vast space. A period with courts of ever-larger territorial ambition playing a central role (M)	Rural oligarchy seeks local rents with some extraversion; merchants are networked spatially across long distances beyond sovereign territories, but also pay tribute to them	Arbitrage in grain, which creates strong connections across both elite groups; arbitrage in textiles, indigo, and spice builds similarly well-networked elites, including sovereign powers; trade in other goods, including possibly people in later militia-led campaigns, some of whom could be mercenaries	Rājya (kingdom) and its rājanya (rules of kingship); mobility and arbitrage	In south India, special cultures around courtly life. But courts also sponsored poets and art. In north India, kāvya was the romantic stories of elite lives with unexpected consequences All over the country, especially in ports but also other strategic market and trading centers, Brahmanism's evolving challenges and assimilation of Śaivite and Vaishnavite traditions, and of	Erosion of parts of forest in the foothills of the Himalayas and elsewhere away from possible crop area control. Still, vast areas of the land remained forested and inhabited by peoples who were ungoverned

1500 CE–2000 CE	Similar to earlier period, with the addition of finance capital and industry, especially since the late nineteenth century. Land conversion to cropland proceeds at an unprecedented pace, especially during the twentieth century, displacing forest peoples everywhere (H)	Globally interlinked but deeply interlocked with local elites through increasingly intricate patterns of extraversion	Rents on capital assets (with land still dominant, but increasingly mediated through finance)	Heightened sense of choice with the emblematic habitus of the shopping mall experience, virtual or real. On the political side, a growing cynicism and withdrawal, anger, and power of visceral populists who sound anti-establishment, or strong hope and belief in the rule of law, however one-sided to one's own advantage it might seem		Yoga and Tantra, as well as successful overthrow of Buddhist access to kingly power A transforming consumer-citizen, increasingly surveilled for the possibility of creating a new category of rent	A sudden and rapid increase in the colonization of land, producing the largest increase in rent to elite arbitragers. Virtual space and identities as data producing new rents
2000 CE–	A tight inner circle of political and financial elites controlling a highly securitized and over-leveraged set of material and informational assets (H)	Planetary linkages, through interlocking local and regional elites, with banks and other financial institutions playing key roles	Traditional as well as new rents from data, energy, and scarce materials, especially those associated with new and emerging technologies for energy and information processing and storage	Expanded version of the previous era, with strong identity association around political affiliation, creed, sexuality, and body self-image	A landscape of frightening, unknown possibilities, largely because of the scope for massive, untoward human-induced destruction and suffering that might ensue. The strong possibility of a "fortress world," an illusion of security from one another, but a cynical one-upmanship to crush		Fully integrated into global markets, but heightened assertiveness around collective memories of nationhood expressed as masculinities and other cultural stereotypes. New styles of "living down," agroecology, virtual deliberative democracies, other intersectional countercultures

Whatever the social processes might be that emerge from the sustained dominance of a given set of elite networks, their effects may only be seen in the longue durée.

Each such pattern in a long historical period has its own particular syndrome of corruption, reflecting variations in the way elite networks were formed and expanded and how accompanying social structures took shape in changing circumstances and geographies to serve privileged forms of rent-generating capital. Around the world, territoriality—the creation of legitimized power over an extensive land area—was the manner in which rival elite networks both protected their interests from each other and colluded through trade and other interlocking strategic connections with others to nourish surpluses. Over time, making their connections global became a necessary and effective strategy for elite networks: it allowed them to remain dominant by linking them across long distances—even though the major eighteenth-century ideology spawned by territoriality, nationalism, was frequently in conflict with economic liberalism and its ally, globalization, which prioritized free trade and movement. Finding appropriate and calibrated forms of managing all of these ideologies became a new obsession for capitalist and political elites around the world.

The territorial limits of ancient Rome and medieval Christianity extended from the Levant across to the far reaches of the British Isles. In early Indian societies, elite network syndromes were found in numerous complexes involving both rigid and unsteady orders of social practice. The boundaries of each network were not easy to represent on a map because they built connections at strategic locations across space, were often mobile, and created subnetworks of mutual favors to maintain overall influence, if not dominance. The early sovereign entities were built on assemblages of many elements: cosmic ideologies (ranging from Ājivika and other beliefs in karmic return or in Brahmanical justification for endogamy and clan hierarchy); a few predominant configurations of traders, priestly classes, generals, and other nobles, forming complex alliances with each other; and most notably, an almost uniform ideal of kingship and courtly traditions whose common feature was their extraordinary grandeur and shows of war readiness, both meant to capture the social imagination and demonstrate distance from the masses (the historical Emperor Aśoka and the mythical Yudhishthira being exceptions or enigmas).

Despite the sense of successful multiculturalism that this picture might convey and that may have been true of some eras in some locations, the more common conditions were that of a successful oligarchy, one that largely kept the peace as long as complaints were slight. What the knitting of alliances across certain groups of elites managed to reproduce were systems of unrelenting physical labor for everyone other than those within these exclusive and powerful groupings. These, in turn, robustly reinforced patently unjust but legal institutions such as patriarchy and slavery. Only those who remained ungoverned—forest peoples and renouncers who managed to escape urban institutions and settled agriculture (agrarian states)—seemed somewhat immune to these laddered social processes. With the birth of industrial capitalism, the latest and most destructive emergent formation of global elite network forms, even they were unquestionably affected, with many experiencing radical changes to their environments and lifestyles. Along with being absorbed in an endless supply of fantasy and other distractions, captured societies have occasionally fallen into periods of *dérèglement,* displaying angry fights and wars over seemingly absurd hurts and otherwise creating a "fortress" mentality around particular groups, alignments, and other factions.[4]

In the Brahmanical tradition as it extended to modern Hindu practices, strict caste endogamy represented a means for keeping intact social classes, including a few elite networks, although inbreeding was probably never fully enforced. Neither was there achieved widespread consent for its dharma codebooks beyond a few self-fashioned dvija communities. Among those who held the reins of serious material and cultural capital, there were growing crises of over-accumulation, given that the rents acquired from both financial and symbolic goods had somehow to be spent and reinvested in new activity for the "machine" to reproduce itself. This usually resulted in the creation of more ideological props that were always accompanied by bodily routines (habitus) that kept the vast multitude complicit in upholding large networks of grand corruption.[5]

Over time, as various types of further elite capture of sovereign power took shape, evolved, and moved on, the morphology of social practice changed as well. From the earliest urban settlement, kingdom, and empire, each successive configuration almost universally represented elite networks of growing sophistication that consolidated and vastly aggrandized control over social formations. Each collective in power ensured its superlative strength through accumulating great wealth that well exceeded that of the typical household. But much of the imbalance was also in the form of cultural resources, which gave elites substantial moral and regulatory control over the general public. In due course, the need to create shared identities through the habitus of exclusion around gender, bloodline, or wealth meant greater investment in tools of cultural representation. Territory formation and the symbolic means to maintain it were critical in this enterprise. Indeed, the true symbol of kingly power throughout has been his unrivaled control over state assets (his sovereignty), more than anything else. Today, a sign of the times is that, in the first two decades of the twenty-first century, the concentration of wealth in just a few hands far exceeds that held by the majority.

I do not expect all my readers to accept this argument. Shaking their head at the hubris of tenured liberal arts professors, some may say, "*Bullshit!*" What sort of grand conspiracy theory is this anyway? Why believe that elites have created *all* we know of history into elaborate social systems of deception over centuries? How much control can a small group have anyway? Why assume that elite networks convey so much power, even if one were to set aside my conspiratorial tone?

But I like to imagine that even diehard skeptics may once or twice recognize patterns—syndromes—I alluded to along the way. Even if my narratives were not all persuasive, I hope each connected history showed that a singular set of arrangements of elite political power endured surprisingly well. Each was also associated with particular social practices over long periods in the forms of domestic routines and public life that ended up creating vast disparities in material and symbolic resources. Collectively, they acquired meaning, creating new languages and cultural practices of respect, admiration, and indifference toward the practices and lifestyles of the most privileged groups in society, who also marked out their distance from others ever so clearly. Their performances returned to a familiar tragic plot that was already written into the institutions responsible for the collection of rents from the rest of the population and that appeared in history books as empires, kingdoms, and, today, modern states and corporations.

Part of the difficulty is accepting my formulation is that many elite groupings served as benign rent collectors while providing useful services to ordinary people. In democratic states today, many of them have our sanction to be where they sit. But we may want to remember some dark events in recent political history. At least since the election into power of the National Socialist Party of Germany in 1932 and the subsequent horrors it committed against humanity, even constitutional democracies should be viewed with some caution. In the late twentieth century, a fossil fuel cartel conspired to spend tens of millions of dollars to spread what its members knew were lies about climate change. They were, and continue to be, supported by governments around the world. And then one must wonder why it is so easy to hold onto the idea that most, if not all, regimes were endorsed through some type of imagined contract among *most* of the people and, indeed, who those people really are.

According to tradition, although there is no way to verify it, around 450 BCE, plebeians in Rome succeeded in their demand that customary practices favoring patricians be superseded by the Twelve Tables. There were many other such democratizing moments, although only few managed to outlast the power of elites sufficiently to place their mark on history. In India, there is scattered evidence that, with the possible exception of the Harappa civilization, it was virtually impossible to bring many itinerant groups in Indian cities into jointly regulated forms of collectively ordered lives. Instead, as loose clientelist societies, within and beyond the palace walls as well as in the hinterland, control was likely maintained through the exchange of small favors among local elites connected through clans or exchange and known for their skills of extraversion in relation to patrons in the larger world. We do not know whether women and men were captive to these networks and what forms of surplus may have been extracted from their labor.

In some instances, however, we can identify elite subgroups as having belonged to specific bloodlines in Vedic practice, such as Brahmins and Kshatriya varnas, and to trade and familial guilds, as well as those with agricultural rights to farm land. Except among the last group, no manorial system as such appeared in India before the Mughal era. This meant that farm-based members of elites were rare; most of the control was likely regulated on the basis of geography with decision-making power closely held within court society in the metropolitan center. Rājās had official "title" to large units of land, but because elite interlocking across territories was necessary, trade networks were inevitably connected to them; these combined networks grew into globally connected forms of networked sovereignty. Kingship was always powerful, however, and in the court we can see the royal power center at work in key councils and palace intrigues for more than two millennia.[6]

Caste and occupation groups marking formalized relative social distance emerged sometime in the first millennium CE in some areas; this process strengthened dominant clans and perhaps other shadowy networks. Trade was continually reworking these into increasingly more dominant elite networks and their mostly dependent populations. Colonialism is one of the most recent but stunningly exposed acts of political corruption in this 4,000-year drama.

Illustrating a few of the manifold changes to land and people, the environmentalist historian Sumit Guha writes,

> In the semi-arid and arid tracts that occupy the greatest part of the Indian sub-continent, herdsmen would have to move from monsoon grazing on the seasonal grasses of the open lands to (or through) the foliage and herbage of the forest tracts. Some pastoralists, like the Banjaras, might cover long distances in their migrations, and become traders, traversing both forest and sown.... Other groups, perhaps due to loss of their livestock, could take up permanent abode in the woodlands.... [Still others] continued to wander, sometimes gaining a reputation as soldiers and/or robbers.... Many foundation legends recorded in the seventeenth or eighteenth centuries recalled great famines, after which the lands had lain fallow, occupied by low people and wandering tribes, before being settled once again by the ancestors of the present holders thus refounding the settled agrarian order, whose task, by definition, was to thrust back the *jangal* [wilderness] and expel the *jangli* [wild].[7]

Taking modern and ancient polities together, their constituent power can therefore be understood as the justificatory dispositif that the elites of a given location might nurture to foster the belief that they—princes, kings, emperors, or even representative governments and their administrative forms—were politically constituted by vast multitudes of popular support or divine sanction; that is, that they were initially given widespread blessing for ordering a collective existence as a state. In its modern form, as I stated earlier, this power appears to have originated sometime during the second millennium in Europe and led to the development of present-day constitutions. At least formally, modern constitutional republics have cut off the king's head by declaring themselves as the people's representatives, but it is by no means clear whose interests are the "people's" and how they are served in lawmaking. This justification that appears as "law" is a category that needs additional examination, or at least should be placed within quotes until further described. Or so I hope this is how the incredulous reader might be persuaded.

Diversion 1: In the United States, Corruption Is in the Public Sphere (Again)

Allow me some diversions that serve to connect my ideas of ancient and medieval India with contemporary events. While starting work on this book, one of the first things I noticed was the strange transition that was taking place within American political culture. The phrase "corruption in America" had suddenly gained prominence. Of course, Zephyr Teachout's book with that very title had just come out. But that was also a few months before Donald Trump announced his intention to run in the US presidential election. As I write these final pages, it is now three years into his presidency, and the US House of Representatives has impeached him for abuse of power, including impeachable bribery, and obstruction of Congress. The Senate has scandalously (corruptly?) exonerated him and removed the case against him. Yet as recently as the 1990s and at least for two decades earlier, it was virtually impossible to find the word "corruption" associated with the United States in mainstream American news media.

Preferred words for the 1972 Watergate burglary and its later cover-up by the Nixon administration, the Pentagon Papers, the $640 toilet seat paid for by the US Department of Defense, and so on, were "scam," "fraud," "theft," and, occasionally, "extortion" but rarely "corruption." In fact, since its inception in the mid-1960s, the academic field of corruption studies (still predominantly confined to the United States and Europe) mostly focused on regimes in the developing world—with all of Africa being a favorite site. Typologies were largely built around theories of patronage, neo-patrimony (both associated with "traditional" rules of heritage), and greed; in the West, only in rare instances, such as in the 1989 Keating Five case involving US senators, were political campaign contributions blamed for incentivizing conditions of quid pro quo resembling corruption.[8]

It was not always like this. At least from the early nineteenth century through the Great Depression, corruption was widely acknowledged as a feature of politics at all levels; before lobbying was made legal and trusts illegal, corruption was generally recognized as being the bane of federal policies, involving backroom deals to enrich railroad investors and other bigwigs. In 1817, James Monroe, during his inaugural speech as the fifth president of the United States, warned darkly, yet familiarly, of the corruption of the people: "It is only when the people become ignorant and corrupt, when they degenerate into a populace, that they are incapable of exercising the sovereignty. Usurpation is then an easy attainment, and an usurper soon found. The people themselves become the willing instruments of their own debasement and ruin."[9]

In the decades that followed, anti-bribery laws were in force at the state and federal levels, but the expansion of territory in the West brought expanded economic opportunities after the Civil War, during the Gilded Age, from the 1870s to around 1900. Millions of freed slaves from the South, along with equally large numbers of immigrants from central and southern Europe, were put to work in factory towns in the Midwest and along the East Coast. An elite nexus of business moguls and members of Congress created enormous rents for oligopolies in railroads, mines, and manufacturing, usually after sufficiently bribing political representatives and occasionally judges. The "spoils" system, in which elected representatives gave special favors to their supporters and families, spawned political machines and often involved underhanded and reciprocal exchanges of courtesies across deep networks.

In response, reform efforts, driven by political mobilization, realized major victories for US democracy: antitrust legislation, labor safety laws, women's suffrage, the New Deal, and later, civil rights laws. But these would not have arisen, and then succeeded, if not for the obvious life-threatening social and economic obstacles faced by the rural poor, small businesses, and industrial workers, especially African Americans, women, and children, in striking contrast to the exclusive lifestyles of the propertied and well-connected few. A sizable group of people engaged in democratizing struggles through civil disobedience, political campaigns, strikes, and sometimes underground violent action. In the post–World War II period, inequality was moderated, social safety nets were well funded, and a bustling economy surged in the tailwind of the growth of new corporate giants, this time automobile and defense, which worked together with other emerging entities such as big banks, finance, and real estate. Business was good because the dollar was strong and backed by elites in the Western alliance.

Even through the Vietnam War and petroleum price shocks in the 1970s, American political commentary largely had a self-congratulatory mood that marveled at the country's exceptionalism and moral leadership in protecting liberties at home while fighting authoritarian governments abroad. Apart from a handful of detractors such as Noam Chomsky, Herbert Marcuse, and Gore Vidal, whose political writings were largely ignored by mainstream media, there was little or no critical public commentary on US domestic and foreign affairs for at least a generation. When scandals broke, they were perceived as the result of deviance, and psychologizing the minds and intentions of criminals became a favorite pastime in popular culture.

In 2008, the financial crisis and its devastating effects on the middle class seemed to be the proverbial last straw that awoke public discourse out of its reverie. Tax reform at state and federal levels had already shrunk the public sector, corporate mergers and takeovers had eliminated jobs, and welfare reform had mostly shredded the social safety net. Meanwhile, insatiable engines of finance capitalism, driven to a large extent by the raw adrenaline of wealth generation, had indulged in reckless and unregulated hyper-speculation. (Remarkably, similar levels of wealth accumulation and inequality are rife yet again at the time of this writing, but with added calamitous peril for a growing global precariat).

Not surprisingly, given the far-reaching connections of elite networks, these processes are rampant in all parts of society. The Trump administration's apparent uncontrolled fusion of public office and private interest has caused many political commentators to claim that the United States is again being ruled by a monarchy. This time, the king may seem crazy, but the operations in the background among a panoply of elite interests are not new: it is just that their work seems more frenzied than ever. Indeed, the oligarchy reaches across the globe, and its deceit is now widely visible. Levels of economic and social inequality are breathtakingly high, corporate and political mischiefs are blatant, and no one seems to take the trouble anymore to hide their crimes. There is carnage on the streets, and yet social conditions seem only to reveal various states of *dérèglement*. The frequency of violence in schools, within families, and by the state apparatus on targeted groups has never been this high in recent memory. But that is not as surprising as the determined popular craze to escape into virtual nirvanas of cycles of consumption fueled by strategic marketing interests.[10]

Diversion 2: Politics Is Personal

My second diversion is personal. As a member of overlapping cultural and, less so, economic, elites, I find it necessary to reflect on comfort zones that allow me to rely on various forms of privilege in different circumstances. Doing so may expose some of my own involvement in this enterprise.

I was born into a large Brahmin family; both of my parents are from the same clan, Aṣṭaśāstra Iyers (Śaivite Brahmins having knowledge of eight śāstras). The clan is claimed to have originated as a sect of 8,000 who were invited to move to south India from central or eastern India by a Chola ruler around the beginning of the second millennium to carry out priestly duties. Both sets of my grandparents were of modest economic means. My mother's father was a schoolteacher and supported more than a dozen children and four of his grandchildren in penurious conditions. My other grandfather was a farmer who died young, leaving behind a second widow with several children and a few acres of paddy and coconut farms in the Kaveri Delta in what is now Tiruchirappalli District. In any event, my grandmother, like women in most parts of India, could not own landed property and had to flee to Madras (now Chennai) rather than get into a dispute with my late grandfather's brothers and sons from his first marriage. Like her, her two daughters were widowed early and were under the care of their sons or brothers. Perhaps remarkably but determinedly, both my parents' families managed to secure access to opportunities for themselves and their kin during a time of great hope in post-independent India.

Today, I have numerous cousins and second cousins who are highly economically successful: there are at least two dozen multimillionaires—in US dollars—and perhaps many more in the extended clan, and several others do well financially and lead comfortable lives. Most are known for their acumen and accomplishments in academia, business, writing, and so on, although none is directly involved in politics. Within my extended family network, several may belong to the global 99th percentile, or the top 1 percent, a category that shot to prominence in the Occupy movements after the 2008 destruction of poor and middle-class assets around the world. Almost everyone else in my extended family circle of more than 200 is at least middle class, with a roof over their heads and a secure if modest future for themselves and their children. Mine is nowhere close to the 1,000 or so prominent family oligarchies in India today, nor is it well known for its pedigree in the form of famous artists, politicians, or businessmen. But my relatives' ability to connect their fortunes to more prestigious and select nodes of power occasionally astonishes me.[11]

I doubt any of them is directly engaged in seeking or providing illegal favors. I take pleasure and pride in meeting my extended family at reunions, where I am moved by the verbal and nonverbal exchanges of food, music, and banter that seal our kinship. But I also recognize that their (and my) remarkable level of comfort and well-being compared to any other random sample of 200 or so close blood relations in the country is an anomaly. Why should the Chella and Swaminathan kin be so unrepresentative in such a vast country like India? And yet, my condition is, of course, hardly unique. There are tens millions of people in similar networks of privilege as my own, and I would hardly consider most of them or my kin as having any meaningful influence to shift the wheels of power. But collectively, it is clear that we make up a significant part of the engine of the regime and play global roles that are out of reach of most people.

Societies are not like atoms moving in Brownian, randomly dispersed, motion to make up diffuse gas-like entities, with any sample of the "gas" having the same properties as any other. Instead, they are made up of agents (actors) who occupy distinct positions in complex fields of meaning and material resources. They form relationships within these patterns of signification, but these meanings are mostly already available to them through long-standing connections of kinship and clientelism—exchanges of favors, usually involving substantially more powerful agents than themselves—as well as the modern rules of economic systems. These connections are made up of laddered arrangements of patronage and wealth creation, resting on a form of arbitrage that relates to inequality in access to different types of resources, including money and cultural goods. In the final analysis, they endow small, well-networked groups with disproportionately high material and symbolic wealth.[12]

Although I could claim that my own modest success in life is attributable to my efforts and luck, some of that luck is surely due to my family connections, starting with the conditions of schooling around my birth and continuing through to the present day when I seek favors from my network to help solve my minor problems relating to buying or selling property, managing health crises, or handling my taxes. My family's upper-caste membership by birth became my inheritance, even though I am technically in violation of virtually all dvija rules specified in the Dharmaśāstra. Neither I nor any of the people in my immediate network of friends and family need to engage in any sort of criminal activity to get things done, but I am aware that less well-connected individuals find it harder to resolve similar difficulties and that others, better connected, have an even easier time.

All this complicates the laddering of elite networks, their interlocking and mobile features; in short, their dynamics. But we can identify features of an inner circle within these networks and our own direct or indirect links to them, if we manage to connect the dots. The economic historian Vivek Chibber writes of a grand coalition of prominent industrialists in 1944 who pledged support for centralized state planning for the young country and gave rise to the Bombay Plan. The plan created the political coalition between the government and business to form a closed and protected economy. Its implementation, however, sheltered the interests of the small number of capitalists who worked with the ruling Congress Party to weaken labor unions and maintain a licensing system that provided select groups monopoly rights to produce industrial goods. Those groups, in turn, often used their licenses strategically to wait for favorable conditions. Regulators directly bargained with firms instead of setting up rules for new investors to come in. All this suggests that the Bombay Plan's authors had concocted a just-in-time strategy to preserve oligarchies, many of which had prospered during the Raj. These authors include several prominent individuals who remain well known even today, but that is not the point. Rather, it is that these fraternities (for they were made up only of men) operated at multiple levels but usually at the same scales of fewer than a hundred or so. They were hierarchically linked, if that could accurately describe the multiply transverse, links to different social classes, political inferiors and clients, and so on. Exchanges of gifts, money, and favors were common, making it possible to engage in investments and exchange around material and symbolic resources to consolidate gains for the oligarchy.[13]

These patterns are familiar in several other contexts of elite networks. In India, one may assume that political and economic power, at least since independence, has largely been about family legacies, remaining within tight kinship patterns for long periods, with these relationships still dominant. Over the longue durée, there were periods when other coalitions of small networks took control of economic and political power and had enormous latitude in organizing dependent social formations. In some cases, they took the form of an urban order; in others, they were tied to esoteric combinations of mantra recitals and ritual sacrifice; in yet others, they described the patterns of financing and sustenance of transnational power networks through trade and arbitrage, creating new forms of capital. These configurations show that there are many levels of order, including several formations of power that control vast territory and have intricate ties involving the everyday operation of the economy, formal and legitimate state power, and extraordinary levels of wealth.

Across history, such manifold syndromes of elite dominance within long time frames were routinely responsible for extracting large amounts of physical and mental labor from vast populations in ways that always heightened social and economic inequality. But they were also frequently contested and, over long periods, created new cultural practices in diverse groups dwelling in many types of ecologies and spatial relationships. The revelations of corruption that I focus on in this book may only be a small fraction of the myriad stories that could perhaps be told. Yet these limited examples do show that, on a few occasions, elite networks or their effects were exposed and contested.

#Elitenetworks: The Trope of Corruption

In the HBO TV series *Westworld*, there are the savage people, designers, evolving characters of the androids, and "corporate," a hidden, dark Leviathan of authority whose protagonists are unnamed. *Westworld*'s plot is simple. Android technology keeps advancing, along with the development of theme parks that involve radical role playing. In its adrenaline-filled re-creation of a fictional Western town, human "visitors" have the ability to create storylines by interacting with the characters, which are programmed to reboot themselves daily. Visitors thereby create emergent social effects for themselves by learning about the best strategies for doing well in the game, while androids presumably cope without any surviving memories.

When the first android character begins to have memories of her past actions from previous days, the narrative is forced to change, generating another emergent process. These evolutionary changes, as the theme park operators discover, are the product of small code insertions that have the effect of deliberately complicating the plot. This "swerve" in their character profiles results in a collective realization of the scale of the betrayal. Still, many androids stay in character and continue acting out their lines with passion and imagination even when there are no visitors.

And so it has been. In the tale I have narrated about the history of corruption in India, one can sense an uninspired repetition of the betrayal of commonly held values when human societies repeatedly organize themselves to accommodate elite interests. And this may occur even when many people are able to recognize how their own ways of living have played key roles in this outcome. Corruption when viewed collectively, across many domains, then feels like a nightmare with its repetitive narrative of *triste:* a mixture of societal sorrow, regret, and disbelief. It might then dawn on us that extremely high stakes are involved, that violent crimes and injustices might go unpunished if they involve a powerful few. This is hardly an unfamiliar narrative to almost any mass of people in history. How should one then investigate the corruption of the people themselves?

As in *Westworld,* the mythology may continue long after the time the characters being exploited (the vast masses) recognize is happening to them and realize how their perpetual motion in "playing the appropriate roles" is harmful to themselves. The existence of this broad pattern, or trope, is not accidental: it has to do with the types of political morphogenesis that Machiavelli associated with many Italian city-states since ancient Rome. In his other book, *Discourses on Livy,* Machiavelli worried repeatedly about the possibility of a corrupted people arising as the anti-political, privatized, and "lumpen" mob comprising individuals who cynically conceive of the political arena in purely instrumental terms as a source of power for advancing their personal interests. But often, the corruption of the people is manifest in their inability to perceive the yoke placed on them: "The same thing happens to a people: since it is used to living under the government of others, not knowing how to reason about either public defense or public offense, neither knowing princes nor known by them, it quickly returns beneath a yoke that is most often heavier than the one it had removed from its neck a little before. It finds itself in these difficulties whenever the matter is corrupt."[14]

What Machiavelli is saying might sound peculiar to commonsensical understandings of the word "corruption." A closer look at classical Rome and other republics clarifies matters. Julius Caesar destroyed the Roman republic, and then a series of lawful and despotic emperors ruled. The bad ones survived and the good ones were quickly destroyed, but Roman civilians had played a role in reinterpreting and justifying ways to interpret Roman law, which ensured republican control over the military.

Machiavelli cautions his reader against those things that a prince ought to refrain from doing to avoid evoking *il odioso o contennendo* (repulsion and contempt) of the people. One of these is not to be a tyrant, of which there are many kinds. Yet there is only one way in which the prince can retain territorial authority or sovereign power: satisfy the people by upholding the law over his throne and promote the separation of powers. In the *Discourses on Livy*, Machiavelli also warns of complacency when city-states have been free for a long time, as Rome was with its republican institutions. The corruption of the people, as I suggested repeatedly, is the trump card that requires vigilant political action.[15]

Corruption stings us because, somehow, a familiar routine of gears operating behind the scenes ends up making almost everyone's life miserable. Even after we collectively discover the existence of a sham and unjust operation, it may already be too late in life for some of us; for example, when decision makers in families cannot afford to risk their projected savings and expectations to make the jump toward alternative ways of living. The sheer inability to maintain my being and support my dependents, even while staying within accustomed modes of existence, is as exhausting as it is fulfilling. Creating transformative institutions to "error-correct" our everyday routines and psychodramas seems unnecessary. And yet, ignoring this challenge is to acknowledge that we may have deceived ourselves about our capacity to democratize ourselves. By failing to call for solidarity, which would involve equality and freedom from all crushing injustice and bodily exploitation, we pretend not to notice the hierarchy of interlocking elite networks in vertical and horizontal dimensions. Our own complicity in the deceit while hiding behind the poor at times to justify our ways of living ("it is a growth-inducing occupation after all!") becomes ever harder to reconcile with our values.

Perhaps the metaphor, corruption as degeneration, is too harsh for some. Or maybe it is just painful because it is true. Still, why assume that all societies are bound to decay? I do not know that they will and want to believe, at least now in the planetary crisis, that this is not inevitable. But there seems to be evidence that elite strategies molded agendas in relatively regular shapes for several millennia. These spawned forms of regulation that constituted societies through exhortation, taxation, provision of services, transformation of land, and sacred rites. Much of what we understand about the captive, dependent non-elites of society is that they were subservient in their activity and yet had relative freedom, even if it was cruelly optimistic at times. There is no way to prove whether ordinary people felt content or were resigned to their conditions of life, which were much harsher than the ways of living of elite inner circles. But some of them realized that they were also entrapped in a web of ideology and restrictions that were severely constrained, perhaps even relative to those of the forest people outside society. A few of them were influential enough to change others and be known for their world-changing legacies: they had names such as Buddha, Kabir, and Gandhi.

The strong associations of *corrumpere* and *oozhal* or "degeneration" with a general unease about the state of affairs in the world can be easily seen today. The rise of populist governments that deny climate change and therefore the need for transformative economic and lifestyle change may not be so coincidental. Perhaps their populist methods are linked to the protection of elaborate though limited global elites and their interlocking networks, from party machines to consultants and big finance. Many tired people may be fed up and want someone to do something and stop fighting. But sometimes fighting in the form of dialogic speech and civil disobedience may be necessary to train ourselves to ask non-caustically if we can be human and pay attention to the mess we have caused. Otherwise, there is no end to the accusations and calls for compensation as revenge.

Scholarship has identified varieties of such tight circles of corporate entities with individual actors at the helm whose operations are key to the ways of the world. As individuals, these elite actors may barely be conscious of what they are doing. But their fattening wallets and prestige and our complicity in excluding the masses of working and striving poor are evident if we seek out the horizon, where a vast and senseless, gurgling machine of late capitalism is gobbling and valuing the planet as a quick buck to be had. I am not proposing that any grand theory of "life" created all these changes. No, there were clearly agents (individuals and those maintaining family legacies) in India's pasts, who over lifetimes and sometimes generations retained certain degrees of extra comfort and well-being compared to a vast majority. They were not necessarily genetically connected nor did they share special traits with each other; it is just that there were swerves and strategic decisions that privileged certain dynasties for a few centuries, after which others arose and took shape. The dominance of certain groups was not entirely accidental, however; for long periods, this power drove and was part of a dispositif that was crafted through ideology, operated through consent and coercion, and changed form and identities with the times. But other groups continued the dance, with the only certainty being a vast and often growing disparity in many measures of symbolic and material wealth, as well as a self-conviction and a story to everyone else that this was what they all wanted in the first place: a kingdom.[16]

In the twenty-first century, we have the image of the legitimate and effective state: it is an abstraction with vast real power, in the form of machinery, employment, and sovereignty, or absolute rights over all bodies in its territory. Its legitimacy lies in its triple set of checks and balances, even as it tries to develop an effective administrative dispositif by taxing citizens, sending them to war, and punishing them for disobeying regulations in the law. It also allocates its money to particular interests and causes that are real and imagined. For Aristotle, *phroenesis,* practical wisdom, is action based on the best available knowledge and means prudence. That also implies, contra Plato, as far as we know, that access to practical or prudent action is not only the best we can do under the circumstances but we can also have faith that our knowledge-action is not misplaced in terms of ethical practice, but is rather defined in the coming together of collective virtues. Recall that Machiavelli interpreted the group of *virtùs* as collective goodwill, at least of finding ways to carry the republic forward, even under the circumstances of a new prince.

The Democratic Alternative: Another World Is Possible

At least three main challenges make up the present planetary crisis. First are planetary boundaries, which have alarmed and shaken many epistemologies and associated forms of knowledge production. This challenge has a generational element that is increasingly framed as an electrifying and shameful ethical accusation made by young people to elders: How dare you leave us this dying world in your reverie! This is complicated by a demographic shift: an increase in the number of disenfranchised youth. The second challenge is growing misery along with heightening inequality of access to cultural, economic, legal, and political goods. The third is the death of the idea that capitalism can get us out of the crisis it has created. Responding to these so-called wicked problems simultaneously seems to demand a transformative change—a cross-scale, cross-sector shift in social organization, behavior, and practices of polity—that must be fair and nonviolent in every possible way. A revolutionary mindset of "toppling" the prevailing order through vaguely defined popular action will likely violate these conditions badly. A better alternative is to foster many different democratizing processes across all segments, through civil action and changes in the law.

These are not easy solutions. There is no magic bullet to assess them or put them together, but models are emerging. Perhaps those creating the models need to learn how to better articulate their endeavors against wily marketing by the oligarchy. Meanwhile, it is useful to wean ourselves away from ongoing corrupt practices. What I hoped to recover in my long history of India are signs of connections between individual actors and their networks and their roles in helping control and deriving power from the social performances that seem to be set into motion. Even elites in the inner circle may be unwitting puppet masters, who have somehow learned to engage in supervisory and other territorially powerful roles that shape societies while aggrandizing their symbolic and material wealth.

It seems logical that Michael Johnston's next book after *Syndromes of Corruption* was his 2014 publication, *Corruption, Contention and Reform: The Power of Deep Democratization*. In it he points out the possibility of fighting corruption through the reassertion of accountability and the mitigation of the power of elite rulers and their networks. Doing so would involve new forms of civic reengagement in the messy and deeply compromised world of contemporary global politics. To neorealists and other scholars and observers of the cynical variety, this may seem near-sighted and naïve. But Johnston reminds his readers that there have been multiple instances in history when surprising forms of citizenship have emerged through people reasserting themselves in the face of power. The examples he provides include confronting the king in thirteenth-century England, resulting in the Magna Carta; the seventeenth-century English Parliament introducing a series of countervailing measures against generations of royal patronage; and anti-corruption struggles to overthrow criminal networks and their bosses in US cities' political machines in the nineteenth and twentieth centuries.[17]

Nonetheless, the collective agency of elite networks and our "maintenance" role in staying connected to them are together discernible as a signature, displaying a particular pattern of predominant political control over territory and social structure that has been developed over an extended period of time. Centuries of such elite-driven social practices that express particular ideologies have been common throughout history. Today, they are expressed in the phrase "too big to fail," among other ideologically loaded idioms intended to foster resignation. Are there chances for change? I do not despair. Perhaps it is still not too late to expose the crooks. But that might mean looking deeply into our social histories from the perspective of our ways of living and considering democratic alternatives to our conditions of life.

Notes

Preface

1. For a succinct interpretation of this viewpoint, see Transparency International, "What Is Grand Corruption and How Can We Stop It?," September 21, 2016, https://www.transparency.org/en/news/what-is-grand-corruption-and-how-can-we-stop-it (accessed November 29, 2019).

1. Introduction

Epigraph: Unnamed Indonesian journalist speaking to the author, cited in Edward Aspinall, *Opposing Suharto: Compromise, Resistance, and Regime Change in Indonesia* (Stanford: Stanford University Press, 2005), 1.

1. United Nations Office on Drugs and Crime, *Estimating Illicit Financial Flows Resulting from Drug Trafficking and Other Transnational Organized Crimes* (Vienna: UNDOC, 2011); Emile van der Does De Willebois, J. C. Sharman, Robert Harrison, Ji Won Park, and Emily Halter, *The Puppet Masters: How the Corrupt Use Legal Structures to Hide Stolen Assets and What to Do about It* (Geneva: World Bank Publications, 2011). See also http://www.worldbank.org/en/topic/governance/brief/anti-corruption (accessed October 23, 2016); Gregg Barak, *Routledge International Handbook of the Crimes of the Powerful* (New York: Routledge, 2015); Steven Hiatt, *A Game as Old as Empire: The Secret World of Economic Hit Men and the Web of Global Corruption* (San Francisco: Berrett-Koehler, 2007); Jeffrey A. Winters, *Oligarchy* (Cambridge: Cambridge University Press, 2011); Andy Coghlan and Debora MacKenzie, "Revealed: The Capitalist Network that Runs the World," *New Scientist,* October 9, 2011, https://www.newscientist.com/article/mg21228354.500-revealed—the-capitalist-network-that-runs-the-world/ (accessed February 8, 2017). Throughout this book, I use the word "network" to signify voluntary and strategically initiated relationships among distinct groups of people, most of whom already enjoy advantages relative to their peers. Over extended periods of time,

these relationships have the potential to congeal into enduring social structures, but these can also shift subsequently. When powered by coercion, their patterns tend to accumulate wealth and political control that set in motion important long-term dynamical structures. See, for instance, John F. Padgett and Christopher K. Ansell, "Robust Action and the Rise of the Medici, 1400–1434," *American Journal of Sociology* 98, no. 6 (1993): 1259–1319; Paul D. McLean, *The Art of the Network: Strategic Interaction and Patronage in Renaissance Florence* (Raleigh, NC: Duke University Press, 2007); Jonathan Shepard, "Networks," *Past and Present* 238, suppl. 13 (2018): 116–157.

2. As I point out in Chapter 2, the standard definition of corruption used by the World Bank and other policy-guiding agencies is more clinically focused on individual wrongdoing, as the "abuse of public office for private gain."

3. Shell companies are an intriguing mix of legal and suspicious elements, sometimes having ludicrous names that barely hide their intent of seeming to be useful or productive enterprises but whose actual purpose is to hide accounts for bigger players. See, for instance, Michael G. Findley, Daniel L. Nielson, and Jason Campbell Sharman, *Global Shell Games: Experiments in Transnational Relations, Crime, and Terrorism* (Cambridge: Cambridge University Press, 2014); Gabriel Zucman, *The Hidden Wealth of Nations: The Scourge of Tax Havens* (Chicago: University of Chicago Press, 2015); and Alexander Cooley, John Heathershaw, and J. C. Sharman, "Laundering Cash, Whitewashing Reputations," *Journal of Democracy* 29, no. 1 (2018): 39–53.

4. "Panama Papers," International Consortium of Investigative Journalists, https://www.icij.org/investigations/panama-papers/ (accessed July 3, 2020); Bruce Buchan, "Our Golden Age of Corruption," *Arena Magazine*, no. 141 (April / May 2016): 24–26; Michael Hudson, Will Fitzgibbon, Emilia Diaz-Struck, and Sol Lauria, "Panama's Revolving Door Shows Global Challenge of Offshore Reform," https://www.icij.org/investigations/panama-papers/20161216-panama-offshore-reform-challenge/ (accessed July 3, 2020); Winters, *Oligarchy;* "If Trump Is Laundering Russian Money, Here's How It Works," https://www.wired.com/story/if-trump-is-laundering-russian-money-heres-how-it-works/ (accessed August 25, 2018). On predatory capitalism, see George A. Akerlof and Robert J. Shiller, *Animal Spirits: How Human Psychology Drives the Economy, and Why It Matters for Global Capitalism* (Princeton: Princeton University Press, 2009).

5. I find the political scientist John Higley's definition of elites useful: "individuals and small, relatively cohesive and stable groups with major decisional power." Elite networks, in the sense in which I use the term in this book, are formed when these persons and groups fuse what are sometimes contingent bonds with each other and the rest of their societies through long-term social processes of consent formation and coercion. Thus, elite networks may comprise members of the "ruling class" and a second stratum of those who are influential and closely linked with ruling elites; together, they establish long-term rules of the

game. In large part because of the ambiguity in the term "elites," I prefer to focus on "elite networks": the institutions spawned and sustained through elite privilege and extended interaction. John Higley, "Continuities and Discontinuities in Elite Theory," in *The Palgrave Handbook of Political Elites,* ed. Heinrich Best and John Higley (London: Palgrave Macmillan, 2018), 25–39. On wealth inequality, see James B. Glattfelder, " Who Controls the World," presented at Tedx Zurich, 2012, https://www.ted.com/talks/james_b_glattfelder_who_controls_the_world?utm _campaign=tedspread&utm_medium=referral&utm_source=tedcomshare (accessed October 22, 2019; Thomas Piketty, *Capital in the Twenty-First Century,* trans. Arthur Goldhammer (Cambridge, MA: Harvard University Press, 2014); Branko Milanović, *Global Inequality: A New Approach for the Age of Globalization* (Cambridge, MA: Belknap Press, 2016).

6. I use the word "tragedy" as a mode of making sense of human action as much as a narrative genre of conflict and bleak endings. Ancient Athenian tragedy was meant to be an allegorical mirror for the audience to reflect on itself and the likelihood of its failure to prevent tyranny. Seeing corruption or societal decay tragically as both preventable in principle but unavoidable as a result of institutional inertia and unforeseen circumstances in history may similarly provide meaningful lessons for the future. Peter Euben, "On Political Corruption," *Antioch Review* 36, no. 1 (1978): 103–118.

7. Michael R. J. Vatikiotis, *Indonesian Politics under Suharto: Order, Development and Pressure for Change* (London: Routledge, 1993); Aspinall, *Opposing Suharto,* 29–30; Raymond Fisman, "Estimating the Value of Political Connections," *American Economic Review* 91, no. 4 (2001): 1095–1102; Benjamin Smith, "'If I Do these Things, They Will Throw Me Out': Economic Reform and the Collapse of Indonesia's New Order," *Journal of International Affairs* 57, no. 1 (Fall 2003): 113–128; David T. Hill, *The Press in New Order Indonesia* (Jakarta: Equinox Publishing, 2006); "The Family Firm," http://www.economist.com/node/598607 (accessed June 7, 2017); Vincent Bevins, "What the US Did in Indonesia," *The Atlantic,* October 17, 2017, https://www.theatlantic.com/international/archive/2017/10/the -indonesia-documents-and-the-us-agenda/543534/ (accessed December 11, 2017); Richard Borsuk and Nancy Chng, *Liem Sioe Liong's Salim Group: The Business Pillar of Suharto's Indonesia* (Singapore: ISEAS Publishing, 2014); *The Act of Killing,* directed by Joshua Oppenheimer, produced by Signe Byrge Sørensen, Joram Ten Brink, Errol Morris, Werner Herzog, André Singer, et al. 2012. Economists were generally optimistic that "good macroeconomic policy" was presumably a sign of "good governance" in Indonesia during the Suharto years. John A. Robinson et al., "Political Foundations of the Resource Curse," *Journal of Development Economics,* 79, no. 2 (2006): 465.

Indonesia's Gini coefficient or index of inequality has hovered between 35 and 40 and was as low as 32 during the Suharto years of prosperity. Poverty fell steeply until Suharto was deposed in 1998; even revised measures show it to be at an impressive 25 percent headcount ratio compared to 80 percent three decades earlier. Anthony B. Atkinson and Salvatore Morelli, "Chartbook of Economic Inequality," *ECINEQ WP* 324 (2014): 28. See also Christopher Hoy, "The Study that Shows Life Is a Lot More Unequal than You (Probably) Think," *The Guardian,* June 6, 2017.

8. For an evocative look at the exceptionally wealthy in the present day, see the Netflix show *Explained: Billionaires,* season 2, episode 2, released October 3, 2019. What is not fully clear is how such patterns cohere into recognizable types over decades, even generations. In the most enduring configurations of corruption, a closely knit but far-reaching set of linkages among elite actors is formed across several domains. As indicated by the Panama Papers case, veritable dens of social networks across countries, areas of occupation, and roles make up grand corruption formations of global size. Just as enigmatic as their appearance, formation, and survival over extended periods is how such networks manage to retain their secrets for a long time, given the massive scale of some of them. On the intergenerational effect of inheritance, see Daniel Halliday, *The Inheritance of Wealth: Justice, Equality, and the Right to Bequeath* (Oxford: Oxford University Press, 2018), 122–154.

9. Chandrashekhar Krishnan and Robert Barrington, *Corruption in the UK: Overview and Policy Recommendations* (London: Transparency International, 2011); Winters, *Oligarchy,* 279; Coghlan and MacKenzie, "Revealed: The Capitalist Network that Runs the World."

10. Sebastian Strangio, "Suharto Museum Celebrates Dictator's Life, Omitting Dark Chapters," *New York Times,* August 13, 2017; Joshua Oppenheimer, "Suharto's Purge, Indonesia's Silence," *New York Times,* September 29, 2015.

11. Winters, *Oligarchy,* 75. He makes the point that "wealth stratification is inherently conflictual, that coercion underlies all property claims and rights (especially when a few hold enormous fortunes while everyone else survives on much less), and that concentrated wealth has the unique characteristic of being a self-sustaining power resource." In contrast to Winters, who treats oligarchy as a special case of elitism, I prefer the term "elite networks" to refer to a collective entity of agents working together but producing emergent effects that cannot be reduced to the analytical effects of individual actors alone. Still, I follow Winters's reasoning that the defense and protection of wealth in all forms are key to the success of elite networks. See also R. Keith Sawyer, *Social Emergence: Societies as Complex Systems* (Cambridge: Cambridge University Press, 2005).

Consider that during the COVID-19 lockdown, elite universities that were forced to go online began to view online education as a very attractive business proposition, boosting their already substantial wealth. The business analyst Scott Galloway says in an interview that the top fifty or so global universities and a few other select ones will form an oligopoly for their brand and campus experiences. In addition to their online offerings, they will have limited enrollment for face-to-face interaction. A large number of people will have a far better and cheaper university education than what they experience today, except that it will be online. Meanwhile, an elite social class will be cultivated as a special selection of campus-based students, even if most of the revenues to the universities come from their online courses. The financing for large-scale online education will come from tech giants such as Apple, Google, and Microsoft, which will likely pour tens of billions of dollars into this space and earn even more. "The cruel truth of what pretends to be a meritocracy but is a caste system is that your degree largely indicates or signals your lifetime earnings. . . . When the government isn't able to bail out America, billionaires step in. But it always comes at a price. Those people become largely untouchable, and they can't be removed from office." "The Coming Disruption," interview with Scott Galloway, *New York,* May 11, 2020, https://nymag.com/intelligencer/2020/05/scott-galloway-future-of-college.html (accessed May 12, 2020).

12. People may simply be accustomed to certain ways of living because the conditions making up their lives are what they are. See J. G. A. Pocock, *The Machiavellian Moment: Florentine Political Thought and the Atlantic Republican Tradition* (Princeton: Princeton University Press, 2009). Pocock demonstrates through Machiavelli's writing and the history of Europe that it is in the very observance of customs that people often deem them good, not the other way around.

13. I am following here a long tradition associated with such a macrosociological position on corruption. See, for instance, Euben, "On Political Corruption"; Peter Euben, "Political Corruption in Euripides' Orestes," in *Greek Tragedy and Political Theory* (Berkeley: University of California Press, 1986), 222–251; Alexander Cooley and Jason Campbell Sharman, "Transnational Corruption and the Globalized Individual," *Perspectives on Politics* 15, no. 3 (2017): 732–753.

14. Cf. C. M. Sinopoli, "The Archaeology of Empires," *Annual Review of Anthropology* 23, no. 1 (1994): 159–180.

15. Robert Michels, *Political Parties: A Sociological Study of the Oligarchical Tendencies of Modern Democracy* (New York: Transaction, 1999 [1962]). As John Higley points out, in complex societies, power is invariably controlled by elites, who typically come from social backgrounds of privilege. John Higley, "Continuities and Discontinuities in Elite Theory," in *The Palgrave Handbook of Political Elites,* ed. Heinrich Best, John Higley, and Maurizio Cotta (London: Palgrave Macmillan, 2018), 25–39. Such control by elites may be accompanied by changes in the rest of society, whose patterns offer clues to different syndromes of corruption. See also Murray Milner Jr., "Theories of Inequality: An Overview and a Strategy for Synthesis," *Social Forces* 65, no. 4 (1987): 1053–1089; and Murray Milner Jr., *Elites: A General Model* (Cambridge: Polity, 2015).

16. The term "accumulation by dispossession" is attributable to David Harvey, who describes violent processes of capitalism to collect tribute or dispossess the poor from their land through acts of imperial force. This can include the general process of creating enclosures of land and other forms of capital. Historically,

enclosures were all types of fenced land and were likely intended initially to protect pastured animals; they later transformed land that was communally administered into a system of agricultural holding with individual ownership. Open fields were thus converted with legal sanction into private property that became a source of rent. There were many forms of resistance to enclosures and their encroachment into what was earlier treated as customary or common land that was farmed collectively by the peasantry. In England, this resistance began in the thirteenth century after passage of the Statute of Merton, which allowed the gentry to take over common land. In response, peasants occupied land or resorted to violence to protest their lack of access to the enclosed land. In the sixteenth century, the growth of the wool trade incentivized large landowners to enclose substantially more land for pasture, driving out many peasants. From the eighteenth century onward, the consolidation of farmland under greater manorial control was enacted by parliamentary acts that numbered in the thousands; nearly seven million acres of common land were converted to increasingly large estates. Enclosures were frequently justified on the grounds that open fields were inefficient, although there was scant evidence for this argument. Michael Turner, "Enclosures in Britain 1750–1830," in *The Industrial Revolution: A Compendium*, ed. Leslie Clarkson (London: Palgrave, 1984), 211–295; David Harvey, *The New Imperialism* (Oxford: Oxford University Press, 2003); Derek Hall, "Primitive Accumulation, Accumulation by Dispossession, and the Global Land Grab," *Third World Quarterly* 34, no. 9 (2013): 1582–1604; Danae Stratou and Yanis Varoufakis, "The Globalising Wall: Globalisation, Conflict and Division," *Architectural Review,* June 2018, https://www.architectural-review.com/essays/the-globalising-wall-globalisation-conflict-and-division/10031408.article (accessed January 7, 2020).

17. Charles Duhigg and David Barboza. "In China, Human Costs Are Built into an iPad." *New York Times,* January 26, 2012; Jim Yardley, "Report on Deadly Factory Collapse in Bangladesh Finds Widespread Blame," *New York Times,* May 22, 2013; Anjali Kamat, "Made in Bangladesh: Behind the Factory Fire," *Al-Jazeera,* October 17, 2016. Cf. Thomas Pogge, "Severe Poverty as a Violation of Negative Duties," *Ethics & International Affairs* 19, no. 1 (2005): 55–83.

18. Ai Weiwei, "How Censorship Works," *New York Times,* May 6, 2017 [emphasis added]. See also James Reeves, Ben Graham, and Bon Philips, dirs. *James Reeves Vlog,* 2017.

19. The morphology—that is, the shape of elite interlocking with different groups—may have many models. Elite global capital networks, according to James Glattfelder and Stefano Battiston, have a complex bow-tie pattern, with a core or strongly connected component and nodes all connected to each other; other less well-connected groups are at both ends. James Glattfelder and Stefano Battiston. "The Architecture of Power: Patterns of Disruption and Stability in the Global Ownership Network," *SSRN,* no. 3314648 (2019).

20. Niccolo Machiavelli, *Discourses on Livy* (Chicago: University of Chicago Press, 2009); Hiroaki Abe, "The Vicissitudes of Government: Machiavelli on Temporality and Pragmatism," paper presented at the Annual Meeting of the American Political Science Association, 2013; Francois Furet, *The Passing of an Illusion: The Idea of Communism in the Twentieth Century,* trans. Deborah Furet (Chicago: University of Chicago Press, 1999); Howard Bodenhorn and David Cuberes, "Finance and Urbanization in the Early Nineteenth-Century," *Journal of Urban Economics* 104, issue C (2018): 47–58, http://www.nber.org/chapters/c9977.pdf (accessed April 18, 2018). Cf. Charles Tilly, "War Making and State Making as Organized Crime," in *Bringing the State Back In,* ed. Peter B. Evans, Dietrich Rueschemeyer, and Theda Skocpol (Cambridge: Cambridge University Press, 1985), 169–191.

21. Barak, *Routledge International Handbook of the Crimes of the Powerful,* 1–2 [emphasis added].

22. Philip Mirowski, *Never Let A Serious Crisis Go to Waste: How Neoliberalism Survived the Financial Meltdown* (New York: Verso, 2013).

23. Stjepan G. Meštrović and Helene M. Brown, "Durkheim's Concept of Anomie as *Dérèglement,*" *Social Problems* 33, no. 2 (1985): 81–99.

24. Barak, *Routledge International Handbook of the Crimes of the Powerful,* 1–52 [emphasis added].

25. In Shakespeare's *Julius Caesar,* the patricians Brutus and Casca as well as their "honest neighbors" are alarmed by Caesar's feigned reluctance to be crowned king.

> Brutus: Was the crown offered him thrice?
> Casca: Ay, marry, was't, and he put it by thrice, every
> time gentler than other, and at every putting-by
> mine honest neighbours shouted.
> 				Julius Caesar, Act I, Scene II.

There is a rich literature on ancient Rome and the medieval Vatican. For examples, see Ramsay MacMullen, *Corruption and the Decline of Rome* (New Haven: Yale University Press, 1988); Eamon Duffy, *Saints and Sinners: A History of the Popes* (New Haven: Yale University Press, 2014); and Mary Beard, *SPQR: A History of Ancient Rome* (New York: Liveright, 2015). I am also aware that my uses of the words "corruption" and "elite networks" in multiple contexts need to remain cognizant of their limited horizon; that is, the meanings I ascribe to them and call on readers to acknowledge arise from my present-day, historically determined, and situated context. See also Hans-Georg Gadamer, *Truth and Method,* trans. Joel Weinsheimer and Donald G. Marshall (London: Continuum, 2004), 336–341.

26. Macmullen, *Corruption and the Decline of Rome;* Euben, "On Political Corruption."

27. In taking this route I follow a critical realist framework, which I consider ecumenically to include many scholars in the social sciences. See, for instance, Carole Pateman, *The Problem of Political Obligation: A Critique of Liberal Theory* (Cambridge: Cambridge University Press, 1985); Margaret Archer, *Realist Social Theory: The Morphogenetic Approach* (Cambridge: Cambridge University Press, 1995); and Margaret Archer, Roy Bhaskar, Andrew Collier, Tony Lawson, and Alan Norrie, eds., *Critical Realism: Essential Readings* (London: Routledge, 1998). See also Rajan, "Practising Theory in the Anthropocene: A Postcolonial Quest for Reliable Knowledge," *Economic & Political Weekly* 52, no. 14 (2017): 72–74.

Responding to the irenic tone taken by fellow scholar and later bishop Mandell Creighton's recently published history of the church, Lord Acton wrote that the popes and their entourage in the thirteenth and fourteenth centuries "instituted a system of Persecution, with a special tribunal, special functionaries, special laws. They carefully elaborated, and developed, and applied it. They protected it with every sanction, spiritual and temporal. They inflicted, as far as they could, the penalties of death and damnation on everybody who resisted it. They constructed quite a new system of procedure, with unheard of cruelties, for its maintenance. They devoted to it a whole code of legislation, pursued for several generations. . . . Power tends to corrupt and absolute power corrupts absolutely. *Great men are almost always bad men, even when they exercise influence and not authority: still more when you superadd the tendency or the certainty of corruption by authority.*" John Emerich Edward Dalberg, Lord Acton, *Acton-Creighton Correspondence* [1887], https://oll.libertyfund.org/titles/acton-acton-creighton-correspondence#-1887 (accessed July 20, 2017), emphasis added.

28. See, for instance, Sunil S. Amrith, *Crossing the Bay of Bengal* (Cambridge, MA: Harvard University Press, 2013); and Peter Frankopan, *The Silk Roads: A New History of the World* (New York: Bloomsbury Publishing, 2015).

29. Ariel Glucklich, *The Strides of Vishnu: Hindu Culture in Historical Perspective* (Oxford: Oxford University Press, 2008), 8–9. In this book, I steer clear of choosing sides between constructionist and primordialist views of Hindu practice—my concern is not with questions of religious identity as such but with the uses of ritual, law, and other social norms in serving to reorganize societies/polities into particular forms. These evolved over long time frames, coeval with the strengthening of different, though often remarkably stable, elite alliances and mutually supportive networks. See also Manu V. Devadevan, *A Prehistory of Hinduism* (Berlin: de Gruyter, 2016).

30. Priya Moorjani, Kumarasamy Thangaraj, Nick Patterson, Mark Lipson, Po-Ru Loh, Periyasamy Govindaraj, Bonnie Berger, David Reich, and Lalji Singh. "Genetic Evidence for Recent Population Mixture in India," *American Journal of Human Genetics* 93, no. 3 (2013): 422–438; Tony Joseph, *Early Indians* (New Delhi: Juggernaut, 2018).

31. Arthur L. Basham and S. A. A. Rizvi, *The Wonder that Was India* (London: Sidgwick & Jackson, 1987); V. S. Naipaul, *India: A Million Mutinies Now* (London: Heinemann, 1990); Ronald B. Inden, *Imagining India* (Bloomington: Indiana University Press, 1990); Sunil Khilnani, *The Idea of India* (New Delhi: Penguin Books India, 1999); Upinder Singh, *A History of Ancient and Early Medieval India: From the Stone Age to the 12th Century* (New Delhi: Pearson Education India, 2009). See also Lisa Lowe, *The Intimacies of Four Continents* (Durham, NC: Duke University Press, 2015); Rajeev Bhargava, "An Ancient Indian Secular Age?," in *Beyond the Secular West*, ed. Akeel Bilgrami (New York: Columbia University Press, 2016), 188–214.

32. There is an enormous literature on the challenges of Indian historiography. See, for instance, Inden, *Imagining India;* Dipesh Chakrabarty, *Provincializing Europe: Postcolonial Thought and Historical Difference–New Edition* (Princeton: Princeton University Press, 2009); Carola Dietze, "Toward a History on Equal Terms: A Discussion of Provincializing Europe," *History and Theory* 47, no. 1 (2008): 69–84; Romila Thapar, *The Past before Us* (Cambridge, MA: Harvard University Press, 2013). Finally, although it might seem that my arguments align with world systems theories, I do not attempt here to tie them together, except in a nonspecific, epigenetic sense that I elaborate on in later chapters. Christopher Chase-Dunn and Peter Grimes, "World-Systems Analysis," *Annual Review of Sociology* 21, no. 1 (1995): 387–417. I do, however, make the case for certain claims about universal and context-specific features of political societies at multiple scales. Cf. Jeroen Duindam, "A Plea for Global Comparison: Redefining Dynasty," *Past & Present* 242, no. Supplement 14 (2019): 318–347.

33. Finn Stepputat and Thomas Blom Hansen, "Sovereignty Revisited," *Annual Review of Anthropology* 35 (2006): 295–315; Piketty, *Capital in the Twenty-First Century*. Perhaps the most persuasive position on the emergence of elite sovereignty, not as a foregone historical conclusion, but as the outcome of strategic success in capture through settled agriculture can be found in James C. Scott, *Against the Grain: A Deep History of the Earliest States* (New Haven: Yale University Press, 2017).

2. Thinking Clearly about Corruption

1. Bob Jessop, *The State: Past, Present, Future* (New York: Wiley, 2015), 123–147.

2. See John Gaventa, *Power and Powerlessness: Quiescence and Rebellion in an Appalachian Valley* (Urbana: University of Illinois Press, 1982); Arnold J. Heidenheimer, Michael Johnston, and Victor T. Le Vine, eds., *Political Corruption: A Handbook* (New Brunswick, NJ: Transaction, 1989); Vincenzo Ruggiero, "'It's the Economy, Stupid!' Classifying Power Crime," *International Journal of the Sociology of Law* 35, no. 4 (2007): 163–177; Vincenzo Ruggiero, "Organised Transnational Crime in Europe," in *Routledge Handbook of European Criminology*, ed. Sophie Body-Gendrot et al. (London: Routledge, 2014), 154–167.

3. Roger Crisp, ed., *Aristotle: Nicomachean Ethics* (Cambridge: Cambridge University Press, 2014), 155. Note that Aristotle's definition of timocracy would be the same as the one used today: participation in governing the people by those who own property, typically land. In this book, I reserve the word "polity" for any organized society, any form of government that would today be termed "state." Athenian democracy was initially conceived and designed by the lawgiver Solon as a graded timocracy with different rules for participation among four social classes, the lowest being serfs. But as the rules of democratic institutions were reformed to become more inclusive, they were eventually engraved in communal sanctuary and watched over by a divinity, namely *Demokratia*. That, in turn, sealed the force of sanctions against elite capture in law. It is conceivable that Demokratia was related to Ma'at, familiar in Pharaonic Egypt more than a millennium earlier. Ma'at was both a concept and a goddess: a concept about principled life and the limits to discretionary power of the king and one's own personal power in ordinary relationships; and a deity confronting *isfet*, denoting chaos, negation, and, curiously, rebellion. Kurt A. Raaflaub, Josiah Ober, and Robert Wallace, eds., *Origins of Democracy in Ancient Greece* (Los Angeles: University of California Press, 2007); Kerry Muhlestein, *Violence in the Service of Order: The Religious Framework for Sanctioned Killing in Ancient Egypt* (Oxford: Archaeopress, 2011).

The political theorist Michael Gagarin writes, "Athenian democracy was brought to an end not by internal forces but by the external power of Philip of Macedon and his son Alexander. The legal system never became autonomous, and the rich sometimes complained that they were victims of unscrupulous litigants, but there is no indication that the people wanted to yield control of the legal process to a professional class, as Plato recommended." Michael Gagarin, *Demosthenes, Speeches 39–49* (Austin: University of Texas Press, 2011), xxviii.

4. The organization of societies into territories is itself neither timeless nor inevitable. Stuart Elden writes, "The idea of a territory as a bounded space under the control of a group of people, with fixed boundaries, exclusive internal sovereignty, and equal external status is historically produced." Stuart Elden, *The Birth of Territory* (Chicago: University of Chicago Press, 2013), 18.

5. Theda Skocpol, *States and Social Revolutions* (Cambridge: Cambridge University Press, 1979); Peter Evans, Dietrich Rueschemeyer, and Theda Skocpol, *Bringing the State Back In* (Cambridge: Cambridge University Press, 1985); Michael Mann, *The Social Sources of Power*, vol. 1: *A History of Power from the Beginning to AD 1760* (Cambridge: Cambridge University Press, 1986); Michael Mann, "War and Social Theory," in *The Sociology of War and Peace*, ed. M. Shaw and C. Creighton (London: Macmillan, 1987), 54–72; Niccolo Machiavelli, *Discourses on Livy* (Chicago: University of Chicago Press, 2009). As Carole Pateman reminds us, not only does the voluntarism posited by a theory of contract legitimize existing coercive relationships but it also mischaracterizes the moral legitimacy and political agency of the *demos*. Carole Pateman, *The Problem of Political Obliga-*

tion: A Critical Analysis of Liberal Theory (Los Angeles: University of California Press, 1985).

6. Charles Tilly, *Contention and Democracy in Europe, 1650–2000* (Cambridge: Cambridge University Press, 2004), ix [emphasis added]. In a similar vein, describing Europe in the sixteenth century, the historian Fernand Braudel writes: "Behind piracy on the seas acted cities and city-states, . . . behind banditry, that terrestrial piracy, appeared the continual aid of lords." Fernand Braudel, *La Mediterranee et le monde mediterraneen a Vepoaue de Philippe II*, vol. 2 (Paris: Armand Colin, 1966), 88–89. Cited in Charles Tilly, "War Making and State Making as Organized Crime," in *Bringing the State Back In*, ed. Evans et al., 173.

7. Paul E. Lovejoy, *International Slave Trade: Causes and Consequences* (New York: New York University Press, 1974). 65; John M. Berry, "Andrew Carnegie and Race," *Diverse: Issues in Higher Education*, June 17, 2008, https://diverseeducation.com/article/11301/ (accessed September 21, 2018); Emma Christopher, *Freedom in White and Black: A Lost Story of the Illegal Slave Trade and Its Global Legacy* (Madison: University of Wisconsin Press, 2018).

8. Pierre Bourdieu. *On the State* (Cambridge: Polity, 2014), 122–149. There can also be multiple sources of resistance to and alliance with sovereign power. These I understand typically as subordinate forms of power that may or may not gain in significance or territorial influence. The subsequent patterns of authority that align themselves to govern societal habits may appear to be circumstantial but are, in effect, the product of deliberate intervention by corrupt elite networks. Bruce Lincoln notes that both persuasion and coercion "exist as capacities or potentialities implicit within authority but are actualized only when those who claim authority sense that they have begun to lose the trust of those over whom they seek to exercise it." Bruce Lincoln, *Authority: Construction and Corrosion* (Chicago: University of Chicago Press, 1994), 6. On kingship and other types of sovereignty, see Dan Philpott, "Sovereignty," in *Stanford Encyclopaedia of Philosophy*, https://plato.stanford.edu/entries/sovereignty/ (accessed October 30, 2018).

9. Murray Milner Jr., *Elites: A General Model* (Cambridge: Polity, 2015). Charles Tilly, *Coercion, Capital, and European Sates, AD 990–1990* (Oxford: Basil Blackwell 1990).

10. On *hierophany*, see Mircea Eliade and Lawrence E. Sullivan, "Hierophany," *Encyclopedia of Religion* 6 (1987): 313–317. John F. Padgett and Christopher K. Ansell, "Robust Action and the Rise of the Medici, 1400–1434," *American Journal of Sociology* 98, no. 6 (1993): 1259–1319; Bob Jessop, *The State: Past, Present, Future* (New York: Wiley, 2015).

11. Susan Rose-Ackerman and Bonnie J. Palifka, *Corruption and Government: Causes, Consequences, and Reform* (Cambridge: Cambridge University Press, 2016).

12. Veena Das, "Corruption and the Possibility of Life," *Contributions to Indian Sociology* 49, no. 3 (2015): 322–343; Akhil Gupta, *Red Tape: Bureaucracy, Structural*

Violence and Poverty in India (Durham, NC: Duke University Press, 2012). Cf. Judith N. Shklar, *Legalism: Law, Morals, and Political Trials* (Cambridge, MA: Harvard University Press, 1986).

13. Scott writes, "Here I have in mind the ordinary weapons of relatively powerless groups: foot-dragging, dissimulation, false-compliance, pilfering, feigned ignorance, slander, arson, sabotage, and so forth. . . . It would be a grave mistake, as it is with peasant rebellions, overly to romanticize these 'weapons of the weak'. *They are unlikely to do more than marginally affect the various forms of exploitation which peasants confront.*" James C. Scott, "Everyday Forms pf Peasant Resistance," *Journal of Peasant Studies,* 13, no. 2 (1986): 6 [emphasis added]. See also E. P. Thompson, "Patrician Society, Plebeian Culture," *Journal of Social History* 7, no. 4 (1976); Fernand Braudel, *The Structures of Everyday Life* (New York: Harper & Row, 1982).

14. Pranab Bardhan, "Corruption and Development: A Review of Issues," *Journal of Economic Literature* 35, no. 3 (1997): 1320–1346; Gupta, *Red Tape.*

15. Edward L. Glaeser and Claudia Goldin, eds., *Corruption and Reform: Lessons from America's Economic History* (Chicago: University of Chicago Press, 2007); Terry Golway, *Machine Made: Tammany Hall and the Creation of Modern American Politics* (New York: W. W. Norton, 2014). To assume that machine politics is ultimately benign or victimless would be erroneous, Philip Gounev and Vincenzo Ruggiero write, "Corruption exacerbates the moral and political de-skilling of the electorate." Vincenzo Ruggiero and Philip Gounev, "Corruption and the Disappearance of the Victim," in *Corruption and Organized Crime in Europe,* ed. Philip Gounev and Vincenzo Ruggiero (London: Routledge, 2012), 19.

16. International IDEA, Money in Politics, https://www.idea.int/our-work/what-we-do/money-politics (accessed May 20, 2020).

17. Alena V. Ledeneva, *Russia's Economy of Favours: Blat, Networking and Informal Exchange* (Cambridge: Cambridge University Press, 1998).

18. Alena V. Ledeneva, *Can Russia Modernize? Sistema, Power Networks and Informal Governance* (Cambridge: Cambridge University Press, 2013), 224.

19. Alena V. Ledeneva, *How Russia Really Works: The Informal Practices that Shaped Post-Soviet Politics and Business* (Ithaca: Cornell University Press, 2006); Mark Galeotti, *The Vory: Russia's Super Mafia* (New Haven: Yale University Press. 2018). Cf. Richard Rose and William Mishler, "Experience versus Perception of Corruption: Russia as a Test Case," *Global Crime* 11, no. 2 (2010): 145–163. In this article, however, the authors focus exclusively on bribe paying in its petty and administrative forms, whose prevalence they contend is low in comparison with the perception of corruption in the country.

20. Francis Fukuyama, *Political Order and Political Decay: From the Industrial Revolution to the Globalization of Democracy* (London: Macmillan, 2014); Zephyr Teachout, *Corruption in America: From Benjamin Franklin's Snuff Box to Citizens United* (Cambridge, MA: Harvard University Press, 2014).

21. There is a wide literature covering these topics. See, for instance, Teachout, *Corruption in America;* Fukuyama, *Political Order and Political Decay,* 435–522; Yiannis Gabriel and Tim Lang, *The Unmanageable Consumer* (Thousand Oaks, CA: Sage, 2015).

22. Michael Johnston, *Syndromes of Corruption: Wealth, Power, and Democracy* (New York: Cambridge University Press, 2005).

23. Ruggiero and Gounev, "Corruption and the Disappearance of the Victim," 15–33. Ruggiero provides an example of normalizing standards for white-collar groups: "Entrepreneurs transferring arms through the export of technology officially destined for civil use may well claim that it is the duty of developed countries to export technology in order to help the economies of developing countries take off." Ruggiero, "'It's the Economy Stupid!' Classifying Power Crimes," 172.

24. Chris C. Ojukwu and J. O. Shopeju, "Elite Corruption and the Culture of Primitive Accumulation in 21st Century Nigeria," *International Journal of Peace and Development Studies* 1, no. 2 (2010): 15–24. On clientelism, see Susan C. Stokes. "Political Clientelism," in *The Oxford Handbook of Political Science,* ed. Robert Goodin (Oxford: Oxford University Press, 2013), https://doi.org/10.1093/oxfordhb/9780199604456.013.0031; Allen Hicken, "Clientelism," *Annual Review of Political Science* 14 (2011): 289–310.

25. In an example of some of the complexities spawned by formal changes in law that further obscure the criminal roles of elite networks, Staffan Andersson and Frank Anechiarico argue that a "reconstitution of the state" has taken place after liberalization, delinking central banks from global trade governance. This has changed the way ideals of public integrity, democratic accountability, and allied values making up social and political justice are viewed. Staffan Andersson and Frank Anechiarico, "The Political Economy of Conflicts of Interest in an Era of Public-Private Governance," in *Routledge Handbook of Political Corruption,* ed. Paul M. Heywood (London: Routledge, 2014), 253–269.

26. The ancient Greek historian Thucydides portrays a number of ways in which the deployment of state wealth and military power by individuals in Athens led to their abuse during the Peloponnesian War in 431–404 BCE. Martin Hammond and P. J. Rhodes, eds., *The Peloponnesian War* (Oxford: Oxford University Press, 2009). See also Chapter 6 for more on the Arthaśāstra.

27. J. Peter Euben, "Corruption," in *Political Innovation and Conceptual Change,* ed. T. Ball, J. Farr, and R. L. Hansen (Cambridge: Cambridge University Press, 1989), 29–31. See also Peter Bratsis, "The Construction of Corruption, or Rules of Separation and Illusions of Purity in Bourgeois Societies," *Social Text* 21, no. 4 (2003): 29.

28. Dean Hammer, "Homer and Political Thought," in *The Cambridge Companion to Ancient Greek Political Thought,* ed. Stephen G. Salkever (New York: Cambridge University Press, 2009), 14–41.

29. In *Politics,* Aristotle refers to democracy destroyed by aggrandizement, arrogance, and demagoguery, resulting in further factional conflict of corrupt oligarchies. *Aristotle's" Politics"* (Chicago: University of Chicago Press, 2013), 202–205. Cf. Moses I. Finley, "Athenian Demagogues." *Past & Present* 21 (1962): 3–24. For the Melian dialogue, see Hammond and Rhodes, *The Peloponnesian War,* 301–307. See also Arlene W. Saxonhouse, *Free Speech and Democracy in Ancient Athens* (Cambridge: Cambridge University Press, 2005).

30. J. Peter Euben, "On Political Corruption," *Antioch Review* 36, no. 1 (1978): 103–118; Geoffrey Ernest Maurice De Ste. Croix, *The Class Struggle in the Ancient Greek World: From the Archaic Age to the Arab Conquests* (Ithaca, NY: Cornell University Press, 1989); Lisa Kallet, *Money and the Corrosion of Power in Thucydides: The Sicilian Expedition and Its Aftermath* (Berkeley: University of California Press, 2001); James M. Buchanan, "Politics as Tragedy in Several Acts," *Economics and Politics* 15, no. 2 (2003): 181–191; Thomas Heine Nielsen and Mogens Hermann Hansen, *An Inventory of Archaic and Classical Poleis* (Oxford: Oxford University Press, 2004); Bruce Buchan and Lisa Hill, *An Intellectual History of Political Corruption* (New York: Macmillan, 2014).

31. Arlene W. Saxonhouse, "To Corrupt: The Ambiguity of the Language of Corruption in Ancient Athens," in *Corruption: Expanding the Focus,* ed. Manuhuia Barcham, Barry Hindess, and Peter Larmour (Canberra: ANUE Press, 2012), 45, 47 [emphasis added].

32. J. Peter Euben, *Corrupting Youth: Political Education, Democratic Culture, and Political Theory* (Princeton: Princeton University Press, 1997).

33. Avner Greif, *Institutions and the Path to the Modern Economy: Lessons from Medieval Trade* (Cambridge: Cambridge University Press, 2006).

34. Niccolo Machiavelli, *Discourses on Livy,* trans. Harvey C. Mansfield and Nathan Tarcov (Chicago: University of Chicago Press, 1996), 48.

35. Machiavelli, *Discourses on Livy,* 48. Machiavelli is critical of what he takes to be Aristotle's inability to read political relations of power correctly but acknowledges his debt to the Greek philosopher's broader framework.

36. J. A. G. Pocock, *The Machiavellian Moment: Florentine Political Thought and the Atlantic Republican Tradition* (Princeton: Princeton University Press, 2009), 204. See also Sara M. Shumer, "Machiavelli: Republican Politics and Its Corruption," *Political Theory* (1979): 5–34.

37. See, for instance, Sara Monoson, "Navigating Race, Class, Polis and Empire: The Place of Empirical Analysis in Aristotle's Account of Natural Slavery," in *Reading Ancient Slavery,* ed. Richard Allston et al. (London: Bristol Classical Press, 2010), 133–151.

38. On "managerialism," see Arvind Sivaramakrishnan, *Public Policy and Citizenship: Battling Managerialism in India* (Delhi: SAGE India, 2011). Without using the term "corruption equilibrium," Robert Klitgaard describes the conditions for a certain level of corruption to be inevitable, given market-like condi-

tions. Robert Klitgaard, *Controlling Corruption* (Berkeley: University of California Press, 1988). These analyses can get more sophisticated, looking into second-order variance across geographical contexts. Jens Chr Andvig and Karl Ove Moene. "How Corruption May Corrupt," *Journal of Economic Behavior & Organization* 13, no. 1 (1990): 63–76. There are, nevertheless, many economic modelers who are cautious. Daron Acemoglu, for instance, points out that political institutions might be the outcome of "various social factors that are not fully controlled for in the empirical models" and that those who hold power then influence the very rules of the game. Such reasoning does not generally go on to ask whether the very framework of "rational" expectations may also be influenced in as yet undetermined ways. Daron Acemoglu, "Constitutions, Politics and Economics; A Review Essay on Persson and Tabellini's 'The Economic Effects of Constitutions,'" *Journal of Economic Literature* 34, no. 4 (2005), 1033.

39. Scholars have often cast doubt on the efficacy of these approaches. See, for instance, Jakob Svensson, "Eight Questions about Corruption," *Journal of Economic Perspectives* 19, no. 3 (2005): 19–42; A. J. Brown, "What Are We Trying to Measure? Reviewing the Basics of Corruption Definition," in *Measuring Corruption*, ed. Charles Sampford, Arthur Shacklock, Carmel Connors, and Fredrik Galtung (London: Routledge, 2006), 57–80; Douglass C. North, John Joseph Wallis, Steven B. Webb, and Barry R. Weingast, *Limited Access Orders in the Developing World: A New Approach to the Problems of Development* (Washington, DC: The World Bank, 2007); Geoffrey M. Hogdson and Shuxia Jiang, "The Economics of Corruption and the Corruption of Economics: An Institutionalist Perspective," *Journal of Economic Issues* 41, no. 4 (2007): 1043–1061; Janine R. Wedel, "Rethinking Corruption in an Age of Ambiguity," *Annual Review of Law and Social Science* 8 (2012): 453–498. Cf. R. Keith Sawyer, *Social Emergence: Societies as Complex Systems* (Cambridge: Cambridge University Press, 2005).

40. Dennis F. Thompson, "Mediated Corruption: The Case of the Keating Five," *American Political Science Review* 87, no. 2 (1993): 369–381; David Schichor and Gilbert Geis, "The Itching Palm: The Crimes of Bribery and Extortion," in *International Handbook of White-Collar and Corporate Crime*, ed. H. N. Pontell and G. Geis (New York: Springer, 2007), 409; Wedel, "Rethinking Corruption in an Age of Ambiguity"; Mark Philp, "The Definition of Political Corruption," in *Routledge Handbook of Political Corruption*, ed. Paul M. Heywood (London: Routledge, 2014), 17–29.

41. Hannes Hechler, Gretta Fenner Zinkernagel, Lucy Koechlin, and Dominic Morris, "Can UNCAC Address Grand Corruption?," *U4 Report* 2011, no. 2 (Stockholm: U4 Anti-Corruption Resource Centre, 2011), https://www.u4.no/publications/can-uncac-address-grand-corruption (accessed January 22, 2017).

42. Anne Krueger, "The Political Economy of the Rent Seeking Society," *American Economic Review* 64 (1974): 291–303. Cf. Peter Gowan, *The Global Gamble: Washington's Faustian Bid for World Dominance* (New York: Verso, 1999).

43. In the late 1970s, as a result of high oil prices and robust revenues from oil producers, Western banks had substantial access to cash that was recycled as debt to developing countries for infrastructure development. With Cold War geopolitics, cronyism and outright theft by autocrats in developing countries, followed by worldwide recession in the early 1980s, the energy sector was severely afflicted by overcapacity in Europe and North America and broken assets almost everywhere else. Power plant equipment manufacturers, fuel companies, and energy contractors were looking for a way out of their dilemma and the solution came in the form of privatization of the electricity sector. By the 1990s, a new mantra was becoming prominent in international energy policy circles: electricity need no longer be a monopoly, with one integrated supplier both generating and transmitting it. Lower investments and competition could result from allowing generators to compete with each other and having distributors bid on zones of collection and billing. Electricity markets were hit by some scandals and rent-seekers, yet they have since stabilized. Navroz K. Dubash and Sudhir Chella Rajan, "Power Politics: Process of Power Sector Reform in India," *Economic and Political Weekly* 36, no. 35 (2001), 3367–3390.

44. Anwar Shah and Jeff Huther, *Anti-Corruption Policies and Programs: A Framework for Evaluation* (Washington, DC: World Bank, 1999). See also World Bank, *World Development Report 2002: Building Institutions for Markets* (New York: Oxford University Press, 2002); Benjamin A. Olken and Rohini Pande, "Corruption in Developing Countries," *Annual Review of Economics*, 4, no. 1 (2012): 479–509. Ranking has the effect of treating countries as more corrupt or less corrupt, which is roughly correlated with wealth, but this hardly describes the overall damage done to polities and societies by systematic abuses of power in both rich and poor countries.

45. Max J. Skidmore, "Promise and Peril in Combating Corruption: Hong Kong's ICAC," *Annals of the American Academy of Political and Social Science* 47, no. 1 (1996): 118–130.

46. Skidmore, "Promise and Peril in Combating Corruption," 125–126. Formal complaints against the ICAC, although frequent, also seem have a relatively low chance of prosecutorial success. According to a recent press release of the independent ICAC Complaints Committee, of twenty-two complaints comprising sixty-six allegations that the committee heard in 2012, only two allegations in two complaints were found to be substantiated and the officers involved were given "appropriate advice." See "ICAC Complaints Committee Annual Report Tabled in LegCo," July 10, 2013, http://www.info.gov.hk/gia/general/201307/10/P201307100308.htm (accessed August 28, 2014). See also Luís de Sousa, Barry Hindess, and Peter Larmour, eds., *Governments, NGOs and Anti-Corruption: The New Integrity Warriors* (London: Routledge, 2012); and the Community Legal Information Centre website: http://www.hkclic.org/en/topics/policeAndCrime/powers_of_ICAC/ (accessed August 28, 2014).

The World Values Survey, for instance, shows that generalized trust in Hong Kong (answers to the question "Can most people be trusted?" to which 40% say yes) is slightly lower than in China (49%), Vietnam (51%), and Thailand (41%) but is higher than in India (21%), Taiwan (24%), and Malaysia (9%). See *World Values Survey Wave 5: 2005–2009*, http://www.worldvaluessurvey.org. The 2011 Bribe Payer's Index for Hong Kong is 7.6 (India's is 7.5, and Netherlands' is 8.8), http://bpi.transparency.org/bpi2011/ (accessed August 28, 2014), but its Corruption Perceptions Index is ranked at 15, next to Japan, http://cpi.transparency.org/cpi2013/results/ (accessed August 28, 2014).

Uslaner uses the Asian Barometer data to show that generalized trust is not a significant determinant of perceptions of corruption in Hong Kong, but that trust in courts and civil servants is important (confidence in courts and civil servants is reported by 82% and 69%, respectively, of respondents). Eric M. Uslaner, *Corruption, Inequality and the Rule of Law* (Cambridge: Cambridge University Press, 2008). Cf. Martin Painter, "Myths of Political Independence, or How Not to Solve the Corruption Problem: Lessons for Vietnam," *Asia & the Pacific Policy Studies* 1, no. 2 (2014): 273–286.

47. Pranab Bardhan, "The Economist's Approach to the Problem of Corruption," *World Development* 34, no. 2 (2006): 341–348. On managerialism, see Sivaramakrishnan, *Public Policy and Citizenship*.

For a sample of the diversity of attempts to broaden meanings of corruption, see J. P. Euben, "Corruption," 220–246; Mark Philp, "Defining Political Corruption," *Political Studies* 45, no. 3 (1997): 436–462; Olivier De Sardan, "A Moral Economy of Corruption in Africa?," trans. Antoinette Tidjani Alou, *Journal of Modern African Studies* 37, no. 1 (1999): 25–52; Johnston, *Syndromes of Corruption*; Manuhuia Barcham, Barry Hindess, and Peter Larmour, eds., *Corruption: Expanding the Focus* (Canberra: ANUE Press, 2012); Veena Das, "Corruption and the Possibility of Life," *Contributions to Indian Sociology* 49, no. 3 (2015): 322–343; Buchan and Hill, *Intellectual History of Political Corruption*; Fran Osrecki, "A Short History of the Sociology of Corruption: The Demise of Counter-Intuitivity and the Rise of Numerical Comparisons," *American Sociologist* (2016): 1–23; R. Fisman and M. Golden, "How to Fight Corruption," *Science* 356, no. 6340 (2017): 803–804.

48. Johnston, *Syndromes of Corruption*; Sardan, "A Moral Economy of Corruption in Africa?"

49. Jean Comaroff, and John L. Comaroff, eds., *Law and Disorder in the Postcolony* (Chicago: University of Chicago Press, 2008); Gupta, *Red Tape*.

50. I draw attention here to Stjepan Meštrović's interpretation of anomie as *dérèglement*, "a condition of madness or a state akin to sin": a serious form of disarrangement in society, affliction, corruption, agitation, and suffering. Stjepan Gabriel Meštrović, *Emile Durkheim and the Reformation of Sociology* (Lanham, MD: Rowman & Littlefield, 1993), 62–63.

51. Luis Moreno Ocampo, "Corruption and Democracy: The Peruvian Case of Montesinos," *Revista: Harvard Review of Latin America* (2002): 26–29.

52. Jeffrey A. Winters, *Oligarchy* (Cambridge: Cambridge University Press, 2011).

53. Quintin Hoare, ed., *Selections from the Prison Notebooks of Antonio Gramsci*, trans. Geoffrey Nowell Smith (London: Lawrence and Wishart, 1971).

54. Johnston, *Syndromes of Corruption*, 12; Alina Mungiu, "Corruption: Diagnosis and Treatment, "*Journal of Democracy* 17, no. 3 (2006): 86–87.

55. Thomas Piketty, *Capital in the Twenty-First Century*, trans. Arthur Goldhammer (Cambridge, MA: Harvard University Press, 2014).

56. Nicholas Lord, *Regulating Corporate Bribery in International Business: Anti-Corruption in the UK and Germany* (Farnham, UK: Ashgate, 2014); Joanna Mckay, "Political Corruption in Germany," in *Corruption in Contemporary Politics,* ed. M. Bull and J. Newell (London: Palgrave Macmillan, 2003), 53–65; Jocelyn A. J. Evans, "Political Corruption in France," in *Corruption in Contemporary Politics,* 79–92; John R. Heilbrunn, "Oil and Water? Elite Politicians and Corruption in France," *Comparative Politics* 37, no. 3 (2005): 277–296. See also James C Scott, "Patron-Client Politics and Political Change in Southeast Asia," *American Political Science Review* 66, no. 1 (1972): 80–84, 91–113.

57. The *Oxford English Dictionary* defines "syndromes" as the concurrence of multiple phenomena that hint at underlying causes, for example, a disease. Corruption syndromes point toward macrosociological emergent entanglements that may require deep forms of investigation that could help interpret sociological conditions in terms of elite networks.

3. The Corruption of Society

1. Adam Masters, "Corruption in Sport: From the Playing Field to the Field of Policy," *Policy and Society* 34, no. 2 (2015): 111–123; Wolfgang Maennig, "Corruption in International Sports and Sport Management: Forms, Tendencies, Extent and Countermeasures," *European Sport Management Quarterly* 5, no. 2 (2005): 187–225; Graham Brooks, Azeem Aleem, and Mark Button, *Fraud, Corruption and Sport* (Berlin: Springer, 2013); Huw Richards, "No Easy Cure for Indian Cricket," *New York Times,* June 5, 2013; Alan Schwarz, Walt Bogdanich, and Jacqueline Williams, "N.F.L."s Flawed Concussion Research and Ties to Tobacco Industry," *New York Times,* March 25, 2016; Emmanuel Bayle and Hervé Rayner, "Sociology of a Scandal: The Emergence of 'FIFAgate,'" *Soccer & Society* (2016): 1–19.

2. Mariah Burton Nelson, *The Stronger Women Get, the More Men Love Football: Sexism and the American Culture of Sports* (Boston: Houghton, Mifflin, 1994); Gertrud Pfister, Verena Lenneis, and Svenja Mintert, "Female Fans of Men's Football: A Case Study in Denmark," *Soccer and Society* 14, no. 6 (2013): 850–871; Stacey

Pope, *The Feminization of Sports Fandom: A Sociological Study* (London: Taylor and Francis, 2017).

3. There is an enormous literature just on the philosophy and sociology of sport. See, for instance, John Wilson, *Playing by the Rules: Sport, Society, and the State* (Detroit: Wayne State University Press, 1994); Pierre Bourdieu, Hugh Dauncey, and Geoff Hare, "The State, Economics and Sport," *Culture, Sport and Society* 1, no. 2 (1998): 15–21; Claudio Tamburrini and Torbjörn Tännsjö, eds., *Values in Sport: Elitism, Nationalism, Gender Equality, and the Manufacture of Winners* (New York: Routledge, 2000); Robert E. Washington and David Karen, "Sport and Society," *Annual Review of Sociology* 27, no. 1 (2001): 187–212; Richard Giulianotti, ed., *Sport and Modern Social Theorists* (Berlin: Springer, 2004); Ben Carrington, "The Critical Sociology of Race and Sport: The First Fifty Years," *Annual Review of Sociology* 39 (2013): 379–398.

4. Some famous instances showing these intricate networks of corruption in sport include the Southern Methodist University college football case (https://en.wikipedia.org/wiki/Southern_Methodist_University_football_scandal, accessed May 8, 2020), the Salt Lake City buyout of the 2002 Olympics (https://en.wikipedia.org/wiki/2002_Winter_Olympic_bid_scandal, accessed May 8, 2020), the Indian Premier League cases (https://en.wikipedia.org/wiki/Controversies_involving_the_Indian_Premier_League, accessed May 8, 2020), and the 2015 FIFA scandal (https://en.wikipedia.org/wiki/2015_FIFA_corruption_case, accessed May 8, 2020). Brett Hutchins, and David Rowe, *Sport beyond Television: The Internet, Digital Media and the Rise of Networked Media Sport,* vol. 40 (London: Routledge, 2012). Hutchins and Rowe are interested in the "intensification of content production, acceleration of information flows, and expansion of networked communication capacity," which vastly amplify the revenues and reach of sport (17).

In *Capital,* Karl Marx poignantly points out that individual capitalists often do not realize that they are collective participants in a system of exploitation. Similarly, workers and consumers in the sports industry may not be aware of the factors that make up their social relations. Karl Marx, *Capital: A Critique of Political Economy,* vol. 1, trans. Ben Fowkes (London: Penguin Classics, 1990), 169–170. See also Michael Burton and John Higley. "The Study of Political Elite Transformations," *International Review of Sociology* 11, no. 2 (2001): 181–199.

5. There is a very broad literature endorsing similar claims. See Mark Granovetter, "The Social Construction of Corruption," in *On Capitalism,* ed. Victor Nee and Richard Swedberg (Stanford University Press: 2007), 152–172 (note especially his use of "network corruption" and "symbiotic patronage networks"); David Rowe and Callum Gilmour, "Sport, Media, and Consumption in Asia: A Merchandised Milieu," *American Behavioral Scientist* 53, no. 10 (2010): 1530–1548; Akhil Gupta, *Red Tape: Bureaucracy, Structural Violence, and Poverty in India* (Durham, NC: Duke University Press, 2012); Jean-Francois Bayart, "Africa in the World: A History of Extraversion," *African Affairs* 99, no. 395 (2000), 217–267. Note that the

relatively subordinate (compared to transnational private and multilateral banks and rich country leaders) exertions of African elites are not treated by Bayart as the defensive tactics of the weak who might use whatever opportunities they can find to make minor gains. Rather, they are well-orchestrated ways of using the external conditions as a major resource for "political centralization and economic accumulation" (219). Indeed, this results in a sort of privatization of the state that sustains multiple sources and forms of authority to generate a complex oligarchy with moguls.

6. Capitalism, seen as a chained set of relationships with contemporary elite networks, is of course a principal player in this mix in the present day. Cf. Francis Fukuyama, "Why Is Democracy Performing So Poorly?," *Journal of Democracy* 26, no. 1 (2015): 11–20.

7. Mary Norris, *Between You and Me: Confessions of a Comma Queen* (New York: W. W. Norton, 2015). This is a familiar theme in social philosophy, although one not typically associated with elite networks. The general idea is that although individuals are free to make their own history, they often end up framing and supporting institutions through their social constructs that ultimately harm themselves. See, for instance, Margaret Gilbert, "Walking Together: A Paradigmatic Social Phenomenon," *Midwest Studies in Philosophy* 15, no. 1 (1990): 1–14; Charles Lemert, "What Is Social Theory?," in *The Routledge Companion to Social Theory,* ed. Anthony Elliott (London: Routledge, 1993), 3–18; Cornelius Castoriadis, *The Imaginary Institution of Society* (Cambridge, MA: MIT Press, 1998); Brian Epstein, "A Framework for Social Ontology," *Philosophy of the Social Sciences* 46, no. 2 (2016): 147–167; Roberto Mangabeira Unger, *False Necessity: Anti-Necessitarian Social Theory in the Service of Radical Democracy* (New York: Verso, 2004).

8. Harold Garfinkel, *Studies in Ethnomethodology* (Englewood Cliffs, NJ: Prentice-Hall, 1967); Roy Bhaskar, *The Possibility of Naturalism: A Philosophical Critique of the Contemporary Human Sciences* (London: Routledge, 2014), 25–79.

9. Nira Yuval-Davis, *Gender and Nation,* vol. 49 (Thousand Oaks, CA: Sage, 1997); Nancy Armstrong, "Some Call It Fiction: On the Politics of Domesticity," in *Literary Theory: An Anthology,* ed. Julie Rivkin and Michael Ryan (Malden, MA: Blackwell, 2004), 567–583; Carole Pateman, *Sexual Contract* (New York: Wiley, 2014).

10. Satish Deshpande, *Contemporary India: A Sociological View* (New Delhi: Penguin Books India, 2004), 2; Emile Durkheim, *The Rules of Sociological Method: And Selected Texts on Sociology and its Methods,* 2nd ed., trans. W. D. Halls (London: Palgrave Macmillan, 2013), 20–28. "Kollywood" refers to the Tamil film industry, an amalgam of Kodambakkam in Chennai and Hollywood.

11. Pierre Bourdieu, "What Makes a Social Class? On the Theoretical and Practical Existence of Groups," *Berkeley Journal of Sociology* 32 (1987): 1–17; Michael

Hanagan, "New Perspectives on Class Formation: Culture, Reproduction, and Agency," *Social Science History* 18, no. 1 (1994): 77–94.

12. Norbert Elias, *What is Sociology?* (New York: Columbia University Press, 1978), 130–133.

13. Roy Bhaskar, *A Realist Theory of Science* (New York: Routledge, 2013), 11–52.

14. Bertrand Russell, "Introduction," in Ludwig Wittgenstein, *Tractatus Logico-Philosophicus* (New York: Routledge, 2002), xx. Speculative realism directly counters this position by asking, "What do we learn from experience?" which bypasses the certainty of cognitive knowledge alone, but nevertheless insists on applying comparable rules of validation. See, for instance, Bruno Latour, "What Is Given in Experience? A Review of Isabelle Stengers *Penser avec Whitehead,*" *boundary 2* 32, no.1 (2005): 222–237.

15. Margaret Archer, "Introduction," in *Critical Realism: Essential Readings*, ed. Margaret Archer et al. (London: Routledge, 1998), 192–193.

16. Gilles Deleuze and Félix Guattari, *A Thousand Plateaus: Capitalism and Schizophrenia*, trans. Brian Massumi (Minneapolis: University of Minnesota Press, 1987), 89–90. See also Jane Bennett, *Vibrant Matter: A Political Ecology of Things* (Durham, NC: Duke University Press, 2010), 23–38.

17. If natural science is reliable in showing us how human action and our recent history of capitalist expansion have led to global warming, the dramatic loss of biodiversity, and severe threats to oceans and the rest of the planet, then perhaps those social mechanisms causing those changes also urgently deserve comparable though not necessarily analogous explanatory models. For a social science to be reliable, it must describe reasonably well a large number of processes making up our lives, including art, political action, speech, urbanizing forms, and climate change.

For an impressive collection on body-oriented sociology and its relation to social action, see Erving Goffman, *The Presentation of Self in Everyday Life* (Harmondsworth: Penguin, 1959); Judith Butler, *Bodies that Matter: On the Discursive Limits of "'Sex"* (London: Routledge, 1993); Harold Garfinkel, *Ethnomethodological Studies of Work* (London: Routledge, 2005); Tony Lawson and Andrew Sayer, "Looking Forward to New Realist Debates," *Dialogues in Human Geography* 3, no. 1 (2013): 22–25.

18. Anthropocene is the term given to the idea that humans have created a new geological age that has superseded the previous one, the Holocene, that began some 10,000 years ago. Paul J. Crutzen, "The 'Anthropocene,'" in *Earth System Science in the Anthropocene*, ed. Eckart Ehlers and Thomas Krafft (Berlin: Springer, 2006), 13–18. See also Donna Haraway, "Anthropocene, Capitalocene, Plantationocene, Chthulucene: Making Kin," *Environmental Humanities* 6, no. 1 (2015): 159–165.

It is also helpful to think of nature as being emergent. This is already a well-known concept in ecology. But while emergent forms in nature and society may seem similar, they are not necessarily related through direct or even indirect mechanisms. Such an ontology avoids the twin traps of reductionism and determinism. Bhaskar, *The Possibility of Naturalism*.

19. George E. Smith, "The Methodology in the *Principia*," in *The Cambridge Companion to Newton*, ed. I. Bernard Cohen and George E. Smith (Cambridge University Press, 2002), 187–238. Cf. Louis O. Mink, "History and Fiction as Modes of Comprehension," *New Literary History* 1, no. 3 (Spring 1970): 541–558.

Isaac Newton was himself hopeful that his method provided a way to discover universal laws everywhere. In *Principia*, Newton writes, "If only we could derive the other phenomena of nature from mechanical principles by the same kind of reasoning! For many things lead me to the suspicion that all phenomena may depend on certain forces by which the particles of bodies, for causes not yet known, either are impelled toward one another and cohere in regular figures, or are repelled from one another and recede. Since these forces are unknown, philosophers have hitherto made trial of nature in vain. But I hope that the principles set down here will shed some light on either this mode of philosophizing or some truer one." Isaac Newton, *The Principia: Mathematical Principles of Natural Philosophy* (Berkeley: University of California, 1999), 382–383.

20. Sheldon S. Wolin, *Politics and Vision: Continuity and Innovation in Western Political Thought–Expanded Edition* (Princeton: Princeton University Press, 2016).

21. Charles Tilly, "War Making and State Making as Organized Crime," in Peter B. Evans, Dietrich Rueschemeyer, and Theda Skocpol, ed. *Bringing the State Back In* (Cambridge: Cambridge University Press, 1985), 169–191; Philip Abrams, "Notes on the Difficulty of Studying the State," *Journal of Historical Sociology* 1, no. 1 (1988): 58–89; John Agnew, "The Territorial Trap: The Geographical Assumptions of International Relations Theory," *Review of International Political Economy* 1, no. 1 (1994): 53–80; Pierre Bourdieu, *On the State* (Cambridge: Polity, 2014); Bob Jessop, *The State: Past, Present, Future* (New York: Wiley, 2015); Thomas Hobbes, *Leviathan* (New York: Routledge, 2016).

22. Even large centralized polities that existed earlier did not have all the present-day elements of state administration with a police force, standing army, a formal structure of law, and clearly defined rules of political order and succession. Adam T. Smith, *The Political Landscape: Constellations of Authority in Early Complex Polities* (Berkeley: University of California Press, 2003).

23. The geographer Stuart Elden writes that territory should be viewed as a political *technology*, a bounded space that entails the violence of exclusion and inclusion, vigilance and mobilization. Stuart Elden, "Land, Terrain, Territory," *Progress in Human Geography* 34, no. 6 (2010): 799–817.

24. J. G. A. Pocock, *The Machiavellian Moment: Florentine Political Thought and the Atlantic Republican Tradition*, vol. 25 (Princeton: Princeton University Press, 2016), 83–113.

25. Machiavelli, *Discourses on Livy*, 176, 193.

26. Tilly writes, "States themselves operate chiefly as containers and deployers of coercive means, especially armed force. Nowadays the development of welfare states, of regulatory states, of states that spend a great deal of their effort intervening in economic affairs has mitigated and obscured the centrality of coercion." Charles Tilly, "The Long Run of European State Formation," in *Visions sur le développement des États européens. Théories et historiographies de l'État modern* (Rome: École Française de Rome, 1993), 140. See also Michael Kearny, *Reconceptualizing the Peasantry: Anthropology in Global Perspective* (New York: Routledge, 1996), 42–72.

27. For a useful description of a bias toward rational choice frameworks and attempts within the modeling community to overcome it, see Robert Keith Sawyer, *Social Emergence: Societies as Complex Systems* (Cambridge: Cambridge University Press, 2005). The political theorist Jon Elster uses analytical reasoning to explain why social norms, of the sort "do x," which make up a sort of cement that binds large groups, are driven by a significant collective motivation to act that cannot be reduced to the rational choices of individual actors. Jon Elster, *The Cement of Society: A Survey of Social Order* (Cambridge: Cambridge University Press, 1989).

28. Catherine Bell, *Ritual Theory, Ritual Practice* (Oxford: Oxford University Press, 1992), 92.

29. Talal Asad, *Genealogies of Religion: Discipline and Reasons of Power in Christianity and Islam* (Baltimore: John Hopkins University Press, 2009), 75–76.

30. Norbert Elias, *Society of Individuals* (New York: Bloomsbury USA, 2001); see also Pierre Bourdieu, "The Genesis of the Concepts of 'Habitus' and 'Field,'" *Sociocriticism* 1 (1985): 11–24.

31. Michel Foucault, *Power/Knowledge: Selected Interviews and Other Writings, 1972–1977* (New York: Pantheon, 1980), 194–195 [emphasis added]. See also Giorgio Agamben, *"What Is an Apparatus?" and Other Essays* (Stanford: Stanford University Press, 2009).

32. Foucault, *Power/Knowledge*, 198, 201 [emphasis added].

33. Peter Brooker, *A Glossary of Cultural Theory* (Oxford: Oxford University Press, 2003), 119–120, 133–136. Benedetto Fontana explains how Antonio Gramsci analyzes the Catholic Church's political strategy. He writes that priests in the Church were constantly maintaining contact with the faithful "in order to prevent the emergence of a 'popular religion' in opposition to the official doctrine of the hierarchy.... The integration of these popular beliefs and practices into the Catholic theological and educational systems is what accounts for the continuity

and stability of the church as a political and social entity: the power of the church is derived from the intellectual and moral force it can generate by means of its 'union' with the ordinary people of the faith.... By means of such a moral and intellectual adaptation, the latter is able to assert and maintain its hegemonic supremacy over the 'community of the faithful.'" Benedetto Fontana, *Hegemony and Power: On the Relation between Gramsci and Machiavelli* (Minneapolis: University of Minnesota Press, 1993), 29.

34. Gaetano Mosca, *The Ruling Class*, trans. Hannah D. Kahn (New York: McGraw-Hill, 1939), 71.

35. Tilly, "War Making and State Making as Organized Crime," 171.

36. Bourdieu, *On the State*, 125, 130. See also Daud Ali, *Courtly Culture and Political Life in Early Medieval India*, vol. 10. (Cambridge: Cambridge University Press, 2004); James B. Glattfelder, "The Bow-Tie Model of Ownership Networks," in *Decoding Complexity* (Berlin: Springer, 2013), 121–148.

37. Michel Foucault, *Security, Territory, Population: Lectures at the Collège de France, 1977–78* (Berlin: Springer, 2007); Gilles Deleuze, *Negotiations, 1972–1990*, trans. Martin Joughin (New York: Columbia University Press, 1995); Paul Rabinow, *Anthropos Today: Reflections on Modern Equipment* (Princeton: Princeton University Press, 2003); Deirdre Niamh Duffy, *Evaluation and Governing in the 21st Century: Disciplinary Measures, Transformative Possibilities* (London: Palgrave, 2017).

38. Michel Foucault, "Truth and Power," interview by A. Fontana and P. Pasquino, in *Power/Knowledge: Selected Interviews and Other Writings, 1972–1977* (New York: Pantheon, 1980), 119.

39. Michel Foucault, *Discipline and Punish: The Birth of the Prison* (New York: Vintage, 1977); Timothy Mitchell, *Rule of Experts: Egypt, Techno-Politics, Modernity* (Berkeley: University of California Press, 2002). Pau A. Shackel and Matthew M. Palus, "The Gilded Age and Working-Class Industrial Communities," *American Anthropologist* 108, no. 4 (2006): 828–841.

40. Bruno Latour, *Reassembling the Social—An Introduction to Actor-Network-Theory* (Oxford: Oxford University Press 2005), 163, 247. Cf. Dave Elder-Vass, *The Causal Power of Social Structures: Emergence, Structure and Agency* (Cambridge: Cambridge University Press, 2010), 121–122.

41. Latour, *Reassembling the Social*, 75.

42. See Joan Wallach Scott, "Fantasy Echo: History and the Construction of Identity," *Critical Inquiry* 27, no. 2 (2001): 284–304. In a related manner, the philosopher Lauren Berlant suggests that agency need not be viewed just in a normative sense of personhood but also as "an activity exercised within spaces of ordinariness." Agency can then be seen as "an activity of maintenance, not making; fantasy, without grandiosity; sentience, without full intentionality inconsistency, without shattering; embodying, alongside embodiment." Lauren Berlant, "Slow Death (Sovereignty, Obesity, Lateral Agency)," *Critical Inquiry* 33, no. 4 (2007): 754–780.

43. C. Wright Mills, *The Power Elite* (Oxford: Oxford University Press, 2000), 288.

44. Mills, *The Power Elite*, 269–297. One helpful way to interpret these dynamics of power elites is to compare them with urban criminal gangs, especially as represented on film and television, where leadership, ritual, and a tight network of trust maintain a precarious but highly profitable underhanded operation. In grand corruption networks as well, there is a need for secrecy and bondage, but the stakes are far higher, implicating those at the extreme end of the affluence spectrum, the top 0.001%. William Foote Whyte, *Street Corner Society: The Social Structure of an Italian Slum* (Chicago: University of Chicago Press, 2012); John Perkins, *The New Confessions of an Economic Hit Man* (San Francisco: Berrett-Koehler, 2016); Anand Giridharadas, *Winners Take All: The Elite Charade of Changing the World* (New York: Knopf, 2018).

45. Stephen P. Borgatti and Virginia Lopez-Kidwell, "Network Theory," in *The SAGE Handbook of Social Network Analysis*, ed. John Scott and Peter J. Carrington (Thousand Oaks, CA: Sage, 2011), 40–54.

46. Mattei Dogan, ed., *Elite Configurations at the Apex of Power*, vol. 85 (Leiden: Brill, 2003), 5; cf. G. William Domhoff, *Who Rules America? The Triumph of the Corporate Rich* (New York: McGraw-Hill, 2014). For a useful approach to mapping elite configurations, see Ursula Hoffmann-Lange, "Methods of Elite Identification," in *The Palgrave Handbook of Political Elites*, ed. Heinrich Best and John Higley (London: Palgrave Macmillan: 2018), 79–92.

47. Michael Woods, "Rethinking Elites: Networks, Space, and Local Politics," *Environment and Planning A* 30, no. 12 (1998): 2106. In Chapter 7, I briefly present the historian Sven Beckert's description of more than a millennium of morphogenesis of cotton actor-networks or assemblages that are tied quite clearly to interlocking elite networks. Sven Beckert, *Empire of Cotton: A Global History* (New York: Vintage, 2015).

48. Michel Foucault, Arnold I. Davidson, and Graham Burchell, *The Birth of Biopolitics: Lectures at the Collège de France, 1978–1979* (Berlin: Springer, 2008); Hubert L Dreyfus, "Being and Power: Heidegger and Foucault," *International Journal of Philosophical Studies* 4, no. 1 (1996): 1–16.

49. Nicholas D., Theodorakis, Daniel L. Wann, Pantelis Nassis, and Tara Beth Luellen, "The Relationship between Sport Team Identification and the Need to Belong," *International Journal of Sport Management and Marketing* 12, no. 1–2 (2012): 25–38; M. J. Melnick, and D. L. Wann, "An Examination of Sport Fandom in Australia: Socialization, Team Identification, and Fan Behavior," *International Review for the Sociology of Sport* 46 (2011): 56–470; Avner Offer, *The Challenge of Affluence: Self-Control and Well-Being in the United States and Britain since 1950* (Oxford: Oxford University Press, 2006); cf. James C. Scott, *Weapons of the Weak: Everyday Forms of Peasant Resistance* (New Haven: Yale University Press, 2008).

50. Michael Carrithers, Steven Collins, and Steven Lukes, eds., *The Category of the Person: Anthropology, Philosophy, History* (Cambridge: Cambridge University Press, 1985; Margaret S. Archer, ed., *Social Morphogenesis* (Berlin: Springer Science, 2013).

51. Christine Delphy, "Patriarchy, Domestic Mode of Production, Gender and Class," trans. Diana Leonard, in *Marxism and the Interpretation of Culture*, ed. Cary Nelson and Lawrence Grossberg (Urbana: University of Illinois Press, 1988), 259–267. Bina Agrawal, *A Field of One's Own: Gender and Land Rights in South Asia*, vol. 58 (Cambridge: Cambridge University Press, 1994).

52. Adam Smith, *An Inquiry into the Nature and Causes of the Wealth of Nations*, vol. 2 (London: W. Strahan and T. Cadell, 1776), 87.

53. These are familiar themes from the early chapters of *Capital*. See also David Harvey, *The New Imperialism* (Oxford: Oxford University Press, 2003). Private property is expansionist in scope because it places solely an instrumental value on land, leaving aside its legacy and intangible affective and symbolic values. A propertyless regime that has never been territorial in scope cannot be imagined in this world.

54. FHWA (Federal Highway Administration), reports of various years. See also https://en.wikipedia.org/wiki/List_of_countries_by_vehicles_per_capita (accessed February 2, 2019). Note that after 2005, partly as a result of the financial crisis but also because of a change in attitudes toward car ownership with the proliferation of ride-hailing and car-sharing alternatives, there was a marked flattening in the trend. Daniel Sperling and Deborah Gordon, *Two Billion Cars: Driving toward Sustainability* (New York: Oxford University Press, 2009).

55. See, for instance, Robert Tillman, "Making the Rules and Breaking the Rules: The Political Origins of Corporate Corruption in the New Economy," *Crime, Law and Social Change* 51, no. 1 (2009): 73–86.

56. M. Sheller and J. Urry, "The New Mobilities Paradigm," *Environment and Planning* 38, no. 2 (2006): 207–226; Sudhir Chella Rajan, "Automobility, Liberalism, and the Ethics of Driving," *Environmental Ethics* 29, no. 1 (2007): 77–90.

57. Joan Didion, *Play It as It Lays: A Novel* (New York: Macmillan, 2005), 13–14.

58. John Platt, "Social Traps," *American Psychologist* 28, no. 8 (1973): 641. I owe this formulation to the transport geographer Madhav Badami. See also Madhav G. Badami, *Restoring Pedestrian Accessibility in Indian Cities* (Mandaluyong: Asian Development Bank, 2009).

59. Cotton Seiler, *Republic of Drivers: A Cultural History of Automobility in America* (Chicago: University of Chicago Press, 2009), 6.

60. Seiler, *Republic of Drivers*; James J. Flink, *The Automobile Age* (Cambridge, MA: MIT Press, 1990); James Howard Kunstler, *Geography of Nowhere: The Rise and Decline of America's Man-Made Landscape* (New York: Simon & Schuster, 1994); Martin Wachs, "Learning from Los Angeles: Transport, Urban Form, and

Air Quality," *Transportation* 20, no. 4 (1993): 329–354; Stan Luger, *Corporate Power, American Democracy, and the Automobile Industry* (New York: Cambridge University Press, 2005).

61. Sudhir Chella Rajan, "Automobility and the Liberal Disposition," *Sociological Review* 54, no. 1 (2006): 113–129. Cf. Louis Althusser, "Ideology and Ideological State Apparatuses (Notes towards an Investigation)," *Anthropology of the State: A Reader* 9, no. 1 (2006): 86–98.

62. Jack Ewing, "Volkswagen Says 11 Million Cars Worldwide Are Affected in Diesel Deception," *New York Times,* September 23, 2015.

Critical writing (or thought) refers to the practice of keeping a consistent exchange of ideas and reasoning across traditions of thought, as expressed in writing, the attempt to exchange ideas or exchange in Socratic questioning. Not viewing automobility critically in public discourse, the media, and academia, in general, is a failure, a "corruption" syndrome in my reading that has emerged in the course of a century. Cf. Joris Vlieghe, "Foucault, Butler and Corporeal Experience: Taking Social Critique beyond Phenomenology and Judgement," *Philosophy and Social Criticism* 40, no. 10 (2014): 109–135.

63. Cf. https://www.carfree.com (accessed May 23, 2017).

64. Hannah Arendt, *The Origins of Totalitarianism* (Boston: Houghton Mifflin Harcourt, 1973); see also Claude Lefort, *Democracy and Political Theory* (Cambridge: Polity, 1988), 45–55; Sudhir Chella Rajan, *The Enigma of Automobility: Democratic Politics and Pollution Control* (Pittsburgh: University of Pittsburgh Press, 1996); Matthew Paterson, *Automobile Politics: Ecology and Cultural Political Economy* (New York: Cambridge University Press, 2007).

65. The academic discipline of economics is itself increasingly an important justificatory discourse for global capitalism. See Jens Maesse, "Globalization Strategies and the Economics *Dispositif,*" *Historical Social Research / Historische Sozialforschung* 43, no. 3 (165 (2018): 120–146. Also, Simon Springer, "Neoliberalism as Discourse: Between Foucauldian Political Economy and Marxian Poststructuralism," *Critical Discourse Studies* 9, no. 2 (2012): 133–147.

66. David Harvey, *Money, Time, Space and the City* (Cambridge: Granta Editions, 1985).

67. The anthropologist Marcel Mauss writes, "*Homo economicus* is not behind us, he is in front us; as the man of morality and duty; as the man of science and reason. Man has been something else for a long time; and it is not long before he is a machine, a complicated calculator."

Marcel Mauss, "Essai sur le don," in *Sociologie et Anthropologie* (Paris: PUF, 1960), 272 [my translation]. See also Karl Polanyi, "The Economistic Fallacy," *Review (Fernand Braudel Center)* (1977): 9–18. Michael Mann, *The Sources of Social Power,* vol. 1: *A History of Power from the Beginning to AD 1760,* 2nd ed. (Cambridge: Cambridge University Press, 2012).

68. Karl Marx, "Historical Tendency of Capitalist Accumulation," in *Capital: Karl Marx and Frederick Engels: Selected Works* (London: Lawrence and Wishart, 2003); Anthony B. Atkinson, Thomas Piketty, and Emmanuel Saez, "Top Incomes in the Long Run of History," *Journal of Economic Literature* 49, no. 1 (2011): 3–71. Michel Callon, *What Does It Mean to Say that Economics Is Performative?* No. 005, Centre de Sociologie de l'Innovation (CSI), Mines ParisTech, 2006, https://halshs.archives-ouvertes.fr/halshs-00091596/document/ (accessed February 2, 2017). Michael J. Sandel, *What Money Can't Buy: The Moral Limits of Markets* (New York: Macmillan, 2012).

69. Karl Polanyi, *The Great Transformation: The Political and Economic Origins of Our Time* (Boston: Beacon, 2001), 56, 146.

70. Polanyi, *The Great Transformation* 202–203 [my translation for *cites ouvrieres*].

71. Polanyi, *The Great Transformation*.

72. David A. Reisman, *Schumpeter's Market: Enterprise and Evolution* (London: Edward Elgar, 2004), 71–96; Philip Mirowski, "Defining Neoliberalism," in *The Road from Mont Pelerin*, ed. Phillip Mirowski, and Dieter Plehwe (Cambridge, MA: Harvard University Press, 2009), 417–450; Daniel Stedman Jones, *Masters of the Universe: Hayek, Friedman, and the Birth of Neoliberal Politics* (Princeton: Princeton University Press, 2014); Simon Springer, Kean Birch, and Julie MacLeavy, "An Introduction to Neoliberalism," in *A Handbook of Neoliberalism* (London: Routledge, 2016), 1–14; Guy Standing, *The Corruption of Capitalism: Why Rentiers Thrive and Work Does Not Pay* (London: Biteback, 2016).

73. Richard Norgaard, "The Church of Economism and Its Discontents," 2015, http://www.tellus.org/pub/The-Church-of-Economism-and-Its-Discontents.pdf (accessed July 13, 2016).

74. Ernesto Dal Bó, "Regulatory Capture: A Review," *Oxford Review of Economic Policy* 22, no. 2 (2006): 203–225, Murray Milner Jr. *Elites: A General Model* (New York: Wiley, 2015), 86–123; Meredith Woo-Cumings, ed., *The Developmental State* (Ithaca, NY: Cornell University Press, 2019).

75. Peter Gowan, *The Global Gamble: Washington's Faustian Bid for World Dominance* (New York: Verso, 1999).

76. Charles Barthold, Stephen Dunne, and David Harvie, "Resisting Financialisation with Deleuze and Guattari: The Case of Occupy Wall Street," *Critical Perspectives on Accounting* 52 (2018): 4–16.

77. See, for instance, Sameer Dasani and Noam Chomsky, "Understanding the Crisis of the Markets, the State and Hypocrisy," *Foreign Policy in Focus,* 2009, http://fpif.org/chomsky_understanding_the_crisis_markets_the_state_and_hypocrisy/ (accessed July 13, 2016); Dean Baker, *The United States since 1980* (New York: Cambridge University Press, 2007).

78. William E. Connolly, *The Fragility of Things. Self-Organizing Processes, Neoliberal Fantasies, and Democratic Activism* (Durham, NC: Duke University Press 2013), 59.

79. Philip Mirowski, *Never Let a Serious Crisis Go to Waste: How Neoliberalism Survived the Financial Meltdown* (New York: Verso, 2013), 92.

4. Early Symptoms of Corruption

Epigraph: Captions of photographs taken at archaeological sites in Harappa (https://www.harappa.com/slide/street-mohenjo-daro and https://www.harappa.com/slide/mound-e-and-et-harappa, accessed July 28, 2015).

1. Adam T. Smith, "Archaeologies of Sovereignty," *Annual Review of Anthropology* 40, no. 1 (2011): 415. The term "landscape" demands some explanation. Archaeologists use it to denote sites of human and material forces operating across some space of a settlement and its environs. As settlements become more connected through larger spatial processes, describing these geographies involves terms that convey emergence, such as "territory," "state," "trade route," and so on. Adam T. Smith, *The Political Landscape: Constellations of Authority in Early Complex Polities* (Berkeley: University of California Press, 2003).

2. Some scholars, including the philologist Asko Parpola, suggest that some Śaivaite traditions, which persist today in Hinduism, might have originated in Harappa. This is based on the discovery of the famous Paśupati seal in Mohenjo-daro, presumably bearing the prototype of the forerunner of Lord Śiva, a seated figure surrounded by wild animals and wearing bull horns. Asko Parpola, *The Roots of Hinduism: The Early Aryans and the Indus Civilization* (New York: Oxford University Press, 2015).

3. Piggott, Stuart, "A Forgotten Empire of Antiquity," *Scientific American* 189, no. 5 (1953): 42–49; Nayanjot Lahiri, *Finding Forgotten Cities: How the Indus Civilization Was Discovered* (Hyderabad, India: Orient Blackswan, 2006).

4. Ian Hodder and Scott Hutson, *Reading the Past: Current Approaches to Interpretation in Archaeology* (Cambridge: Cambridge University Press, 2003); Adam T. Smith, "Archaeologies of Sovereignty," *Annual Review of Anthropology* 40, no. 1 (2011): 415.

5. Yashodhar Mathpal, *Prehistoric Painting of Bhimbetka* (Chikhili, India: Abhinav, 1984); Dilip K. Chakrabarti, *India: An Archaeological History: Palaeolithic Beginnings to Early Historic Foundations* (Oxford: Oxford University Press, 2009), 91–116; Mark M. Jarzombek, *Architecture of First Societies: A Global Perspective* (New York: John Wiley, 2014). Jane McIntosh notes that, unlike elsewhere, Bhimbetka suggests that there was a continuity and a symbiotic relationship between forager-hunters and settled farmers, involving some type of sharing of resources between the two. Foragers would often trade forest products for grain

with farmers. Jane McIntosh, *The Ancient Indus Valley: New Perspectives* (Santa Barbara, CA: ABC-CLIO, 2008), 55.

6. James C. Scott, "Four Domestications: Fire, Plants, Animals, and . . . Us," Tanner Lectures on Human Values, delivered at Harvard University, May 2011; James C. Scott, *Against the Grain* (New Haven: Yale University Press, 2017). Scott describes how foragers and hunters were held captive on farms to grow grains, a socialization that radically altered diets and human physiognomy for the worse. See also S. R. Walimbe, "Population Movements in the Indian Subcontinent during the Protohistoric Period: Physical Anthropological Assessment," in *The Evolution and History of Human Populations in South Asia*, ed. M. D. Petraglia and B. Allchin (Dordrecht: Springer, 2007), 297–319; Kathleen D. Morrison, "Foragers and Forager-Traders in South Asian Worlds: Some Thoughts from the Last 10,000 Years," in *The Evolution and History of Human Populations in South Asia*, 321–339. Dilip Chakrabarti uses the term "Kot Diji occupation," suggesting that a collective style, which developed along sites near the Hakra plain due east of the later Mohenjo-daro (*c.* 2600 BCE), may have re-created urban forms using much more advanced technology drawing on their gathering, engineering, and material resources. Chakrabarti, *India: An Archaeological History,* 117–204; "Kot Diji Gold Phase Sequins," https://www.harappa.com/indus5/32.html (accessed March 20, 2016).

Fairservis writes, "On the present evidence it seems reasonable to assume that the Harappan civilization stemmed from the developing village complex characteristic of much of Iran in the third millennium before Christ. Apparently economic advantages inherent in the Indus Valley situation motivated the production of surpluses, the proliferation of populations, the amplification and multiplication of non-farming specialists, and, in turn, the improvement or elaboration of traits already possessed or received by that population." W. A. Fairservis Jr., "The Origin, Character and Decline of an Early Civilization," *American Museum Novitates,* no. 2302 (1967): 15. Cited in Gregory L. Possehl, "Revolution in the Urban Revolution: The Emergence of Indus Urbanization," *Annual Review of Anthropology* 19 (1990): 267.

7. Trade extended as far as Mesopotamia from about the third millennium BCE. Shereen Ratnagar. *Trading Encounters: From the Euphrates to the Indus in the Bronze Age* (Oxford: Oxford University Press, 2004); Gregory L. Possehl, "Revolution in the Urban Revolution: The Emergence of Indus Urbanization," *Annual Review of Anthropology* 19 (1990): 262.

8. Large amounts of material were transported to and from Harappan sites. See, for instance, Brad Chase, P. Ajithprasad, S. V. Rajesh, Ambika Patel, and Bhanu Sharma, "Materializing Harappan Identities: Unity and Diversity in the Borderlands of the Indus Civilization," *Journal of Anthropological Archaeology* 35 (2014): 63–78.

9. Edward Soja, *Postmetropolis: Critical Studies of Cities and Regions* (Oxford: Wiley-Blackwell, 2000); George L. Cowgill, "Origins and Development of Urbanism: Archaeological Perspectives," *Annual Review of Anthropology* 33 (2004): 525–549.

10. Ian Hodder, "The Vitalities of Çatalhöyük," in *Religion at Work in a Neolithic Society: Vital Matters* (Cambridge: Cambridge University Press, 2016), 1–32.

11. Katherine I. Wright, "Domestication and Inequality? Households, Corporate Groups and Food Processing Tools at Neolithic Çatalhöyük," *Journal of Anthropological Archaeology* 33 (2014): 1–33.

12. Scott, "Four Domestications," 185.

13. During the Pleistocene, when there were abundant forest lands, good soil conditions and their biodiverse ecologies typically provided more than sufficient food for foragers and hunters. Peter J. Richerson, Robert Boyd, and Robert L. Bettinger, "Was Agriculture Impossible during the Pleistocene but Mandatory during the Holocene? A Climate Change Hypothesis," *American Antiquity* 66, no. 3 (2001): 387–411; Thomas P. Leppard, "Social Complexity and Social Inequality in the Prehistoric Mediterranean," *Current Anthropology* 3 (2019): 283–308.

Scott writes, "There is evidence, for example, that quasi-sedentary populations in the Mesopotamian alluvium during the Younger Dryas cold spell adopted more mobile subsistence strategies as the abundance of local subsistence forage dwindled." Scott, *Against the Grain*, 136.

14. Scott, *Against the Grain*, 106 [emphasis added]. Cf. Norbert Elias, *The Civilizing Process*, trans. Edmund Jephcott (Oxford: Blackwell, 1994), 65. There is a large literature on the relationship between the control of water and the rising power of political institutions. See, for instance, Christine Bischel et al., eds., "Water Infrastructure and Political Rule," special issue, *Water Alternatives* 9, no. 2 (2016): 168–372.

15. Hodder, "The Vitalities of Çatalhöyük," 107

16. Michael Mann, *The Sources of Social Power*, vol. 1: *A History of Power from the Beginning to AD 1760* (Cambridge: Cambridge University Press, 1986), 37–70. See also Jeremy Waldron, "Property and Ownership," https://plato.stanford.edu/entries/property/ (accessed April 20, 2020).

17. Karl Polanyi, Conrad M. Arensberg, and Harry W. Pearson, eds., *Trade and Market in the Early Empires: Economies in History and Theory* (Glencoe, IL: The Free Press, 1957); Adam T. Smith, *The Political Landscape: Constellations of Authority in Early Complex Polities* (Berkeley: University of California Press, 2003). Also, John Agnew shows that even contemporary definitions of state sovereignty fall into such a "territorial trap"—the false belief that territory is the only way in which to understand spatial politics. John Agnew. "Revisiting the Territorial Trap," *Nordia Geographical Publications* 44, no. 4 (2015): 43–48.

18. Karl Butzer, *Early Hydraulic Civilization in Egypt: A Study in Cultural Ecology* (Chicago: University of Chicago Press, 1976); Robert C. Allen, "Agriculture and the Origins of the State in Ancient Egypt," *Explorations in Economic History* 34, no. 2 (1997): 135–154; Juan Garcia Carlos Moreno, ed., *Ancient Egyptian Administration* (Leiden: Brill, 2013).

19. See Charles Tilly, "Cities, States, and Trust Networks," in *Contention and Trust in Cities and States*, ed. Michael Hanagan and Chris Tilly (Dordrecht: Springer Netherlands, 2011), 1–16. There is a lively debate around the concept and topology of early complex polities in relation to states. See, for instance, Gary M. Feinman and Joyce Marcus, eds. *Archaic States* (Santa Fe, NM: School of American Research Press, 1998); Smith, *The Political Landscape*; Norman Yoffee, *Myths of the Archaic State: Evolution of the Earliest Cities, States, and Civilizations* (Cambridge: Cambridge University Press, 2005); Adam T. Smith, "Archaeologies of Sovereignty," 415.

20. The smallest weight measure was 13.64 grams. The remaining measures were in ratios of 1; 2; 8/3; 4; 8; 16; 32; 64; 160; 200; 320; and 640. Units of length were similarly standardized. How these standards were enforced across the region remains a puzzle. Possehl, "Revolution in the Urban Revolution," 268. See also McIntosh, *The Ancient Indus Valley*, 150–151.

21. Farid A. Khan, "Excavations at Kot Diji," *Pakistan Archaeology* 2, no. 2 (1965): 22, cited in Gregory L. Possehl, "Sociocultural Complexity without the State: The Indus Civilization," in Feinman and Marcus, *Archaic States*, 261–291.

22. B. B. Lal, "Aryan Invasion of India: Perpetuation of a Myth," in *Indo-Aryan Controversy*, ed. Edwin Bryant and Laurie Patton (New York: Routledge, 2005), 58.

Evidence of at least some violence in Harappa is indicated by an analysis of a small sample of skeleton remains in Gwen Robbins Schug, Kelsey Gray, V. Mushrif-Tripathy, and A. R. Sankhyan, "A Peaceful Realm? Trauma and Social Differentiation at Harappa," *International Journal of Paleopathology* 2, no. 2 (2012): 136–147. Although only about 4% of the skeletons examined show signs of trauma, the authors point out that the "rate at Harappa is significantly greater and is the highest recorded rate in the prehistoric period thus far recorded" (145). Most of the violent deaths occurred in the post-urban period, from Cemetery H. Exclusion and social differentiation appear to be important in determining who was most likely to suffer from violent injury from others; this puts the lie to the portrayal of Harappan society as an exceptionally peaceful realm with little or no social stratification or systematic violence. The element of performance is critical to understanding the ritual power of forming "communitas" in Harappan society. See also Ratnagar, *Harappan Archaeology*.

23. T. S. Subramanian, "The Rise and Fall of a Harappan City," *Frontline*, June 18, 2010, available at https://archaeologynewsnetwork.blogspot.com/2010/06/rise-and-fall-of-harappan-city.html (accessed May 28, 2018).

24. Jonathan Kenoyer, "Bead Technologies at Harappa, 3300–1900 BCE: A Comparative Summary," http://www.harappa.com (accessed July 30, 2016); Upinder Singh et al., "Early Neolithic Tradition of Dentistry: Flint Tips Were Surprisingly Effective for Drilling Tooth Enamel in a Prehistoric Population," *Nature* 440 (2006), 755–756. Cf. Shereen Ratnagar, "An Aspect of Harappan Agricultural Production," *Studies in History* 2, no. 2 (1986): 137–153.

25. Yoffee, *Myths of the Archaic State*, 35.

26. McIntosh, *The Ancient Indus Valley*, 235–237. See also Michael Jansen, "Water Supply and Sewage Disposal at Mohenjo-Daro," *World Archaeology* 21, no. 2 (1989): 177–192. Jansen concludes his engineering assessment of these systems by noting that they "were developed to a degree of perfection which was to remain unsurpassed until the coming of the Romans and the flowering of civil engineering and architecture in classical antiquity, more than 2000 years later" (192). Cf. Shereen Ratnagar, "The Drainage Systems at Mohenjo-Daro and Nausharo: A Technological Breakthrough or a Stinking Disaster?," *Studies in People's History* 1, no. 1 (2014): 1–6.

27. Bridget Allchin and Raymond Allchin, *The Rise of Civilization in India and Pakistan* (Cambridge: Cambridge University Press, 1982), 193. The Allchins attribute the term "competent dullness" to the archaeologist Stuart Piggott.

28. For a detailed illustration of one of the sites, Chanhudaro, see Jane Mackay's account from 1937 of a fresh set of excavations, http://a.harappa.com/category/author-article/dorothy-mackay (accessed November 25, 2014). See also Shereen Ratnagar's lecture on Harappa, https://www.harappa.com/video/science-versus-social-science-did-rains-do-harappans (accessed August 4, 2016).

29. Ratnagar points to the use of microweights as being evidence of high-value goods in transaction. Shereen Ratnagar, *Harappan Archaeology: Early State Perspectives* (Delhi: Primus Books, 2016), 100–101. Akkadian accounts from the twenty-fourth century BCE suggest that ships from Meluhha were docked far up the Euphrates River. Beads, pottery, cubical weights, and seals from the region have been found there, but the accounts speak of imports also of animals and plants, carnelian, copper, ebony, lapis lazuli, and ivory brought by the Harappans. At Eshnunna, a Harappan-style toilet has been found, and there are references to Meluhhan people throughout Sumer at least until the twenty-first century. See McIntosh, *The Ancient Indus Valley*, 182–191.

30. It has also been hypothesized that there was continuity with the second wave of urbanization that started about a millennium later further east, in the Indo-Gangetic plain. See also Andrew Lawler, "Indus Collapse: The End or the Beginning of an Asian Culture?," *Science* 320, no. 5881 (2008): 1281–1283. This question is at the heart of a major political contestation between Hindutva activists who claim that Vedic culture has Harappan roots and the view of several scholars who question such a strong connection given the major differences in their material cultures.

31. McIntosh, *The Ancient Indus Valley*, 91.

32. Hermann Kulke and Dietmar Rothermund, *A History of India* (London: Psychology Press, 2004), 29–31.

33. Lal, "Aryan Invasion of India," 59.

34. For reviews, see Possehl, "Sociocultural Complexity without the State," and Nayanjot Lahiri, *The Decline and Fall of the Indus Civilization* (New Delhi: Permanent Black, 2000).

35. Chase et al., "Materializing Harappan Identities."

36. Chase et al., "Materializing Harappan Identities," 74.

37. On elite lifestyles in Harappa, see Massimo Vidale, "Aspects of Palace Life at Mohenjo-Daro," *South Asian Studies* 26, no. 1 (2010): 59–76; Massimo Vidale, *The Lady of the Spiked Throne: The Power of a Lost Ritual* (Trieste: Gnutti Eural, 2011).

38. See Yoffee, *Myths of the Archaic State*, 42, whose description is more apt in characterizing the Vedic than the Harappan period.

39. Daniel Miller, "Ideology and the Harappan Civilization," *Journal of Anthropological Archaeology* 4, no. 1 (1985): 34–71.

40. Jonathan M. Kenoyer, "Indus Seals: An Overview of Iconography and Style," *Ancient Sindh: Annual Journal of Research* 9 (2006–2007), 7–30. Also see Jonathan M. Kenoyer and Richard H. Meadow, "Inscribed Objects from Harappa Excavations, 1986–2007," in *Corpus of Indus Seals and Inscriptions*, vol. 3, ed. A. Perpola et al. (Helsinki: SuomalainenTiedeakatemia, 2010). Both available at http://a.harappa.com (accessed November 26, 2014). See also Frenez Dennys and Massimo Vidale, "Harappan Chimaeras as 'Symbolic Hypertexts': Some Thoughts on Plato, Chimaera and the Indus Civilization," *South Asian Studies* 28, no. 2 (2012): 107–130. Their study suggests that the chimeric motifs on the seals served as hypertexts with multiple levels of referentiality within a complex symbolic universe. Significant effort has gone into deciphering the script on the seals. Rajesh P. N. Rao, Nisha Yadav, Mayank N. Vahia, Hrishikesh Joglekar, R. Adhikari, and Iravatham Mahadevan, "Entropic Evidence for Linguistic Structure in the Indus Script," *Science* 324, no. 5931 (2009): 1165–1165; Steve Farmer, Richard Sproat, and Michael Witzel, "The Collapse of the Indus-Script Thesis: The Myth of a Literate Harappan Civilization," *Electronic Journal of Vedic Studies* 11, no. 2 (2004): 19–57 (available at www.safarmer.com/fsw2.pdf; accessed December 1, 2017). Until the semantic rather than symbolic significance is clear, the writing on the seals remains a tantalizing mystery.

41. McIntosh, *The Ancient Indus Valley*, 257.

42. McIntosh, *The Ancient Indus Valley*, 82.

43. Fairservis cited in Possehl, "Sociocultural Complexity without the State," 282. See Monica L. Smith, "The Archaeology of South Asian Cities," *Journal of Archaeological Research* 14 (2006): 97–142. See, also, Vidale, "Aspects of Palace Life at Mohenjo-Daro," 59–76. Vidale concludes that in each of the sites, elite

groups were maintained in individual, citadel-like walled enclosures and perhaps competed with one another for political supremacy.

44. Adam Smith, *The Political Landscape*, 81.

45. Adam Smith, *The Political Landscape*, 108; Adam Smith, "Archaeologies of Sovereignty."

46. Cf. Yoffee, *Myths of the Archaic State*.

47. Daniel Miller suggests that it is because of the very absence of alternatives that the so-called priest-king and dancing girl figures keep appearing in contemporary accounts of the Harappan civilization. Daniel Miller, "Ideology and the Harappan Civilization," *Journal of Anthropological Archaeology* 4, no. 1 (1985): 34–71.

48. Heather M.-L. Miller, "Associations and Ideologies in the Locations of Urban Craft Production at Harappa, Pakistan (Indus Civilization)," *Archeological Papers of the American Anthropological Association* 17, no. 1 (2007): 37–51.

49. Catherine Bell, *Ritual Theory, Ritual Practice* (Oxford: Oxford University Press, 2009), 69–93.

50. Miller, "Ideology and the Harappan Civilization," 61 [emphasis added]. See also Paul Rissman, "Public Displays and Private Values: A Guide to Buried Wealth in Harappan Archaeology," *World Archaeology* 20, no. 2 (1988): 209–228.

51. Miller, "Ideology and the Harappan Civilization," 37–38.

52. Randall Law, "Moving Mountains: The Trade and Transport of Rocks and Minerals within the Indus Valley region," *Space and Spatial Analysis in Archaeology* (2006), 301–313. Law points out that "the scale of Harappan lithic transportation system might best be described as extensive but not necessarily labour intensive in regard to single loads." Were foragers and others in the vicinity deployed for this purpose? See Sudeshna Guha, "Recognizing 'Harappan': A Critical Review of the Position of Hunter-Gatherers within Harappan Society," *South Asian Studies* 10, no. 1 (1994): 91–97.

53. Chase et al., "Materializing Harappan Identities"; Ratnagar, *Harappan Archaeology*. Cf. Richard W. Scott and John W. Meyer, *Institutional Environments and Organizations: Structural Complexity and Individualism* (Thousand Oaks, CA: Sage, 1994), 207–300.

54. James C. Scott, "Everyday Forms of Resistance," *Copenhagen Journal of Asian Studies* 4, no. 1 (2008): 45–46.

5. The Vedic Period

Epigraph: Michel Foucault, *The Archaeology of Knowledge* (New York: Routledge, 1989), 21.

1. Rajendra Chandra Hazra, *Studies in the Puranic Records on Hindu Rites and Customs* (New Delhi: Motilal Banarsidāss, 1987), 193–214; Brian K. Smith, *Reflections on Resemblance, Ritual and Religion* (New Delhi: Motilal Banarsidāss, 1998); Frits Staal, *Discovering the Vedās: Origins, Mantras, Rituals, Insights* (New Delhi:

Penguin Books India, 2008), 87–102; Elaine M. Fisher, *Hindu Pluralism: Religion and the Public Sphere in Early Modern South India* (Oakland: University of California Press, 2017). Cf. Frances A. Yeats, *The Art of Memory: Selected Works of Frances Yeats,* vol. 3 (London: Routledge, 1966); Dorothy M. Figueira, *Āryans, Jews, Brahmins: Theorizing Authority through Myths of Identity* (Albany: State University of New York Press, 2002).

2. Staal, *Discovering the Vedās,* 71; Theodore Proferes, *Vedic Ideals of Sovereignty and the Poetics of Power* (New Haven, CT: American Oriental Society, 2007). Note that "bráhman" and "brāhmanas" are distinct in that the first is a concept and the second refers to an endogamous group of learned men. The proper noun "Brāhmanas" refers to a series of texts from the Vedic age that instructed brāhmanas on proper means of ritual.

3. Michael Witzel, "Autochthonous Āryans? The Evidence from Old Indian and Iranian Texts," *Electronic Journal of Vedic Studies* 7, no. 3 (2001): 3–107. See also Alf Hiltebeitel, "Hinduism," in *The Religious Traditions of Asia: Religion, History and Culture,* ed. Joseph Kitagawa (London: Routledge, 2002), 11–48. What seems relevant to note here is what the philologist Johannes Bronkhorst has termed *orthoepic diaskeuasis,* the commitment to memory of a single authoritative version, following editorial practice over centuries to produce that redacted form. This was perfected into precise pronunciation through rules embedded in the stanzas and was orally preserved in *śakhas,* or schools, which must have developed in the early post-Rigvedic age, most likely before the eighth century BCE. Each śakha belonged to a particular chieftainship whose Brahmin community and territory belonged to a specific tribe or subtribe. Their hymns, prose aphorisms, instructions, and invocations were ultimately consolidated into a finite set of redactions maintained by the śakhas, numbering anywhere from about a half-dozen verses for some texts to more than a hundred for others. Johannes Bronkhorst, "The Orthoepic Diaskeuasis of the Rigveda and the Date of Pānini," *Indo-Iranian Journal* 23 (1981): 83–95.

4. Bronkhorst, "The Orthoepic Diaskeuasis." See also Sheldon Pollock, "The Revelation of Tradition: śruti, smrti, and the Sanskrit Discourse of Power," in *Boundaries, Dynamics and Construction of Traditions in South Asia,* ed. Federico Squarcini (London: Anthem Press, 2011), 41–62. On the character of Vedic society, see Michael Witzel, "The Development of the Vedic Canon and Its Schools: The Social and Political Milieu," in *Inside the Texts, beyond the Texts: New Approaches to the Study of the Vedās: Proceedings of the International Vedic Workshop,* ed. Michael Witzel (Cambridge, MA: Harvard University Press, 1997), http://archiv.ub.uniheidelberg.de/savifadok/volltexte/2008/110 (accessed January 20, 2015).

In *Vedic Ideals of Sovereignty,* Proferes claims that the word "people" more accurately characterizes the Rigvedic *viś, jana, carsani,* and *krsti* than "tribe" or even "clan." The word "people" has its own important political overtones given its invocation for mobilizing claims to power.

5. Until the fourteenth century, there is no evidence for a Sanskrit manuscript having been created. Sanskrit commentaries on the Rigveda date back earlier, to the fourteenth century. One of the early translations from the Vedic corpus was that of the Upaniśads from Sanskrit to Persian during the reign of Shah Jahan in the seventeenth century. *The Rigveda: The Earliest Religious Poetry of India*, trans. Stephanie W. Jamison and Joel P. Brereton (New York: Oxford University Press, 2014), 18.

6. Stephanie W. Jamison and Michael Witzel, "Vedic Hinduism," in *The Study of Hinduism*, ed. Arvind Sharma (Columbia: University of South Carolina Press, 2003), 65–113; Sheldon Pollock, *The Language of the Gods in the World of Men: Sanskrit, Culture, and Power in Premodern India* (Berkeley: University of California Press, 2006).

7. Studies in Brahmanism, varna, and the caste system are legion. See, for example, Susan Bayly, *Caste, Society and Politics in India: From the Eighteenth Century to the Modern Age* (Cambridge: Cambridge University Press, 1999); Sekhar Bandyopadhyay, *Caste, Culture and Hegemony: Social Dominance in Colonial Bengal* (Delhi: Sage: 2004); Braj Ranjan Mani, *Debrahmanising History: Dominance and Resistance in Indian Society* (Delhi: Manohar Publishers, 2005); Gail Omvedt, *Seeking Begumpura: The Social Vision of Anticaste Intellectuals* (New Delhi: Navayana, 2008); Valerian Rodrigues, *The Essential Writings of B. R. Ambedkar* (Delhi: Oxford University Press, 2019).

8. For instance, there is a rich literature in Vedic studies on the sound of hymns and their meter, the role of tonal memory of syllabic and nonsyllabic sounds in Vedic transmission, and the experience of conducting sacrifice and following later Vedic strictures on endogamy and bodily discipline. See, for example, Hermann Oldenberg, *Prolegomena on Metre and Textual History of the Rigveda* (New Delhi: Motilal Banarsidās, 2005); Staal, *Discovering the Vedās*; Annette Wilke, "Sound," in *Brill's Encyclopedia of Hinduism*, vol. 5, ed. Knut A. Jacobsen (Leiden: Brill, 2013), 134–149. See also the idea of authority as inventive discourse: Yameng Liu, "Authority, Presumption, and Invention," *Philosophy & Rhetoric* 30, no. 4 (1997): 413–427.

9. Asko Parpola, *The Roots of Hinduism: The Early Āryans and the Indus Civilization* (New York: Oxford University Press, 2015); David Reich, Kumarasamy Thangaraj, Nick Patterson, Alkes L. Price, and Lalji Singh, "Reconstructing Indian Population History," *Nature* 461, no. 7263 (2009): 489; Edwin Bryant and Laurie Patton, eds., *The Indo-Āryan Controversy: Evidence and Inference in Indian History* (London: Routledge, 2005); Upinder Singh, *A History of Ancient and Early Medieval India: From the Stone Age to the 12th Century* (New Delhi: Pearson Education India, 2009), 186; Vagheesh M. Narasimhan, Nick J. Patterson, Priya Moorjani, Iosif Lazaridis, Lipson Mark, Swapan Mallick, Nadin Rohland, et al., "The Genomic Formation of South and Central Asia," *bioRxiv* (2018): 292581; Tony Joseph, *Early Indians: The Story of Our Ancestors and Where We Came From* (New

Delhi: Juggernaut, 2018). Pointedly, within Vedic liturgy and ritual practice, time itself is cyclical, which has helped reinforce a long-standing view among some Hindus that the Vedās are timeless and therefore immune to attempts to historicize them.

10. Jamison and Witzel, "Vedic Hinduism," 65–113; *The Rigveda: The Earliest Religious Poetry of India*, trans. Stephanie W. Jamison and Joel P. Brereton (New York: Oxford University Press, 2014); Parpola, *The Roots of Hinduism*. The terms "peasants," "servants," and "slaves" demand explanation. Peasants can be understood as those working on the land, typically without choice, but over time consenting to being bound to it. Servants are dependent on employment for food, and slaves have similar properties but are also treated as the property of their owners.

11. The similarities between the two include the use of chariots and horses, fire sacrifice accompanied by sacred hymns, and close phonetic roots for key terms. But some words have stark differences in meaning between Avestan and Sanskrit. Parpola, *The Roots of Hinduism*; Kumkum Roy, *The Emergence of Monarchy in Northern India, Eighth to Fourth Centuries BC* (Oxford: Oxford University Press, 1994).

12. In the area of Narhan, in today's Gorakhpur District in Uttar Pradesh, remains of domesticated horses were found, dated to 1300–800 BCE. Singh, *A History of Ancient and Medieval India*, 223–225; George Erdosy, ed., *The Indo-Aryans of Ancient South Asia: Language, Material Culture and Ethnicity*, vol. 1 (Amsterdam: Walter de Gruyter, 2012); Shareen Ratnagar, "Trails, Footprints, Hoofprints," *Journal of Biosciences* 44, no. 56 (2019).

13. Rakesh Tiwari, "The Origins of Iron Working in India: New Evidence from the Central Ganga Plain and the Eastern Vindhyas," *Antiquity* 77, no. 297 (2003): 536–545; Witzel, "Autochthonous Āryans?," 1–115; Johannes Bronkhorst, *Greater Magadha: Studies in the Culture of Early India* (Leiden: Brill, 2007).

14. Romila Thapar, *India: Historical Beginnings and the Concept of Āryan* (New Delhi: National Book Trust, 2006); Parpola, *The Roots of Hinduism*; Staal, *Discovering the Vedās*, 71; Bryant and Patton, *The Indo-Āryan Controversy*. Cf. Singh, *A History of Ancient and Early Medieval India*, 102–131, 157–158, 239.

15. Diana L. Eck, *Benares: City of Light* (New York: Columbia University Press, 1999); Bronkhorst, *Greater Magadha*; Singh, *A History of Ancient and Early Medieval India*, 334–336, 497.

16. Singh, *A History of Ancient and Early Medieval India*, 211–255.

17. See Ariel Glucklich, *The Strides of Vishnu: Hindu Culture in Historical Perspective* (New York: Oxford University Press, 2008), 27. The first written reference to Vedic people, or rather to the gods worshipped by them, comes not from South Asia but from Anatolia in 1380 BCE. There, a treaty between a Mitanni king and a Hittite ruler invokes *Mitra, Varuna* and *Indra*, familiar gods in the Vedic pantheon. Alongside it was a horse-training manual with a number of words identified as Proto-Indo-European. Roger D. Woodard, *Indo-European Sacred Space: Vedic and Roman Cult* (Urbana: University of Illinois Press, 2010), 18.

18. Balakrishna Ghosh, "Max Muller's Introduction to the Rigveda-Pratiśakhya," *Indian Historical Quarterly* 3, no. 3 (1927): 611–624; Bronkhorst, "Orthoepic Diaskeuasis," 83–95. See also Paul Kiparsky, "Pānini, Variation, and Orthoepic Diaskeuasis," *Asiatische Studien* 66, no. 2 (2012): 327–335.

19. Gonda, *Vedic Literature*; Witzel, "Vedās and Upaniśads"; Laurie Patton, *Bringing the Gods to Mind: Mantra and Ritual in Early Indian Sacrifice* (Berkeley: University of California Press, 2005), 59–87; Staal, *Discovering the Vedās*, 127–128.

20. The dozen or so texts known as *Mukha*, or principal, Upaniśads appeared before the turn of the millennium, and several others were composed during the first millennium of the Common Era. The word "Upaniśad" means "to place two things together." Many Upaniśads are rendered in dialogic or story form and constitute a broad philosophical commentary on human society and godly providence. Much of the early interpretation of the Vedās (but considered part of the corpus itself) occurs in the Upaniśads, particularly the Brihadaranyaka and Chandogya Upaniśads, also considered the oldest of these texts. These are expressed as elucidations on breath, ritual chants, sleep and speech, but all are directed toward the act of recognizing the true nature of the Self. The Self is seen as the interplay of personal selfhood, or *ātman*, and universal consciousness, or *bráhman*: "And take what people call '*bráhman*'—clearly, it is nothing but this space here outside a person. And this space here outside a person—clearly, it is the same as this space here within a person. And this space here within a person—clearly, it is the same as this space here within the heart; it is full and nondepleting. Anyone who knows this obtains full and nondepleting prosperity." Chandogya Upaniśad: 3.12.7–3.12.9. Patrick Olivelle, *The Early Upaniśads: Annotated Text and Translation* (Oxford: Oxford University Press, 1998), 207.

21. Romila Thapar, *Interpreting Early India* (Oxford: Oxford University Press, 1993), 307.

22. Jamison and Brereton, *The Rigveda* (X.90): 1540.

23. Further details can be collected from Śatapata Brāhmana (text) and also Dharmasutras, Manava Dharmaśāstra. Cf. Johannes Bronkhorst, *Buddhism in the Shadow of Brahmanism* (Leiden: Brill, 2011), 27–97. Bronkhorst points out that at least in the Buddhist canon, although Brahmins are frequently mentioned, there is no evidence for the existence of four varnas until after Aśoka's inscriptions, circa the third century BCE. Was there a "Sanskritization" process that enabled early non-dvija communities that were not initiated into Brahmanical codes to create identities and transform themselves into endogamous groups? I do not explore the origins or meanings of the word "caste" in this book and prefer to use the word *jāti* instead (for clan-based groups) and *varna*, where appropriate. On Sanskritization, see M. N. Srinivas, *The Cohesive Role of Sanskritization* (Delhi: Oxford University Press, 1989), 56–72; Johan Frederik Staal, "Sanskrit and Sanskritization," *Journal of Asian Studies* 22 (1963): 261. For an exploratory use of the term "Sanskritization," involving attempts by Kuru elites to use ritual order to

consolidate infrastructure, communication, and control in the mid- to late Vedic period, see Michael Witzel, "Early Sanskritization: Origins and Development of the Kuru State," *Electronic Journal of Vedic Studies* 1, no. 4 (2016): 1–26.

24. Singh, *A History of Ancient and Early Medieval India,* 186; Thapar, *India;* Michael Witzel, "Vedās and Upaniśads"; Parpola, *The Roots of Hinduism,* 308–360.

25. F. R. Allchin, ed., *The Archaeology of Early Historic South Asia: The Emergence of Cities and States* (Cambridge: Cambridge University Press, 1995).

26. Cf. Norman Yoffee, "Too Many Chiefs? (or, Safe Texts for the '90s)," in *Archaeological Theory: Who Sets the Agenda?* ed. Norman Yoffee and Andrew Sherratt (Cambridge: Cambridge University Press, 1993), 60–78.

27. *The Rigveda,* VII.18 (5,11) and VII.33 (3). Peter A. Coclanis, "Power and Control," in *Rice: Global Networks and New Histories,* ed. Francesca Bray, Peter A. Coclanis, Edda L. Fields- Black, and Dagmar Schäfer (Cambridge: Cambridge University Press, 2015), 275–278. See also, R. S. Sharma, *Material Culture and Social Formations in Ancient India* (Delhi: Macmillan, 1983), 105.

28. Francesca Bray, "Patterns of Evolution in Rice-Growing Societies," *Journal of Peasant Studies* 2, no. 1 (1983): 3–33; Te-Tzu Chang, "The Impact of Rice on Human Civilization and Population Expansion," *Interdisciplinary Science Reviews* 12, no. 1 (1987): 63–69.

29. Dorian Q. Fuller, Ling Qin, Yunfei Zheng, Zhijun Zhao, Xugao Chen, Leo Aoi Hosoya, and Guo-Ping Sun, "The Domestication Process and Domestication Rate in Rice: Spikelet Bases from the Lower Yangtze," *Science* 323, no. 5921 (2009): 1607–1610.

30. Singh, *A History of Ancient and Early Medieval India;* Romila Thapar, *From Lineage to State: Social Formation in the Mid-First Millennium B.C. in the Ganga Valley* (Bombay: Oxford University Press, 1984), 23 and 75; Michael Witzel, "Vedās and Upaniśads"; Dorian Q. Fuller, "Pathways to Asian Civilizations: Tracing the Origins and Spread of Rice and Rice Cultures," *Rice* 4, no. 3–4 (2011): 78–92. There are debatable references to rice (or barley) porridge in the Rigveda, but these are not in the so-called family books, which were likely composed before the first millennium BCE.

31. Michael Mann, *The Sources of Social Power,* vol. 1: *A History of Power from the Beginning to AD 1760,* 2nd ed. (Cambridge: Cambridge University Press, 2012), 44–45.

32. Romila Thapar, *Interpreting Early India,* 2nd ed. (Oxford: Oxford University Press, 1993), 76.

33. Kumkum Roy, "The King's Household: Structure / Space in the Sastric Tradition," *Economic and Political Weekly* (1992): WS55–WS60; Romila Thapar, *From Lineage to State: Social Formations in the Mid-First Millennium BC in the Ganga Valley,* 2nd ed. (Oxford University Press, 1999).

34. Staal, *Discovering the Vedās;* Joseph, *The Early Indians;* cf. Elden, Stuart Elden, *The Birth of Territory* (University of Chicago Press, 2013).

35. Singh, *A History of Ancient and Early Medieval India;* Thapar, *From Lineage to State,* 23, 75; Michael Witzel, "Vedās and Upaniṣads."

36. Mann, *The Sources of Social Power,* 47.

37. James C. Scott, *The Art of Not Being Governed: An Anarchist History of Upland Southeast Asia* (New Haven: Yale University Press, 2009).

38. SB III.1.1.9 cited in Naama Drury, *The Sacrificial Ritual in the Śatapatha Brāhmana* (Delhi: Motilal Banarsidāss, 1981).

39. Sylvian Lévi, cited in Patrick Olivelle, *The Aśrama System: The History and Hermeneutics of a Religious Institution* (New York: Oxford University Press, 1993), 38; e.g., SB 2.2.2.16; Smith, *Reflections on Resemblance, Ritual and Religion,* 86.

40. Brian K. Smith, "Ritual, Knowledge, and Being," *Numen* 33, no. 1 (1986): 68.

41. One of last few verses of the tenth mandala of the Rigveda, the *Dhruva Anghirisa,* or Royal Consecration, hymn goes thus:

> I have brought you here: be among (us). Stand firm, without wavering.
> Let all the clans want you. Let kingship not fall away from you.
> Be only here; do not budge—unwavering like a mountain.
> Like Indra, stand firm here; here uphold your kingship . . .
> And now Indra will make the clans bring tribute only to you.
> *RV* X.173.1–6

See also Thapar, *From Lineage to State,* 27, 32.

42. Brian Black, *The Character of the Self in Ancient India: Priests, Kings, and Women in the Early Upaniṣads* (Albany: State University of New York Press, 2007), 102.

43. Brian Hayden, *Shamans, Sorcerers and Saints: A Prehistory of Religion* (Washington, DC: Smithsonian Books, 2003), 258–266.

44. Theodore Proferes points to evidence of intertribal conflict in his work, "Kuru Kings, Tura Kāvaseya, and the -Tvāya Gerund," *Bulletin of the School of Oriental and African Studies* 66, no. 2 (2003): 210–219; *The Rigveda,* 55.

45. In these instances of territorial consolidation, it is likely that monastic austerity and separation by lineage enabled the appropriation of certain roles. These new roles were supported by the continuation of the Brāhmana or ritual literature through a proliferation of texts around sacrifice (Śrauta and Grhya Sutras) and, still later, the epics and Puranas, or stories of yore describing genealogies of particular clans and their traditions of worship. By the end of the Vedic period and the beginning of Buddhist discourses, rule-based literature became prominent in the areas of law, aesthetics, grammar, and government. Witzel, "Early Sanskritization," 1–26; Michael Witzel, "Rigvedic History: Poets, Chieftains and Politics," in *Language, Material Culture and Ethnicity: The Indo-Āryans of Ancient South Asia,* ed. George Erdösy (Berlin: De Gruyter, 1995), 307–352.

46. *Aitareya Brāhmana* VIII.10.24; *Śatapatha Brah* XIII 7.1.15 cited in Thapar, *From Lineage to State*, 28.

The forest has been a recurrent tale in India over countless generations. In the Rigveda, dozens of storm deities known as the Maruts are praised for their ability to cross over many realms: "As you smite the steadfast to the far distance and you set the heavy to rolling, o men, you drive across the forests of the earth and across the regions of the mountains" (*RV* I.38.11 and I.39.3).

47. Thapar, *From Lineage to State;* Namita Sugandhi and Kathleen Morrison, "Archaeology of Hinduism," in *The Oxford Handbook of the Archaeology of Ritual and Religion* (Oxford: Oxford University Press, 2011), 919–931.

48. Romila Thapar, *Early India: From the Origins to AD 1300* (Berkeley: University of California Press, 2002), 137, 146–150. The historian Kumkum Roy emphasizes the manner in which sacrificial rituals became increasingly grander and more somber, culminating in the *agnistoma* and other performances described in the Śrauta Sutras, which required more than a dozen priests and lasted several days. Roy, *The Emergence of Monarchy in Northern India*. See also Jarrod Whitaker, *Strong Arms and Drinking Strength: Masculinity, Violence, and the Body in Ancient India* (New York: Oxford University Press, 2011), 9.

49. Olivelle, *The Aśrama System*.

50. Witzel, "Early Sanskritization," 21.

51. Roy, *The Emergence of Monarchy in Northern India*, 56. Upinder Singh points to the metamorphosis of the clan chieftain to the hereditary king as sanctified by the Purusha Sukta hymn. Upinder Singh, *Political Violence in Ancient India* (Cambridge: Harvard University Press, 2017), 23–25.

52. Proferes, *Vedic Ideals of Sovereignty*, 31. Cf. Thapar, *From Lineage to State*, 23, 75; Michael Witzel, "Vedās and Upaniśads."

53. Proferes, "Kuru Kings, Tura Kāvaseya, and the -Tvāya Gerund," 210–219. In Chapter 6, I define more precisely what "court" may mean in different contexts, but here I use it loosely to imply the inner circle of the Kuru rājās. See for example, Rigveda II.1.2, II.36.

54. Wendy Doniger, *The Hindus: An Alternative History* (New York: Penguin Press, 2009); Michael Witzel, "Vedās and Upaniśads"; Thapar, *From Lineage to State*.

55. Stuart Hall, ed., *Representation: Cultural Representations and Signifying Practices* (Thousand Oaks, CA: Sage, 1997), 2.

56. Hall, *Representation*, 4. On the foundations (dharman) of Rigvedic kingship, see Alf Hiltebeitel, *Dharma: Its Early History in Law, Religion, and Narrative* (Oxford: Oxford University Press, 2011), 66–78.

57. On the token minority status of women and Śudras in the Vedic period, see Ananya Vajpeyi, "The Śudra in History: From Scripture to Segregation," in *South Asian Texts in History: Critical Engagements with Sheldon Pollock*, ed. Yigal

Bronner, Whitney Cox, and Lawrence McCrea (New York: Columbia University Press, 2011), 337–353.

58. *Rigveda,* 60–61; Gonda, *Vedic Literature,* 90.

59. Early Vedic sacrificers (*yajamāna*) were priests and warrior-kings who conducted the ritual in an effort to both emulate and please the gods. In the fourth mandala, King Trasadāsyu refers to himself both as Indra and Varuna, but also as their gift: "Because the wife of Purukutsa served you two with oblations and acts of homage, o Indra and Varuṇa, so then to her you two gave King Trasadāsyu, who smashes obstacles (and) who is half a god" (IV.42.9). This verse, thematically similar to many others in the Rigveda, provides sanction for the rājā's authority as a male worthy of Indra and Varuna and then seals the deal by conducting yajna in their name. Toward the end of the Vedic age, Kuru chieftains may well have wanted to canonize hymns that highlighted hypermasculine qualities, which legitimized their own political authority. Whitaker, *Strong Arms and Drinking Strength,* 27, 166.

60. R. W. Connell, *The Men and the Boys* (Berkeley: University of California Press, 2000). Connell refers to masculinity as a certain type of "configuration of gender practice" involving a set of linguistic codes and bodily dispositions that try to align themselves with institutional norms.

61. Chandogya Upaniṣad 8.5.1; Olivelle, *The Āśrama System,* 277–279.

62. Except for the much-cited female sage Gargi, there is little or no evidence of women having access to Vedic mantras. Rigvedic patriarchy was also a type of disciplinary power built around limits on women's movements and sexual expression. See Uma Chakravarti, "Conceptualising Brahmanical Patriarchy in Early India: Gender, Caste, Class and State," *Economic and Political Weekly* 28, no. 14 (April 1993), 581; Olivelle, *The Āśrama System,* 184; Smita Sahgal, "Niyoga [Levirate]: Conflict Resolution to Bruised Masculinity in Early India," *International Journal of Social Science and Humanity* 6, no. 4 (2016): 303–308.

63. Sukumari Bhattacharji, "Motherhood in Ancient India." *Economic and Political Weekly* 25, nos. 42–43 (October 1990), WS56. Uma Chakravarti writes, "The Śatapatha Brāhmana expresses the fear that the wife might go to other men [SBI 3.1.21J]. Most significantly there is a very embryonic notion of ultimate control over women's sexual behaviour being asserted by the king. The Salapatha Brāhmana [1.15.20] states that the divine 'rājā' Varuna seizes the woman who has adulterous intercourse with men other than her husband." Chakravarti, "Conceptualising Brahmanical Patriarchy in Early India," 581.

64. In some passages, dasyus are portrayed as demons or perhaps as just having demonic characteristics, and continual refrains are either invocations to Indra to strike them down or descriptions of how Indra did in fact strike them down. Indra's sworn enemy is *Vrtra,* the demon that creates obstacles, who is said to be a dāsyu. In a hymn praising Indra for his various deeds, the poet says, "You tore off

the one wheel of the Sun for Kutsa; the other you made into wide space for driving. You crushed the Dāsyus mouthless with your murderous weapon; you wrenched those of slighting speech down into a woeful womb" (V.34.6) It is unclear whether the dasyus are depicted here as linguistic aliens (hence, "mouthless"); and there are many other references to their language as being crude though not incomprehensible. In the quoted verses, rendering "those of slighting speech" mouthless is perhaps a reference to trouncing into mute submission those with foreign accents and patterns of speech. Elsewhere in the Vedās there are many references to dāsas and dasyus getting destroyed by Indra, Agni, and even Soma.

Elsewhere, Indra is praised for having "split the seven autumnal strongholds, their shelter, [when] he smote Dāsa clans, doing his best for Purukutsa (the Purus)" (VI.21.10). Or, "having smashed the Dāsyus, he aided the Ārya hue" (III.34.9). And again, "You scattered down the dark fifty thousand." (IV.16.13). *Rigveda* (V.29.10), 54–57. Wash Edward Hale, *Ásura-in Early Vedic Religion* (New Delhi: Motilal Banarsidāss, 1986), 146–169.

65. Ram Sharan Sharma, *Śūdras in Ancient India: A Social History of the Lower Order Down to Circa A.D. 600* (New Delhi: Motilal Banarsidāss, 1980).

66. In RV III.34.9, Indra is said to have aided the ārya hue by smashing the dasyus. In RV V.30.9, the dāsas are said to have made women their weapons, but Indra saw through their ploy and advanced on the dasyus to fight. In RV VI.18.3 Indra is said to have tamed the dasyus for the ārya. In RV VII.5.6 Agni is said to have dispelled the dasyus from their place, thereby producing great light for the ārya. In RV VIII.89.1–4 the Maruts (Indra's companions and fierce divine warriors) are invoked in a chant to Indra, his battle song, to destroy Vrtra, the dāsyu demon of obstacles: "You will smite Vṛtra; you will win the sun." In the Aitreya Brāhmana 7.18, Visvamitra assists the eastern Iksvaku king Harischandra by symbolically adopting local "barbarian" tribes (dāsyu), such as the Andhra, Pundra, and Sabara "who live in large numbers beyond the border."

67. Bronkhorst, *Buddhism in the Shadow of Brahmanism*, 42.

68. The early roots of this intention may be detectable in the Rigvedic gendered project and its treatment of insiders and outsiders. Rigvedic patriarchy was militaristic and expansionist, argues Jarod Whitaker:

> Rigvedic tribes had a heavily ritualized martial ideology driving their migratory progress. The social and historical implications of the dominant masculine ideology would have been realized in Āryan migratory expansionism, in securing and maintaining natural resources, such as pastoral lands and waterways, and in the union or subjugation of competing Āryan and non-Āryan peoples. Rigvedic poet-priests clearly propagate a violent masculine ideology—a Rigvedic warrior ethic—wherein all males, whether young or old, become real men by participating in the ritual tradition and by being strong, tough, and dominant.

Whitaker, *Strong Arms and Drinking Strength*, 161. See also Uma Chakravarti, "Conceptualising Brahmanical Patriarchy in Early India."

69. See Bruce Lincoln, *Authority: Construction and Corrosion* (Chicago: University of Chicago Press, 1994). Cf. Lalan Prasad Singh, *Tantra: Its Mystic and Scientific Basis* (Delhi: Concept Publishing, 1976), 14.

70. Olivelle, *The Āśrama System*, 184.

71. Cf. Balmurli Natrajan, *The Culturalization of Caste in India: Identity and Inequality in a Multicultural Age* (London: Routledge, 2011).

6. Dharma Yuga

Epigraph: Gautama Dharmasutra (11.27–28).

1. Brahmin poets of that period and beyond referred to it as the start of the Age of Strife or *Kaliyuga*, a time that was long anticipated with dread for its widespread forms of social degeneration and disorder in a world ruled by barbarians (*mlecchas*) and replete with affliction and disease.

2. Upinder Singh, *A History of Ancient and Early Medieval India: From the Stone Age to the 12th Century* (New Delhi: Pearson Education India, 2009), 276, 279, 329; Hermann Kulke and Dietmar Rothermund, *A History of India* (London: Routledge, 2016), 30, 39, 50–105. On the introduction of rice cultivation in South Asia, see Dorian Q. Fuller and Ling Qin, "Water Management and Labour in the Origins and Dispersal of Asian Rice," *World Archeology* 41, no. 1 (2009): 88–111; Dorian Q. Fuller, "Pathways to Asian Civilizations: Tracing the Origins and Spread of Rice Cultures," *Rice* 4 (2011): 78–92.

3. James C. Scott, *Against the Grain* (New Haven: Yale University Press, 2017). Elsewhere, Scott writes, "Encouragement of sedentarism is perhaps the oldest 'state project,' a project related to the second-oldest state project of taxation. It was at the center of Chinese statecraft for millennia through the Maoist period, when People's Liberation Army soldiers by the thousands were digging terraces to get the 'wild' Wa to plant irrigated wet rice." James C. Scott, *The Art of Not Being Governed: An Anarchist History of Upland Southeast Asia* (New Haven: Yale University Press, 2009), 340, note 12. See also Uma Chakravarti, *Social Dimensions of Early Buddhism* (New Delhi: Munshiram Manoharlal, 2002), 7–64; Anne T. Mocko, *Demoting Vishnu: Ritual, Politics, and the Unraveling of Nepal's Hindu Monarchy* (Oxford: Oxford University Press, 2016). For a quick visual overview of the multiple territorial shifts across India's longue durée, see https://www.youtube.com/watch?v=QN41DJLQmPk (accessed June 18, 2018).

4. Norman Yoffee, "Too Many Chiefs? (or, Safe Texts for the '90s)," in *Archaeological Theory: Who Sets the Agenda?* ed. Norman Yoffee and Andrew Sherratt (Cambridge: Cambridge University Press, 1993), 60–78.

There is a rich literature on the second wave of urbanization. See, for instance, Dilip K. Chakrabarti, *The Archaeology of Ancient Indian Cities* (New York: Oxford

University Press, 1995); Upinder Singh, "Cults and Shrines in Early Historical Mathura (c. 200 BC—200 AD)," *World Archaeology* 36, no. 3 (2004): 378–398; John Heitzman, *The City in South Asia* (London: Routledge, 2008). Recall that Harappa was not available to the collective memory of later Vedic and other traditions.

5. Strabo, *Geography* (London: Loeb Classical Library 241, 1930), 63 (15.1.36).

6. The Aiterya and Śatapatha Brāhmanas associate rājasuya with the anointment of the king as the guardian of dharma: he was the overlord to whom everyone comes came seeking law and order. Similar symbolic, but now territorial, functions are were associated with the aśwamedha, where "'with my two shins and my two feet I am the *dharma*, the king fixed firmly on his people." Taitereya Brāhmana 2.6.5, cited in Adam Bowles, *Dharma, Disorder, and the Political in Ancient India: The Āpaddharmaparvan of the Mahābhārata*, vol. 28 (Leiden: Brill, 2007), 92–93.

7. Notwithstanding the Vedic legend of the "Battle of the Ten Kings," the formation of the mahājanapādas need not be seen as an outcome of war or conquest, but rather as mutual recognition of territory among elites while collectively delivering notice to the "barbarians at the gate" (comparable, loosely, it the treaty of Westphalia in 1648). See Michael Mann, *The Social Sources of Power*, vol. 1: *A History of Power from the Beginning to AD 1760* (Cambridge: Cambridge University Press, 1986), 73–189; John Lukacs, "Interpreting Biological Diversity in South Asian Prehistory: Early Holocene Population Affinities and Subsistence Adaptations," in *The Evolution and History of Human Populations in South Asia*, ed. M. D. Petraglia and B. Allchin (Dordrecht: Springer, 2007), 271–296.

8. Because I have not yet used the term "social forces" in this book, I define it briefly as emergent forms of social coordination and control made possible by different dominant configurations of power.

9. Cf. Stuart Elden, *The Birth of Territory* (Chicago: University of Chicago Press, 2013). Elden's book exclusively follows the genealogy of territory within Europe, which he describes in terms of multiple syndromes of spatialized power.

10. Sovereign authority is hegemonic to the extent that consent is widespread, that is, through moral intellectual leadership, principally through the law. But this has a Centaur-like relationship with organized violence, hence the "force of law." That legal reasoning may differ by circumstance becomes apparent on examining the political foundations of law across traditions. See E. P. Thompson, "Patrician Society, Plebeian Culture," *Journal of Social History* 7, no. 4 (1976): 382–405; Sally Engle Merry, "Legal Pluralism," *Law & Society Review* 22 (1988): 869; Jacques Derrida. "Force of Law: The 'Mystical Foundation of Authority,'" *Cardozo Law Review* 11 (1990): 961–973; Richard A. Posner, *The Problems of Jurisprudence* (Cambridge, MA: Harvard University Press, 1993); Benedetto Fontana, *Hegemony and Power: On the Relation between Gramsci and Machiavelli* (Minneapolis, MN: University of Minnesota Press, 1993). On the instrumental uses of law, see Ejan Mackaay, "History of Law and Economics." *Encyclopedia of Law and Economics* 1 (2000), 65–117.

On the popular foundations of constituent power, see Andreas Kalyvas, "Popular Sovereignty, Democracy, and the Constituent Power," *Constellations* 12, no. 2 (2005): 223–244; Mattias Kumm, "Constituent Power, Cosmopolitan Constitutionalism, and Post-Positivist Law," *International Journal of Constitutional Law* 14, no. 3 (2016): 697–711. See also Andrew Arato and Jean Cohen, "Banishing the Sovereign? Internal and External Sovereignty in Arendt," *Constellations* 16, no. 2 (2009): 307–330.

11. The fact that rules of deliberation in legislatures and courts typically follow common principles of justice and serve the vast majority of people in most ordinary situations across the world is one of the triumphs of republican political forces across recent history. Nevertheless, blind spots, indeed significant failures in social and political justice, also seem to persist in every modern constitutional republic. See Bob Jessop, *The State: Past, Present, Future* (New York: Wiley, 2015), 53–90. In a series of lectures on the state at the College of France, Pierre Bourdieu points out that the abstraction of the state that is as familiar as the story of the market in contemporary cultures is a "great fetish . . . constituted on a bank of symbolic capital." In so doing, he finds a different way to focus on Jessop's first and second features. Pierre Bourdieu, *On the State* (Cambridge: Polity, 2014), 123.

12. Catherine Bell, *Ritual Theory, Ritual Practice* (Oxford: Oxford University Press, 1992), 21–25; Lars Fogelin, "The Archaeology of Religious Ritual," *Annual Review of Anthropology* 36 (2007): 55–71; Talal Asad, *Genealogies of Religion: Discipline and Reasons of Power in Christianity and Islam* (Baltimore: Johns Hopkins University Press, 2009); Talal Asad, "Thinking about Tradition, Religion and Politics in Egypt Today," *Critical Inquiry* 42, no. 1 (2015): 166–214.

13. M. H. Crawford, "Twelve Tables," in *Oxford Classical Dictionary,* 4th ed., ed. Simon Hornblower, Antony Spawforth, and Esther Eidinow (Oxford: Oxford University Press), 1521.

14. One of the earliest known references to law is from nineteenth-century BCE Egypt, during the rule of Sesostris III, referring to the treasurer Mentuhotep:

> Hereditary prince, vizier and chief judge, attached to Nekhen, prophet of Mat (goddess of Truth), giver of laws, advancer of offices, confirming the boundary records, separating a land-owner from his neighbor, pilot of the people, satisfying the whole land, a man of truth before the Two Lands, accustomed to justice like Thoth, his like in satisfying the Two Lands, hereditary prince in judging the Two Lands, supreme head in judgment, putting matters in order, wearer of the royal seal, chief treasurer, Mentuhotep.

James Henry Breasted, *Ancient Records of Egypt,* vol. 1 (Urbana: University of Illinois Press, 1906), 255–256. Notice how royal authority imbues nearly every phrase in this description.

Whereas Roman law emerged out of a political struggle between plebeians and patricians, which ended up defining and defending people's rights, as initially laid out in the Twelve Tables, Egyptian law had its origins in the pharaoh's court in relation to organizing revenue collection, which began by identifying and defining property rights for land. To be sure, Roman law also defined rights to land and the right to taxation, but the protection of individual bodily liberty was an important concession that plebeians extracted from patricians. George Mousourakis, *Roman Law and the Origins of the Civil Law Tradition* (Berlin: Springer, 2015). Cf. Elden, *The Birth of Territory*.

15. Derrida, "Force of Law," 943, 925; Simon Glendinning, "Derrida and the Philosophy of Law and Justice," *Law and Critique* 27, no. 2 (2016): 187–203. On speech act theory, see Mitchell Greene, "Speech Acts," Stanford Encyclopedia of Philosophy, https://plato.stanford.edu/entries/speech-acts/ (accessed May 20, 2020).

16. Donald R. Davis Jr., *The Spirit of Hindu Law* (Cambridge: Cambridge University Press, 2010), 128. See also Benjamin R. Barber, "Misreading Democracy: Peter Euben and the Gorgias," in *Demokratia: A Conversation on Democracies, Ancient and Modern*, ed. Josiah Ober and Charles Hedrick (Princeton: Princeton University Press, 1996), 361–376.

17. Many erstwhile Brahmins were prominent in Buddhism later, so it is not a stretch to assume that breaking the ranks was rare but not unusual.

18. See, for instance, the depiction of legal and political order in the epics and lyrical literature like the Buddhacharitra, mostly appearing in the second half of Dharma Yuga, when political consolidation through dharma socialization was established but was also being treated with skepticism. Upinder Singh, *Political Violence in India* (Cambridge, MA: Harvard University Press, 2017), 95–176.

19. Dorian Q. Fuller and Ling Qin, "Water Management and Labour in the Origins and Dispersal of Asian Rice," *World Archaeology* 41, no. 1 (2009): 88–111.

20. Kulke and Rothermund, *A History of India*, 58. Although no agricultural implements have been found from this period, the Pali term "ayo nangala" (iron plow) was used in texts then. Sharma, *Śudras in Ancient India*, 95. See also Susan E. Alcock et al., eds., *Empires, Perspectives from Archaeology and History* (Cambridge: Cambridge University Press, 2001).

21. Johannes Bronkhorst, *Greater Magadha: Studies in the Culture of Early India* (Leiden: Brill, 2007), 271. The skills that Brahmin priests needed to perfect were complex, but the benefits were correspondingly high.

22. Johannes Bronkhorst, "Is There an Inner Conflict of Tradition?," in *Aryan and Non-Aryan in South Asia: Evidence, Interpretation, and Ideology; Proceedings of the International Seminar on Aryan and Non-Aryan in South Asia*, University of Michigan, Ann Arbor, October 25–27, 1996, vol. 3 (Harvard University Department of Sanskrit and Indian Studies, 1999).

23. Johannes Bronkhorst, "Brahmanism: Its Place in Ancient Indian Society," *Contributions to Indian Sociology* (2017): 363.

24. Sudarsan Seneviratne, "The Mauryan State," in *The Early State*, ed. Henri Claessen and Peter Skalnik (The Hague: Mouton Publishers, 1978), 381–402; Romila Thapar, *Aśoka and the Decline of the Mauryas* (London: Oxford University Press, 1961), 66. Recall Adam Smith's definition of rent cited in Chapter 3.

25. Matsya Purana 10.6,7. The mlecchas were churned out by Brahmins from the dead body of the lecherous and robber, King Vena, who had mixed pedigree:

> Black as soot the barbarian race that came out of Vena was the outcome of the evil qualities of his mother, and from the portion of the good qualities of his pious father, appeared out of the right hand of the dead king, a most brilliant figure, wearing armour, studded with precious stones, and armed with bow and arrow in one hand and holding a club in the other. An illustrious figure thus produced, after so much difficulty, was named Prthu. King Prthu was anointed by the Brāhmanas, but even then he performed severe austerities.

B. D. Basu, *Sacred Books of the Hindus*, vol. 27, part 1: *Matsya Purana 8–10*, 29 (New York: AMS Books, 1916). See also https://www.wisdomlib.org/definition/mleccha (accessed December 17, 2018).

26. Hegel to Niethammer, October 13, 1806, *The Letters*, cited in Steven B. Smith, *Hegel's Critique of Liberalism: Rights in Context* (Chicago: University of Chicago Press, 1991), 96.

27. Ernst Kantorowicz, *The King's Two Bodies: A Study in Medieval Political Theology*, vol. 22. (Princeton: Princeton University Press, 2016). In Shakespeare's *Hamlet*, this is Hamlet speaking after having unwittingly killed the king's counselor Polonius (act 4, scene 2 [emphasis added]):

> Yes, sir, a sponge that soaks up the king's approval, his rewards, and his decisions. Officers like that give the king the best service in the end. He keeps them in his mouth like an ape. First he moves them around, then he swallows them. When he needs what you have found out, he can just squeeze you like a sponge and you'll be dry again.
> ... The body's with the king, but the king's not with the body. *The king's a thing ... A thing of no importance.* Take me to him.

It is possible to make comparisons of kingship across cultures because of their remarkable similarities, especially in relation to dynasty. Jeroen Duindam, *Dynasties: A Global History of Power, 1300–1800* (Cambridge: Cambridge University Press, 2016).

28. Lanny Bell, "Luxor Temple and the Cult of the Royal Ka," *Journal of Near Eastern Studies* 44, no. 4 (1985): 251–294.

29. Charles S. Spencer, "Territorial Expansion and Primary State Formation," *Proceedings of the National Academy of Sciences* 107, no. 16 (2010): 7119-7126; Gideon Shelach and Yitzhak Jaffe, "The Earliest States in China: A Long-Term Trajectory Approach," *Journal of Archaeological Research* 22, no. 4 (2014): 327-364; Roderick B. Campbell, John Baines, Rowan Flad, Tang Jigen, Li Min, John W. Olsen, and Roderick B. Campbell, "Toward a Networks and Boundaries Approach to Early Complex Polities: The Late Shang Case," *Current Anthropology* 50, no. 6 (2009): 821-848.

30. Norman Yoffee, "Too Many Chiefs? (or, Safe Texts for the '90s)," in *Archaeological Theory: Who Sets the Agenda?* ed. Norman Yoffee and Andrew Sherratt (Cambridge: Cambridge University Press, 1993), 60-78; Jeroen Duindam, "Pre-Modern Power Elites: Princes, Courts, Intermediaries," in *The Palgrave Handbook of Political Elites* (London: Palgrave Macmillan, 2018), 161-179.

31. Jonathan Barnes and Melissa Lane, *Aristotle's Politics: Writings from the Complete Works: Politics, Economics, Constitution of Athens* (Princeton: Princeton University Press, 2016), 20, 109. On masculinities in Vedic contexts, see Uma Chakravarti, "Conceptualising Brahmanical Patriarchy in Early India: Gender, Caste, Class and State," *Economic and Political Weekly* (1993): 579-585; Smita Sahgal, "Situating Kingship within an Embryonic Frame of Masculinity in Early India," *Social Scientist* 43, no. 11/12 (2015): 3-26.

32. Ali Daud, "Violence, Courtly Manners and Lineage Formation in Early Medieval India," *Social Scientist* 35, no. 9-10 (2007): 3-21.

33. See, for example, Kesavan Veluthat, *The Political Structure of Early Medieval South India* (New Delhi: Orient Longman, 1993).

34. Ali Daud, *Courtly Culture and Political Life in Early Medieval India*, vol. 10 (Cambridge: Cambridge University Press, 2004). On cultures of refinement and social distancing, see Pierre Bourdieu, *Distinction: A Social Critique of the Judgement of Taste* (Cambridge, MA: Harvard University Press, 1984), 28-35; Norbert Elias, *The Court Society* (New York: Pantheon, 1983), 87.

35. Daud, *Courtly Culture,* 22, 70.

36. Maurice Halbwachs, *On Collective Memory* (Chicago: University of Chicago Press, 1992), 123.

37. The use of Greek in Kandahar highlights the Hellenization of the northwestern part of the subcontinent. Kenneth R. Norman, "Notes on the Greek Version of Aśoka's Twelfth and Thirteenth Rock Edicts," *Journal of the Royal Asiatic Society* 104, no. 2 (1972): 111-118; Nayanjot Lahiri, *Aśoka* (Cambridge, MA: Harvard University Press: 2015), 167-172.

38. Thapar, *Aśoka and the Decline of the Mauryas,* 317.

39. Pillar Edict VII: "The advancement of *Dhamma* amongst men has been achieved through two means, legislation and persuasion. But of these two, legislation has been less effective, and persuasion more so." Thapar, *Aśoka and the Decline of the Mauryas,* 266. The Eightfold Path includes the following elements:

right understanding, intention, speech, action, means of livelihood, effort, mindfulness (involving right awareness and right memory), and meditative absorption.

40. Thapar, *Aśoka and the Decline of the Mauryas*, 255–256.

41. Upinder Singh, "Governing the State and the Self: Political Philosophy and Practice in the Edicts of Aśoka," *South Asian Studies* 28, no. 2 (2012): 137. The logical progression in the edicts and the Arthaśāstra is the same, The king forms the center; his bureaucracy and administration occupy the inner circle; their roles are to manage the economy; collectively they seek to address interstate relations, including forest peoples and other renegades, while always being prepared for war. Aśoka creates an interesting variant in this logic by spreading the message of dharma as "love" or compassion, indeed, the very opposite of war. See also Lahiri, *Aśoka*.

42. D. D. Kosambi, *An Introduction to the Study of Indian History*, 2nd ed. (Hyderabad: Sangam Books, 2004), 206. See also Aloka Parasher-Sen, "Perceptions of Time, Cultural Boundaries and 'Region' in Early Indian Texts," *Indian Historical Review* 36, no. 2 (2009): 183–207.

43. See, for instance, Arthaśāstra 1.2. Forests and forest people were reviled and feared in virtually all narratives of territorial elites. Aloka Parasher-Sen, "Of Tribes, Hunters and Barbarians: Forest Dwellers in the Mauryan Period," *Studies in History* 14, no. 2 (1998): 179–180; Brajadulal Chattopadhyaya, "The State's Perception of the 'Forest' and the 'Forest' as 'State' in Early India," in *The Concept of Bharatavarsha and Other Essays* (Albany: State University of New York Press, 2019), 57–76.

44. Archaeologists have pointed to the discontinuous geography of empire and non-uniformity of internal administration under the Mauryas, indicating a networked view of disarticulated control at strategic points, such as mines, trade routes and ports, urban centers, and monasteries. See Carla M. Sinopoli, "Imperial Landscapes of Asia," in *Archaeology of Asia*, ed. Miriam Stark (New York: Wiley, 2008), 324–329; Namita Sugandhi, "Between the Patterns of History—Rethinking Mauryan Imperial Interaction in the Southern Deccan" (PhD diss., University of Chicago, 2008); Namita Sugandhi, "Conquests of Dharma: Network Models and the Study of Ancient Polities," *Archeological Papers of the American Anthropological Association* 1, no. 22 (2013): 145–163.

45. Lahiri, *Aśoka*, 200. See also Singh, "Governing the State and the Self," 135–136; Thapar, *Aśoka and the Decline of the Mauryas*, 252. The presence of Northern Black Polished (NBP) Ware in multiple parts of the empire, but in very small quantities, may indicate its use as a luxury or prestige good that was only given to elites as a gift for loyalty to the emperor.

46. Carla M. Sinopoli, "On the Edge of Empire: Form and Substance in the Satavahana Dynasty," in *Empires: Perspectives from Archaeology and History*, vol. 122, ed. Susan E. Alcock, H. D. John, Terence N. D'Altroy, Kathleen D. Morrison, and Carla M. Sinopoli (Cambridge: Cambridge University Press, 2001), 155–178. Burton

Stein writes, "According to Buddhist cosmology, castes were created after kings: the brahmans, who lived in the forests and studied the vedas, the vis (*vessa* in Pali), who married and produced and traded goods, and the *sudda* (shudras), who worked for vessa masters and hunted in the forests. In addition to these there were ascetics (*sramana*), who might come from any caste." Burton Stein, *A History of India* (New York: Wiley, 2010), 61.

47. Lahiri, *Aśoka*, 197–201.

48. Romila Thapar, "The State as Empire," in *The Study of the State,* vol. 35, ed. Henri J. Claessen and Peter Skalník (Berlin: de Gruyter, 1981), 409–426.

49. Joel P. Brereton, "Dharman in the Rgveda," in *Dharma: Studies in Its Semantic, Cultural and Religious History,* ed. Patrick Olivelle (New Delhi: Motilal Banarsidass, 2009).

50. Brereton, "Dharman in the Rgveda." The legal scholar Robert Lingat suggests something similar: "Dharma is what is firm and durable, what sustains and maintains, what hinders fainting and falling." Robert Lingat, *The Classical Law of India* (Delhi: Oxford University Press, 1993), 3. Lingat goes on to treat dharma in the Vedās as cosmic law, but see Patrick Olivelle, "Dharmaśāstra: A Textual History," in *Hinduism and Law: An Introduction,* ed. Timothy Lubin, Donald R. Davis Jr., and Jayanth K. Krishnan (Cambridge: Cambridge University Press, 2010), 28–57. Olivelle points out that Lingat's and other historians' back-projection of the importance of dharma onto the Vedic literature is misguided: they ignore the actual texts and use third-century Mīmāmsā interpretations. See also Timothy Lubin, "Vratá Divine and Human in the Early Veda," *Journal of the American Oriental Society* 121, no. 4 (2001): 565–579.

Lubin identifies three registers of vratá or "resolution" by post-vedic times: rule, divine attribute, rule of ritual observance. These are transformed from foundations through divine law to fixed principles and the merit accorded by proper performance of rites. Cf. Michael Witzel, "Moving Targets? Texts, Language, Archaeology and History in the Late Vedic and Early Buddhist Periods," *Indo-Iranian journal* 52, no. 2–3 (2009): 287–310.

51. Bharadvaja Śrauta Sutra (9.8.14) cited in Patrick Olivelle, "The Semantic History of Dharma in the Middle and Late Vedic Periods," *Journal of Indian Philosophy* 32, no. 5–6 (2004): 491–511. On the other hand, the Upaniṣads frequently ridiculed the ritualism of the Vedic tradition of which they themselves were a part:

> Surely, they are floating unanchored,
> these eighteen forms of the sacrifice,
> the rites within which are called inferior;
> The fools who hail that as the best,
> return once more to old age and death.
> *Mundaka Upaniśad,* 1.2

Cited in Patrick Olivelle, "The Renouncer Tradition," in *The Blackwell Companion to Hinduism*, ed. Gavin Flood (New York: Wiley, 2003), 276. Olivelle argues that the aśrama system (orders of life for a dvija man), in its earliest form, which sanctioned the vocation of an ascetic among other choices, was probably the outcome of this anti-ritualistic strand within Brahmanism to institutionalize renunciation into the tradition during the middle of the first millennium BCE. Patrick Olivelle, *The Āśrama System: The History and Hermeneutics of a Religious Institution* (Oxford: Oxford University Press on Demand, 1993).

52. Olivelle makes this case on the basis of references to yavanas or people of Greek origin in the Gautama Dharmasutra, a term he argues could at the earliest appear in the middle of the third century BCE. Patrick Olivelle, ed., *The Dharmasutras: The Law Codes of Ancient India: The Law Codes of Ancient India* (Oxford: Oxford University Press, 1999).

53. The four aśramas were that of a Vedic student, the householder, retirement in the forest, and renunciation.

54. Gautama Dharma Sutra 11.1–11; Olivelle, *The Dharmasutras*, 96.

55. See also Kumkum Roy, "Defining the Household: Some Aspects of Prescription and Practice in Early India," *Social Scientist* 2 (1994): 3–18. In numerous rites in the Grhya Sutras, the *gotra* name or patrilineage is critical for the ceremony to continue. Like dharma, the concept of gotra or patrilineage shows up relatively late in Vedic literature. In the Rigveda, the word appears several times associated with "cowpen" or "herd." By the time of the Chandogya Upaniṣad, gotra has its more contemporary meaning specifying agnate relationships. Similarly, the evolution of the word, vratá, is emblematic of this change. Arthur Anthony Macdonell and Arthur Keith Berriedale, *Vedic Index of Names and Subjects*, vols. 1 and 2 (New Delhi: Motilal Banarsidass Publishers, 1995), 1:235, 2: 341. See also Lubin, "Vratá Divine and Human in the Early Veda."

56. Āpastamba Sutra 1.1.9; Olivelle, *The Dharmasutras*, 7.

57. Among other markers of patriarchy in the Dharmasutras were inheritance laws, which required the performance of *srddha* rites or funeral oblations, but these were in turn only open to those permitted to perform sacrifice. Since women were barred, they were logically also barred from inheritance. See Mary McGee, "Ritual Rights: The Gender Implications of *Adhikara*," in *Jewels of Authority: Women and Textual Tradition in Hindu India*, ed. Laurie Patton (Oxford: Oxford University Press on Demand, 2002).

Similarly, regarding Śudras, the Gautama Dharmasutra (53–63) says,

> The Śudra is the fourth class with a single birth ... He should make ancestral offerings; support his dependants; be faithful to his wife; serve the upper classes; seek his livelihood from them; use their discarded shoes, umbrellas, clothes, and mats and the like; and eat their leftovers. He may also support himself by working as an artisan. The ārya whom he serves must support

him even when he is unable to work, and under similar circumstances he should support the upper-class man using his savings for that purpose.

Olivelle, *The Dharmasutras*, 95–96.

58. Patrick Olivelle, "The Semantic History of Dharma," *Journal of Indian Philosophy* 32 (2004): 491–511. Olivelle suggests that the instructional genre was not necessarily part of the Vedic śakhas but developed autonomously during a phase of post-Vedic society, when the locus of ritual shifted toward the household and away from grand ceremony. Note also that the word *dharmasta* or court (among other legal terms) is found in both the Arthaśāstra and the Dharmaśāstra. Patrick Olivelle, "Manu and the Arthaśāstra: A Study in Śāstric Intertextuality," *Journal of Indian Philosophy* 32, no. 2–3 (2004): 281–291.

59. While an ārya woman became an outcaste for having sex with a Śudra man, the latter could be castrated and lose his property or his life as well. In his introduction to his translation of the *Mānava Dharmaśāstra*, Olivelle writes,

> Reading the *MDh* one cannot fail to see and feel the intensity and urgency with which the author defends Brahmanical privilege. A major aim of Manu was to re-establish the old alliance between priesthood and royalty, an alliance that in his view would benefit both the Brahmin and the king, thereby reestablishing the Brahmin in his unique and privileged position within society.... The reason why foreign ruling classes, such as the Greeks, Sakas, Persians, and Chinese, have fallen to the level of Śudras, once again, is their lack of devotion to Brahmins.

Patrick Olivelle, *Manu's Code of Law: A Critical Edition and Translation of Mānava Dharmaśāstra* (Oxford: Oxford University Press, 2005), xliii.

60. Bourdieu, *Distinction*, 97–256.

61. A Brahmin "may, however, make a Śudra, whether he is bought or not, do slave labor; for the Śudra was created by the Self-existent One solely to do slave labor for the Brahmin." Mānava Dharmaśāstra 8.413; Olivelle, "Manu and the Arthaśāstra," 189. See also Sharma, *Śudras in Ancient India*, 191–240.

62. The forest hermit's life was integral to varnāśramadharma. The historian B. D. Chattopadhyaya suggests that this explains why the early janapādas both asserted their right to the space of the forest and perceived it as being a threat to their moral authority because the autonomous power of its wilderness could affect life in urban centers. Chattopadhyaya, "The State's Perception of the 'Forest' and the 'Forest' as 'State' in Early India," 65–66, 70.

63. Olivelle, *Manu's Code of Law,* 31. We discover a lot about the significance of the Dharmaśāstra in the commentaries of a ninth-century CE expert, Medhatithi. In Manubhasya, or Commentaries on Manu, Medhatithi drew a direct line from

the Vedās to the Mānava-Dharmaśāstra, which appeared at least a half-millennium before his time. Davis, *The Spirit of Hindu Law* (2010): 29.

What was to be later attributed to the Vedās, dharma was more than the actual occurrences of the term in the texts, but also later statements uttered by the learned and their practices. *Mimāmsā*—the scholastic interpretation of the Vedās—provided the foundation for their infallible authority of the Vedās, interpreting dharma as ritual obligations that needed to be properly performed to maintain harmony in the world.

64. Although it is tempting to compare the Arthaśāstra directly with Machiavelli's *The Prince* there are important differences between the two. *The Prince* may have been written as a supplication to Lorenzo the Medici, but Machiavelli proved to be too shrewd a republican for it to be read straightforwardly. Kautilya's strategies mirror what Machiavelli describes as those the ideal Prince must deploy, as someone compelled to hold onto newly acquired territory. Still, the Prince's qualities and the circumstances in which he finds himself are the primary focus for Machiavelli: he seems to suggest that together they lead to emergent and often unintended outcomes. This is therefore no mirror-of-princes manual but a study in political sociology and history. See, for instance, Isiah Berlin, "The Question of Machiavelli," *New York Review of Books,* November 4, 1971; J. G. A. Pocock; *The Machiavellian Moment: Florentine Political Thought and the Atlantic Republican Tradition* (Princeton: Princeton University Press, 2016). For a comparison that sees both the Arthaśāstra and *The Prince* as expressing arguments for securing legitimacy for kingship, see Stuart Gray, "Reexamining Kautilya and Machiavelli: Flexibility and the Problem of Legitimacy in Brahmanical and Secular Realism," *Political Theory* 42, no. 6 (2014): 635–657.

65. Patrick Olivelle, trans., *King, Governance, and Law in Ancient India: Kauṭilya's Arthaśāstra* (Delhi: Oxford University Press, 2013), 78.

66. Olivelle, *King, Governance, and Law,* 272 (6.1.8; see also sections 2.1.2, 2.3; 2.4. and 6.1.1). James C. Scott (2017) writes: "Tribes are, in the first instance, an administrative fiction of the state; tribes begin where states end. The antonym for 'tribe' is 'peasant': that is, a state subject." James C. Scott, *Against the Grain: A Deep History of the Earliest States* (New Haven, CT: Yale University Press), 235.

67. Sumit Guha, *Environment and Ethnicity in India, 1200–1991,* vol. 4 (Cambridge: Cambridge University Press, 1999), 44.

68. Chattopadhyaya, "The State's Perception of the 'Forest' and the 'Forest' as 'State' in Early India," 65–66, 70. See also Singh, *Political Violence in India,* 367–459.

69. Chattopadhyaya, "The State's Perception of the 'Forest' and the 'Forest' as 'State' in Early India," 66–68.

70. Mark McClish and Patrick Olivelle, *The Arthaśāstra: Selections from the Classic Indian Work on Statecraft* (Indianapolis: Hackett, 2012), lxxi.

71. One might, for instance, interpret Sheldon Pollock's notion of a "Sanskrit cosmopolis" to describe a long-term process of bringing high culture to the masses through stories of kings and their courts that were transmitted widely while performing the function through the content of *kāvya*, or literature, of mobilizing the exclusive sounds of Sanskrit itself. Sheldon Pollock, *The Language of the Gods in the World of Men: Sanskrit, Culture, and Power in Pre-Modern India* (Berkeley: University of California Press, 2006), 39–258.

72. The tales in the Rāmāyana and Mahābhārata are intricate but too well known to be recounted here. For quick summaries, see their respective Wikipedia pages. R. K. Naryayan's *Indian Epics Retold* provides enchanting narratives from both. Rasipuram Krishnaswamy Narayan, *The Indian Epics Retold: The Rāmāyana, the Mahābhārata, Gods, Demons, and Others* (New Delhi: Penguin Books India, 2000).

73. As Daud Ali points out, by the time of the epics, kingship was rarely the sole site of political action. Rather, the trajectories of the corpus of the king must be treated as a grand distraction from the court, which was an arena of intense activity, involving the production of discourses and supporting a whole class of elites who generated distinct cultures of the court—social practices that created distinctions and other forms of power relations. Ali, Daud, *Courtly Culture*. Cf. Jeroen Duindam, "Pre-Modern Power Elites," 161–179.

74. K. R. Subramanian, *Origin of Saivism and Its History in the Tamil Land* (New Delhi: Asian Educational Services, 2002); Peter C. Bisschop, "Buddhist and Śaiva Interactions in the Kali Age: The Śivadharmaśāstra as a Source of the Kāraṇḍavyūhasūtra," *Indo-Iranian Journal* 61, no. 4 (2018): 396–410.

75. A religious action is visible as a social action resulting from collectively organized faith-based ritual practices. On these power-laden elements of religious practices, Talal Asad writes in the context of early Christianity:

> Augustine was quite clear that power, the effect of an entire network of motivated practices, assumes a religious form because of the end to which it is directed, for human events are the instruments of God. It was not the mind that moved spontaneously to religious truth, but power that created the conditions for experiencing that truth.

Asad, *Genealogies of Religion*, 35. Aśoka's seemingly paradoxical imperial role in spreading a gentle message Buddhism as the very symbol of territorial power is, therefore, an appropriately significant theme within scholarly work on his rule.

76. In spite of the Buddha's own initial reluctance to induct nuns into the order, the involvement of women in the Sangha was established early through the intervention of his apostle, Ananda. See Akira Hirakawa, *A History of Indian Buddhism: From Śākyamuni to Early Mahāyāna* (Delhi: Motilal Banarsidass, 1993). The religion scholar Rita Gross points out, however, that misogyny and

patriarchy were in fact rife for long within Buddhism, although some social practices did become somewhat more progressive over time. Rita M. Gross, *Buddhism after Patriarchy: A Feminist History, Analysis, and Reconstruction of Buddhism* (Albany: State University of New York Press, 1993).

77. Patrick Olivelle, *The Life of the Buddha* (New York: New York University Press, 2008), 29, 1.75 [emphasis added].

78. Frances Wood, *The Silk Road: Two Thousand Years in the Heart of Asia* (Berkeley: University of California Press, 2002); Jason Neelis, *Early Buddhist Transmission and Trade Networks: Mobility and Exchange within and beyond the Northwestern Borderlands of South Asia* (Leiden: Brill, 2017), 25.

79. For a summary of these various positions, see Greg Bailey and Ian Mabbett, *The Sociology of Early Buddhism* (Cambridge: Cambridge University Press, 2003), 13–30. Cf. Brian Black. "Ambaṭṭha and Śvetaketu: Literary Connections between the Upaniṣads and Early Buddhist Narratives," *Journal of the American Academy of Religion* 79, no. 1 (2010): 136–161. On Buddhism's re-appropriation of Brahmanical language and ideas, see Sheldon Pollock, *The Language of the Gods in the World of Men: Sanskrit, Culture, and Power in Premodern India* (Berkeley: University of California Press, 2006), 51–59.

80. Yudhishthira is the eldest of the Pāndavas and was king for a while before losing his kingdom and his dignity in a fateful game of dice with his Kaurava cousins. Alf Hiltebeitel, "Aśvaghoṣa's Buddhacarita: The First Known Close and Critical Reading of the Brahmanical Sanskrit Epics," *Journal of Indian Philosophy* 34, no. 3 (2006): 233.

81. On the Bhagavad Gita's many interpretations see Richard H. Davis, *The "Bhagavad Gita": A Biography* (Princeton: Princeton University Press: 2014). Śankara used different lines of reasoning to question the foundations of Buddhist realism and skepticism. In doing so, he may have rocked the intellectual vanguard of Buddhism, which was engaging in Sanskrit discourses, at least in India. By then, however, Buddhist practice was long past its death knell and was already out the door. On the *Gita* and dharma, see Alf Hiltebeitel, *Dharma: Its Early History in Law, Religion, and Narrative* (Oxford: Oxford University Press, 2011), 553–568.

82. Gurucharan Das, *The Difficulty of Being Good: On the Subtle Art of Dharma* (Oxford: Oxford University Press: 2010), 258–261; Hiltebeitel, *Dharma*, 411–480. Hiltebeitel follows the philosopher Bimal K. Matilal in identifying a paradigm shift in the meaning and uses of dharma in the Mahābhārata, because the text identifies genuine moral dilemmas for agents where *fortuna* or chance is as important for determining outcomes as *virtù*, or personal fortitude and commitment to the formal rules of dharma. In some cases, however, as in Yudhishthira's grief, the social circumstances are such that what seems like right action (renunciation of the throne) is inappropriate and might cause harm to many others. Hiltebeitel, *Dharma*, 20–29.

83. Śāntiparvan, (59) 78; (7.3–7), cited in Bowles, *Dharma, Disorder, and the Political in Ancient India*, 140; Olivelle, *The Dharmasutras*, 97–98 [emphasis added]. See also Nick Sutton, "Aśoka and Yudhisthira: A Historical Setting for the Ideological Tensions of the Mahābhārata?," *Religion* 27, no. 4 (1997): 333–341.

84. (38.1–2, 4). Cited in Bowles, *Dharma, Disorder, and the Political in Ancient India*, 146.

85. (15.49.50). Cited in Bowles, *Dharma, Disorder, and the Political in Ancient India*, 143.

86. The cultural theorist Milind Wakankar describes an "an ever so slight turn from mainstream religion in the work of these low-caste poets," such as Kabir and Ravidas. M. Milind Wakankar, *Subalternity and Religion: The Prehistory of Dalit Empowerment in South Asia* (London: Routledge, 2010), viii. See also Gail Omvedt, *Seeking Begumpura: The Social Vision of Anticaste Intellectuals* (New Delhi: Navayana, 2008). That there were multiple Rāmāyanas, in particular, has animated scholars and activists in India, particularly after the violence and destruction in 1992 of a Mughal-era mosque in Ayodhya, identified as the legendary birthplace of Rāma. Paula Richman, ed., *Questioning Rāmāyanas: A South Asian Tradition* (Berkeley: University of California Press, 2001); Mandakranta Bose, ed., *The Rāmāyana Revisited* (Oxford: Oxford University Press, 2004).

87. The religious studies scholar John Stratton Hawley writes, "'Bhakti,' as usually translated, is devotion, but if that word connotes something entirely private and quiet, we are in need of other words. Bhakti is heart religion, sometimes cool and quiescent but sometimes hot—the religion of participation, community, enthusiasm, song, and often of personal challenge. John Stratton Hawley, *A Storm of Songs: India and the Idea of the Bhakti Movement* (Cambridge, MA: Harvard University Press, 2015), 2.

88. Reference should also be made here to the materialist school (interchangeably named Lokayata and Charvaka), about which virtually nothing is known. Founded around the time of the Buddha, it stood in direct opposition to authority of the Vedās or to any other claims to otherworldliness. It viewed perceptive experience as the only source of knowledge and saw the mind as simply another expression of matter. On the Śaiva Age, see Alexis Sanderson, "The Śaiva Age: The Rise and Dominance of Śaivism during the Early Medieval Period," in *Genesis and Development of Tantrism*, ed. Shingo Einoo (Tokyo: Institute of Oriental Culture, 2009), 41–349.

89. Gavin Flood, "The Śaiva Traditions," in *The Blackwell Companion to Hinduism*, 200–28. The Puranas were a set of stories that may have been orally transmitted to the nobility, but over time became the vehicle through which the arcane language of Brahmanical thought could become more accessible by drawing on popular myths and stories. It also served the purpose of linking multiple folk traditions to the Vedās by providing biographies for Vishnu, Śiva, and other minor gods. Freda Matchett, "The Puranas," in *The Blackwell Companion to Hinduism*, 130–143.

90. Matchett, "The Puranas," 207.

91. The esoteric Tantric practices may have seemed similar to Brahmanism, but they broke the varna barrier by suggesting that they practices were open to anyone willing to engage in strenuous bodily effort and asceticism, regardless of birth. It is also noteworthy to contrast the Tantric view of nonduality with that of Adi Śankara. See also Gavin D. Flood, *The Tantric Body: The Secret Tradition of Hindu Religion* (London: I. B. Tauris, 2005). The revelation of these types of ascetic experience in the writings of Patanjali in the second century BCE had already signaled the presence of the world of the outsider, a theme that traveled widely in lore and practice in the figure of the śramana. The śramana was a mendicant who was appropriated into the varnāśrama system (proper ways of living for dvija men) only in later periods in post-Vedic society. See Olivelle, *The Āśrama System*.

92. Sanderson, "The Śaiva Age," 253 [emphasis added]. The fifteenth-century Kabir was born into a Muslim weaver caste and sang songs of divine ecstasy while ridiculing both Brahmanical and ascetic practice. But "Kabir" also became a sign for multiple subaltern poets signing their name to their songs of *bhakti* and commentary on their contemporary social conditions. Omvedt, *Seeking Begumpura*.

93. It is well beyond my ambit to explore the relationships among types of urbanization, forestry and water bodies, forms of territoriality, systems of legality, and special sites of elite power, such as the palace and the temple. Yet, it is, of course, vital to engage in these very explorations to produce a clearer view of the processes of elite network formation and their emergent social and ecological effects during the Age of Dharma.

7. Trade Winds

Epigraph: Anonymous, probably sixteenth century, England.

1. Simo Parpola, Asko Parpola, and Robert H. Brunswig Jr., "The Meluhha Village: Evidence of Acculturation of Harappan Traders in Late Third Millennium Mesopotamia?," *Journal of the Economic and Social History of the Orient* 20 (1977): 131.

2. For instance, Strabo, the first-century BCE geographer, was surprised that although India was "the greatest of all nations and the happiest in the lot," its potential was not apparent to its inhabitants: "It is said that in the country of Sopeithes there is a mountain of mineral salt sufficient for the whole of India. And gold and silver mines are reported in other mountains not far away, excellent mines, as has been plainly shown by Gorgus the mining expert. But since the Indians are inexperienced in mining and smelting, they also do not know what their resources are, and handle the business in a rather simple manner." *The Geography of Strabo,* Loeb Classical Library (Cambridge, MA: Harvard University Press, 1968), 2:5–32; 15: 1–30.

3. The social process and political economy of trade have sometimes been characterized in terms of their premodern and modern features, respectively, but to great scholarly detriment. For a review, see Rahul Oka and Chapurukha M. Kusimba, "The Archaeology of Trading Systems; Part 1: Towards a New Trade Synthesis," *Journal of Archaeological Research* 16, no. 4 (2008): 339–395.

4. Kauṭilya spends a lot of effort in *Arthaśāstra* identifying different strategies for maintaining sovereign authority in relation to foreign allies and adversaries. His *mandala* or "circle of kings" strategy involves recognizing that one's immediate neighbors are one's natural enemies but the second circle beyond constitutes enemies of enemies and therefore potential allies. Trade policy involved a number of organizing principles, or technologies and a dispositif, including setting standards for weights and measures, protection or security along trade routes, and tolls, monopolies, and so on. Kauṭilya describes how by following common law principles of promoting peace, not being openly unfair, and shirking negligence and laziness, the ruler can avoid "impoverishment, greed, and disloyalty of his subjects." Patrick Olivelle, trans., *King, Governance, and Law in Ancient India: Kauṭilya's Arthaśāstra* (Delhi: Oxford University Press, 2013), 43–47, 143–158, 271–291.

5. On reviews on legitimation, see the philosopher Jurgen Habermas, who represents it as a form of communicative power: the ability to control discourse. Contradictory stimuli might ensue in some operations where the system goes into crisis. Jurgen Habermas, *Legitimation Crisis,* vol. 519 (Boston: Beacon, 1975). In comparison, Bruce Lincoln points to the deployment of authority to back legitimating discourses, with political resistance frequently being "acts of sabotage" against them. But the persuasive role of authority generates authorizing discourses, similar to Habermas. Bruce Lincoln, *Authority: Construction and Corrosion* (Chicago: University of Chicago Press, 1994).

6. There is a substantial branch of scholarship that views the very category of "Hinduism" as having been produced through the colonial encounter between British administrators and Brahmin elites. Gauri Viswanathan, "Colonialism and the Construction of Hinduism," in *The Blackwell Companion to Hinduism,* ed. Gavin Flood (New York: Wiley, 2003), 23–44.

7. See, for instance, Vijay Nath, "From 'Brahmanism' to 'Hinduism': Negotiating the Myth of the Great Tradition," *Social Scientist* 29, no. 3 (2001): 19–50.

8. Geoffrey Poitras, "Arbitrage: Historical Perspectives," in *Encyclopedia of Quantitative Finance* (New York: Wiley: 2010). The historian John Keay describes how in the seventeenth century, nutmeg and mace found in Indonesia could be sold in Europe for a profit of 32,000 percent. This enormous price difference dropped subsequently when the East India Company began expanding plantations elsewhere in South and South Asia. John Keay, *The Honourable Company: A History of the English East India Company* (New York: Scribner, 1994), 4.

9. It is useful to build an image of the intricate morphology of such networks by comparing them with elite power networks in the contemporary United States. The political scientist William Domhoff writes, "The corporate rich and the power elite build on their structural power, their status power, their storehouse of policy recommendations, and their success in the electoral arena to dominate the federal government on the issues they care about. Lobbyists from corporations, law firms, and trade associations, working through the special-interest process, play a crucial role in shaping government policies on narrow issues of concern to wealthy families, specific corporations, or business sectors. At the same time, the policy-planning network supplies new policy directions on major issues, along with top-level governmental appointees to implement those policies." William Domhoff, *Who Rules America?* (New York: McGraw-Hill: 2014), 162.

10. The coevolution of trade networks with Buddhist transmission has received considerable attention in recent scholarship. Two notable works are Xinru Liu, *The Silk Road in World History* (Oxford: Oxford University Press, 2010); and Jason Neelis, *Early Buddhist Transmission and Trade Networks: Mobility and Exchange within and beyond the Northwestern Borderlands of South Asia* (Leiden: Brill, 2017). Liu points out that commoners in Han China were prohibited from wearing embroidered silks, so they became prestige items for the court. But Buddhist ceremonies also used silks, which made them both sacred and an object of patronage as well as wealth among some priests and the wealthy. These exchanges and elite power networks spawned significant theological and institutional changes in Buddhism from the sixth century CE onward. For possible later variants of such kin-based patronage, see Kaiwan Munshi and Mark Rosenzweig, *Why Is Mobility in India so Low? Social Insurance, Inequality, and Growth*, no. w14850, National Bureau of Economic Research, 2009; Philip Oldenburg, "Middlemen in Third-World Corruption: Implications of an Indian Case," *World Politics* 39, no. 4 (1987): 508–535; Abhijit Banerjee and Lakshmi Iyer, "History, Institutions, and Economic Performance: The Legacy of Colonial Land Tenure Systems in India," *American Economic Review* 95, no. 4 (2005): 1190–1213.

11. Jean-François Bayart and Stephen Ellis, "Africa in the World: A History of Extraversion," *African Affairs* 99, no. 395 (2000): 217–267; Mattei Dogan, ed., *Elite Configurations at the Apex of Power* (Leiden: Brill, 2003).

12. How both elites and their supporters participate in supportive modes of power appears as the very expression of ideology. The social philosopher Louis Althusser notes that it "is so much present in all the acts and deeds of individuals that it is indistinguishable from their 'lived experience.'" Louis Althusser, *Philosophy and the Spontaneous Philosophy of the Scientists* (New York: Verso, 1990), 25.

13. Eric Hobsbawm, *The Age of Revolution* (New York: Vintage, 1996), 33–42; Prasannan Parthasarathi, *Why Europe Grew Rich and Asia Did Not: Global*

Economic Divergence, 1600–1850 (Cambridge: Cambridge University Press, 2011), 23–27, 130.

14. Sven Beckert, *Empire of Cotton: A Global History* (New York: Vintage, 2015), 84. See also Giorgio Riello and Prasannan Parthasarathi, eds. *The Spinning World: A Global History of Cotton Textiles, 1200–1850* (Oxford: Oxford University Press, 2011).

15. Beckert, *Empire of Cotton*; Daniel Wells and Jennifer R. Green, eds., *The Southern Middle Class in the Long Nineteenth Century* (Baton Rouge: Louisiana State University Press, 2011).

16. George Kateb, *The Inner Ocean: Individualism and Democratic Culture* (Ithaca, NY: Cornell University Press, 1992); George Kateb, "Democratic Individualism and its Critics," *Annual Review of Political Science* 6, no. 1 (2003): 275–305.

17. Bronislaw Malinowski, "Kula, the Circulating Exchange of Valuables in the Archipelagos of Eastern New Guinea," *Man* 20 (July 1920), 97–105; Pierre Bourdieu, "Symbolic Power," *Critique of Anthropology* 4, no. 13–14 (1979): 77–85; Marcel Mauss. *The Gift: The Form and Reason for Exchange in Archaic Societies* (London: Routledge, 2002); Mary Douglas. "No Free Gifts," foreword in Mauss, *The Gift*, ix–xxi.

18. Karl-Gustaf Lofgren, Torsten Persson, and Jorgen W. Weibull, "Markets with Asymmetric Information: The Contributions of George Akerlof, Michael Spence and Joseph Stiglitz," *Scandinavian Journal of Economics* 104, no. 2 (2002): 195–211; Michael Mann, *The Social Sources of Power*, vol. 1: *A History of Power from the Beginning to AD 1760* (Cambridge: Cambridge University Press, 1986), 47. On the Silk Road, see Liu, *The Silk Road in World History*. Tribute was not demanded spontaneously but by the authority of kinship and rank. On early tariffs as a type of tribute, see Hironori Asakura, *World History of the Customs and Tariff* (Brussels: World Customs Organization, 2003), 24–106. Cf. Karl Polanyi, "The Economistic Fallacy," *Review (Fernand Braudel Center)* (1977): 14.

19. Çatalhöyük (6250–5400 BCE) shows the earliest signs of imported shells from the Mediterranean, along with a variety of precious and semiprecious stones from other areas. See Richard L. Smith, *Premodern Trade in World History* (London: Routledge, 2009), 15, 40–51.

20. Simo Parpola, Asko Parpola, and Robert H. Brunswig Jr., "The Meluḫḫa Village: Evidence of Acculturation of Harappan Traders in Late Third Millennium Mesopotamia?," *Journal of the Economic and Social History of the Orient* (1977): 129–165; Shereen F. Ratnagar, "Theorizing Bronze-Age Intercultural Trade: The Evidence of the Weights," *Paléorient* 29, no.1 (2003): 79–92.

21. Mann, *The Social Sources of Power*, 64–68, 113; Colin Renfrew, "Trade as Action at a Distance," in *Ancient Civilization and Trade*, ed. J. Sabloff and C. C. Lamberg-Karlovsky (Albuquerque: University of New Mexico Press, 1975), 3–59.

22. Kathleen D. Morrison, "Commerce and Culture in South Asia: Perspectives from Archaeology and History," *Annual Review of Anthropology* 26, no. 1 (1997): 87–108. Many lay donors as well as elites sponsored temple and monastery complexes. Merchant titles abound in Buddhist inscriptions, including "*sārthavāha/sathavāha* (perhaps denoting a merchant involved in long-distance trade), *vaṇij/vāṇiya* (probably traders in basic goods), *negama* (members of guilds of traders or artisans), *hairaṇyaka/heraṇika* (goldsmiths or treasurers), *gandhika* (usually translated as 'perfumers' but broadly meaning merchants and shopkeepers), and *vyāvahārika* (a general term for a businessman)." Neelis, *Early Buddhist Transmission and Trade Networks*, 25.

23. Smith, *Premodern Trade in World History*, 84–98. Neelis, *Early Buddhist Transmission and Trade Networks*, 225, cites Pliny the Elder, the first-century CE commentator and companion to the Roman emperor, as being outraged by the cost to the treasury of the trade in luxury goods with Asia: "And by the lowest reckoning India, China and that peninsula [Arabia] take from our empire 100 million sestertii each year. That is the sum which our luxuries and our own women cost us. For what fraction of these imports, I ask, gets to the gods or to the lower world?"

24. Hermann Kulke and Dietmar Rothermund, *A History of India* (London: Psychology Press, 2004), 43.

25. See Philip D. Curtin, *Cross-Cultural Trade in World History* (Cambridge: Cambridge University Press, 1984), 90–135. The historian Kenneth Hall writes that Malay sailors were the "nomads of the Southern Ocean, and they played a role in history that in some ways resembles that of the nomads of the northern steppe. They were prime movers in the links created between larger centers, as well as potential impediments to those links once they were created." Kenneth Hall, *A History of Early Southeast Asia: Maritime Trade and Societal Development, 100–1500* (Lanham, MD: Rowman & Littlefield: 2011), 5.

26. Tan Chung, "Ageless Neighbourliness between India and China: Historical Perspective and Future Prospects," *China Report* 15, no. 2 (1979): 3–37; Sing C. Chew, *The Recurring Dark Ages: Ecological Stress, Climate Changes, and System Transformation* (Walnut Creek, CA: Altamira, 2006), 111–165.

27. Stein, *A History of India*, 105–138.

28. Stein, *A History of India*, 121.

29. See Kenneth R. Hall, *Trade and Statecraft in the Ages of Colas* (New Delhi: Abhinav, 2003). The anthropologist Mattison Mines points out that the power and wealth of weavers fluctuated over time and also varied greatly among them, as it continues to do so today among those having different skill levels all the way to ascendant cloth merchants. Mattison Mines, *The Warrior Merchants: Textiles, Trade and Territory in South India* (Cambridge: Cambridge University Press, 1984), 150.

30. Cf. Thomas Hobbes, *Leviathan* (Longman Library of Primary Sources in Philosophy) (London: Routledge, 2016). Hobbes's vision of the political configuration

leading to a demand for centralized authority generates an enchanting image of ordered elite control and associated alliances of finance and territorial power, typically through military dominance. But his civil society is open-ended and has many unexplored democratizing dimensions, intended to keep the beast in check as it were. See also Charles de Montesquieu, *The Spirit of the Laws* (Cambridge: Cambridge University Press, 1989).

31. M. A. Friedman and S. D. F. Goitein, *India Traders of the Middle Age: Documents from the Cairo Geniza India Book* (Leiden: Brill, 2008), 38, 155, 162.

32. Kulke and Rothermund, *A History of India*, 124–125; Smith, *Premodern Trade in World History*, 140.

33. Describing Muhammad Sayyid, the archetypal merchant prince or portfolio capitalist, Bayly and Subrahmanyam write, "Muhammad Sayyid carved out an unusually sizeable but not unique enterprise. Based in the interior fortress town of Gandikota, he managed a substantial prebend, kept a close control over diamond production and trade in the area, and at the same time maintained interests on the coast and overseas. Besides, he maintained a personal bodyguard of five thousand men and employed several European cannon-founders and artillerymen." Sanjay Subrahmanyam and Christopher A. Bayly, "Portfolio Capitalists and the Political Economy of Early Modern India," *Indian Economic & Social History Review* 25, no. 4 (1988): 410.

34. There is a substantial literature on this history. See, for instance, Yannis Varoufakis, *Talking to My Daughter about the Economy: A Brief History of Capitalism* (London: Bodley Head, 2018).

35. Peri-Cene is also the name of a research project led by Joe Ravetz to investigate peri-urbanization in relation to climate and environmental change. See https://peri-cene.net/ (accessed July 10, 2020).

36. Peter M. Vitousek, Harold A. Mooney, Jane Lubchenco, and Jerry M. Melillo, "Human Domination of Earth's Ecosystems," *Science* 277, no. 5325 (1997): 494–499. On food security, see for instance, Lester R. Brown, "World Population Growth, Soil Erosion, and Food Security," *Science* (1981): 995–1002; Paul R. Ehrlich and Anne H. Ehrlich, *The Population Explosion* (New York: Simon & Schuster, 1990); cf. Stephen J. Scanlan, "Feeding the Planet or Feeding Us a Line? Agribusiness, 'Grainwashing' and Hunger in the World Food System," *International Journal of Sociology of Agriculture & Food* 20, no. 3 (2013).

37. Ellen Meiksins Wood writes, "Instead of a centralized public authority, the feudal state was a network of 'parcelized sovereignties,' governed by a complex hierarchy of social relations and competing jurisdictions, in the hands not only of lords and kings, but also of various autonomous corporations, to say nothing of Holy-Roman emperors and popes." Ellen Meiksins Wood and Larry Patriquin, eds., *The Ellen Meiksins Wood Reader* (Leiden: Brill, 2012), 148.

38. Cited in Alan Everitt, "Farm Labourers," in *The Agrarian History of England and Wales: 1500–1640,* vol. 4, ed. Joan Thirsk (Cambridge: Cambridge University

Press, 1967), 406–407. See also Roger B. Manning, *Village Revolts: Social Protest and Popular Disturbances in England, 1509-1640* (Oxford: Clarendon, 1988). By the sixteenth century wool cloth became far more attractive as an export than raw wool because of the high export taxes imposed on wool by the monarchy from 1275 onward, which had ironically hoped to collect rents from the growing profitability of the wool trade.

39. John Locke, *Two Treatises of Government and a Letter Concerning Toleration* (New Haven, CT: Yale University Press, 2003), 111–121.

40. See Ronald Findlay and Kevin H. O'Rourke, *Power and Plenty: Trade, War, and the World Economy in the Second Millennium* (Princeton: Princeton University Press, 2009); Orlando Patterson, *Slavery and Social Death* (Cambridge, MA: Harvard University Press, 1982), 28. See also Stephen L. Carter, "The Dialectics of Race and Citizenship," *Transition* 56 (1992): 80–99; John Bodel and Walter Scheidel, eds., *On Human Bondage: After Slavery and Social Death* (New York: Wiley, 2016); cf. Judith N. Shklar, *American Citizenship: The Quest for Inclusion* (Cambridge, MA: Harvard University Press, 1995).

41. André Wink, *Akbar* (London: Oneworld Publications, 2012), 52–53, 71. The anthropologist Anand Pandian suggests that there were two modes of territoriality in Mughal and British attempts to create subservient nobles and awed subjects, respectively. Each was expressed in their respective royal hunts. For the Mughals, the hunt was symbolic of the emperor's awesome magnificence and his ability to capture and subdue even menacing predators, while reminding his subordinates that he could pursue and kill treasonous enemies within the territory. For the later British, however, the audience for the hunt was the village subjects, who were threatened by man-eating tigers and could be shown protection by officers engaging in elaborate rituals of sportsmanship. Tapan Raychaudhari and Irfan Habib write, "The Mughal revenue demand is estimated at 50 percent or more of the gross produce of the land. Of this, in 1647, 61.5 percent went to 445 *mansabdars* [mansab rank-holding officers] and about a quarter of that amount was effectively their personal income." Tapan Raychaudhari and Irfan Habib, *The Cambridge Economic History of India*, vol. 1, *c. 1200-c. 1750* (Cambridge: Cambridge University Press, 1982), 266.

42. Kulke and Rothermund, *A History of India*, 196–203; Santhi Hejeebu, "The Colonial Transition and the Decline of the East India Company, C. 1746–1784," in *A New Economic History of Colonial India*, ed. Anand Swamey and Tirthankar Roy (London: Routledge, 2015), 33–51. Under one of its directors, Sir Josiah Child, the company had entered into a ruinous war with Emperor Aurengzeb in 1688, which ended in disgrace and resulted in the payment of a fine to the emperor, only after which trading privileges were restored.

43. Robert Eric Frykenberg, "Elite Groups in a South Indian District: 1788–1858," *Journal of Asian Studies* 24, no. 2 (1965): 261–281; Susan Neild-Basu, "The Dubashes of Madras," *Modern Asian Studies* 18, no. 1 (1984): 1–31; Lakshmi Subramanian,

"Capital and Crowd in a Declining Asian Port City: The Anglo-Bania Order and the Surat Riots of 1795," *Modern Asian Studies* 19, no. 2 (1985): 205–237.

44. There were different attempts to not be influenced by the court; see, for instance, Keay, *The Honourable Company*; Marie Antoinette Petronella Meilink-Roelofsz, *Asian Trade and European Influence in the Indonesian Archipelago between 1500 and about 1630* (Berlin: Springer, 2012). See also Sudipta Sen, *Empire of Free Trade: The East India Company and the Making of the Colonial Marketplace* (Philadelphia: University of Pennsylvania Press, 1998).

45. Bayly, "Portfolio Capitalists," 4–5. See also Sen, *Empire of Free Trade*.

46. There is a profusion of writing on Gandhi's political thought. Here are some examples that may not all speak to each other coherently, but nevertheless capture different elements of his democratic motif. Partha Chatterjee, *Nationalist Thought and the Colonial World: A Derivative Discourse?* (London: Zed Books, 1986); Thomas Pantham, "Thinking with Mahatma Gandhi: Beyond Liberal Democracy," *Political Theory* 11, no. 2 (1983): 165–188; Vivek Dhareshwar, "Politics, Experience and Cognitive Enslavement: Gandhi's Hind Swaraj," *Economic and Political Weekly* 95, no. 12 (2010): 51–58; Nishikant Kolge, *Gandhi against Caste* (Delhi: Oxford University Press, 2017).

47. In a succinct description of the social electricity of the Gandhian moment, Bayly writes, "On the fringes of the colonial state Indian capital, peasant colonists and inferior administrators played a vital part in the subordination of tribal and nomadic peoples and culture to the discipline of production for the market. Indian gentry, now transformed into landlords, and scribal people also supported a political framework within which the conflicts which arose from these social changes could be accommodated. India was made tributary to the capitalist world system, but the dynamism of its deeper social changes and the endemic resistance of its rural leadership helped determine the nature and extent of the subcontinent's tribute." Bayly, "Portfolio Capitalists," 6. Cf. E. P. Thompson, "The Moral Economy of the English Crowd in the 18th Century," *Past & Present* 50 (February 1971): 76–136.

48. Guy Standing, *The Corruption of Capitalism: Why Rentiers Thrive and Work Does Not Pay* (London: Biteback, 2016); Domhoff, *Who Rules America*, xii.

8. Conclusions

Epigraphs: Bryan Bender, "From the Pentagon to the Private Sector," *Boston Globe*, December 26, 2010, http://archive.boston.com/news/nation/washington/articles/2010/12/26/defense_firms_lure_retired_generals/; Samuel Osborne, "Nigeria's Ex-Oil Minister Reportedly Arrested in London for Money Laundering," *The Independent,* October 3, 2015, https://www.independent.co.uk/news/uk/nigerias-ex-oil-minister-reportedly-arrested-in-london-for-money-laundering-a6678136

.html; James Wallis Simons, "How Interpol Got into Bed with FIFA," *Politico*, March 5, 2015, https://www.politico.eu/article/fifa-funded-interpol-policing/; Margaret Badore, "EPA Ruling on Roundup Pesticides Heavily Swayed by Monsanto-Backed Studies," November 6, 2015, http://www.treehugger.com/environmental-policy/epa-ruling-roundup-pesticides-heavily-swayed-monsanto-backed-studies.html; "About the Paradise Papers Investigation," International Consortium of Investigative Journalists, November 5, 2017, https://www.icij.org/investigations/paradise-papers/about/; Jessica Chia, "Whopping 70% of Trump Property Buyers Are Utilizing Shell Companies to Keep their Identities Secret—Compared to Just 4% of Buyers Three Years Ago," *Daily Mail,* June 15, 2017, https://www.dailymail.co.uk/news/article-4607896/70-Trump-property-buyers-using-shell-companies.html.

The similarities in these headlines may become more evident if one considers that the entities they refer to may even share "risk managers" in spite of their wide variation across contexts, places, and forms of elite alliance that harm larger publics.

1. For instance, Thucydides, *The Peloponnesian War* (Oxford: Oxford Classics, 2009), 3.2–6, 3.50, 5.85–116. The political theorist Pierre Manent shrewdly points out that grieving the end of liberalism is futile, because its origins lay in a stopgap series of solutions to match the end of the ancien regime and the bodies politic of Europe and its colonies. Liberal, or constitutional democracy, was a governing order brought in hurriedly to replace the failing institution of European monarchy with a new set of elites. Pierre Manent, "The Crisis of Liberalism," *Journal of Democracy* 25, no. 1 (2014): 131–141; cf. Francis Fukuyama, "States and Democracy," *Democratization* 21, no. 7 (2014): 1326–1340.

2. See, for instance, Philip Abrams, "Notes on the Difficulty of Studying the State (1977)," *Journal of Historical Sociology* 1, no. 1 (1988): 58–89; Pierre Bourdieu, *On the State: Lectures at the Collège de France, 1989–1992* (New York: Wiley, 2018).

3. The ontological turn in the human sciences is also associated with this change. See, for instance, Erle C. Ellis. "Ecology in an Anthropogenic Biosphere," *Ecological Monographs* 85, no. 3 (2015): 287–331; Heather Anne Swanson, Marianne Elisabeth Lien, and Gro B. Ween, eds., *Domestication Gone Wild: Politics and Practices of Multispecies Relations* (Durham, NC: Duke University Press, 2018); Adelene Buckland, "'Deficit Subjects': Realism and Species Belonging," *Cambridge Quarterly* 48, no. 4 (2019): 365–371.

4. Slave society and African American society after the antebellum, for example, shared a conjoint relation with fragmentation and unity through a shared identity. Philip Page. *Dangerous Freedom: Fusion and Fragmentation in Toni Morrison's Novels* (Oxford: University Press of Mississippi, 1995).

5. On overaccumulation, see David Harvey. *The Limits to Capital* (New York: Verso, 2018).

6. See, for instance, Javier Moro, *Passion India: The Story of the Spanish Princess of Kapurthala* (New Delhi: Full Circle Publishing, 2007).

7. Sumit Guha, *Environment and Ethnicity in India, 1200–1991*, vol. 4 (Cambridge: Cambridge University Press, 1999), 47–48.

8. "Watergate Breakup," *New York Times*, editorial, April 20, 1973; Jack Smith, "$37 Screws, a $7,622 Coffee Maker, $640 Toilet Seats: Suppliers to Our Military Just Won't Be Oversold," *Los Angeles Times* July 30, 1986. Cf. Dennis F. Thompson, "Mediated Corruption: The Case of the Keating Five," *American Political Science Review* 87, no. 2 (1993): 369–381.

9. James Monroe, Inaugural Address, March 4, 1817. Cited in Zephyr Teachout, *Corruption in America: From Benjamin Franklin's Snuff Box to Citizens United* (Cambridge, MA: Harvard University Press, 2014), 113. Monroe's remarks are influenced by Montesquieu, claims Teachout, but there are also distinct echoes of Machiavelli.

10. See, for instance, Juliet Schor, *Born to Buy: The Commercialized Child and the New Consumer Culture* (New York: Simon & Schuster, 2004).

11. "India Home to 101 Billionaires, Mukesh Ambani Tops List: Forbes," *Businessworld*, March 21, 2017; Philip Oldenburg, "Political Elites in South Asia," in *The Palgrave Handbook of Political Elites*, ed. Heinrich Best and John Higley (London: Palgrave Macmillan, 2018), 203–223. Academia has even more select networks with linkages to power, in spite of meritocracy. This is not to say that upper castes are exclusive to all such networks, although, sadly, that is mostly true. Many individuals with rags-to-riches stories reach these heights in academia, business, or politics, but those remain the exceptions that illustrate the rule.

12. For a useful description of the multiple layers of social structure, see Pierre Bourdieu, "Social Space and Symbolic Power," *Sociological Theory* 7, no. 1 (1989): 14–25. See also Jeroen Duindam, "Pre-Modern Power Elites: Princes, Courts, Intermediaries," in *The Palgrave Handbook of Political Elites* (London: Palgrave Macmillan, 2018), 161–179.

13. Chibber writes, "Much like Syngman Rhee [president of South Korea from 1948–1960] used the instruments at his disposal to consolidate his base among Korean industrialists, so Indira [Gandhi]—and especially Sanjay [her son]—used the licensing regime to reward their friends, and to exact punishment on their enemies. . . . [In] the Gandhi era, the very purpose of the system was substantially transformed, from a developmental apparatus to an instrument for the exchange of favors within patron-client networks." Vivek Chibber, *Locked in Place: State-Building and Late Industrialization in India* (Princeton: Princeton University Press, 2003), 251; cf. James Glattfelder and Stefano Battiston, "The Backbone of Complex Networks of Corporations: Who Is Controlling Whom?," *arXiv*:0902.0878, 2009.

14. Niccolò Machiavelli, *Discourses on Livy* (Chicago; University of Chicago Press, 2009), 44.

15. Machiavelli, *Discourses on Livy*, 48

16. Stephen Greenblatt, *The Swerve: How the World Became Modern* (New York: W. W. Norton, 2011).

17. Michael Johnston, *Corruption, Contention and Reform: The Power of Deep Democratization* (Cambridge: Cambridge University Press, 2014).

Acknowledgments

It took a small village to write and produce this book, although the usual disclaimer applies.

I am, first of all, very grateful to Sharmila Sen and Heather Hughes at Harvard University Press for being by my side every step of the way and for their conviction that a readable and worthwhile book was indeed in the offing.

My close readers and editors, Sujatha Byravan, Janani Ganesan, Nalini Rajan, and Lalitha Zachariah patiently helped me reorganize and also redirect my stray sentences toward more intelligible expression. Plenty of others gave me appropriately useful feedback on earlier versions of the manuscript. They include Sneha Anaverappu, Sannihit Bathula, Dipesh Chakraborty, Gail Naron Chalew, Anjali Kamat, Aditya Kolachana, Mathangi Krishnamurthy, Jayanth Krishnan, Śamīk Malla, Prasannan Parthasarathi, Sree Hari Purushothaman, V. Rajesh, Kripa Raman, Joe Ravetz, Shobha Sharma, Upinder Singh, Arvind Sivaramakrishnan, Kalyani Subbiah, Rani Unnamalai, and M. S. Visakh. Still others, too numerous to recount here, gave me plenty to chew on in classrooms, seminar halls, and coffee shops.

Well before this project began, Sujatha was my constant interlocutor as we put together an array of interconnected ideas around society, politics, and the material world. Many of these were pivotal in shaping the concepts advanced in the book. Her forbearance, care, and constant engagement and encouragement formed the ground on which the project evolved to its present form.

To all my students and colleagues at the Department of Humanities and Social Sciences and the Indo-German Centre for Sustainability at IIT Madras I am thankful for encouraging me in every possible way during this long endeavor. I am equally indebted to the administration for providing me with an open academic environment in which to conduct research with no fixed agenda.

Index

Ancient Egypt: and the birth of territory, 125; and divine kingship, 204; and empire, 248; laws of, 337n14; Ma'at, 300n3; trade with, 246, 248

Ancient Greece: democracy in, 32, 46–48, 51; and the legend of the Judgment of Paris, 45–46; and tragedy, 293n6

Ancient Rome: corruption in, 22–23, 47–51, 284–285; historian from, Strabo, 188; and the origins of law, 195, 276–277; trade with, 240, 250

Aristotle: on corruption, 32–33, 50; on kingship, 205; on phroenesis or practical wisdom, 287

Arthaśāstra: on bribery and embezzlement, 45; as court manual and textual law on kingship, 200, 219–222, 239

Āryan / Ārya (noble): conflict with dāsas and dasyus, 175, 178–179; distinction, 216–220; invasion theory, 134; settlement and expansion, 164–165

Aśoka, 208–213, 215, 219–220, 225–227

Automobility, 88, 96–101, 108

Bayly, Christopher, 255, 262

Bodily / Body: autonomy of, 99, 223, 227, 233; cosmic (Purusha), 159, 166–167, 180, 222; on display, 167, 205, 207, 311n17; dispositions and practice, 22, 84–85, 99, 115, 118, 123, 143, 148, 150, 153, 173, 178, 182, 184, 191, 207, 218, 233, 268, 273 (*see also* Habitus); disciplined, docile, 88, 146, 167, 177, 184–185, 194, 201, 214, 216, 223, 270–271; exploitation, violence, 15, 69, 183, 210, 225, 245, 250; presence, representation, 35, 66–68, 203, 205–206, 208; purity, 183, 185, 203, 250

Bourdieu, Pierre, 83, 87, 218

Bráhman, 148–149, 151, 159, 229

Brāhmanas, 149, 163, 172–174, 180, 215

Brahmanism, Brahmanical: definition of, 151–152; ideology of, 168–170, 180; institutions of, 175, 183–185, 250; revival / re-appropriation of, 223, 229, 231–234, 240; ritual, 167; threats to, 215, 217–218, 223, 226–227, 239

Brahmins: and Buddhists, 199, 209–213, 226–227; as a kinship group, 149–153, 170; and Mīmāmsā, 229; and pollution, 185; as providers of ritual services and as scholars, 165–167, 180–181, 200–201; in the Rig Veda, 159, 160; roles in kingship, 169–171, 186, 196, 222, 223; roles in law books, 216–218, 220; and Śaivism, 232, 234

Buddhism, 26, 91, 151, 224–228; and law (dharma / dhamma), 192, 219; and the Middle Path, 209, 210, 226; its monasteries / sangha, 172, 224, 226, 249–250; proselytization and influence, 165, 184, 213, 233–234, 239, 251–252; role in trade and urbanization, 156, 218

Christianity, 23, 76, 215, 346n75

Clientelism, 44, 53, 59, 105, 275, 281

Collective memory, 17, 28, 109; of the "good king," 206, 208, 212; of Vedic liturgy, 150–152, 203

Democracy: and corruption / criminal control of, 32, 34, 40, 46, 51, 266, 274, 275; institutions of, models of, 16, 32, 116, 196, 278, 288–289; spirit of xi, 11, 24, 65, 83, 245, 263–264, 275, 285

Dérèglement (collective disorder, anomie): descriptions of, 21, 57, 273; processes leading up to, 60, 78, 268; relations with other social phenomena, 110
Dharma: definitions of, 186, 226–227; evolution of from Vedic corpus, 213–219; as ideology, 191, 235; of the king/rājadharma, 221, 240; as law, 190–198, 203; in the Mahābhārata, 223, 228–231; proselytizing, 211–212; as ways of living/rules of, 160, 191, 210, 255
Dispositif/Apparatus/Assemblage, 76–77, 85, 88; of automobility, 96–101; of cotton, 243–245; as driver of social practice, 88–89, 93–109; of the economy, 20–21, 101–109; of kingship, 207–208; of law, 193; of the state, 193, 287; Vedic, 197
Durkheim, Émile, 21, 57, 78
Dvija (twice-born): definition, 158; role in ritual, 182, 194, 201, 233; rules of endogamy, 182, 185, 215–217, 239; and social hierarchy, 169, 179, 203

Economism, 101–109, 262
Elias, Norbert, 72, 89, 206, 267
Elite networks: court societies as, 206–207, 219, 235; definitions of, 8–9, 16, 36, 168, 266; and interlocking, 91, 110; morphology and social structure, 16, 69, 76, 87–90
Emergence, 29, 75–77, 89, 93, 99, 102, 109, 121, 143–147, 154, 206, 243. *See also* Dispositif
Endogamy. *See* Familial: lines
Everyday: objects, 96, 136, 138, 142–143, 218; routines and transactions, 43–44, 55, 61, 69–71, 78, 84, 99, 101–111, 218
Extraversion, 243–244, 262, 275

Familial/Family/Household: books of the Rig Veda, 157, 168, 214; lines (*Endogamy, Kinship*), 127, 131, 140, 145, 149, 151, 160, 164, 180, 203, 281; partnerships, 169, 250, 275; ritual practice (*see* Grhya Sutras)
Figuration, 72–73, 85, 89, 206, 208
Foucault, Michel, 85, 87, 88, 92, 103

Ganges, 155, 187, 188, 198, 199, 249
Ghaggar-Hakra (Sarasvati), 119, 130, 133, 134
Grhya Sutras, 149, 177, 180, 181, 192, 214–217, 223, 224, 240. *See also* Familial: ritual
Gupta dynasty, 186, 207, 221, 227, 250, 251, 253

Habitus: of agriculture, 123; of automobility, 97, 99, 101; of Brahmanism, 169, 174, 177, 184–185; of the court, 206–208; definitions of, 83–84, 91–92, 97, 269–271, 273–274; of landscape architecture, 118, 143–144; of religiosity, 194
Hegemony, 61, 85–86; of Brahmanism, 183; of the state form, 190–191, 197, 267
Household. *See* Family, Grhya Sutras
Hydraulic society, 123, 125, 204, 238

Ideology: of Brahmanism, 182–184, 219; of capitalism and economism, 18, 105, 272; of contract, 21, 33, 275, 276; as corruption syndrome, 16; of individualism, 21–22, 99, 101; of kingship, 204, 221, 239, 267; meanings of, 83, 85–86, 139; of nationalism, 29, 272; of neoliberalism, 104–109; of ordered sociospatial life—urbanism, 127, 141–144, 168
Indus, 26, 118–119, 128, 130, 133–134
Inheritance, 9, 94, 208, 219, 282, 343n57

Janapādas, Mahājanapādas, 161, 172, 182, 187, 189–190, 198–202
Jāti (birth name or group lineage, frequently translated as "caste"), 219, 221, 239, 242, 250, 252, 255, 262, 276
Johnston, Michael, 59–60, 62–64, 104, 288

Kingship (rājanya): for Aristotle, 32; as divine, 175, 204; as dynastic wealth protection, 204–206, 222; and elite networks, 185, 222, 223, 235, 276; and its logic of territoriality, 189, 199, 206, 221, 235, 238; as paternalism, 205
Kinship. *See* Familial: lines

Land (*cf.* Sedentarism): law, 239; as source of revenue, 36, 95, 202 (*see also* Rent); as territory, 125–127, 152, 191 (*see also* Kingship)
Law: as constitutionality, 32–33, 51; as dharma, 160, 191–198, 217; as legitimizing injustice, 42; manipulation of, 9, 18, 106; moral foundations of, relationship with justice, 195, 223, 228–231; of property, 95, 259–260; Roman, 45; rule of, 43, 48, 81, 190; of territory, 219–233, 239; violation of, 38, 44, 58
Lothal, 116, 119, 131, 149
Luxury goods, 126, 135, 141, 189, 238, 240–241, 249–251

Index

Machiavelli, Niccolo, 48–51, 81–82, 195, 263, 284–285
Mahābhārata, 172, 221, 222–224, 228–231
Managerialism, 52–58
Marx, Karl, 72, 86, 103, 119, 264, 267, 309n4
Masculinities, 67, 176–177, 181, 205, 225
McIntosh, Jane, 133, 138
Media, 4, 7, 9, 44, 66–68, 277, 279
Mesopotamia, 116, 120, 123, 125, 132, 135, 146, 237
Mleccha, mlecchajāti (outsiders), 201, 203, 218, 219, 221
Mohenjo-daro, 115, 129, 132, 133, 140
Monopoly: over violence, 140, 241; markets, 259, 261, 282; rents, 101

Normalization: of automobility, 100; of bondage and exploitation, 16, 21, 24, 35, 67; of bribery, 39; of factory life, 103–104; of inequality, 9, 17, 21; of sovereignty, 206, 267

Oligarchs, oligarchy: as degeneration of aristocracy, 32; dominance of, 12, 238; iron law of, 16; as rentiers, 41, 61, 81, 104, 245; violence caused by, 15, 87, 279
Olivelle, Patrick, 183, 219, 222

Panama Papers, 4–5, 18
Patriarchy: in Buddhist society, 225; and Hindu law, 197, 216–217; and inheritance, 94, 247; and sport, 67, 71; as universal form, 15, 78, 205; in Vedic society, 155, 161, 175–178, 183
Patronage, 6–8, 14, 23, 60, 207, 233, 239, 242, 252, 262, 266, 270, 277, 281
People (*popolo, plebeian*), 48, 79, 82, 195, 302, 336; corruption of the, 12, 20, 33, 46, 50–51, 82, 83, 93, 238, 278
Politics: and anti-politics, 50–51, 101; as biopolitics/biopower, 51, 79; of corruption, 19–24; meanings of, 14–15, 31, 78–79; and patronage, "machine," 6–7, 40–43; tragedy of, 47
Polity: definition of, 80; early complex, 140–141; Harappan, 138–140
Power elite, 90, 201, 351n9
Property: claims to and protection of, 31, 94–95, 245, 249, 294n11; political rights based on, 32; as a source of rent, 95; symbolic, 182; women as, 94. *See also* Inheritance

Ratnagar, Shareen, 132, 247
Rent: as corruption ("rent-seeking"), 56, 104, 110, 262; definition of, 94–95; sources of, 107, 109, 124–126, 162, 175, 185, 190, 202, 212, 243, 249, 256, 258
Rice cultivation: bondage from, 162; origins, 161–163, 187, 198; rents from, 162
Ritual: ascetic form, 142–144, 233; bonding, 67, 121, 171; in domestic life, 136; as intensive form of communication through repetitive practice, 83; mating, 70–71; as reaffirmation of kingship, 171–172, 174, 177; sacrifice, 149–150, 163, 166–169

Śaivism, 148, 224, 231–234, 240, 252
Sarasvati. *See* Ghaggar-Hakra
Scott, James C., xi, 38, 122–123, 146, 197
Sedentarism, 122–123, 125, 162, 187, 211
Slavery, 20, 35, 103, 175–180, 245
Sovereign Power. *See* Kingship
Sport and corruption, 66–68
State: definition, 79–80; genealogy of, 123–124; from lineage to, 171–172; performative role, 82, 137; qualities of the modern, 192–193; as racketeering network, 87
Śudra: in Rigveda, 159; becoming one through loss of dvija status, 167; in the Dharma texts, 217; origins of, 179; status of, 183, 218
Suharto, Muhamad, 6–8, 10–11, 41, 60, 62, 83, 108
Synekism, 120, 122, 127, 144

Tantra, 184, 224, 231–234
Thapar, Romila, 158, 171, 172, 209
Tilly, Charles, xi, 34, 36, 79, 86–87, 297
Trust: betrayal of, loss of, 8, 10, 24, 51, 57, 181; in geographical elite networks, 125, 127, 199, 242; meanings of, 33, 35, 100

Vaishnavism, 148, 252
Vatican, 22–23, 108, 257

White-collar crime, 20–22, 43, 83

Yoga, 177, 184, 224, 231–234, 271, 333